영화 드라마 속

살아있는 영어 표현 15000

영화 드라마 속

살아있는
영어 표현 15000

인쇄일 2015년 3월 11일
발행일 2015년 3월 20일

저 자 서효진 문지선 공편
발 행 인 윤우상
책임편집 윤병호 최준명
발 행 처 송산출판사
주 소 서울특별시 서대문구 통일로 32길 14 (홍제동)
전 화 (02) 735-6189
팩 스 (02) 737-2260
홈페이지 http://www.songsanpub.co.kr
등록일자 1976년 2월 2일. 제 9-40호
북디자인 DesignDidot 디자인디도

ISBN 978-89-7780-222-3 13740

이 도서의 국립중앙도서관 출판예정도서목록(CIP)은 서지정보유통지원시스템 홈페이지(http://seoji.nl.go.kr)와 국가자료공동목록시스템(http://www.nl.go.kr/kolisnet)에서 이용하실 수 있습니다.
(CIP제어번호 : CIP2015006777)

우리말로 생각하고 바로바로 영어로!

영화 드라마 속

살아있는 영어 표현 15000

서효진 문지선 공편

송산출판사

들어가는 말

이 책을 작업하면서 문득 몇 해 전 일본 여행 중에 있었던 일이 생각이 났다. 일행과 떨어져 혼자 시내를 돌아다니던 중에 출출함이 느껴지는데 일본 라멘을 꼭 먹어보고 싶었다. 식당은 여기 저기 많은데 일본어를 모르니 도대체가 어디를 들어가야 라멘 맛을 볼 수 있나 하고 한참을 기웃거리다 너무 배가 고파서 라멘을 팔 것 같이 보이는 식당을 들어 갔더니 젊은 웨이츄레스가 메뉴판을 건넨다. 이 정도 현대식 식당에 근무하는 아가씨면 영어를 하겠구나 싶어 영어로 라멘있냐고 하니, 완전 달나라 말을 듣는 듯한 표정이다. 가장 쉬운 영어 단어를, 나중에는 손짓 발짓까지 해 설명을 해대도 전혀 못 알아먹고, 나 역시 그녀의 일본어와 손짓, 발짓을 도저히 이해할 수가 없었다. 결국 더 시간 끌다 굶어 죽을 것 같아. 메뉴판의 아무 글씨나 가리키고 달래서 받아보니 돈까스! 연 이틀 동안 삼시세끼 돈까스를 먹었는데 또 돈까스다. '라멘되나요?' 라는 표현 정도만 알았다면 그런 상황은 없었을 텐데,,,

지금이야 영어가 익숙하니 영어권 나라에 가도 문제가 없지만, 영어를 한참 배울 때는 위와 같이 웃지도 울지도 못할 상황들이 참으로 많았다. 예를 들어, 첫 미국 여행 중 LA 국제공항에서 생긴 일이다. 공항에서 피닉스로 가기 위해 기다리던 중에 미국 본토에서 맥도널드 햄버거를 꼭 먹어봐야겠다는 마음이 들었다. 햄버거 가게에서 내 차례를 기다리며 열심히 메뉴판을 보고 주문연습을 하였다 드디어 내 차례가 되어 "치즈버거 하나 주세요."라고 하니 음료는 무엇으로 할 거냐고 묻는다. 당연히, "Cola."했다. 주문을 받던 여자가 'What?" 하고 눈을 똥그랗게 뜨고 묻는데 왜 이렇게 당황이 되던지…. 잘 안 들렸다 보나 하고 다시 한 번, "Cola." 했다. 역시 또 "What?"이다. 첫 해외여행이라고 갖은 멋을 부리며 차려 입었는데 기다리던 모든 사람들이 나를 주시했다. '뭐야, 뭘 잘못했지? 맞는데…' 하며 땀까지 흘리며 한참을 고민하다 내 대답이 너무 짧은 것 같아 길게 답해줬다, "Coca cola" 그 때서야 "Oh, coke!" 한다. 사람들의 시선과 이 여자의 킥킥거림으로 입맛을 잃고 햄버거와 콜라는 바로 쓰레기통 신세가 되었던 그 때 나에게 이런 책이 있었다면!

이런 일이 비단 나에게만 일어나겠는가? 벌써 위에 써진 일화를 보고 피식 웃음이나 박장대소를 하였다면 당신 역시 짧은 외국어 실력 때문에 해외여행지에서 혹은 외국인과의 대화에서 땀을 한 바가지나 흘리면서 "뭐라고 말해야 돼?" 하고 안절부절 해 본 경험이 있는 사람일 것이다.

이런 당황스러움과 민망함을 겪지않고, 그리고 영어 앞에서 참을 수 없는 내 존재의 가벼움(?)을 겪지 않도록 돕기 위해 쓰였다.

2014년 8월

편저자

이 책의 특징

1. 원하는 표현을 찾기 쉽도록 사전식 나열 방식이다.

원하는 단어를 사전에서 쉽게 찾는 방법에서 아이디어를 얻어 영어 회화 표현을 사전식으로 나열하였다. 각 문장에서 군더더기는 제외하고 핵심 단어로 시작함으로 한글 자음, 모음 순으로 찾으면 된다.

2. 수록된 표현은 미국드라마에 쓰이는 생생한 표현이다.

그 시대에 사용되는 언어는 TV를 보면 알 수 있다는 말이 잇다. 따라서 구어식, 혹은 다른 영어 나라권 표현이 아닌 미국 본토에서 생생하게 사용되는 회화식 표현을 배울 수 있도록 현재 케이블 TV에서 방영하는 영어 표현을 수록하였고, 특히 많이 사용되는 표현은 음영을 처리하여 여러분에게 시각적 효과를 주고자 하였다.

3. 같은 한글 문장도 상황에 따라 다른 영어 표현이 될 수 있다.

"가." 라는 한국말도 상황에 따라서는 다른 의미를 가진다. 즉 영어 표현이 다르다는 의미이다. 이를 위해 각 한글 표현마다 상황 표시를 하며 그 상황에 다르게 사용되는 영어 표현을 제시하여 여러분이 잘못된 영어 표현을 하여 더욱 당황스러운 상황에 빠지지 않도록 하였다.

4. 아주 많은 표현이 수록되었다.

자칫 부담스러운 양으로 받아들여질 수 있겠지만, 공부하는 학생에게 단권화를 강조하는 것처럼 이 책 한 권이면 거의 모든 상황에서 자연스럽게 영어를 구사할 수 있을 것이라 자신한다. 영어 사전도 한 권 사서 거의 평생을 이용할 수 있는 것처럼 이 책 역시 여러분을 든든히 지켜주는 영어회화 사전이 될 것이다.

마지막으로 여러분이 자신 있게 웃으며 영어로 이야기 할 수 있기를 기원한다.

Good Luck!

[영화 드라마 속 살아있는 영어 표현] 학습방법

Step1 전체내용을 읽으면서 살아있는 언어표현을 느껴보세요.

이 책은 우리말로 생각하고 바로 찾아 영어로 말하는데 많은 도움이 되는 참으로 방대한 내용을 담고 있습니다. 학습자는 먼저 소설 읽듯이 처음부터 끝까지 한 번 쭉 읽어본 후 사전식 배열을 활용하여 마음에 드는 표현을 읽히면서 원어민의 어감을 느껴보세요.

Step2 한국어 표현을 보고 영어로 말해보면서 노트에 정리해보세요.

이 책은 영화 드라마 대본을 집중분석하고 이를 우리말 가나다순서로 배열하여 다양한 영어 표현을 확인할 수 있도록 찾기 쉽게 정리되어 있습니다. 영화 드라마 속에서 보았던 살아있는 표현들처럼 달달 외워서 말해보거나, 그때그때 말하고 싶었던 영어 표현만 따로 모아서 노트에 정리해 활용해 보세요.

Step3 자투리 시간을 활용하여 한국어-영어 동시 녹음 Mp3를 꾸준히 들으세요.

15,000여개 예문을 우리말과 영어를 동시 녹음한 MP3가 제공됩니다. 원어민의 음성을 들어보면 보석 같이 빛나는 표현이 쏟아지며, 한번만 들어봐도 영어에 빠지는 마력(魔力)이 있습니다. 라디오로 드라마를 듣는 것처럼 부담감 없이 꾸준히 반복해서 들으세요

• 본 교재에 사용된 부호 •

- ☞ : 찾아보기
- [ ] : 예문의 상황설명
- ➡, ⬅ : 두 사람의 대화연결
- // : 한국어 및 영어 예문구분

차례

가

ㄱ

가!	① [어떤 장소로] Move! = Leave! ② [떠나기를 재촉함] Go! // Go! The bus is here! (~, 버스 왔어!) ③ [귀찮음 · 쫓아버림] Go away! ☞ 꺼져!
가겠습니다.	I'll get there. // I'll definitely get there. (꼭~)
가격도 저렴합니다.	The price is low, too. = It's also cheap. = It's a bargain as well. = It's inexpensive, too.
가격이 너무 비쌉니다.	The price is too high. = It's very expensive. = It's too steep.
가고 싶습니까?	Would you like to go? ➡ Where would you like to go tomorrow? (내일 어디~) ➡ I'd like to go to Jeju Island.(제주도에요.) ➡ Where would you like to go next? (다음에 어디를~) ➡ I'd like to go to Texas. (텍사스요)
가고 싶은 데가 있습니까?	Is there any place you'd like to go to? ➡ There's a place I'd like to go to. (내가 가고 싶은 데가 한군데 있습니다.) ➡ I haven't thought about it. (아직 생각 안 해봤는데요.)
가고 있는 중 입니다.	I'm on my way. ☞ 가는 길입니다.
가까스로	With difficulty. ☞ 간신히
가까운 병원은 어디에 있습니까?	Is there a hospital near here? ➡ Where is the nearest hospital? (여기에서 가장~) ➡ Go straight from here. Turn left at the corner and you'll see it. (여기에서 곧바로 가다가 첫 번째 길목에서 왼쪽으로 돌면 바로 나옵니다.)

ㄱ

가까운 이웃이 먼 일가보다 낫다.	[속담] A good neighbor is better than a brother far away. ☞ 먼 친척보다 이웃사촌이 낫다.
가까운 지하철역은 어디에 있습니까?	Is there a subway station near here? ➡ Where is the nearest subway station? (가장~) ⓐ Five miles from here. (전방 5마일이요.) ⓑ Turn right, and you'll see it in one mile. (우회전해서 1마일 안에 있습니다.)

가까이 다가오지마!	① Don't come close!
	// Don't come close, or I'll jump off! (~, 아니면 뛰어내린다!)
	② [가까이 붙는 경우] Don't come any closer!
	// Don't come any closer! Do you wanna see her die? (~이 여자 죽는 거 보고 싶어!)
	③ [혼자 있고 싶어 함] Leave me alone!

가까이 와봐!	Come close! // Come closer! (좀~)
	// Come a little closer! (좀 더~)
	// Come close to the middle! (가운데로~)

가난한 집 제사 돌아오듯 한다.	[속담] When it rains, it pours. ☞ 설상가상. // 엎친 데 덮친 격이군!
가난합니다.	I'm poor. // The man is so poor. = The man is as poor as a church mouse. (그 남자는 너무 ~)
가는 길에 상점 좀 들려 주세요.	Stop by the store on your way, please.

가는 길입니다.	I'm on the way.
	// I'm on the way there. (그리로~)
	// I'm on my way. I'm almost home. (~집에 다 왔습니다.) ☞ 가고 있는 중입니다.

가는 데까지 데려다 줄게요.	[차로] I'll take you where you want to go.
가다가 우회전하면 됩니다.	Go straight and turn right. // Go straight down and turn right. (앞으로 곧장~)

ㄱ

가던 길이나 가시지!	① [간섭에 대한 시비] Just go your way! // <비속어> Fuck, just go your way! (시발, ~) ② [쓸데없는 간섭에] Never mind! Just go! ③ [귀찮음] Go away! ④ [신경을 끄라는 의미] **Don't bother!** ⑤ Mind your own business! ☞ 끼어들지 마세요.
가도 됩니까?	Can I go now? ➡ Sure, you can. (가도 됩니다.)
가득 따라 드리겠습니다.	[술] I'll fill the cup full. = I'll fill the cup to the top. = I'll fill the cup all the way.
가득 채워주세요.	① [술] **Fill the cup full, please.** ② [주유소] Fill the gas tank full, please. ☞ 기름을 가득 채워주세요.
가든지 남든지 마음대로 해! // 가든지 말든지 맘대로 해!	I don't care whether you leave or stay! = I don't care whether you go or not!
가랑비에 옷 젖는 줄 모른다.	[속담] Many drops make a flood.
가래침 뱉기 금지!	[경고문] No spitting!
가래침을 함부로 뱉지 마세요.	[경고문] Don't spit.
가려고 합니다.	① [의지] I intend to go. ② [바람 · 생각] I'm thinking of going to Seoul. (서울에~) // I'm thinking of going next year. (내년에~) ③ [예정] I'm going to go to Seoul. (서울에~) ④ [계획] I'm planning to go to Beijing. (북경에~)
가려던 참입니다.	① [자리를 뜸] I'm about to take off. ② [어떤 장소에] I'm leaving.
가려워!	It's itchy!

가로막아!	Block the way! // Block his way! (그 사람~)

가르쳐 주세요.	① [학습] Please teach me.
	// Please teach me Chinese. (저에게 중국어를~)
	// Please teach me how to use computers. (컴퓨터를 어떻게 사용하는지 좀~)
	② [지도 · 지적] Please teach me.
	= Please let me know.
	// Please don't hesitate to teach me. (주저마시고~)
	➡ You're modest. (겸손하십니다.)
	③ Please help me.
	// Please help me out with directions. (길을~)

가리지 마세요.	[시선이나 앞길을] Don't block my way, please.
가만!	① [대화중에 다른 생각이 떠올라서] Wait a minute! ② [가는 상대방을 멈춰 세움] Just a moment! ☞ 잠깐만! ③ [대화의 정지] Give me a break!
가만 좀 내버려 둬!	[혼자 있고 싶음] Leave me alone! // Leave me alone! You're annoying! (~귀찮아!)

가만두지 않을 거야.	① [용서치 않음] I won't forgive.
	// I won't forgive him. (절대로 그 사람~)
	// He won't forgive us. (그가 우릴~)
	// If Mom finds it out, she'll never forgive. (엄마가 아시면~)
	② [용서치 않음] I won't tolerate it.
	// I'll never tolerate it. (절대로~)
	③ [재발에 대한 경고] I won't let it go.
	// If it happens again, I won't let it go. (또 그러면~) ☞ 가만있지 않을 거야!
	④ [복수를 다짐] I'll pay you back.
	= I'll get you back.
	⑤ [승복하지 않음] I can't take it.
	⑥ [위협] I'll get you back.
	// I have a power. I'll get you back. (난 그런 능력 있어. ~)

ㄱ

ㄱ

	⑦ [손 떼지 않음] I won't give it up.
가만있어!	① [간섭] Don't disturb me! ② [얌전히] Cut it out! (좀~) ③ [말참견] Don't interfere! ④ [동작] Stop it! ⑤ [말대답 제지] Shut up! ⑥ [붙잡힌 사람에게 위협] Don't move!
가만있어 봐!	① [생각] Let me think! ② [잠시 대기] Well, well. // Well, well. What should we do? (~어떻게 하지?)
가만있지 않을 거야!	I won't let it go. ☞ 가만두지 않을 거야!
가망 없어!	① It's hopeless! ② [경기 결과] Not a chance!
가망 있습니까?	Is it hopeful? = Is there any hope? ➡ ⓐ Yes, it is hopeful. (가망 있습니다.) ⓑ No, it's hopeless. (가망 없어요.)
가면 안 됩니다.	① [허가 · 가능] You can't go. ② [금지] You must not go.
가면서 길을 안내해 드리겠습니다.	[차 안에서] I'll show you the way while I'm driving.
가방 조심해!	Watch the bag! // Watch your bag! (너~)
가방 가지고 슈퍼에 들어가도 됩니까?	Can I take my bag with me into the market? ➡ ⓐ Sure, you can. (예.) ⓑ No, you can't. (안 됩니다.)
가방끈이 짧습니다.	I'm not well-educated.
가방은 보관함에 넣어주세요.	[슈퍼에서] Please leave your bag in a locker.

ㄱ

가방을 들어주실래요?	Would you hold my bag? ➡ Sure. (그러죠.)
가버려!	Go! ☞ 가! // 꺼져!
가버렸습니까?	Gone? // Has he gone? (그 사람~) ➡ Yes, he has.

가보겠습니다!	[작별인사] I'm taking off!
	// I'm taking off now! (그만~)
	// We're taking off now! (우리 그만~)
	➡ Bye. Take care. (살펴가세요.)

가보면 압니다.	① You'll know it when you get there. ② [잠시 후에] You'll know it in a bit. = You'll find it out in a bit.

가본 적 있습니까?	[경험] Been there? = Have you ever been there?
	// Been to Shanghai? (상해에~)
	➡ ⓐ Yes, I have. (가봤어요.)
	// I have been there. (전에 가본 적 있습니다.)
	ⓑ No, I haven't. (아니요.)
	ⓒ I haven't been there. (가본 적 없어요.)
	ⓓ I have never been there.
	(한 번도 가본 적 없어요.)

가봐!	① [목적지로] Leave now! ② [재촉] Go now! (그만~) ③ [귀찮아 함] Go away! ☞ 꺼져!

가봐야겠습니다.	① [의지] I must get going.
	// I must get going now. (그만~)
	② [시간이 돼서] It's time to say good-bye.
	= I'm leaving. // I'm leaving now. (그만~)
	// I'm sorry, but it's time to say good-bye now. (미안합니다, 그만~)
	➡ Why don't you stay a little more?
	(좀 더 계시지 않고요.)
	③ [의무] I must leave.

	// I must leave before you. (저 먼저~)
	// Sorry, but I must leave now. (미안합니다. 그만~)
	// I must leave for home. (집에~)
	➡ ⓐ Why don't you stay a little more?
	(좀 더 있다가 가세요.)
	ⓑ Please stay with me. It's still early.
	(좀 더 놀다가세요. 시간이 아직 이른데요.)
	☞ 가보겠습니다!

가봤습니까?	① [경험] Been there? = Have you ever been there? (거기~) ➡ ⓐ Yes, I have. (가봤습니다.) ⓑ No, I haven't. (아니요.) ⓒ I haven't been there. (못 가봤습니다.) ② [얼마 전에] Did you go there? ➡ Yes, I did. (가봤어요.)
가서 누워있겠습니다.	I'll go and lie down. // I'll go and lie down for a while. (잠시~)
가서 물어봐!	Go and ask! // Why don't you go and ask? (네가 좀~)
가서 일보세요.	You can go back to your work.
가서 자라.	Go to bed.
가서 전하세요.	Go and say this.
가서 확인해!	Go and check! // Please go and check! (좀~)

가셨습니다.	① [자리를 뜸] Gone.
	// He's gone already. (그분은 벌써~)
	② [죽음] Passed away.
	// He's already passed away. (그분은 벌써~)

가스 안 끄고 나왔네.	① I didn't turn off the stove. ② [갑자기 생각남] Oh, my! I forgot about the stove! (이런! ~)

가슴이 아픕니다.	**It's breaking my heart.** = It's hurting my heart. = It's painful for me. // It's breaking my heart so much. (너무~)
가시겠습니까?	① [자리를 뜸] Do you want to go? ② [떠남] Are you leaving? ➡ Yes. (예.)
가시는 길 순조롭길 바랍니다.	① Safe trip. ② [배를 타고 떠나는 경우] Good luck on your sailing.
가시는 길 평안하시길 바랍니다.	① Safe trip. ☞ 가시는 길 순조롭길 바랍니다. ② [비행기를 타고 떠나는 경우] Good luck on your flight.
가실 겁니까?	① [시간] Will you go? // When will you go? (언제~) ➡ In the afternoon. (오후 시간에요.) ② [교통수단] How will you go? (어떻게~) ➡ By bus. (버스 타고요.)
가야겠습니다!	**I must get going.** ☞ 가봐야겠습니다.
가야만 합니까?	Do you have to go? // Should you have to go? (꼭~) ➡ ⓐ Yes. (가야합니다.) ⓑ Certainly. (꼭 가야 합니다.) ⓒ I should hurry. (급히 가야만 합니다.)
가야합니까?	① [질문] Should you go? (꼭~) ② [시간] How long will it take? (얼마나~) ➡ About ten minutes. (대략 10분이요.) ③ [교통수단] How can I go? (어떻게~) // How can I get to Myeongdong? (명동에 어떻게~) ➡ Take the subway. (지하철을 타세요.)
가요!	① [호출에 대한 대답] **I'm coming!** // I'm coming now! (바로~)

ㄱ

ㄱ

	② [상대방에게] Please go! // Please come with me! (나와 ~)
가세요.	① [부탁] Please go! ② [허락 · 허용] You can go.
가운데로 좀 지나가겠습니다.	I will go through the middle.
가위, 바위, 보!	Rock! Paper! Scissors!

가위, 바위, 보로 정하자.	Decide by rock-paper-scissors.
	// Let's decide by rock-paper-scissors. (우리~)
	관련표현
	Rock (주먹) // Scissors (가위) // Paper (보)
	Rock beats scissors, scissors beat paper and paper beats rock.
	= Stone blunts scissors. Scissors cut paper. Paper wraps stone.
	(주먹은 가위를 이기고, 가위는 보를 이기고, 보는 주먹을 이긴다.)

가을 단풍이 아름답습니다.	Maple leaves are beautiful. // Maple leaves are really beautiful. (정말~)
가이드가 필요합니다.	① [여행] I need a tour guide. ② [삶의 조언] I need guidance.
가장 가까운 길로 가주세요.	Please take a shortcut.
가장 중요한 일입니다.	It's most important. // This is most important. (이것은~)
가전제품을 보러 갑시다.	Let's go and see some household appliances.
가정교사	a tutor ☞ 과외선생
가정부가 필요합니다.	I need a house maid.

가져갑니까?	① [방법] Will you take it?
	// How will you take it? (어떻게~)
	➡ Wrap it up, please. (싸주세요.)
	② [이유] Are you taking it?
	// Why are you taking this? (이거 왜~)
	➡ I need to use it. (쓸데가 있어서요.)

가져다 쓰세요.	① You can take it. ② 〈경어〉 Would you take it and use it, please?
가져다 주세요.	① [물건을 부탁] Please bring it. ② [상점 등에서 물건을 찾음] Please bring it to me. ③ [전달] Please take it to him. (그에게~)
가져다 줄게요.	① I'll get it. // I'll get some medicine right away. (약을 바로~) ② [도움] I'll get it for you.
가족들에게 안부 전해주세요.	Say hello to your family, please.
가족은 다 편안하시죠?	Is everybody in your family doing well? ➡ Yes. Thank you. (고맙습니다. 다들 잘 지냅니다.)
가족은 몇 식구입니까?	How many are there in your family? ☞ 식구는 몇입니까?
가주세요.	① [택시] Let's go. // Let's go to this place. = Please take me to this place. (여기로~) ② Please leave me. (그만~) ③ Go away! ☞ 가!
가증스러운 인간!	You're heinous!
가지 많은 나무에 바람 잘 날 없다.	[속담] A mother with a large brood never has a peaceful day.
가지고 가실 겁니까?	[패스트푸드점] Here or to go? = For here or to go?

ㄱ

ㄱ

	➡ ⓐ To go. (가지고 갑니다.) ⓑ For here. (여기서 먹을 겁니다.)
가지고 갈 물건 잘 챙기세요.	Take all of your belongings with you. // Take all of your belongings with you tomorrow. (내일~)
가지고 오겠습니다.	I'll bring it. // I'll bring it more. (더~)
가지고 오는 걸 깜박했습니다.	I forgot to bring it.
가지고 와!	Bring it! // Go and bring it! (가서~)
가지고 가!	① [간단한 물건 등] Have it with you! ② [받기를 강권] Take it!
가지고 가세요.	① [몸에 지니기] Take it with you, please. ② [선물로 줌] You can take it. // You can take it, ma'am. (아주머니~) ③ [구매] You can have it for ten dollars. (10달러에~)
가지고 가시겠습니까?	[패스트푸드점] Here or to go? ☞ 가지고 가실겁니까? ➡ ⓐ To go, please. (갖고 갑니다.) ⓑ For here, please. (여기에서 먹겠습니다.)
가지 마세요.	① [떠남] Don't leave! ② [어떤 장소에] Don't go! ➡ OK. (알았어요.) ③ 〈경어〉 Would you please not leave?
가지 마시고 함께 식사합시다.	[남아서] Don't go. Let's eat together.
가출했습니다.	Ran away. // She ran away. (그녀가~) ➡ That can't be true! (그럴 리가요?)
가화만사성.	[속담] When one's home is harmonious, all goes well. ☞ 집안이 화목해야 만사가 잘된다.

ㄱ

각

각별히 조심하도록!	Take good care of yourself!
각자 계산합시다. // 각자 냅시다. // 각자 부담합시다.	Let's pay individually. = Let's go Dutch. = Let's split the bill. ☞ 더치페이로 합시다.

간

간 좀 더하세요.	Put in some more salt. = Add a little more salt. // It's not salty enough. Put in some more salt. (너무 싱거우니, ~)
간다!	① [자리를 뜸] I'm leaving! (나~) ② [어떤 장소에] I'm coming! (나~) ☞ 갑니다!
간단하게 말하세요.	Speak briefly, please. = Briefly, please. = Please cut it short. ➡ Yes, I will. (그러지요.)
간단하게 말할게.	[긴 이야기를] Let me keep it short.
간단한 일이 아닙니다.	It's not simple. // It's not that simple. (그렇게~)
간단합니다.	① It's simple. // It's very simple. (아주~) // This is very simple. (이건 매우~) // This is pretty simple. (이거 아주~) ② [일처리] It's easy.
간덩이가 부어도 단단히 부었구나!	How dare you!
간섭하지 마세요.	Don't bother me! // Don't bother me any more! (더 이상~)
간식을 먹고 싶습니다.	I want some snacks.

ㄱ

간신히.	With difficulty. ☞ 가까스로
간에 기별도 안 갑니다.	It's hardly enough.
간장 있습니까?	Do you have soy sauce? ➡ ⓐ Yes. What kind are you looking for? (예, 어떤 종류를 찾으세요?) ⓑ No. But I will buy one right away. (없습니다. 바로 가서 사올게요.)
간장에 찍어야 합니다.	Dip it in the soy sauce.
간지럼 태우지 마세요.	Don't tickle me.

갈

갈 겁니다.	① [어떤 장소에] I'll get there.
	// I'll surely get there. (꼭~)
	// He'll certainly get there. (그는 꼭~)
	② [자리를 뜸] I'm leaving.

갈 길이 멀어요.	I have a long way to go. = I have miles to go. (나는 ~)
갈 데는 있습니까?	Do you have any place to go? ➡ ⓐ Yes. (있습니다.) ⓑ No. (없어요.)
갈수록	More and more.
갈수록 태산.	① From bad to worse. ② [속담] Hills over hills and Alps on Alps arise.
갈피를 못 잡다.	I don't get the point.

감

감기 걸렸어요.	I got a cold. = I have a cold. = I caught a cold.

감기에 걸린 것 같습니다.	Seems like I have a cold. = I feel like I've got a cold.
감동 많이 받았습니다.	I was so moved. = I was deeply impressed.
감사는 제가 해야지요.	I should thank you.
감사드려야 할지 모르겠습니다.	How can I ever thank you? = I don't know how to thank you. // I don't know how to thank him. (그에게 어떻게~)

감사합니다!	Thank you! // Thank you so much! (정말~)
	// Thank you very much! (너무~)
	// Thank you a great deal! (정말 너무~)
	➡ ⓐ You're welcome. = Don't mention it.
	= Never mind. (천만에요.)
	ⓑ No problem! = Not at all! (별말씀을요!)
	☞ 고맙습니다!

감히 네가!	① [무례함을 질책] How could you! ② [반역] How dare you!

갑

갑니까?	Are you leaving? = Are you taking off? ➡ ⓐ Yes. (갑니다.) ⓑ No. I can't. (못 갑니다.) // No, I'm not. (안 갑니다.)
갑니다!	① [자리를 뜸] I'm leaving! ➡ ⓐ Why the hurry? (뭐가 급해요?) ⓑ Why don't you stay a bit longer? (좀 더 있지 않고요?) ② [어떤 장소에] I will get there. // I will get there for sure. (꼭~) ③ [오던 곳으로 돌아감] I'm coming back! ④ [작별인사] Bye for now!

갑시다!	[자리를 뜸] Let's go! // Let's go now! (우리 그만~)

ㄱ

갓

갓 온 물건	a new arrival.

갔

갔다 올게요.	Bye. // Bye for now. (그럼~)
갔다 왔습니다.	① [귀가] I'm home. ② I'm back from France. (프랑스에~) ➡ How was it? (잘 갔다 왔니?) ③ [경험] Been there. // I have been to France once. (프랑스에 한 번~)
갔습니다.	① [어떤 장소에] I went there. ② [자리를 뜸] He's off. (그는~)
갔었습니다.	[그 장소에] I went there.

강

강도야!	Robber! = Burglar!
강심장이네!	Bold! // So bold! = Bold as brass! (정말~)
강요하지 마세요.	Don't push. // Don't push me, then. (그럼 나한테~)
강요한 적 없어요.	[협박해서] I didn't push. // I didn't push you. (당신에게~)

같

같은 걸로 주세요.

[주문] The same here.
// The same as hers. (그녀와~)
➡ Sure. Wait a minute, please.
(알았습니다. 잠시 기다려주세요.)
// The same as that. (저것하고~)

같은 학교 출신이었네요.

We are from the same school.
= We are colleagues.
// I just figured out we are from the same school. (알고 보니 우린~)

같이 가겠습니까?

Will you go with me?
// Will you go downtown together with me?
(시내에 가려는데~)
➡ ⓐ Sounds good. (좋습니다.)
ⓑ No. (아니요.)
ⓒ I have no time today. (오늘 시간 없어요.)

같이 갑시다.

Let's go together with me.
= Why don't we go together?
// Why don't you go with me. (나와~)

같잖은 놈!

<비속어> Worthless asshole!

개

(몇) 개

① one (한 개) // two (두 개) // three (세 개)
// four (네 개) // five (다섯 개) // six (여섯 개)
// seven (일곱 개) // eight (여덟 개)
// nine (아홉 개) // ten (열 개)
// a thing = one thing (물건 하나)
// two things (물건 두 개)
② this thing (이 물건) // that thing (저 물건)
// these two things (이 두 개의 물건)
// those three things (저 세 개의 물건)

개 같은 놈! // 개 같은 자식!	〈비속어〉 Son of a bitch! ☞ 개새끼!
게도 구럭도 다 놓치다.	[속담] If you run after two hares, you will catch neither.
개 버릇 남 못 줍니다.	[속담] From the cradle to the grave. = What is learned in the cradle is carried to the tomb. = Habit is a second nature. = Old habits die hard.
개교기념일 입니다.	Today's the school's anniversary. // It's the school's anniversary today. (오늘은 우리 학교~)
개구리 올챙이 시절 생각 못한다더니.	You forgot what you were.
개구리 올챙이 적 생각 못한다.	[속담] Danger past, God forgotten. = The parish priest forgets that ever he has been a holy water clerk. = He forgets where he came from.
개똥도 약에 쓰려면 없다.	When you really need it, you can't find it.
개똥 밭에도 이슬 내릴 날이 있다.	[속담] Every dog has its day. ☞ 쥐구멍에도 볕들 날이 있다.
개를 좋아합니까?	Do you like dogs? ➡ ⓐ Yes, I do. (좋아합니다.) ⓑ No, I don't. (싫어합니다.)
개새끼! // 개자식!	〈비속어〉 Son of a bitch! ☞ 개 같은 놈!
개소리!	〈속어〉 Nonsense! = Rubbish! = Poppycock! = Bullshit!
개수작 그만해!	〈속어〉 Stop the bullshit!

ㄱ

개었습니다.	It is clear. (날씨가~)
(몇) 개월 정도 됩니다.	It's been months. // It's been a month. (1~)
개인기 좀 보여줘.	Show your talents! // Show your talents, too. (너도~)
개천에서 용난다.	[속담] It is a case of a black hen laying white eggs.
개판 친 이 꼴 좀 봐라.	Look! What an awful mess you made. = Look at the mess. // Look at the mess here. (여기~)
개판이야!	It's a terrible mess!
개 팔자가 상팔자	[속담] A dog's lot in the happiest gall.

객

객실	① [가정집] guest room ② [호텔 등 숙박시설] room

거

거기 가만히 있어.	① Stay there. ② [정지] Stop there.
거기서!	① [정지] Stop! ② [명령] Stop! = Don't move! ③ Hold on!
거드름 피우지 마세요.	Don't put on airs.
거들어 주세요.	Please help me. ☞ 도와주세요.

ㄱ

거봐!	① [상황이 사실로 확인되는 경우] Look!
	= I told you so! = You see?
	= Didn't I tell you? = Did you get it?
	= See?
	// Didn't I tell you? You have a cold.
	(~감기 걸렸지?)
	// You see? I told you. (~내가 말했지.)
	// I told you so! You are stubborn!
	(~고집은!)
	② [단념하라는 말] I told you, just forget it!

거수로 정하자!	Let's decide by raising hands!

거스름돈 여기 있습니다.	[주인이 손님에게] Here is your change.
	// Here is your change, 10 cents. (10센트~)
	// You just gave me 10 dollars. Here is the change, 50 cents. (10달러 받았습니다, 50센트~)

거스름돈은 필요 없습니다.	Keep the change. ☞ 잔돈 필요 없습니다.
거시기 말인데.	[알려주고 싶음] You know what?
거의 다 됐습니다.	Almost done.
거저 드립니다.	It's like free. = It's a steal.
거저 주는 거나 다름없네.	It's like for nothing.
거저 먹으려고!	You want to take it for nothing! (네 놈이~)
거절합니다.	No, thank you.
거지됐구나!	You're broke! // You're so broke! (정말~)
거짓말!	① Lie! = Not true! = False! = Fib! ② [허풍] Brag!

거짓말이야!	① [비난] It's a lie!
	// You are a pack of lies! (네가 한 말 다~)
	// He's talking out of his ass. (그가 한 말 다 ~)

	② [놀림] It's not true. (그건~) // This is not true. (이건~)
거짓말하지 마세요.	Don't lie. // Don't lie anymore. (더 이상~)
거칠어요!	[행동이] Rough! // Too rough! (너무~)
거하게 쏠게.	[초대해서] I will treat you well.

걱

걱정 끼쳐드려서 죄송합니다.	I'm sorry for troubling you. // I'm sorry for troubling you, all. (모두에게~)
걱정도 팔자다.	① You worry too much. ② [안심] Don't worry.

걱정됩니다.	I am worried.
	// I am worried about you. (당신이 정말~)
	// I'm so worried. (정말~)

걱정하지 마세요.	① [심려] Don't worry.
	// Don't worry too much. (너무~)
	// Don't worry about me. (절~)
	// Don't worry because of me. (저 때문에~)
	② [대개 부모님에게] Don't worry, please.
	③ [골치 아픈 일에] Don't worry about things.
	④ [안심] Take it easy. ☞ 안심하세요.
	⑤ [별일 없음] No worries. ☞ 괜찮습니다.

걱정할 필요 없습니다.	Don't need to worry. = Shouldn't worry.
	= You don't have to worry.
	// You don't need to worry about me. (제~)
	// You don't have to worry about it. (그 일로~)
	// You don't need to worry because of me. (저 때문에~)
	// Don't worry. I'm here with you. (~곁에 제가 있습니다.)

걱정했습니다.	I was worried. // I was so worried. (많이~)

ㄱ

건

건강은 어떻습니까?	How are you? = How do you feel? // How have you been these days? (요즘~) ➡ ⓐ Fine. (건강합니다.) ⓑ So so. (그저 그렇습니다.) ⓒ Not good. (건강이 안 좋습니다.) ⓓ Much better. (많이 좋아졌습니다.)
건강이 빨리 회복되시길 바랍니다.	I hope you get better soon.
건강이 제일입니다.	Your health is the most important thing. // Don't be angry. It's not good for your health. (화내지 마세요. ~)
건강하세요.	① [일반적인 안부인사] Please take care. ② Please take care of your health.
건강하시고 아름답게 사세요.	May you live a healthy and beautiful life. // May you live a healthy and beautiful life forever. (평생~)
건강하시고 장수하세요.	May you enjoy a long and healthy life! // May you enjoy a long and healthy life, Mother! (어머님, ~)
건달!	Loafer! ☞ 양아치!

건들지 마세요.	① [말상대] Don't interfere me.
	// Don't bother him. (그 사람~)
	// Don't bother me today. (오늘 나~)
	② [몸이나 물건 등] Don't touch it.
	③ [성질나게] Don't bug me.
	// Don't bug him. (그 사람~)
	④ [귀찮게] Don't be annoying.

	= Don't disturb me. ⑤ [금지] Stop disturbing me!
건망증도 있습니다.	I'm forgetful, too. // She's forgetful, too. (그 여자는~)
건망증이 심해졌습니다.	I'm so forgetful. = I have a bad memory.
건방져!	You are such a snob! (넌 너무~)
건방진 것!	① Snob! ② [사극에서] How impudent!
건배!	[잔을 비움] Cheers!
건배하지 마시고 주량 것 드십시오.	Please drink as much as you can.
건배합시다.	Let's toast. (우리~) // Let's toast all together. (우리 다같이~)
건의가 있습니까?	① Any suggestions? (무슨~) // Any good suggestions? (무슨 좋은~) ➡ I have suggestions. (건의사항이 있습니다.) ② [단정] Do you have some suggestions? (무슨~) ➡ No. (없습니다.)
건의에 반대합니다.	I'm against the suggestion. // I'm against his suggestion. (그의~)
건조합니다.	[날씨] It's dry. // It's too dry. (너무~)

걸

걸립니까?	How long does it take? (얼마나~) // How long does it take to go downtown? (시내중심까지 얼마나~)

ㄱ

	// How long does it take to get to the airport? (공항까지 얼마나~)
	// How much longer does it take? (더 얼마나~)
	➡ ⓐ Forty minutes. (40분이요.)
	ⓑ At least an hour. (적어도 1시간이요.)

걸립니다.	① It takes about 15 minutes on foot. (걸어서 15분쯤~)
	② [시간소요] It takes 5 days. (5일~)
	// It takes about 4 or 5 days. (약 4~5일쯤~)
	// It takes 5 hours to Busan. (부산까지 다섯 시간~)
	// It might take about 1 hour. (아마 한 시간쯤~)
	③ [교통수단] It takes 5 hours. (5시간~)

걸어서 갑니다.	I walk. = I go there on foot.
걸어서 약 20분 걸립니다.	It takes about 20 minutes on foot.
걸어주세요.	① [전화] Call me, please. // Please call me again later. (이따가 다시~) ② [발로] Walk, please. ③ [옷걸이 등에] Hang it on the rack. (옷걸이에~)
걸으실 수 있습니까?	① [가능] Can you walk? ➡ ⓐ Sure. (그럼요.) ⓑ I can walk. (걸을 수 있습니다.) ② [피곤 · 부상] Is it OK to walk? ➡ No problem. (문제없습니다.)

검

검사해 봅시다.	Let's test it. // Let's give it a try. (한번~) // Let's have her checked out. (그녀를 ~)
검은머리 파뿌리 되도록 행복하게 사십시오.	[결혼] Grow old together. ☞ 백년해로하시길 바랍니다.

검토해 보겠습니다.	I'll examine it. // Don't rush. I'll examine it. (서두르지 마십시오. ~) ➡ Was the matter solved? (그 일은 해결되었습니까?)

겁

겁대가리 없구나!	① You're fearless! ② [분위기 파악이 안 되는 사람에게] You have guts! (이놈이 정말~)
겁 안 난다야!	I'm not scared!
겁 안 나요.	I'm not afraid. // I'm not afraid of anything. (아무것도~)
겁나요.	I'm scared. ➡ Why scared? (무섭기는!)
겁이 많구나!	You are such a coward! ☞ 소심하구나!
겁쟁이!	① You, chicken! (이~) ② Coward!

게

게으름 피우지 마세요.	Don't be lazy. = Don't squander your time.
게임 때문에 할 일을 소홀히 하지 마세요.	[컴퓨터] Don't neglect your work because of computer games.
게임은 끝났습니다.	The game is over. // The game is already over. (이미~)
게임이 안됩니다.	① [상대가 약해서] I'm the winner. ② [상대가 강해서] You can't compete.

ㄱ

겨

겨울 날씨는 춥습니다.	The weather is cold in winter.
겨울방학은 12월 말입니다.	The winter vacation is at the end of December.
겨울은 춥습니까?	Is it cold in winter? = Is the weather cold in winter? ➡ ⓐ Yes, it's cold. (춥습니다.) ⓑ No, it's not so cold. (별로 춥지 않습니다.)
겨울이 지나지 않았는데 봄이 오겠는가.	Spring can't come before winter is gone.
겨자를 넣어주세요.	Please put in some mustard. // Would you put in some mustard? (좀~)

견

견딜 수 없습니다.	① [심리 · 정신] I can't stand it. ② [패자의 울분] I can't take it. ③ [인내] I can't put up with this. // I can't put up with the smell. (냄새를 ~)
견본 있습니까?	Do you have a sample?
견본이 있습니다.	① [책자] I have a sample. // I have a sample here. = Here is a sample. (여기~) ② [견본품] Sample. = Tester.
견해가 똑같습니다.	Same here. // We have the same opinion. (우리는~)

결

결과에 신경 쓰지 마세요.	Don't care about results. // Don't care about results too much. (너무~)
결국 이겼습니다.	I won in the end! // We won in the end! (우리가~)
결론을 속단하지 마세요.	Don't jump to conclusions. = Don't make a hasty conclusion.
결론적으로 말해서	In conclusion = To sum up = As the last thing
결백합니다.	① [결백 및 순수] I'm innocent. (전~) ➡ Who's gonna believe it? (누가 믿어?) ② [무고한 고소] I'm falsely accused. (전~) ☞ 억울합니다! ③ I'm clean.
결심했습니다.	① [결정] I made a decision. ② [확고함] I am determined this time. (이번엔 정말~)
결자해지.	[속담] One who has tied a knot must untie it. = Solve the problems you create.
결재방식은 어떻게 합니까?	How would you like to pay? ➡ ⓐ By cash. (현금으로 합니다.) ⓑ On credit. (카드요.)
결재했습니다.	Paid. // He paid. (그가~)
결정내리지 못했습니다.	I haven't reached a decision. // I haven't made a decision yet. (아직~)
결정해!	Decide! = Make a decision! // Make a decision about that important thing! = That important thing is up to your decision! (큰 것은 자네가~)

결정했습니까?	Have you decided? ➡ Yes, I have. (결정했습니다.)
결정했습니다.	① [결정] I've decided on this house. = I have my mind set on this house. (이 집으로~) ② [약속 · 합의] We've reached a decision. = We've made a deal. (우리는 ~)
결혼 1주년을 축하합니다.	Congratulations on your first wedding anniversary.
결혼 50주년을 축하합니다.	Congratulations on your 50th wedding anniversary. (두 분의~)
결혼기념일을 축하합니다.	Happy wedding anniversary!
결혼 상대는 있습니까?	[남녀공용] Do you have a soul mate? ➡ ⓐ Yes. (예.) ⓑ I'm married to my job. (일과 결혼했어요.) ⓒ Not yet. (아직요.)
결혼은 언제 할 겁니까?	[결혼] When will you get married? = When are you planning to get married? ➡ ⓐ Soon. (금방이요.) ⓑ No plans yet. (아직 계획 없습니다.)
결혼을 축하합니다.	Congratulations on your marriage. = Wish you a happy marriage.
결혼을 허락해주세요.	① Let me marry. = Allow me to get married. ② 〈경어〉 Would you please allow us to get married? // Would you allow me to marry her? (그녀와~)
결혼해주세요.	① [남자가 여자에게] Will you be my wife? ② [여자가 남자에게] Will you be my husband?
결혼해주시겠습니까?	Will you marry me?

	= Please marry me. (저와~) ➡ ⓐ Yes, I will. (그래요.) ⓑ Sure. (그럴게요.)
결혼했습니까?	Are you married? = Are you taken? ➡ ⓐ Yes. (결혼했습니다.) ⓑ Not yet. (아직 안했습니다.)

겸

겸손해!	① [충고] Be modest! ② [남에게 배우는 자세를 요구] Don't be too proud of yourself.

경

경거망동하지 마세요.	[주의를 당부함] Don't act like a kid, please. = Please act your age. // What I would like to tell you all is act your age, please. (모두에게 일러두고 싶은 것은 제발~)
경고하는데.	I'm warning you. = I'm giving you a warning. // I warn you not to bother me again. (~앞으로 내 일에 참견하지 마세요.) ➡ I don't wanna bother you. (나도 참견하고 싶지 않아.)
경극을 보고 싶습니다.	I'd like to see a Chinese opera.
경기 결과에 깨끗이 승복해야 합니다.	You should be willing to accept the result of the game. // Everybody should be willing to accept the result of the game. (모두가 ~)
경기가 형편없어!	This game sucks!
경례!	① Bow! ② [허리를 굽혀하는 절] Bow deeply!

ㄱ

경사났네!	Hooray!
경솔하게 판단하지 마세요.	Don't make a hasty judgement.
경찰 불러!	Call the cops! // Call the cops now! (어서~)
경찰관님!	Officer!
경찰에 신고해 주세요.	Please report it to the police. // Please hurry and report it to the police. (빨리~)
경찰을 불러주세요.	Call the police, please. = Please call the cops. ➡ They'll be here soon. (곧 옵니다.)
경찰이 떴어요!	Cops are coming! = Cops are around here!
경치가 참 아름답습니다.	Quite a view. = The scenery is beautiful. // A beautiful scenery here. (이곳~)
경험은 지혜를 낳는다.	[속담] People learn from experience. = Experience leads to wisdom. = Experience bears wisdom. = Experience makes even fools wise.

곁

곁에 있어줘!	Please stay with me! (내~) // Please stay with me forever! (앞으로도 쭉 내~)

계

계단에서 넘어졌습니다.	I fell on the stairs.
계란으로 바위치기.	① That's out of the question. ② 〈직역〉 Breaking a rock with eggs.

계산서 가지고 오세요.	Can I have the bill, please. = Please get me the bill.
계산서가 틀린 것 같습니다.	The bill seems to be wrong.
계산서 주세요.	Please give me the bill.
계산이 잘못된 것 같습니다.	The bill seems to be wrong here. (여기~)
계산이요!	① [음식점] I'm ready to pay! = I'll pay the bill now! ② Here is the money!
계산하는 곳은 어디에 있습니까?	Where can I pay the bill? = Where is the cashier? ➡ First floor. (1층입니다.)
계산해!	[음식값] You pay! = Pick up the check!
계속해봐!	[말 · 동작] Go on! = Keep going!
계십니까?	① [존재확인] Anyone here? ➡ Yes. (예.) ② [누군가를 찾음] Is Mr. I there? (이 선생 거기~) ➡ ⓐ Yes. (예.) ⓑ No. (아니요.) ③ [확인] Is Mr. I there?(이 선생 거기~) // Is Mr. I at home? (이 선생 집에~) ➡ ⓐ Yes. (예.) ⓑ Who's there? (누구세요?) ⓒ Who are you looking for? (누굴 찾으세요?) ④ [거주] Are you in Seoul? (서울에~) = Do you live in Seoul? ➡ Yes. (예.) ⑤ Where are you now? (지금 어디에~) ➡ I'm at school. (학교에 있습니다.)
계약기간은 몇 년입니까?	How long is your contract?

ㄱ

	➡ A year. (1년입니다.)
계약서에 서명했습니다.	I signed the contract.
계약합시다.	Let's sign the contract.
계절을 제일 좋아합니까?	Which season do you like most? = What's your favorite season? (어느~) ➡ ⓐ I like spring. (봄을 좋아합니다.) ⓑ I like summer. (여름을 좋아합니다.) ⓒ I like fall. (가을을 좋아합니다.) ⓓ I like winter. (겨울을 좋아합니다.)
계좌를 개설하고 싶습니다.	[은행] I'd like to open an account.
계좌를 개설하려면 어떻게 합니까?	[은행] How can I open an account? ➡ Bring your id to the bank and fill out an application form. (신분증을 가지고 은행에 가서 신청서를 쓰시면 됩니다.)
계좌번호를 불러주세요.	Say your bank account number, please. (당신의~)
계좌에 잔고가 얼마나 있는지 확인하고 싶습니다.	[은행] I want to know my balance.
계집년!	〈비속어〉 Bitch! // You, fucking bitch! (이 우라질~)
계집은 남의 것이 곱고 자식은 제 새끼가 곱다.	[속담] The grass always looks greener on the other side of the fence. ☞ 남의 떡이 커 보인다.
계획이 바뀌었습니다.	The plan was changed.

고

고개를 돌리지 마세요.	Don't turn your head.

고개를 들어!	Head up!
고기가 너무 질깁니다.	The meat is tough. // This meat is tough. (이~)
고기가 참 부드럽습니다.	The meat is very tender.
고기는 몇 인분 드릴까요?	How many servings of meat do you want?
고단수야!	So clever!
고독합니다.	I'm lonely.

고등학교 몇 학년이야?	What year are you in high school?
	➡ I'm a freshman. (고등학교 1학년입니다.)
	// I'm a junior. (고등학교 2학년입니다.)
	// I'm a senior. (고등학교 3학년입니다.)

고등학교에 다닙니다.	I'm a high school student.
	= I go to high school.
	// He goes to high school. (그는~)
	// My older sister goes to high school. (누나는~)

고래싸움에 새우 등 터진다.	[속담] Suffer a side blow in a fight. = An innocent bystander gets hurt in a fight.
고르겠습니까?	Which one do you want? (어느 것을~) ➡ That one on the left. (왼쪽에 있는 저거요.)
고마운 일이 다 있나!	Thank you so much! // Oh, my! Thank you so much. (이런~)
고만고만합니다.	[상황이] So so.
고맙기는!	You're welcome! = No problem! = Don't mention it! ➡ Thank you very much. (대단히 감사합니다.)
고맙습니다!	Thank you! // Thank you very much! (대단히~) // Thank you a great deal! (정말 대단히~)

ㄱ

	➡ ⓐ You're welcome. = No problem. = Don't mention it. (천만에요.) ⓑ That was nothing! (고맙기는요!) ☞ 감사합니다!

고민 있습니까?	① Do you have worries?
	// Do you have any worries? (무슨~)
	➡ No. (없어요.)
	② [단정] You're worried.
	// You're worried about something. (무슨~)
	➡ No. I'm fine. (괜찮아요.)

고백할 일이 있습니다.	I have something to tell you. // To be honest with you, I have something to tell you. (당신한테 솔직히~)
고백해!	Tell me! = Confess to me! // Tell me the truth! (사실대로~)
고생 끝에 낙이 온다.	[속담] No pain, no gain. ☞ 고진감래.

고생 많았습니다.	① [수고] Well done.
	= Thank you for your work. = Good job.
	② [고생] You have done well.
	// You have done so well. (정말 ~)
	// You have done well so far. (그동안~)

고생을 해봐야 성공한다.	[속담] Adversity makes a man wise.
고소하다!	You deserve it! = It serves you right! // It serves him right! (그놈~) ☞ 쌤통이다!
고속버스는 얼마 만에 한 대씩 있습니까?	How often does the express bus run? // How often does the express bus to Chicago run? (시카고에 가는~) ➡ Once an hour. (한 시간요.)
고속버스와 기차 중 어느것이 더 빠릅니까?	Which is faster, the express bus or the train? ➡ ⓐ Both are fast. (둘 다 빠릅니다.) ⓑ They're both the same. (다 비슷합니다.)

고스톱만 쳤습니까?	① [카드 · 화투] Have you only played cards these days? (요즘에~) ② 〈직역〉 Do you only play cards these days? (요즘에~)
고양이 목에 방울걸기.	① 〈직역〉 The mouse's hanging a bell on the cat's neck. ② 〈의역〉 Attempting something dangerous.
고양이 보고 반찬 가게 지키라는 격.	[속담] That's like setting the wolf to guard the sheep. = It's like having the fox guard the hen house. ☞ 도적에게 열쇠를 주다.
고양이와 개의 관계이다.	They're like cats and dogs. = They fight like cats and dogs.
고양이 쥐 생각.	Being the hypocrite.
고양이 쥐 생각 해주는거야!	[위선] You're a hypocrite!

고의로 그런 게 아닙니다.	① I didn't do it on purpose.
	= I didn't mean it.
	= I didn't do it intentionally.
	= It was a mistake.
	// I really didn't mean it. (정말~)
	// I didn't mean it, either. (저도~)
	② I didn't do it again on purpose. (제가 또~)

고인물이 썩는다.	[속담] A rolling stone gathers no moss. ☞ 흐르는 물은 썩지 않는다.

고장 났습니다.	Something's wrong. = Out of order.
	= Not working. = It doesn't work.
	// Something's wrong with the computer. (컴퓨터가~)
	// The copy machine doesn't work. (복사기가~)
	// Partially out of order. (약간~)

고장입니까?	① Is it out of order? = Isn't it working? = Doesn't it work?

ㄱ

	② Something wrong with it? // Anything wrong with it? (무슨~)
고정하세요.	Calm down. = Stay calm. = Don't panic! ☞ 냉정하세요. // 흥분하지 마세요.
고지식한 사람입니다.	Guileless person. = Stupidly honest. // He's very guileless. (그는 너무~)
고진감래.	[속담] No pain, no gain. ☞ 고생 끝에 낙이 온다.
고집불통.	Stubborn!
고집 하난 세구나! // 고집이 정말 세구나!	[소고집] You're stubborn! // You're very stubborn! (정말~)

고집부리지 마!
// 고집피우지 마!
	① You're sitting too tight!
	= Don't be too stubborn!
	// Don't be stubborn anymore! (더 이상~)
	② [자녀에게] Don't be too stubborn!
	= You're too pigheaded!
	// Don't be stubborn anymore. (더 이상~)

고칠 수 있습니다.	I can fix it. // I can fix it right away. (곧바로~)
고통없이 얻어지는 건 없다.	No pain, no gain. ☞ 경험은 지혜를 낳는다.
고통스럽습니다.	It's painful. // I'm in a lot of pain. = Too much pain. = It's very painful. (아주~)
고향은 어디입니까?	① Where were you born? = What is your hometown? ➡ My homtown is Seoul. (제 고향은 서울입니다.) ② [출신] Where are you from? ☞ 어디서 왔습니까?

곤

곤란하게 해드려 정말 죄송합니다.	Sorry for the troubles. = I'm sorry I got you in troubles.

	➡ That's OK. (괜찮아요.)
곤란하게 됐습니다.	I'm in an awkward situation.

곤란합니다.	① It's hard. // This is hard. (이건 좀~)
	// It's hard. (그건 좀~)
	// I am at a loss what to do because of this.
	= I am in a real fix because of this.
	(이 일 때문에 정말~)
	② [문제 해결] It's troublesome.
	// This is a real problem. (이 일은 정말~)

골

골 때린다!	① Outrageous! ② [일 처리] It's like banging my head against a brick wall! = It drives me up the wall! // **This gets on my nerves.** (이 일 진짜~) ③ [머리가 아픔] It's a headache! // This is a headache! (이 일 진짜 사람~)
골라봐!	Choose! = Make a choice! = **Make a pick!** ☞ 선택해!
골라주세요.	Please choose for me. = Please pick for me.
골인!	Goal! = Score!
골치 덩어리입니다.	Troublemaker. // He's a troublemaker. = He's a real pain. = **He's a pain in the neck.** (그는~)
골치 아파 죽겠습니다.	① [두통] I have a terrible headache. ② [힘든 일] It gives me a headache.
골치 아프게 됐습니다.	I'm in an awkward situation. = It's given me a headache. ☞ 곤란하게 됐습니다.

ㄱ

골치 아픈 일입니다.	It's a real pain. // This is a real pain. (이 일은 정말~)

골치 아픕니다.	① I'm troubled. // I'm very troubled. (정말~)
	// It's really painful. (그건~)
	// I'm troubled this time. (이번엔~)
	② You'll be troubled if you do it.
	= If you do it, you'll get troubles. (그러면~)

골프 치는 것을 좋아합니다.	I like to play golf.

곪

곪은 상처 같다.	It's like a festering wound.

곯

곯아 떨어졌습니다.	He fell into a deep sleep. (그는 깊은 잠에~)

곰

곰곰이 생각한 끝에 내린 결정이에요.	It's a decision I made after my fullest consideration.

곱

곱빼기로 주세요.	Give me a large helping, please. = May I have a large helping?

공

공든 탑이 무너지랴.	[속담] Hard work will be rewarded.
공부는 늙어 죽을 때까지 한다.	You never stop learning.
공부를 열심히 해야 한다.	You must study hard. // Students must study hard. (학생은~)
공부한 셈 쳐!	[사고를 통해 교훈을 터득함] Think you've learned a lesson from the experience! // Lucky you. Think you've learned a lesson from the experience! (됐어. ~)
공부합니까?	Do you study? // How many hours do you study? (하루에 몇 시간~) ➡ Ten hours. (10시간이요.)
공사 중 접근 금지!	[경고문] Under construction!
공연은 몇 시에 시작합니까?	When does the concert start? // When will the concert start tomorrow? (내일~) ➡ At ten in the morning. (오전 10시에요.)
공연이 시작됩니다.	It's starting. // It's starting right now. (곧바로~)
공연이 있습니까?	Do you have concerts? // Do you have concerts today? (오늘~) ➡ Yes. (있습니다.)
공연합니까?	[연극] Do you show plays? // How long is the show? = How long does the show run? (모두 몇시간 ~) ➡ Two hours. (2시간입니다.)
공원에 산책하러 갑니다.	I'm taking a walk in the park. // We're taking a walk in the park. (우리는~)

공은 공이고 사는 사입니다.	Public is different from private.
공자 앞에서 문자 쓴다.	[속담] To teach a fish how to swim. = To teach one's grandmother how to suck eggs.
공정하게 해!	You must be fair! = Play fairly!
공중전화가 어디에 있습니까?	Where are the payphones? = Where are the public phones? ➡ In front of you. (앞쪽에요.)
공중화장실이 있습니까?	Where are the public restrooms? ➡ Over there. (저쪽에요.)
공짜는 없어요.	Nothing is free. = Everything costs. = There's no such thing as a free lunch. // Nothing is free in this world. (세상에 ~)
공짜 밥 먹으려고, 꿈도 꾸지마!	Don't even think about a free meal! ➡ I didn't come here to eat but to talk. (밥 먹으러 온 게 아니야. 급히 너와 상의할 일이 있어서.)
공짜로 줘도 싫습니다.	I don't want it even if it's free.
공짜입니다.	① [술집 등] This is on the house. (이것은~) ② This is a free gift. = For nothing. (이것은~) ☞ 서비스입니다.
공처가입니다.	He's whipped. (그는~)
공항까지 가는 택시를 불러주세요.	Call me a cab to the airport, please.
공항까지 얼마나 걸립니까?	How long does it take to the airport? ➡ An hour. (1시간이요.)
공항버스를 타야합니까?	Should I take the airport shuttle? // Where should I take the airport shuttle? (어디에서 ~)

	➡ Four miles ahead. (앞쪽으로 4마일 가세요.)
공항에 갑니까?	Is it going to the airport? // Is this bus going to the airport? (이 버스는~) ➡ Yes, it is. (공항에 갑니다.)
공항에 어떻게 갑니까?	How can I get to the airport? = How can I go to the airport? ➡ ⓐ Go straight. (앞으로 곧장 가세요.) ⓑ There's a shuttle ahead of you. (앞쪽에 공항버스가 있습니다.)
공항이용권은 어디서 삽니까?	Where can I buy airport admission tickets? = Where can I get an airport admission ticket? ➡ At the ticket booth. = At the ticket counter. (표 파는 창구요.)
공항이용권은 어디에서 냅니까?	Where should I turn in my airport admission ticket? ➡ Over there. (저쪽입니다.)

ㄱ

과

과거는 과거일 뿐이야!	The past is in the past!
과대평가하지 말아요.	Don't overestimate me. (저를 ~)
과로하지 마세요.	Don't overwork. // Don't work too much. (너무~)
과묵한 사람입니다.	He's a very quiet person. (그는~)
과부 사정은 과부가 안다.	① 〈직역〉 It takes a widow to know a widow's difficulties. ② I can empathize with you.
과소평가하지 말아요.	Don't underestimate me. (저를 ~)

과속에 걸렸습니다.	I got a speeding ticket.
과속했습니다.	I drove too fast. = I was speeding.
과식했습니까?	Did you overeat? = Did you eat too much? = Did you eat to excess? ➡ ⓐ Yes, I think so. (그런 것 같습니다.) ⓑ No. (아니오.) ⓒ Kinda strange if I don't. (안 그러면 이상하죠?)
과연 너 답다!	① It's so you to do such a thing! ② [빈정거림] You've done a great job!
과연 듣던 대로입니다.	You are just like what we were told.
과외선생	a tutor
과외선생으로 일주일에 세 번 가르칩니다.	I tutor three times a week. = I'm a tutor teaching 3 times a week.
과용하셨습니다.	① You spent too much. // You spent too much today. = You overspent today. (오늘~) ➡ That's OK. (뭘요.) ② You spent a lot. How kind! (~친절도 하시지.) ➡ I just did what I should do. (받으세요. 당연히 그래야죠.)
과일 드세요.	Have some fruit.
과장하지 말아요.	Don't make a mountain out of a molehill. = You're exaggerating it. = Don't make a big deal out of it.
과찬이십니다!	[과분한 칭찬에 대해] I am so flattered! = You overpraise me! = That's very flattering! = That's too much praise!

관

관계없는 일입니다.	Have nothing to do with it.
	// None of your business. (당신과~)
	// This is none of my business. (이건 저와~)

관계입니까?	Are you related? // How are you related to him? (당신은 그 사람과 무슨~) ➡ Nothing! (아무 관계 아니에요.)
관계자 외 출입금지!	[경고문] Off limits! = No admittance except on business!
관계할 일이 아닙니다.	None of your business. // This is none of your business. (이건 당신이~)
관광 명소를 가르쳐주세요.	Please tell me what places I should visit. = Please tell me some good places to visit. // Please recommend some good places to visit. (필수~)
관광안내 지도를 살 수 있습니까?	Can I get a tour map? = Can I buy a tour guide map? ➡ I'll send it to you later. (잠시 후에 보내드리겠습니다.)
관대한 처분을 바랍니다.	Please show me some generosity.
관두겠습니다.	I will quit.
관두세요.	① [제지 · 중지] Stop it. // Stop it, then. (그럼~) ② [배려나 초대를 거절] No, thank you. ③ [방임] Leave me alone. ☞ 내버려둬요.
관리 잘하세요.	Take good care. // Take good care of it. (그거~)
관심 없습니다.	I'm not interested. // I'm not interested in it. (그런 거에~)

	// I'm not interested in cars. (자동차에~) // Nothing interests me. (무슨 일을 하든~)

관심 있습니까?	① Are you interested?
	// What are you interested in? (무엇에~)
	➡ Soccer. (축구요.)
	② Are you interested in me? (저한테~)
	// Are you still interested in me? (아직도 저한테~)
	➡ Who said that? (누가 그래요?)

관점이 틀렸습니다.	Wrong point of view. // Your point of view is wrong. (당신의~) ➡ What's the matter with it? (뭐가 문제입니까?)

괘

괘씸한 놈!	You're disgusting! = You, traitor!
괘씸합니다.	You're so ungrateful!

괜

괜찮습니까?	① [사태 · 부상] Are you all right? = Are you OK? = Didn't you get hurt? = Are you alright? ➡ I'm OK. = I'm fine. (괜찮습니다.) ② [건강 · 질병] How do you feel? = Are you alright? = Do you feel better? ➡ I feel better. = I'm fine. (괜찮아요.) // I feel a little bit better. (좀~) ③ [신경 안 씀] Does it matter? ➡ No. It doesn't matter at all. (괜찮아요.) ④ [동의] Is it OK with you? = Is it alright with you?

= Does it work out for you?
= Do you agree? = Is it fine with you?
= Is it good with you?

➡ It's OK. = It's good with me. (괜찮아요.)

⑤ [만족] Is it good for you?

➡ It's good. (괜찮아요.)

⑥ [질병 · 부상 정도] How do you feel?

➡ ⓐ I feel better. (좀 괜찮아요.)
ⓑ I am fine. (전 괜찮아요.)
ⓒ Fine. (괜찮아요.)

⑦ [적당한 약속시간] Is it OK with you?
= Does it work for you?
// Does two o'clock work for you? (두시가~)

➡ Yes. (괜찮아요.)

⑧ [문제] Is it OK?

➡ Yes, it is. (괜찮아요.)

괜찮습니다.

① Fine. = Good. = OK. = Alright.
// I'm alright. (전~)
// I'm very good. (전 정말~)

➡ Fine, then. (그럼 됐어요.)

② [건강 · 기분] I feel good.

③ [상황 · 수준] It's alright.

④ [신경 안 씀] It doesn't matter at all.
// I don't care. (저야~) ☞ 신경 쓰지 않아요.

⑤ [동의] I agree.

⑥ [칭찬 · 만족] Great. = Good. = Excellent.
// Not bad. (그런대로~) // Very good. (아주~)
// Everything is good. (다~)
// This is very excellent. (이거 정말~)

⑦ [거절] No, thanks.

⑧ [선택] I like that one. (그거~)
// I like that day. (그날은~)
// I can make it at two. (두시가 ~)

⑨ [사양] No, thanks. = No. Thank you.
= I'm fine. // No. Thank you. (~감사합니다.)

⑩ [활동에 지장 없음] I'm alright.

ㄱ

괜찮지요?	① [상황 · 수준] Is it OK? // Is it OK yet? (아직~) ② [만족] Isn't it good? ③ [부상정도] Are you alright? = Are you OK? = Did you get hurt? ➡ I'm OK. = I'm fine. = I didn't get hurt. (괜찮아요.) ④ [몸살] Do you feel better? = Have you recovered? (좀~) ➡ Yes. I feel a little better. (좀 괜찮아요.) ⑤ [사태] Is everything OK? // Is everything really OK? (정말~) ➡ It's really fine. (정말 괜찮아요.)
괜한 걱정 마세요.	Don't worry. = Don't trouble yourself with useless worries.
괜한 걱정했습니다.	I am worried for no reason at all.
괜한 소리 마세요.	Don't say things like that.
괜히 물어봤네.	It was stupid to ask such a question. = I shouldn't have asked the question.
괜히 좋아했네.	[약속이나 일정 등이 취소됨] It was stupid of me to be happy like that. = I got my hopes up for nothing.

괴

괴로워하지 마세요.	Don't be hard on yourself.
	// Don't get distressed too much. (너무~)
	// Don't be distressed by that. (그 일로 더 이상~)

괴롭습니다.	I feel distressed. = I am sad. = I am unhappy. = It's troubling me. // I am so sad. (정말~) // She's very sad because her pet died. (그녀가 키우던 애완동물이 죽어서 무척~)
괴롭히면 안 됩니다.	Don't harrass. = Stop harrassing. // Don't harrass others. (사람을~)

괴롭히지 마세요.	① [귀찮게 함] Stop nagging me. ② [언어나 폭력] Don't bully me. ☞ 귀찮게 하지마세요.

ㄱ

굉

굉장하다!	① [칭찬] Outstanding! = Awesome! // Very excellent! (정말~) ☞ 대단하다! ② [탄복] Great! = Awesome!

교

교양이 없네요.	No manners. = Bad manners.
	= Bad-mannered.
	// Really bad-mannered. (정말~)
	// Very bad manners. (너무~)

교통사고가 났습니다.	① [당사자] I had a car accident. // He had a car accident yesterday. (어제 그는~) ② [목격] There was a car accident.
교통은 편리합니까?	Is the traffic OK? // Is the traffic OK here? (이 근처~) ➡ Yes, it is. (편리합니다.)
교통카드 있습니까?	① [버스] Do you have a bus pass? ➡ Yes, I do. (있습니다.) 관련표현 daily pass (일정액원) weekly pass (주정액권) monthly pass (월정액권) ② [뉴욕 지하철 등] Do you have a Metro Card?
교통카드는 어디서 사용할 수 있습니까?	Where can I use my pass? ➡ Both subway and bus. (지하철과 버스에 다 사용할 수 있습니다.)

교통카드에 10달러 충전해주세요.	I'd like to deposit ten dollars in my card.
교통편을 이용해야 합니까?	Do I have to use public transportation? // What form of transportation should I use to go to Seoul? (서울까지 가려면 어떤~) ➡ The train is most convenient. (기차가 제일 간편합니다.)
교통 체증에 발이 묶였어요.	I was caught in a traffic jam.
교활한 놈!	Cunning fellow! = Sly old fox! = Crafty man! = Cunning as a fox!

구

구(9) 번을 누르세요.	[전화] First, press number 9, please. (먼저~)
구간버튼을 누르고 돈을 넣으면 됩니다.	[지하철] Please press your destination and deposit your money.
구경 갈까요?	Wanna go sightseeing? // Wanna go sightseeing with me? (같이~) ➡ ⓐ Yes, I do. (같이 가지요.) ⓑ Later. (나중에요.)
구경하고 싶습니다.	I want to go sightseeing. = I want to look around. // I want to go sightseeing at Gyeongbok Palace. (경복궁을~)
구경하고 있어요.	I'm just looking around. = I'm just browsing. = I'm just window-shopping. (저 그냥 ~)
구관이 명관이다.	[속담] Better the devil you know than the devil you don't know.
구급차를 불러주세요.	① Call the ambulance. ② [구조대] Call 911.

ㄱ

구두는 한 치수 작은 것 있습니까?	Do you have a smaller pair of the shoes? = Do you have the shoes in a smaller size? ➡ Yes. Wait a minute. (예, 잠시 기다리세요.)
구두쇠!	Stingy! = Miser! = Cheapskate!
구르는 돌에는 이끼가 끼지 않는다.	[속담] A rolling stone gathers no moss.
구면입니다.	I know her. (나와 그녀는~)
구슬이 서 말이라도 꿰어야 보배.	① [속담] No pain, no gain. ☞ 고진감래 ② 〈직역〉 Nothing is complete unless you put it in final shape.
구역질 난다!	Disgusting! // Really disgusting! (정말~) // This is disgusting. = This nauseates me! = This makes me nauseous! (이건~)
구입은 어디에서 합니까?	Where can I buy things? ➡ Upstairs. (위층이요.)
구정	Lunar New Year's Day = Chinese New Year
구정연휴에 무슨 계획이 있습니까?	Do you have any plans for Chinese New Year? ➡ I plan to visit my hometown. (고향에 다녀오려고 합니다.)
구정은 언제입니까?	When is the Chinese New Year? ➡ January first on the lunar calendar. (음력 1월 1일입니다.)

구제불능이야!	Disaster! = Complete failure!
	// Horrible disaster! (정말~)
	// You are a disaster!
	= You are a complete failure. (넌 정말~)

구질구질한 날씨야!	The weather is bad! = The weather is awful! = The weather is horrible! = The weather is terrible!

ㄱ

구체적으로 말씀해주실래요?	Can you say it in detail? ➡ OK. (그러죠.)
구체적인 얘기는 하지 마세요.	Please don't say it in detail. // Please don't say it in great detail. (너무~)
구취가 심합니다.	You have bad breath. = Your breath smells bad.
구태여 그럴 필요 있겠습니까!	Why bother? = It's not necessary to do so. ➡ You don't need to do so. (그럴 필요 없습니다.)
구토가 심합니다.	I vomited too much. = I threw up too much.
구해주세요.	Please save me. = Please help me. // Come quickly and save me. (빨리 와서~)

구했습니까?	① [물건이 생김] Did you get it?
	② [티켓 · 물건 · 돈 등을 어렵게 구함] Did you find it?
	// Where did you find it? (이거 어디서~)
	// Where did you find such a thing? (이런 걸 어디서~)

국

국경일입니다.	Today is a public holiday. = Today is a national holiday. // The first of October is a national holiday. (10월 1일은~)
국물 한 그릇 추가입니다.	Let me have one more bowl of soup. = I'd like to have one more bowl of soup. = Give me one more bowl of soup, please.
국비장학생으로 유학왔습니다.	I'm an international student with a state scholarship.
국산품입니까, 수입품입니까?	Domestic or import? ➡ Import. (수입품입니다.)

국수 먹으러 갑시다.	Let's have noodles.
국수는 언제 먹습니까?	① When will we have noodles? ② [결혼] When are you planning on getting married? ☞ 결혼은 언제 할 겁니까?
국제전화는 어떻게 겁니까?	How can I make an international call? ➡ Ask it over there. (저쪽에 가서 물어 보세요.)
국제전화를 하려고 합니다.	I'd like to make an international call. = I wanna make an international call. = I have an international call to make.

군

군불에 밥 짓기.	[속담] To catch two pigeons with one bean. = To kill two birds with one stone.
군자는 대로 행.	[속담] A wise man never takes a short cut.
군침이 돕니다.	My mouth is watering. = It's making my mouth water. = I am salivating.

굴

굴러들어온 복을 차버린 것 아닌가요?	[연애] Did I make a stupid mistake in dumping this guy? (저란 사람이~)

굶

굶은 놈이 이 밥 저 밥 가리냐.	[속담] Beggars can't be choosers. = Beggars can't be picky.

굿

굿 아이디어!	Good idea! = That's a good idea! (좋은 생각이야!)

궁

궁금한 게 있습니다.	I'm wondering about something. // I have a question. (한 가지~)
궁금합니까?	① [질문이나 의문] Do you have questions? ➡ Yes. (네.) ② [호기심] Are you curious? ➡ I'm curious. (궁금해요.)

궁금했습니다.	① I have been wondering about you.
	(줄곧 당신에 대해 ~)
	// I've been so wondering about how you're doing. (어떻게 지내는지 정말~)
	② [호기심] I have been curious.
	// I have been really curious. (정말~)
	// I have been very curious. (무척~)

궁하면 통한다.	[속담] Necessity is the mother of invention.

권

(몇) 권	book
	① a / one book (한 권의 책) // two books (두 권의 책)
	// three books (세 권의 책)
	② this book (이 책) // that book (저 책)
	// these two books (이 두 권의 책)
	// these three books (이 세 권의 책)
	// those three books (저 세 권의 책)

귀

귀 막아!	Block your ears! = Plug your ears!
귀 좀 그만 파!	Stop picking your ears!
귀가가 늦습니까?	Will you go home late? // Will you go home late today? (오늘~) ➡ I think so. (그럴 겁니다.)
귀가가 늦습니다.	I'll be late home. // I'll be late home today. (저 오늘~) ➡ OK. (알았어요.)
귀국하다니 섭섭합니다.	I'm sorry to see you leave. // I'm sorry to see you leaving now. (벌써~)
귀국합니까?	When will you return home? // When will you return to Korea? (언제 한국에~) ➡ Next year. (내년이요.)
귀국합니다.	I'm returning. // I'm returning tomorrow. (내일~)
귀동냥으로 들었습니다.	I overheard.
귀머거리 삼 년 벙어리 삼 년 장님 삼 년.	① [속담] No pain, no gain. ☞ 고진감래 ② 〈직역〉 3 years deaf, 3 years dumb and 3 years blind.
귀먹었어?	Are you deaf? = Can't you hear me? = Don't you hear me? ➡ ⓐ Yes. (그래.) ⓑ You are deaf! (너나 귀먹었지!)
귀신같은 녀석!	Real wizard! = You must be a psychic!
귀신같이 알고, 이럴 때 전화를 했네.	[신통력] Such a wonder you called at the best timing. = Your timing is wonderful.

귀신이 곡할 노릇이네.	① It's strange! // It's so strange! (정말~) ② [의문] It's mysterious.
귀싸대기 갈긴다!	I will slap you on the face! ➡ Go ahead! (때려봐!)
귀에 걸면 귀걸이, 코에 걸면 코걸이.	[속담] It depends on the circumstances.
귀에 걸면 귀걸이, 코에 걸면 코걸이인지 알지.	You know it depends on circumstances. // Such a thing differs with circumstances. (이런 일일수록~)
귀여운 녀석! // 귀염둥이!	Cutie! = My dear! = Sweetie! = My darling!
귀여워 죽겠어요.	Super cute.

귀엽다!	① [생김새가 귀여움] Cute! = Sweet! = Lovely!
	// Very cute! (너무~) // Really cute! (정말~)
	// Your daughter is really cute! (따님이 정말~)
	② [남자가 성적인 매력을 지님] The guy over there is cute! (저기 저 남자 ~)

귀중품을 여기에 맡길 수 있습니까?	Can I leave my valuables here? = Can you hold my valuables? ➡ Of course. (그럼요.)
귀중한 의견을 많이 내주세요.	Please give us your precious ideas. = I'm looking forward to your comments.
귀찮게 굴지 마라!	Stop bugging me!
귀찮게 굴지 말고, 저리 가!	Stop bugging me. Go away! = Stop bugging me. Leave me alone!

귀찮게 하지 마세요.	① Don't bother me.
	// Don't bother me anymore. (다시는 나를~)
	// Don't bother me here. (여기서 날~)
	② [기분을 건드림] Don't bug me.

귀찮게 해서 죄송합니다.	Sorry to bother you.

	➡ That's OK. (괜찮아요.)
귀찮아 죽겠네.	Annoying! = Irksome! = Bothering! // I'm sick and tired of him. (그 사람 때문에~) // Who's calling me? What a nuisance! (누가 전화하는 거야?~)
귀청 떨어지겠네.	It's very loud. = It's deafening.
귀한 자식 매 한 대 더 때린다. // 귀한 자식 매로 키워라.	[속담] Spare the rod and spoil the child.

귤

귤 주스를 마시겠습니다.	I would like some tangerine juice.

그

그 스승에 그 제자.	[속담] Blue comes from indigo.
그 시간, 그 장소에서 만나!	[약속] See you then.
그 아버지에 그 자식이네.	Like father, like son. ☞ 부전자전입니다.
그 정도는 아닙니다.	Not like that. // Not like that yet. (아직~)
그건 그렇습니다.	① [동의] I agree. ② [말씀이] That's right.
그건 맞는데.	You're right. = That's the way.
그건 문제가 안 됩니다.	[걱정할 일이 아님] That's not a problem.
그건 안 됩니다.	No way.

ㄱ

그걸 말이라고 해요?	① That doesn't make sense. = What nonsense! = What the hell are you talking about? ② [말로 상처를 입히는 경우] Stop talking like that! ③ [비꼬는 말투] Do you know what you're saying?
그것 좀 봐라!	[비난] See what's happened?
그것도 그러네.	[듣고 보니 일리가 있음] That sounds reasonable. = That sounds logical. = That makes sense.
그게 그거지 뭐?	① [별거 아님] It's like nothing. ② [같음] It's the same. ③ [비김] It's a tie.
그게 꼭 그런 건 아닙니다.	It doesn't always go that way. = It's not always happening like that. = It's always the same.
그게 무슨 뜻입니까?	What do you mean by that? ➡ Nothing. (아무 뜻 없어요.)
그게 아닙니다.	① [사실과 다름] That's not true. ② [의미] It's not like that. ☞ 그런 게 아닙니다.
그게 어디 되겠습니까?	Do you think it's possible? ➡ We should make it happen. (안 되면 되게 해야 합니다.)
그게 어쨌다는 거야?	[시비] So what?
그길로 나가라!	[빈정거리는 말투] Go for it!
그까짓 게 대수냐?	Does it matter? = Is it a big deal?
그냥 그대로 두세요.	① [건들지 말고] Leave it alone. (그거~) ② [물건을] Leave it there. (그곳에~)
그냥 그대로야.	[생활의 변화가 없음] Nothing special. = Same as before.
그냥 그래요.	[병세나 상황의 변화가 없음] Neither better nor worse.

그냥 나왔습니다.	[외출] I just came out. = I'm not going anywhere. ➡ Where are you going? (어디 가십니까?)
그냥 돌아다닙니다.	[산책] I'm just walking around. = I'm just taking a walk.
그냥 하는 소리입니다.	It's just meaningless. = I didn't mean anything at all.
그냥 해 본 소리가 아닙니다.	I meant something. = It's not just meaningless. = I said it on purpose.
그놈하고 같이 있냐?	[교제] Are you with him?
그는 안 됩니다.	[능력부족] Not him.
그대로네.	① [상황이나 모습이 변화가 없음] Same here. = Nothing has changed. = It looks the same as before. = Same as usual. = Nothing special. ② [내용 · 형식 · 수법 등이 옛날 그대로 변화가 없음] Same as before.
그동안 대단히 감사했습니다.	Thank you so much.
그동안 어디 갔었니?	Where have you been?
그때 봅시다!	See you then!
그때 그때 달라요.	It depends on the circumstances. = It varies. = It depends on the situation. ➡ What do you mean? (그게 무슨 말입니까?)
그때 그때 얘기해!	Tell me whenever you want to! // Don't hold your tongue. Tell me whenever you want to! (참지 말고, ~)
그때는 그때고, 지금은 지금입니다.	It's not the same as before. = That was then, this is now. = Let bygones be bygones.

ㄱ

ㄱ

그래 그럼.	[동의] Certainly. = Surely.
그래 그래!	① [마지못해 하는 동의] OK. ② [호응] Sure. = Why not?
그래야지.	That's it. = That's the way it goes.
그래요.	① [동의] Right. = All right. ☞ 좋습니다. ② Fine. ← How's everybody? (다들 잘 있습니까?) ③ [확인] Yes. Of course. (~당연하죠.)
그랬어요.	[사실을 인정함] Yes, it was. = You're right. = That's right.
그랬었구나!	① [이해] Oh, I see! = I got it! ② [이상할 것 없음] No wonder! ③ [짐작함] I already knew it! ☞ 어쩐지!
그랬으면 좋겠습니다.	① [바람] I hope so. = I'm looking forward to it. = I'm longing for it. // If so, it couldn't be better. (만약~) ② [간절한 바람] I really wish for it.
그러게 말이야.	① [상대 의견에 동의] You can say that again. = I agree with you. = You're right. = Quite so. = That's right. = I said so, too. ← Stop it! (그만둬 해!) ② Quite right. = Surely it is. = Quite so. ☞ 그렇고 말고요!
그러기만을 바랍니다.	I'm looking forward to it.
그러기야?	This is hilarious! = This is outrageous!
그러네요.	[어떤 상황이나 일에 대한 판단] That's the way it goes.
그러는 게 좋겠습니다.	It's better to do so.

그러니까!	① [호응] That's why! ② No wonder! ☞ 어쩐지!
그러든지!	[판단 후의 동의] As you said so!
그러려니 하세요.	[시비하지 말고] Never mind. // Never mind him. (그놈은~)
그러죠.	① [동의] Sure. ② [마지못해 하는 동의] OK.
그러지 마세요.	① [행위] Stop it. = Cut it out. = Stop acting like that. ② [상투적인 행위] Please don't do it. ③ [예의차림에] Please no. // That's too much. (너무~) ④ [사양] No, thank you.
그러지 뭐!	OK, I will!

그러지 않겠습니다.	① I'll never do it again. (다시는~)
	// From now on, I'll never do it. (다음부터~)
	② [무례한 행위를] I won't do it.
	// I won't do it again. (다시는~)
	// I won't do it next time. (다음부터는~)
	// I will be careful next time. I won't do it. (다음번에는 꼭 주의해서, ~)

그러지요.	[동의] Sure. = OK.
그럭저럭 지냅니다.	I'm fine. = Not too bad. = Just so-so.
그럭저럭.	① [수입 등이] Manageable. ② [상황] Fine. ③ [생활] Nothing special. ③ [정도 · 수준] So so.
그런 거야.	Such is the way. = That's the way it goes. // That's always the way it goes. (다~)
그런 거였군요!	Oh, I see! = I got it! ☞ 그랬었구나!

그런 거지 뭐.	You knew it.
그런 것 같습니다.	I think so.
그런 게 아닙니다.	① [사실과 다름] That's not the case. // That's not true. (일이~) ② It's not what you're thinking. (당신이 생각하는~)
그런 게 어디있어!	[헛소리] Nonsense!
그런 눈으로 쳐다보지 마세요.	Stop looking like that. // Stop looking at people like that. (사람을~) // Don't look at me like that. (절~) // Don't give my mom that strange look again. (다시는 우리 엄마를~)
그런 뜻으로 말한 게 아닙니다.	① I didn't mean it that way. (저는~) ② I never meant it that way. (저는 결코~)
그런 말씀 마세요.	① [감사에 대한 대답] Don't mention it. = It was nothing. ② Stop saying it. ③ [제지] Don't say such a thing.
그런 소리하지 마세요.	Don't say such a thing. ☞ 그런 말씀 마세요.
그런 식으로 말하지 마세요.	① Don't talk that way. = Stop talking like that. ② [경고] You must not talk that way!
그런 일 없습니다.	① Nothing like that. = It didn't happen. // It never happened. (정말~) ② [비존재] No such a thing.
그런가봐요.	① [추측] Maybe that's right. ② [생각] I think so, too.
그런대로.	① [만족 · 수준] So so. ② [생활 · 일처리] It's OK.
그런데 (말이야).	① [대화시작] By the way. ② [대화중에 일의 결말 말함] You know what?

	= Guess what happened?
그런데!	[의견 제기] However!
그런데?	[다음 대화를 유도] So? = What happened? ➡ Nothing. (없어.)
그럴 가치도 없습니다.	No need. = **It's not worth it.**
그럴 겁니다.	① [추측] It might be. ➡ Isn't it good? (그거 괜찮지?) ② Maybe.
그럴 기분 아닙니다.	**I'm not in the mood.** = I don't feel like it.

그럴 리 없습니다.	① [추측] It's not possible. = That can't be.
	// That can never be possible. (절대~)
	// That's forever impossible. (영원히~)
	⬅ He stole something from others.
	(그가 다른 사람의 물건을 훔쳤어요.)
	② [불신] I don't think so.
	③ [불가능] Never.
	// This never happened. (이건~)
	☞ 그런 일 없습니다.

그럴 리가요?	① [가능] That can't be possible. ② [상대의 걱정에 대해] No way! ③ [믿기지 않음] **That can't be!** ➡ Why not? (왜 아니겠어요!)
그럴 줄 알았습니다.	① [예측이 맞음] I already knew it. ② [별일 없었을 것에 대한 짐작] I was aware of it.
그럴지도 모릅니다.	① [우려 · 걱정] That might be true. ② [추측] That could be possible.
그럴 필요 없습니다.	① [필요] **That's not necessary.** ② You don't need to do so. // You don't need to do so. Thank you so much anyway. (~대단히 감사합니다.)

그럴 필요 있을까요?	[필요] Is it necessary? ➡ Yes, it is necessary. (그럴 필요 있습니다.)
그럼 그렇게 합시다.	[결정] Let's do it that way.
그럼 됐어요.	[안심] Fine.
그럼 이만!	① [자리를 뜨며 하는 작별인사] Bye for now. ② [정중한 작별인사] Good bye. ③ [전화대화의 맺는 말] Bye.
그럼(요)!	① [동의] That's right! ② [당연] Of course! = Certainly! = Surely! ☞ 당연하지. ③ Bye for now! ☞ 그럼 이만! // 그렇고말고요.
그렇게 비쌉니까?	Is it that expensive? ➡ Because it's high-quality and imported. (품질이 우수하고, 수입부품이기 때문입니다.)
그렇게 생각 안 합니다.	① I don't think so. = I don't think that way. ② [의심] I doubt.
그렇게 생각합니까?	Do you think that way? // Why do you think that way? (어째서~) ➡ Don't you know why? (왜 그런지 몰라요!)
그렇게 생각합니다.	I think so. // I think so, too. (저도~)
그렇게 안 보입니다.	① [판단] You don't look like that. ② [나이] You don't look that old. = You look younger than your age. = You don't look your age.
그렇게 잘났나?	[상대의 교만에 대해] Do you think you are that special? = Do you think you're something? ➡ Yeah, I am that special. (당연히 잘났지.)
그렇게 좋으냐!	How happy you are! = You like it too much! = You are so happy!

그렇게 좋으냐?	Do you like it that much? ➡ ⓐ Yes. (예.) ⓑ Of course. (당연하죠.) ⓒ Can't you believe it? (안 믿기세요?)
그렇게 하겠습니다.	[분부나 지시대로] I'll do it. = OK. = No problem. = Sure thing.
그렇게 하도록 하겠습니다.	I'll do it.
그렇게 하세요.	[처리] Go ahead. // I like it. Go ahead. (좋아요, ~)
그렇게 합시다.	① [제안에 동의] OK. = That's good. = That sounds great / good. = Great. = Good. ② [결정] Let's do it that way. // OK. Let's do it that way. (좋아요, ~)
그렇게나 빨리!	[일을 빨리 끝냄] How fast! = You have done it so fast! = You are so fast!
그렇게는 생각하지 않습니다.	I don't think so. = I don't think that way.
그렇게는 안 되지요.	[대가를 요구함] I can't take it. = That's not that easy.
그렇게는 안 됩니다.	[반대] I don't get it.
그렇고 말고!	① [동의] Yes! ② [호응] That's right! = Right!= That's true! = Exactly! ③ [확인] You're right! ④ [두말할 필요 없음] You can say that again! ⑤ [말에 일리가 있음] That sounds right. = That's a good point! ⑥ [구두약속] OK! ⑦ [상대의 의견에 대한 동감] I agree! = I couldn't agree more! = That's exactly what I think!

ㄱ

	⬅ It's so hard to handle kids these days. (요즘 애들은 다루기 힘들어요.) ☞ 그럼!
그렇군요.	[사실을 듣고 나서] I see.
그렇다고 말할 수 있습니다.	You can say that again.
그렇다고 봐야죠.	It's so.
그렇다고 생각합니다.	I think so.
그렇다고 할 수 있습니다.	That's true.
그렇습니까?	① [확인] Is it true? ➡ Yes. = Surely. (그렇습니다.) ② [동의] Do you agree? ③ [의견 확인] Do you think so?
그렇지 않습니까?	① Don't you think so? ➡ Yes, I think so! (그래요!) ② [동의] Don't you agree? ➡ Yes, I agree. (그렇습니다.)
그렇지 않습니다.	① I don't think so. ② [추측] I don't think it's possible. ③ [상태] It is not. ④ [확인] No.
그리	Not Particularly. ☞ 별로
그리 비싸지 않습니다.	It's not that expensive.
그리고요?	And then? ➡ No. That's it. (없어요. 이것뿐이에요.)
그리웠습니다.	I missed you.
그림을 잘 그립니까?	① Are you good at drawing / painting? ➡ ⓐ Just so so. (그저 그렇습니다.)

	ⓑ Not so good. (별롭니다.) ② Is he a good painter? (그는~) ➡ ⓐ Yes, he is. (잘 그립니다.) ⓑ No, he isn't. (못 그립니다.)
그림의 떡입니다.	[속담] **It's a pie in the sky.** // This is like a pie in the sky. (이런 방법은 다만~)
그만 가보겠습니다!	I must leave now! ☞ 가보겠습니다!

그만 끊겠습니다.	① [전화] I have to say bye now.
	// OK. I have to say bye now. (예. ~)
	// I have to say bye for now. (그럼~)
	② [더 귀찮게 않겠다는 전화 인사말] I'll let you go.

그만 마셔요.	① [제지] Stop it now.
	② Stop drinking. You can't drink that much. (~술 마시지도 못 하면서.)
	// Stop drinking. You will get drunk. (~취합니다.)
	// Stop drinking. Let's go. (~우리 갑시다.)

그만 먹을래요.	I want to stop eating now. = **I've had enough.**
그만 울어!	Stop crying!

그만 좀 해!	① [정신적인 괴롭힘] **That's enough!** = Cut it out!
	② [잔소리나 잘난척하는 꼴] Stop acting like that!
	// Stop acting like that! I'm sick and tired of it. (~이제 지겨워.)
	③ [장난이 심함] Don't!
	④ [난리나 소란 피움] Stop it!
	// Stop it, please! (제발~)
	⑤ [말을] Don't say any more words!
	= Don't talk!
	➡ Why not? (왜 안돼요?)

그만두겠습니다.	① [일을] I'll quit. ② [단념] I give up.

ㄱ

ㄱ

그만두자! / 그만둡시다.	① [말이나 행위를 제지] Let's not do it. // No way. Let's not do it. (아니요, ~) ② [말이나 행위를] Let's stop it.
그만둬!	① Stop it! ② [비난] Cut it out! ☞ 그만해!
그만뒀습니다.	① [일을] I gave it up. ② [회사를] I quit. // He already quit. (그는 벌써~)
그만합시다.	① [대화를 끝냄] Let's finish our conversation. = Let's end our conversation. (우리~) ➡ What? (무슨 소리야?) ② [대화 제지] Stop it. // Stop it now. Please leave. (~그만 가주세요.) ③ [회의] Let's finish the discussion now. ☞ 그만두자!
그만해!	① [말을] Stop it! = Cut it out! = Stop talking! ② [만족] That's enough! = Enough! ☞ 됐습니다! ③ [싸움을 제지] Stop it! // Stop it now! (어서~) ④ [귀찮게 같은 동작이나 말을 반복하는 경우] That's enough! ⑤ [지나친 언행에 대해] Shut up! ☞ 입 닥쳐! ⑥ [말 같지도 않은 말에 대해] Cut the crap out! ⑦ [대화 제지] No more words! ⑧ [소란 · 장난] Stop the fuss! ⑨ Cut it out! ☞ 그만 좀 해!
그밖에 다른 것 있습니까?	[상점] Do you have anything else? ➡ No. (더 없어요.)
그분도 한국 사람입니다.	He is Korean, too.
그분에게 볼 일이 있으십니까?	Do you have something to do with him? ➡ Yes, I do. (일이 좀 있어서요.)
그분은 중국인입니까?	Is he Chinese? ➡ ⓐ Yes. (예.)

ⓑ No. He's Korean. (아니오, 그는 한국사람 입니다.)

그저 그렇습니다.	Neither better nor worse. = Nothing special. // I go to work and come back home. It's just nothing special. (~출근하고 퇴근하고.)

ㄱ

근

근데.	① [편하게 질문함] Well. = By the way. ② [본 화제로 돌림] Anyway.
근무 중입니다.	On duty. // We're on duty. (우리 ~)
근무시간 아닙니까?	Aren't you on duty now? = Isn't it your working hours? ➡ Yes. (예.)
근방에 삽니다. // 근처에 삽니다.	I live nearby. // I live nearby. Right ahead of you. (~바로 앞쪽입니다.)
근처 어디에 운동장이 있습니까?	Is there a playground near here? ➡ There is one in a mile. (1마일 안에 운동장이 있습니다.)

근처에 있을 겁니다.	① [당연] Must be around here.
	// He must be around here. (그 사람은~)
	② [추측] Might be around here.
	// My mom might be around here.
	(저희 엄마가 ~)

글

글쎄요.	① [정확기 말하기 어려움] I don't know. = Well. ② [상대방의 관점을 부정] You can't be for sure. ③ [가능성이 높음] That's possible.

	④ [자세히 모름] Let me see. ⑤ [결정 내리지 못함] Let me think.
글씨를 쓸 줄 모릅니다.	I don't know how to write.

금

금강산도 식후경.	[속담] A loaf of bread is better than the song of many birds. = The belly has no eyes. = In any situation, eating comes first.
금방 갑니다.	① [대답] I'm coming. ② [자리를 뜸] Yes. I'm going there.
금방 오겠습니다.	I'll be right back. = I'll be back here soon.
금상첨화.	It's like icing on the cake.
금시초문입니다.	① I've never heard of it before. = I didn't know it. = I didn't expect it. = That's quite news to me. // This is quite news to me. (이 일은~) ☞ 처음 듣습니다. ② [기발한 생각이나 언행에 대해] That's a revelation to me.
금연!	[경고문] No smoking!
금연석으로 주세요.	Non-smoking, please.
금연입니다.	I quit smoking. // I quit smoking from today. (오늘부터~)
금의환향하시기를 바랍니다.	I wish your returning home in glory. // I wish you gloriously return home as soon as possible. (하루 빨리~)

급

급성맹장염입니다.	You have acute appendicitis.
급한 용건입니까?	Do you have something urgent? = Is it urgent? ➡ Yes. (예.)
급한 일로 당신을 찾고 있습니다.	Looking for you in urgent needs.
급한 일이 생겨서 먼저 가보겠습니다.	Something urgent came up, so I am leaving. // Something urgent came up, so I must leave now. (~먼저 가봐야겠습니다.)
급할수록 돌아간다.	[속담] Make haste slowly. = The more haste, the less speed.
급해 죽겠네!	So busy!
급행열차는 몇 시입니까?	What time will the express train come? // What time will the next express train come? (다음~) ➡ At five thirty. (5시 반입니다.)
급히 가야 합니다.	I must hurry up.

긍

긍정적으로 생각하세요.	[속담] Please think positive. = Please look at the bright side. = Every cloud has a siver lining. ☞ 좋은 쪽으로 생각하세요.

기

기가 막혀서!	① [어의가 없음] Dumbfounded! = Shocking! ② [방법이 없음] No way!

	③ [믿기 어려움] **Unbelievable!** // Really unbelievable! (정말~)
기가 막힙니다.	① [부합] I'm rather taken aback. ② [놀람] I can't believe this. = I'm shocked.
기간만료가 언제입니까?	When is the expiration date? = When does it expire? = When will it expire? ➡ You have seven days. = It will expire in seven days. (아직 7일 남았습니다.)
기간을 연장해 줄 수 없습니까?	**Can you give me an extension?** ➡ No, I can't. (안 됩니다.)
기내에서 파는 물건은 모두 면세품입니까?	Are goods in the airplane duty free? ➡ Yes, they are. (그렇습니다.)
기내에서는 핸드폰 사용이 금지되어 있습니다.	You can't use cellphones in airplanes. = You're not allowed to use cellphones in airplanes.
기념일을 축하합니다.	Congratulations on your anniversary.
기념품 좀 사고 싶습니다.	I'd like to buy some souvenirs.
기다려 보세요.	Wait, please. // Wait some time, please. (좀~)
기다려 봅시다.	① [일을 뒤로 미룸] Let's wait. ② [인내] Let's have some patience. = Let's be patient. (인내심을 갖고 더~)
기다려야 합니까?	① How much more do I have to wait? (얼마나~) ➡ About two hours. (약 두 시간이요.) ② Until what time should I wait? (언제까지~) ➡ Just for some time. (잠깐이면 됩니다.)
기다려요.	Wait. = **Hold on.** // Wait a moment. (잠깐~)

기다리게 해서 미안합니다.	I'm sorry to keep you waiting. ➡ That's OK. (괜찮습니다.)
기다리겠습니다.	I'll wait. // I'll wait here. (여기서~)

기다리고 있어!	Wait there! (그 자리에~)
	// Wait here! (여기서~)
	// Wait here until I am back. (나 올 때까지 여기서~)

기다리고 있었습니다.	① [사람] I've been waiting for you. (마침 당신을~) // He's been waiting for you. (그가 쭉~) ② I've been waiting for your call. (당신의 전화를~)
기다리다가 방금 갔습니다.	He waited for a long time, but just left. (그가 한참~)
기다리세요.	[전화표현] Hold on, please. = Just a minute, please. = Hang on, please. (잠깐만~)
기다린 보람이 있었네요.	It was worthwhile waiting.
기다릴 겁니다.	I will wait.
기대가 큰 만큼 실망도 큽니다.	The higher the expectation, the bigger the disappointment.
기대하지 마세요.	Don't expect. = Don't look forward to it. = Don't anticipate. // Don't expect too much. (너무 크게 ~)
기똥차다.	It's surprising. = It's amazing. // It's very surprising. (정말~)
기름을 가득 채워주세요.	Please fill it up. // Please fill up the gas tank. (오일탱크에~)
기름이 떨어졌어요.	Out of oil. = No oil.
기름진 요리에 익숙하지 않습니다.	I'm not used to oily food.

ㄱ

ㄱ

기막힙니다.	① [감탄] It's amazing! ② [기발한 생각이나 언행에 대해] Unbelievable. = Incredible.
기분 나쁩니까?	Are you upset? // Why are you upset? (왜~) ➡ No reasons! (이유 없어!)
기분 나쁩니다.	I'm upset. = I feel bad. // I'm very upset. (몹시~) // It's upsetting me. = That sounds very bad. (그 소리 아주~)
기분 잡치네.	[술자리] It's spoiling all the fun. // It's really messed up. (정말~)
기분 좋습니까?	Are you happy? ➡ Yes, I am happy. (기분 좋아요.)
기분 좋습니다.	① I am so happy. (너무~) ② [만족] I'm so satisfied. (너무~)
기분 나빠 말아요.	Don't be upset. ➡ Nothing to be upset about. (기분 나쁜 거 없어.)
기분 나빠하지 말아요.	Don't be upset.
기분이 어떻습니까?	① [안부] How are you? ➡ ⓐ Good. (좋습니다.) ⓑ Not bad. (그런대로요.) ② How do you feel? ➡ ⓐ Great! (아주 좋습니다.) ⓑ Not bad. (그런대로요.)
기분이 좋습니다.	I'm very fine now. (지금 매우~) // I'm fine now. (오늘~)
기분이 좋아 보입니다.	① You look happy. // You look surprisingly upbeat today. (오늘 놀랍도록~) ② [건강] You look quite good today. (오늘은 꽤~)

기쁩니다.	I'm happy. = I feel great. // I feel so good. (너무~)
	// I'm really happy. (정말~)
	// I feel so good today. (오늘은 너무~)

기사아저씨!	① [정중하게] Sir! = Mr.! ② [낮춰부름] Driver!
기숙사가 밝고 깨끗합니다.	The dorm is clean and bright.
기억났습니까?	Did you remember? ➡ ⓐ Yes, I remembered. (기억났습니다.) ⓑ No. (아니요.)
기억력이 좋네요. // 기억을 잘 하십니다.	You have a good memory. = You remember well.
기억에 남는 것은 무엇입니까?	What do you remember? // What do you remember most? (가장~) ➡ Having Chinese food. (중국음식 먹은 겁니다.)
기억이 없는데요.	[인상] I can't remember. = No memories.

기억하고 있습니까?	Do you remember? // Do you still remember? (아직도~) // Do you remember me? (절~)
	➡ ⓐ Yes, I do. (기억합니다.) // Of course, I remember. (당연히 기억하죠.)
	ⓑ No. (아니요.)
	ⓒ Yes, I kinda remember. (기억나는 것 같습니다.)

기억해!	[당부] Remember it! = Keep it in mind!
기온은 몇도입니까?	What's the temperature today? (오늘~) ➡ Eighteen degrees at the highest, and ten degrees at the lowest. (최고기온은 18도이고, 최저기온은 10도입니다.)
기왕이면 다홍치마.	[속담] Better a castle of bones than of stones.

ㄱ

기운 내!	① [격려] Cheer up! ② [응원] Go! = Way to go! = Come on! ☞ 파이팅! // 힘내!
기운 내세요.	① [격려] Cheer up. ② [환자에게] I hope you feel better.
기재해 주세요.	① Please fill it out. // Please fill out the chart. (이 표에~) ② 〈경어〉 Would you please fill out this form? (이 양식에~)
기절하겠네.	I'm dying. = I feel like I'm passing out.
기절했습니다.	He passed out. = He felt faint. (그는~)
기죽지 마세요.	Don't lose your courage. = Don't get discouraged. // Don't get discouraged too much. (너무~)
기차 타고 갑니까, 비행기 타고 갑니까?	Will you use the train or the airplane? ➡ I'll use the train. (기차 타고 갑니다.)
기차 타고 갑시다.	Let's go by train.
기차를 놓쳤습니다.	I missed the train.
기차를 타는 게 좋을까요, 고속버스가 좋을까요?	Which is better, the train or the express bus? ➡ The train is better. (기차가 좋지요.)
기차를 타면 몇 시간 걸립니까?	How long does it take by the train? ➡ Twenty hours. (20시간이요.)
기차역에 가려면 어떻게 갑니까?	How can I get to the train station? ➡ ⓐ Nearby ahead of you. (앞쪽으로 얼마 안 가서 있습니다.) ⓑ Turn right and then turn left at the second traffic light. (우측으로 돌아서, 두 번째 신호등에서 좌회전하면 됩니다.)

기차역은 여기에서 멉니까?	Is the train station far from here? ➡ A few steps from here. (몇 걸음 안 됩니다.)
기차와 고속버스 중 어느 것이 더 빠릅니까?	Which is faster, the train or the express bus? ➡ The train is faster. (기차가 더 빠릅니다.)
기차표 두 장 주세요.	Two tickets, please.
기차표는 몇 시 겁니까?	What time is your ticket for? (당신의~) ➡ Ten thirty at night. (밤 10시 반 차입니다.)
기침도 나고 목도 아픕니다.	I have a cough and a sore throat.
기침도 나고 식은 땀도 납니다.	I'm coughing and sweating.
기침약을 먹었습니다.	I had cough drops. = I took cough medicine.
기침약을 주세요.	Please give me cough medicine.
기침을 심하게 합니다.	I have a bad cough.
기침이 그쳤습니다.	My coughing has stopped. = I stopped coughing.
기침이 멈추지 않습니다.	I can't stop coughing.
기침이 심합니까?	Is your cough bad? ➡ ⓐ Yes, it is. (기침이 심합니다.) ⓑ No, it isn't. (심하지 않습니다.)
기침하고 콧물나고 머리도 아픕니다.	I have a cough, a runny nose and a headache.
기회는 또 올 겁니다.	You'll have another chance. // You'll have another chance again. (앞으로~)
기회는 또 있을 겁니다.	There will be another chance.
기회는 많습니다.	There are many chances.

ㄱ

	// There will be more chances from now on. (앞으로~)
기회를 놓쳤습니다.	① I missed the chance. ② [자신의 과오] I blew the chance.
기회를 놓치지 마세요.	① I'll never miss out on any opportunity. (결코~) ② [속담] Make hay while the sun shines.
기회를 놓치지 말고, 잘해요.	[절호의 기회] Don't miss a chance. Cheer up.
기회를 한번 주세요.	[간청] Please give me a chance. (제발~)
기회만 엿보고 있습니다.	I'm waiting for a chance now. (지금~)
기후는 어떻습니까?	① How's the weather in Korea? = What's the weather like in Korea? (한국의~) ➡ ⓐ It's humid. (습기가 많습니다.) ⓑ It's very good. (기후는 참 좋습니다.) ② How's the weather there? (그곳의~) ➡ Spring in all seasons. (사계절이 봄 같습니다.)

긴

긴급 상황입니다.	It's an emergency. // This is an emergency. (이건~)
긴말 할 것 없어!	① Don't say any more words! = Cut it short! ② [쓸데없는 말에] No more useless words!
긴장 풀어요.	① [이완] Relax. ② [편안함] Feel at home. ③ [위로] Take it easy.
긴장됩니다.	I'm nervous. // I'm so nervous. (아주~) // I'm most nervous when I get my report card. (성적표 받을 때가 가장~)

길

길 맞은 편에서 타세요.	Take the bus across from here.
길 좀 가르쳐 주세요.	Would you give me directions?
길 좀 묻겠습니다.	Can I ask you for directions?
길고 짧은 것은 대봐야 안다.	[속담] You can't always tell from appearances. = You can't tell which is longer unless you measure them against each other.
길목에 세워 주세요.	Please stop the car at the corner. // Please stop the car at the front corner. (앞쪽 저기~) ➡ No parking here. (여긴 주차금지입니다.)
길에서 우연히 만났습니다.	I met him on the street by chance. = It was coincidental that I met him on the street. = I ran into him on the street by chance. = I bumped into him on the street by chance. (그를 ~)
길옆에 세워 주세요.	Please stop the car on the side of the street.
길을 안내하겠습니다.	I'll show you the way. (제가~) ➡ Thank you, but I can go by myself. (감사합니다만 혼자 갈 수 있습니다.)
길을 압니까?	Do you know the way? // Does he know the way? (그가~) ➡ Yes. (잘 압니다.)
길을 잃었습니다.	I got lost. = I'm lost.
길이 미끄러우니, 조심하세요.	Please be careful of slippery roads.
길조심하세요.	Please be careful. = Take care. = Take care of yourself.

ㄱ

김

김밥 옆구리 터지는 소리하고 있네!	What the hell are you talking about again? (또~)
김밥이 맛있습니다.	① [한식] *gimbap* is delicious. ② [일식] The California roll is delicious.
김빠집니다.	It sounds boring. = It sounds dull.
김치맛이 어떤가요?	How do you like *gimchi*? ➡ I don't like *gimchi* much. (김치가 입맛에 안 맞습니다.)
김치찌개 주세요.	Let me have *gimchi* soup, please.
김칫국부터 마신다.	[속담] Don't count your chickens before they're hatched.

깁

깁니까?	Is it long? [길이] // How long is it? (얼마나~) ➡ Five feet. (5 피트입니다.)

까

까놓고 말하다.	I'm totally honest with you. = To be frank with you. (너한테~)
까다롭게 굴긴!	Don't be picky! = Don't be choosy! = Don't be particular!
까마귀 날자 배 떨어진다.	[속담] It is just a coincidence that the two events have happened at the same time.
까마귀가 백로되기를 바란다.	[속담] Once a devil, always a devil. = Once a knave, and ever a knave.

	☞ 헛물만 켜는 거야.
까먹었습니까?	[망각] Did you forget? ☞ 잊어버렸습니까?
까불지 마!	① What a cheek! = Well, of all the cheek! ② 〈속어〉 Stop the bullshit! ③ [소란] Don't make a fuss! ④ [시비] Stop picking fights! ⑤ [어떻게 해 볼 생각] Don't be so boisterous!

깍

깍두기 좀 갖다 주세요.	Please give me some radish *gimchi*.
깍쟁이!	① You, shrewd! ② [부정적] You, sly dog!
깍깍!	Caw, caw!

깎

깎아주세요.	① [머리] Have my hair cut like this picture. (이 사진대로~) ② [과일을] Please peel the fruit. (과일을~) ③ [가격] Would you give me a discount. ☞ 싸게 좀 해주세요.
깎아줄래요?	① [가격] Can you lower the price? (좀 더~) ➡ I can't. No profits with more discount. (더 깎아드리면 남는 게 없습니다.) ② [할인] Can I get it at a discount? ➡ ⓐ Sure. (그럼요.) ⓑ No. (안 됩니다.) ③ [과일 등] Can you peel the fruit? ➡ OK. (좋아요.)

	④ [연필 등] Can you sharpen my pencil? ⑤ [손톱 등] Can you clip my fingernails?
깎을 수 있습니까?	[가격을] Can I get it cheaper? = **Can I get a discount?** = Can I get it at the lower price? (좀 더~) ➡ ⓐ It's already cheap enough. = It's reduced already. (충분히 깎아드렸습니다.) ⓑ No more. (더 싸게는 안 됩니다.)

깔

깔깔!	[웃음소리] Chortle, chortle!

깜

깜빡할 뻔 했네요.	I almost forgot. ☞ 잊을 뻔 했네요.

깜빡했습니다.	I forgot. // Sorry. I forgot. (죄송합니다. ~)
	// I forgot I had something to do. (일 있는 걸~)
	// I forgot to bring the textbook.
	(교과서를 가져오는 걸~)

깜짝 놀랐습니다.	I was surprised. ☞ 놀랐습니다.

깨

깨끗이 닦아 주세요.	① [걸레로] Wipe it out, please. ② [세탁] Clean it up, please.
깨우지 마세요.	Don't wake me up, please. // Don't wake up Mr. I, please. (이씨를~)
깨워주세요.	[모닝콜] **Please give me a wake-up call.**

	// Please wake me up at six. (아침 6시에~) // Please wake me up early tomorrow morning. (내일 아침 일찍~)
깨지는 물건 취급 주의	Fragile. = Handle with care.

꺼

꺼내지 마세요.	① [말] Don't talk about it. ☞ 말 마세요. ② [물건] Don't take it out.
꺼벙하긴!	Idiot! = Stupid! = Fool! = Foolish!
꺼억!	[트림소리] Burp!

꺼져!	① [옆에 있지 말고] Go away!
	② [멀리 쫓아냄] Get out! = Out!
	// You, get out! (넌~)
	// You, get the hell out of here! (네가 꺼져, 새끼야!)
	③ 〈속어〉 Get the hell out of here! ☞ 사라져!

껄

껄껄!	[웃음소리] Chuckle.

껌

껌 값이지!	It's very cheap! = It's knockout! // It's as cheap as kids' bubble gum. (정말 애들~)

껴

껴안아 주세요.	Please hug me. // Please hug me tight. (꼭~)

꼬

꼬끼오!	[닭소리] Cock-a-doodle-doo!
꼬락서니하고는!	① [놀람] **Look at you!** = What a sight! = What's wrong with you? // What's wrong with him today? (저 친구 오늘~) ② [더러움] How dirty you are! ③ [비난 및 경멸] **Shame on you!** = What a plight!
꼬르륵!	[배에서 나는 소리] Rumbling!
꼬마야!	Hey, boy!

꼭

꼭 나오세요.	[약속] Please make it there. = Please show up there.
꼭 돌아와야 합니다.	Please come back. = Make sure you come back.
꼭꼭 씹어서 먹어요.	Please chew the food well.

꼴

꼴값 떨고 있네.	[제3자에게] Look at that shameless face! That sly one pretends not to know. (~저 놈 시치미만 떼고 있어.)
꼴도 보기 싫어!	① I don't wanna see you! // I don't wanna see you again! (다시는 너~) ② [강한 어조] **I hate your ass!**
꼴좋다!	It serves you right! = You deserve it!

= You've got what you deserved!
☞ 고소하다! // 꼬락서니하고는!

ㄱ

꼼

꼼짝 마!	Freeze! = **Don't move!** = Hold still!
꼼짝 말고 있어요.	Stay here, please. // Don't go anywhere. Stay here, please. (어디 가지 말고 ~)

꽁

꽁무니를 빼다.	I chickened out of it. = I shrank from it. = I stepped back.

꽃

꽃에 물을 좀 주세요.	Water the flowers, please.

꽈

꽈당!	[넘어지는 소리] Boom!

꽉

꽉 물어!	[입으로] Bite it! = Hold it in your mouth! // Bite it! (그걸~)
꽉 잡아!	**Hold it tight!** // Hold me tight. (날~)

ㄱ

꽝

꽝!	[문 닫는 소리] Bang!
꽝이야!	① [공백] Blank! ② [마음에 들지 않음] It's nothing after all! = It's useless! = It's in vain! = It's futile! // It's really useless! (아주~)

꽥

꽥꽥!	[오리나 개구리 소리] Quack quack!

꾀

꾀병 부리지 마세요.	Don't pretend to be sick.

꾸

꾸물대지 마!	Don't waste time! = Why are you so slow!
꾸벅꾸벅 졸지 마세요.	Don't fall asleep. = Don't doze off! = Stop nodding off.
꾸어 온 보릿자루.	① [속담] It's like a cat in a strange garret. ☞ 꿔다놓은 보리자루. ② Idiot! ☞ 못난 놈! // 바보같은 놈!
꾸중을 들었습니다.	I was scolded. // I was scolded by the teacher. = I got in trouble with the teacher. (선생님한테~)

꿀

꿀 먹은 벙어리.	Dumb.

꿀 먹은 벙어리가 됐냐?	Did you become dumb? // Why are you being dumb now? (어쩨~) ➡ You are dumb. (너나 그렇겠지.)
꿀꺽꿀꺽!	[물먹는 소리] Gulp gulp!
꿀꿀!	[돼지 울음소리] Oink, oink!

꿇

꿇어!	① [무릎] Kneel down! = On your knees! = Get down on your knees. = Down on your knees! ② [항복] Surrender to me!

꿈

꿈 깨! // 꿈 깨시지!	① [비난] Are you dreaming? ② [부정 · 거절] Wake up!
꿈꾸고 있네!	[비난] Are you dreaming? ☞ 꿈 깨!
꿈도 야무져!	[실현 불가능한 이상적인 생각] You are such a dreamer!
꿈에도 생각지 못했습니다.	I've never dreamed of it. // I never dreamed of meeting you here. = I never dreamed I would meet you here. (여기에서 당신을 만날 줄은~)
꿈은 이뤄진다.	Your dreams will come true.
꿈인지 생시인지?	Is this a dream or what? = Am I dreaming?

ㄱ

꿍

꿍꿍이 속이 뭐야?

What the hell are you thinking about?
// What on earth are you thinking about?
(도대체~)

꿔

꿔다 놓은 보리자루.

It's like a cat in a strange garret.
☞ 꾸어 온 보릿자루.

꿩

꿩 먹고 알 먹기네.

[속담] To catch two pigeons with one bean.
= To kill two birds with one stone.

끈

끈 떨어진 연이네.

It's like a kite with no string.

끊

끊는다!

[전화] I'll hang up the phone!

끊어!

[전화] Hang up the phone!

끊지 마세요.

[전화] Hold on, please.
= Don't hang up the phone, please.

끌

끌어들이지 마세요.	Don't get me in. = I don't want to get involved. = I don't want to get in the middle of this. = Don't involve me. (나를~)

끝

끝나갑니다.	[일이] It's almost done. = It's almost finished. (거의~)
끝납니까?	[회의 · 공연 등] Is it over? // When is it over? (몇 시에~) ➡ At two. (두시입니다.)
끝났습니까?	[일 등이] Done? = Is it done? ➡ ⓐ Yes. It will be done soon. (곧 끝나갑니다.) ⓑ Not yet. (아직요.)
끝났습니다.	① [회의 · 공연 등] It's over. ② [이별] We're done. = We split up. = We broke up. = We ended things. (우리~) ③ [일 등을] It's all finished. (전부~) ④ [대화나 일 등] Done. ➡ We're not done yet. (우리 대화 끝나지 않았어.)
끝내준다!	① [생김새] Awesome! = Fabulous! ② [완벽함] Perfect! ③ [중독] I'm totally into it! (정말~)
끝냅시다.	Let's finish. // Let's finish quickly. (어서~)
끝이 없네.	[잔소리가] There's no end to the lecturing.
끝장났습니다.	[망함] We're finished. = We're doomed. = We're ruined. // We're doomed now. (이번에는~) ☞ 망했어요.

끝장났어!	[경고] You're dead! (넌~)
끝장냅니다.	Let's finish. // Let's finish today. (오늘~) // Let's finish here. (차라리 여기서 다~)
끝장입니다!	Done now! ☞ 이번에는 끝장입니다!

끼

끼가 있습니다.	He is musically talented. (그는 음악에~)
끼는데요.	[옷 등이] It's tight. // Very tight here. (여기가 꽉~)
끼니 거르지 마!	Don't skip meals! // Never skip meals! (앞으로~)
끼어들어 죄송합니다.	① [대화중에] I'm sorry to cut in on the conversation. ☞ 끼어들지 마세요. ② [차 안에서] I'm sorry I cut you off. = I'm sorry for cutting you off.
끼어들지 마세요.	① [대화중에] Don't interfere. // Don't interrupt. Wait till he finishes talking. (끼어들지 말고, 그와 말을 끝낼 때까지 기다려주세요.) ② [남의 일에] Mind your own business. = Don't interfere. // Don't interfere with this thing. (이 일에~) ③ Don't cut in line. ☞ 새치기하지 마세요.
끼워주세요.	① [게임이나 경기에] Count me in, please. (나 좀~) ② [목걸이 · 반지 등을] Put it on for me, please.
끼익!	[차가 멈추는 소리] Screech!

나

나 원 참!	① [불평이나 어이가 없음] Damn it! ② [웃김] This is hilarious! = This is outrageous! ☞ 그러기야?
나 좀 봐요.	① [눈으로 응시] Look at me, please. = Take a look at me, please. ② [불러냄] Have some time? = Can I see you now? = Can you give me a minute?
나가!	① [밖으로] Out! = Get out! = Off! ② [경기에] You're out! ③ [쫓아버림] Go away! = Get out! = Get the hell out of here. ☞ 꺼져!
나가 뒈져!	〈비속어〉 Fuck off!
나가버려!	[명령] Out! = Get out! = Leave now! // Get out now! (썩~)
나가보겠습니다.	I'm going out now. = I am off now. // I'm going out before you. (먼저~)
나가보세요.	You can leave now. = You can go now.
나가서 일보세요.	① Go and work. = You can leave now. ☞ 나가보세요. ② [상사 등이 회의나 소집을 해산] Dismissed.
나가지 마세요.	Don't go away. = Don't leave me. = Don't go out.
나갑니다. // 나가겠습니다.	I'll be out. // I'll be right out. = I'll be out soon. (곧 ~)
나갔다 오겠습니다.	① [자리에서] I want some fresh air. ② [외출] I'll be out. // I'll be out for some time. (좀~)

나갔습니다.	He's out. = He's off. (그는~) // He's out with work. (그는 일이 있어서~)
나그네가 도리어 주인노릇 한다.	[속담] It's like putting the cart before the horse.
~나누기 3은 2입니다.	Six divided by three equals two. = Six divided by three is two. (6~)

나도 그래.	① [긍정] So am / do I. = Me, too. = Same here. = Likewise.
	← I am hungry. (배고파요.) // I love you. (사랑해요.)
	② [부정] Neither am / do I. = Me, neither.
	← I am not hungry. (배 안고파요.) // I don't love you. (당신 사랑 안 해요.)

나도 사랑해!	I love you, too!
나도 압니다.	I know it, too.
나도 잘 지냅니다.	I am fine, too.
나무는 보고 숲은 보지 못한다.	[속담] Cannot see the wood for the trees.

나무라지 마세요.	Don't blame. // Don't blame me. (절~)
	// Don't blame her. (그녀를~)
	// Don't blame. I am sorry. (~잘못했어요.)
	☞ 탓하지 마세요.

나무랄 데가 없습니다.	① [만족] I'm very satisfied. ② Nothing to complain about.
나무에 잘 오르는 놈이 떨어지고 헤엄 잘 치는 놈이 빠져죽는다.	[속담] Good swimmers are at length drowned. = The best swimmers are the most drowned. = Even Homer sometimes nods. = A good marksman may sometimes miss.
나쁜 년!	〈비속어〉 Bitch! = Whore! = Slut!
나쁜 놈!	〈비속어〉 Asshole! = Son of a bitch!

ㄴ

	= Bastard! = Scumbag! = Wretch! // You, son of a bitch! (이~)
나쁜 소문은 금방 퍼져도 좋은 소식은 잘 퍼지지 않는다. // 나쁜 일은 천리밖에 난다.	[속담] Bad news travels fast / quickly.
나쁜 자식!	① <비속어> You, bastard! = Son of a bitch! ☞ 나쁜 놈! ② [점잖은 표현] Bad man!

나아질 겁니다.	[상황] It will be better.
	// It will certainly be better. (반드시~)
	// It will be much better later. (다음에 더~)

나야!	It's me! = Me! ⬅ Who's that? (누구야?)
나오지 마세요.	① [밖으로] Don't come out. ➡ Please come forward. (앞으로 나오세요.) ② [손님이 전송 나온 주인에게] Don't come out. = Don't step out. = You don't need to send me off. ⬅ Take care. (살펴가세요.) ☞ 멀리 못나갑니다. ➡ Please go inside. (들어가세요.)
나와 무슨 상관입니까?	None of my business. = It doesn't concern me. // It's none of my business. = I have nothing to do with it. (그게~) ➡ It surely is. (당연히 상관있지요.)
나와!	[밖으로] Out!
나이 값 좀 해라.	Act your age. = Don't behave like a kid. = You've got to know better. // Are you a kid or what? Act your age. (네가 애냐, ~)
나이가 몇 살이니?	How old are you?

	// How old are you this year? (올해~) ➡ I'm nine. = I'm nine years old. (9살입니다.)
나이가 어떻게 됩니까?	How old are you? ➡ ⓐ I'm eighteen. = I'm eighteen years old. (올해 18살입니다.) ⓑ I'm twenty-three. = I'm twenty-three years old. (23살입니다.) ☞ 연세가 어떻게 되십니까?
나이스 볼!	Nice ball! (멋진 볼!)
나이스 플레이!	Nice play! (멋진 경기!)
나중에 다시 전화하겠습니다.	① [이따가] I'll call you later again. ② [다른 날에] I'll call you back.
나중에 봅시다.	① [다른 날을 잡아서] See you later. ② [잠시 후에] See you soon. ☞ 이따가 봅시다. ③ [후일을 기약] See you. (우리~)
나중에 얘기합시다.	① [이따가] Let's talk later. ② [다른 날에] Let's talk some time later.
나하고 무슨 상관이야?	Why should I care? // Why should I care about this? = This is none of my business. (이게~) ➡ Yes, you should. (당연히 상관있지요.)

낙

낙수 물이 바위를 뚫는다.	[속담] Little drops of water make the mighty ocean.
낙타가 바늘구멍 나가기는 어렵다.	It's difficult for a camel to go through the eye of a needle.

낚

낚시하러 갑니다.

Let's go fishing.
// Let's go fishing this Sunday. (일요일에~)

난

난리 났어!

[사고가 일어남] **Something terrible happened!**
☞ 야단났네!

난처해 죽겠어요!

① I'm so embarrassed!
② [망신당함] <비속어> I'm so pissed off!
③ [웃음거리가 됨] I was so ridiculed!
= I was made the laughingstock.
// I was made the laughingstock of my school. (학교에서 ~)

날

날씨가 어떻습니까?

① How's the weather?
= What's the weather like?
// How's the weather today? (오늘~)
// How's the weather here? (이곳~)
➡ ⓐ Very good. (아주 좋습니다.)
ⓑ Fine. (괜찮습니다.)
ⓒ It's a little cold. = It's a little chilly.
= **It's a little nippy.** (약간 서늘해요.)
② How will the weather be tomorrow?
= What will the weather be like tomorrow? (내일~)
➡ ⓐ It'll be sunny tomorrow. (내일은 맑은 날씨래요.)
ⓑ It'll be cloudy tomorrow. (내일 흐리답니다.)
ⓒ It will rain tomorrow.
= It'll be rainy tomorrow. (비 온답니다.)

	ⓓ It will be sunny and cloudy later. (맑았다가 구름이 낀답니다.)
날씨가 좋다!	What a nice day! = It's good! // It's very good! // It's really good today! (오늘 정말~)
날씨가 좋습니까?	Is the weather good? // Is the weather good today? (오늘~) ➡ ⓐ It's very good today. (오늘 날씨가 정말 좋습니다.) ⓑ It's good today. (오늘 날씨가 좋습니다.) ⓒ It's a very fine day today. (오늘 날씨가 정말 괜찮습니다.) ⓓ It's nice today. (오늘 날씨가 정말 편안합니다.)
날씨가 좋습니다.	The weather is good. = It's good. // It's good today. (오늘~)
날이 저물었습니다.	It's already dark.
날치기야!	Robber! = Thief!
날치기 조심하세요.	Be careful of robbery. = Watch out for robbery.

남

남은 것은 싸주세요.	[음식점] I'd like to take my leftovers. = Can I have a bag for my leftover food?
남의 떡이 커 보인다.	[속담] The grass is always greener on the other side of the fence. = The apples on the other side of the wall are the sweetest. ☞ 게집은 남의 것이 곱고 자식은 제 새끼가 곱다.
남의 장단에 춤추다.	To dance to other's tune.
남이 사!	None of your business! = Leave me alone! ☞ 내버려둬요. // 관두세요.

남이냐?	Don't I know you? = Am I a stranger to you? (내가~) ☞ 우리가 남인가요?
남자는 다 늑대야.	Men are all wolves.
남자입니다.	I am a man. (저는~)
남자친구하고는 이미 깨졌습니다.	I broke up with my boyfriend. = I split up with my boyfriend.

ㄱ

낫

낫 놓고 기역자도 모른다.	[속담] He's too ignorant to know his ABCs. = He doesn't know A from B. (그는 ~)

낭

낭만적이야!	It's romantic! // He's so romantic! (그는 아주~) // How romantic! (너무 ~)

낭비하지 마세요.	Don't waste.
	// Don't waste your time. (시간을 ~)
	// Don't squander your money. (돈을 ~)

낮

낮말은 새가 듣고 밤말은 쥐가 듣는다.	① Walls have ears. = Fields have eyes, and woods have ears. ② 〈직역〉 Birds hear at daytime and mice hear at night.
낮잠 잘 잤습니까?	Did you have a good nap? = Did you enjoy your nap? ➡ ⓐ Yes, I did. (잘 잤습니다.) ⓑ Sort of. (그런대로요.)

낯

낯가립니다.	She's shy in front of people she doesn't know. = She's afraid of people she doesn't know. (그녀는~)
낯은 알아도 마음은 모른다. // 열 길 물속은 알아도 한 길 사람의 속은 모른다.	〈직역〉 You can sound water ten fathoms deep, but you cannot sound the human heart a single fathom.
낯짝도 없는 놈!	〈비속어〉 Shameless bastard!

낳

낳은 정보다 기른 정.	〈직역〉 The foster parents are closer than the biological parents.

내

내 것이 아닙니다.	Not mine. // It's not mine. = It doesn't belong to me. (그것은~)

내 것입니다.	Mine.
	// This is mine. = This belongs to me. (이것은~)
	// It's mine. = It belongs to me. (그것은~)

내 코가 석자.	I have got myself into a hell of a fix, so I can't afford to help others.
내가 한 말이 다시 나한테 돌아온다.	① To cut off one's nose to spite one's face. ② [속담] Curses like chickens come home back to roost.
내겠습니다.	① [접대] I'll treat you. = I'll pick up the tab. = I'll pay the bill. = It's on me.

	= This one's on me. (제가~)
	// I'll treat you today. (오늘 제가~)
	☞ 사겠습니다.
	② [제출] I'll turn it in. = I'll submit it. (제가~)
	// I'll turn it in today. (오늘은 제가~)

내기하자고?	Wanna bet? ➡ Sure. (좋아.)
내기합시다.	Make a bet. = Let's bet on it. // Let's make a bet. (우리~)
내년에 결혼할 생각입니다.	I'm planning on getting married next year.
내년에 졸업합니다.	I am graduating next year. = I am expecting my graduation next year.
내놔요!	① [요구] Give me! ☞ 주세요! ② [반환] Give it back to me! ☞ 돌려주세요. ③ [물건을 꺼내서] Take it out! ④ [가져간 물건을] Return it! // Return it right now! (당장~)
내려가세요.	① [차 등에서] Get off, please. ② Step down, please.
내려놓으세요.	[물건을] Put it down, please.
내려오세요.	Come down, please.
내려주세요.	① [정차] Drop me off, please. ② [업고 있는 경우] Let me down, please. (날~)
내버려둬요.	① [상대] Leave him alone, please. (그 사람~) ② [방임] Give him some time, please. (걔 잠시~) ③ [건들지 말고] Leave me alone. (날~) ④ Leave him alone. (그 사람~) ☞ 냅둬요!
내숭떨기는!	Pretending you're naive!

	➡ What pretending? (누가 떨었다고!)
내오지 마세요.	[접대다과] Please don't bother! = You don't need to do so. ➡ I'm fine. = I'd love to do. = It's my pleasure. (제가 좋아서 그럽니다.)
내일 봅시다.	[작별인사] See you tomorrow.
내일 저녁 어떻습니까?	How about tomorrow evening? ➡ ⓐ Good. (좋습니다.) ⓑ No, I can't. (안 됩니다.)

냄

냄새 좀 맡아봐!	Smell it!
냄새 좋다!	[음식 등] Smells good!
냄새가 고약합니다.	It smells bad.
냄새가 독합니다.	It smells terrible.
냄새가 역겹습니다.	It smells disgusting.

냅

냅둬요!	Leave me alone!
냅킨은 어디에 있습니까?	Where are napkins? ➡ On the table. (테이블 위에 있습니다.)

냉

냉면 두 그릇 주세요.	Give me two bowls of cold noodles, please.

	= Let me have two bowls of cold noodles, please.
냉수 먹고 이쑤시기.	〈직역〉 Pretending as if one had a full stomach. = Pretending as if one were well-off.
냉수도 불어 먹는다.	〈직역〉 Blow on even cold water before drinking.
냉장고에 음료수가 있습니다.	There are drinks in the refrigerator.
냉정하세요.	[진정] Keep cool. = Calm down. = Chill out. = Stay calm. // Calm down, please. (좀~)

너

너 때문이야.	① [비난] Your bad! // It's all your fault! (다~) ② [배려] Thanks to you. = I owe you one. (다~)
너 말이야!	[불만] I'm talking about you! = It's all about you!
너 없이 못살아!	I can't live without you!
너구나!	It's you!
너그럽게 봐주십시오.	[용서를 구함] Please forgive me!
너나 잘해!	You take care of your business!
너답다!	① [칭찬] Great! ② [비난] It's so you!
너도 참!	① [어이가 없음] You! ② [불만] Do you have mind?
너무한다!	You're going too far! = That's too much!
너였구나!	It's you! = You did it!
너 죽고 나 죽자.	Both you and I die.

ㄴ

넌

넌 누구냐?	Who are you? ➡ It's me, Yujin. (난 유진이야.)
넌 몰라!	You didn't know it!
넌 뭐야?	[시비] Who the hell are you?

널

널리 양해 바랍니다.	Please understand it.

넘

넘어질 뻔 했습니다.	I almost fell down.
넘었습니다.	① It's past 7. (7시가~) ② [시간이] It's over already. (벌써~)

넣

넣어두세요.	① [물건 등을 줌] Please take it. ② [물건을 서랍에] Please keep it inside. = Please put it inside. // Please keep it inside. Hurry. (얼른~)

네

네미!	<비속어> Damn it! = God damn!
네미럴!	① <비속어> Damn it! = God damn! ② [다른 사람들을 두고] Damn you! = Son of a bitch!

넥

넥타이가 비뚤어졌습니다.	The tie is crooked.
넥타이를 맸습니다.	I've put my tie on. = I wear a tie.

노

노래 못 부릅니다. // 노래 못합니다.	I don't sing well. = I'm not a good singer. = I'm not good at singing.
노래 잘한다!	[칭찬] Great singing! = You're good at singing! = What a singer! = You sing well! // You sing very well! (너무~)
노래방에 갑시다.	Let's go to a singing room! (우리~)
노려보지 말아요.	Don't look at me like that. = Stop eyeballing me. = Stop glaring at me. (나를 ~)
노력해!	① [응원 · 격려] Try harder! ② [학습] Study harder! // Keep trying hard! (계속~) ③ [일] Keep working on it! = Keep it up! (계속~)
노출이 심한 옷을 입지마세요.	Please don't expose so much skin.
노크하는 것 같은데.	Seems someone's knocking on the door. = I think someone's knocking on the door. = I think someone's at the door. (누가~)

녹

녹차 한 잔 주세요.	① Can I have a glass of green tea? ② 〈경어〉 Would you give me a glass of green tea?

놀

놀고 있네!	① [농담에 대해] You're kidding! = You're joking! = Are you pulling my leg? ② [소란에 대해] What a fuss!
놀고 자빠졌네.	How silly! = How hilarious!

놀다가세요.	① [권유] Please have fun here.
	= Please enjoy yourself here.
	// Please have some more fun here. (좀 더~)
	// It's still early. Please have some more fun here. (시간이 아직 이른데, 좀 더~)
	➡ No, thank you. (아닙니다.)
	② [여유 있음] Please stay and enjoy here. (좀 더~)

놀라게 해드려 죄송합니다.	① I'm sorry to surprise you. ② [소란으로] I'm sorry to surprise you with this fuss. // I'm sorry to surprise you, guys. (여러분을~)
놀라지 마세요.	Don't be surprised.

놀랐습니다.	① [놀람] I was surprised.
	// I was so surprised. (너무~)
	// I was really surprised. (정말~)
	② [충격] I was shocked. = I was astonished.
	③ [무서움] I was frightened.

놀랐잖아요.	① [뒤에서 놀래주는 경우] You surprised me. = You frightened me. // I was really surprised this time. (이번엔 정말~)

	② I was surprised at you. (방금 당신 때문에~) ➡ Really? It's a wonder you were surprised. (그래요? 당신도 놀랄 때가 다 있네요.)
놀랐지!	① Surprise! // Surprise, all! (모두들~) ② [이벤트 선물] Surprise! = Tadah!
놀래라! // 놀랬어! // 놀랬어요!	① What a surprise! ② [깜짝 놀라거나 두려운 감정이 듦] You scared me! (너 때문에 놀랬어.)
놀러갑시다.	Let's go to play. = Let's have some fun. (우리~)

놀러오세요.	Please come. // Please come again. (또~)
	// Please come often when you're free.
	(시간 나면 자주~)
	// Please come either on business or for fun.
	(일이 있건 없건~)
	// Please come more often. (앞으로 자주~)
	// Please come. (꼭~)
	// Please come next time. (다음에 꼭~)

놀리는 거야?	[놀림 · 말장난] ① Are you kidding me? = You're pulling my leg. = Are you teasing me? // Are you kidding me now? (지금 날~) ➡ ⓐ Am I doing what? (놀리다니요?) ⓑ I don't think so. (그럴 리가요?) ⓒ Why should I? (내가 왜요?) ② You must be kidding. (지금 날~) ➡ No way. How can I? (그럴 리가요? 제가 감히 어떻게?)
놀리지 마세요.	① [농담] Don't pull my leg. = No kidding. = No joking. = Stop pulling my leg. ② [놀림 · 말장난] Don't pull my leg. = No kidding. = No joking. = Stop pulling my leg. = Stop talking like that. = Don't laugh at me. = Don't make fun of me.

	③ [비웃음] You gotta be kidding.
놀아줘요.	Please play with me. (나하고 좀~) // Please play with the kid. I'm begging you! (그 애하고 좀~ 부탁이야!)

농

농구를 아주 잘합니다.	Good at basketball! = What a player!
농구를 할 줄 모릅니다.	I don't know how to play basketball.
농담 그만하세요.	No kidding. ← I can fly down from the second floor. (2층에서 날라서 내려올 수 있습니다.)
농담 아닙니다.	① [농담] I'm not kidding. ② [심각함] I'm serious. = I mean it.
농담입니다.	I'm just kidding. = I'm just joking. // It's just a joke. (다만~)
농담하지 마세요.	Don't pull my leg! = No kidding! = No joking! = Stop pulling my leg!

누

누가 그래?	Who said that? → Well, I don't know. (잘 모르겠습니다.)
누가 알겠어요!	① Who knows it! = Only god knows it! ② [나는 모름] How could I possibly know? ③ Nobody knows! (아무도 모릅니다.)
누구냐?	Who are you? // Who the hell are you? (넌 대체~)

ㄱ

누구누구입니까?	Who are they? ➡ Mr. Brown, Mr Smith and Mr. Johnson. (브라운씨와 스미스씨, 그리고 존슨씨요.)
누구를 닮았습니까?	Who do you resemble? = Who do you look like? ➡ I resemble my father. = I look like my father. (아버지를 닮았어요.)
누구를 찾습니까?	Who are you looking for? ➡ I'm looking for Mr. Henson. (헨슨 선생님을 찾습니다.)
누구세요?	① Who are you? // Who is he? (그는~) ➡ He's my father. (제 아버지입니다.) ② [전화] Who's calling, please? ③ [문앞] Who's calling, please?
누구십니까?	[전화] Who's this? = Who's calling? // Excuse me, who's calling, please? (실례지만, ~)
누구야?	① [확인] Who's that? ☞ 누구세요? ② [상대방] Who are you? ➡ Your colleague. (동창생이잖아.)
누구입니까?	Who is he? (그는~) ➡ He is Mr. Choe. (그는 최 선생님입니다.)
누구 편입니까?	Whose side are you on? ➡ I'm on your side. (당신편이죠.)
누룽지 좋아합니다.	I like crispy rice.
누우세요.	Please lie down.
누워서 떡먹기야.	It's a piece of cake. = Piece of cake. = It's a snap. = It's a cinch. = It's easy. = It's like nothing.
누워서 쉬세요.	Stay in bed and rest. // Don't get up. Please stay in bed and rest. (일어나지 말고, ~)

누워서 침 뱉기.	① Cut off your nose to spite your face. ② 〈직역〉 Lie down and spit.
누이 좋고 매부 좋고. // 누이 좋고 매부 좋은 겁니다.	[속담] What's good for the goose is good for the gander.

눈

눈 가리고 아웅 한다.	Bury one's head like an ostrich in the sand.
눈 감아보세요.	① Close your eyes. = Shut your eyes. // Close your eyes first. (먼저~) ② 〈경어〉 Would you close your eyes, please.
눈 속에 넣어도 아프지 않다. // 눈에 넣어도 아프지 않다.	The apple of one's eye.
눈도 없냐!	Can't you see? = Are you blind?
눈물 닦아!	Wipe your tears!
눈에 너무 띕니다.	It's too outstanding. = It's too noticeable. = It's distinguishing.
눈에 넣어도 아프지 않은 게 자녀다.	The kid is the apple of the parents' eye.
눈에 넣으세요.	[안약] Please drop some in your eyes.
눈에 콩깍지가 씌다.	So wrapped up in someone. ➡ She's so wrapped up in him, so she can't see his faults. (저 남자한테 눈에 꽁깍지가 씌어서 그의 잘못을 보지를 못해요.)
눈에 튀지 않아요?	[의복 등이] Doesn't it stand out too much?
눈엣가시	speck in the eye

눈이 꽤 왔습니다.	So much snow here.
눈이 내립니다.	[눈이 내리고 있음] It's snowy.
눈이 더 나빠졌나요?	Did your eyes get worse? ➡ Yes. (예.)
눈이 삐었구나!	You must have bad eyesight! = Are you blind or what?
눈이 옵니다.	[일기예보] It's snowing. = It's snowy. // It will snow tomorrow. (내일~) ☞ 눈이 내립니다.
눈치없게!	You have no sense! // Oh, my. You have no sense! (뭐야? 그렇게~)

눕

눕고 싶습니다.	I want to lie down.

느

느끼합니다.	[요리] It's greasy. = It's oily. // It's too greasy. = It's too oily. (너무~)
느낌이 어떻습니까?	How do you feel? = How are you? = How's it going on? ➡ ⓐ Fine. = Not bad. = OK. = Good. (괜찮습니다.) ⓑ So so. (그런대로요.) ⓒ Not good. = Bad. (별로입니다.) ⓓ Very bad. (안 좋습니다.)

늘

늘 바쁩니다.	I'm busy as usual.
늘 운동합니다.	I always exercise. = I always work out.

늙

늙고 병든 몸은 눈먼 새도 안 앉는다.	[속담] Long life has long misery.

능

능청 떨지 마세요.	Don't play innocent! = Don't pretend you're innocent!

늦

늦게 와서 미안합니다.	I'm sorry for being late. = I'm sorry I'm late. ➡ Why were you late? = What took you so long? = What made you so late? (왜 이렇게 늦었어?)
늦겠다.	[상대방] You're gonna be late. [자신] I'll be late.
늦어도 안 하는 것보다 낫다.	[속담] Better late than never.
늦어서 먼저 갈게!	I'm late. I'm leaving now!
늦어서 죄송합니다.	I'm sorry for being late. = I'm sorry I'm late.
늦었습니다.	I'm late. = I'm running late.

	// I'm just five minutes late.
	= I'm running just five minutes late. (다만 5분~)
	// I'm thirty minutes late. (30분~) ☞ 지각했어요.

늦잠 자면 안 됩니다.	You shouldn't get up late. // You shouldn't get up late today. (오늘~)
늦잠 자지 마세요.	Don't get up late, please.

ㄱ

다

다 귀 대봐!	① Put your ears here! ② [경청] Everybody, listen!
다 끝나갑니다.	[완성] I'm almost done. = I'm almost finished. // It's almost finished. = It's almost done. (거의~)
다 나 때문이야!	It's all because of me!
다 내 잘못입니다. // 다 내 탓입니다.	It's all my fault. = It's all my bad. ➡ No. It's my fault. (아닙니다, 제 잘못입니다.)
다 너 때문이야!	[원망] It's your fault! = It's your bad! // This is your fault! = This is your bad! (이건~)
다시 말해주세요.	Would you say that again? = Excuse me? = Sorry? = Pardon me? = I beg your pardon? = Repeat, please? = Come again?
다 썼습니다.	[글씨] I'm done with writing. = I have finished writing. // I have almost finished writing. (거의~)
다 왔습니다.	① [도착] We're almost there. (거의~) // We're almost there. Just a little more to go. (~조금 더 가면 됩니다.) ② Here we are. = We arrived.
다녀오겠습니다.	Good bye. = Bye. = Bye bye.
다녀왔습니다.	[귀가] I'm back. = I'm home.
다 되어갑니다.	It's almost ready. = It's almost done. = It's almost finished. // Dinner is almost ready. (저녁밥이~)
다들 잘 있습니까? // 다들 잘 지내십니까?	How's everybody? ➡ ⓐ They're fine. (잘들 있습니다.) ⓑ So so. (그럭저럭.)

다들 조심해.	Be careful, everybody.
다른 거 더 필요하십니까?	Do you need anything else? = Anything else? ➡ ⓐ No. (아니요.) ⓑ I'm fine. (됐습니다.) ⓒ Nothing. (없습니다.)
다른 거 또 필요합니까?	Do you need something else? = Anything else? ☞ 다른 거 필요합니까?
다른 거 없습니다.	① [소유] I have nothing else. ② [필요] I need nothing else.
다른 거 필요합니까?	Do you need something else? = Anything else do you need? ➡ ⓐ A cup of coffee. (커피 한 잔이요.) ⓑ I'm fine. Thank you. (됐습니다.)
다른 약속이 생겼습니다.	① [변호사, 의사, 미장원, 교수 등과의 약속] I have another appointment. ② [친구, 애인, 가족 등과의 약속] I have another plan.
다른 약속이 있습니까?	Do you have another appointment? ➡ No. (없습니다.)
다리 벌려봐!	Put your legs apart!
다리가 부러졌습니다.	I have a broken leg. = My leg is broken.
다리가 붓기 시작합니다.	My leg is swollen.
다리가 아파요.	My legs hurt. // My legs are killing me. (너무 ~)
다리가 저립니다.	My leg fell asleep. (제~)
다리를 밟았습니다.	You stepped on my foot. (제~) ➡ I'm sorry. (미안합니다.)
다리를 삐었어요.	I have a sprained leg. = My leg is sprained. = I've sprained my ankle.

ㄷ

다리에 쥐가 납니다.	I've had a cramp in my leg.
다리에 타박상을 입었습니다.	I've got a bruise on my leg. = My leg is bruised.
다림질하고 있었어요.	I'm ironing.
다시	Again. ☞ 또
다시 말해서.	① By the way. ☞ 그런데 (말이야). ② To say that again. = In other words.
다시 말해 주세요.	① [일반적] What did you say? = Say that again? = I'm sorry? = Excuse me? ② 〈경어〉 Pardon me? = I beg your pardon? = Would you say that again? ③ [의성] Huh?
다시 해봐!	① [시도] Try it again! = Give it another shot! ② [시범] Do it again!
다음 역에서 내려야 합니다.	I'll have to get off at the next stop.
다음 역에서 내립니다.	I'll get off at the next stop.
다음 주 금요일 걸로 예약됩니까?	Can I make a reservation for next Friday? // Can I reserve a table for next Friday? (한 테이블 ~) ➡ ⓐ Sure. (그럼요.) ⓑ Of course. (물론이죠.)

다음 주라면 시간이 될 것 같네요.	I think I'll be free next week.
	= I think I'll have some time next week.
	관련표현
	next week = upcoming week (다음 주)
	// next Monday (다음 주 월요일)
	// next Tuesday (다음 주 화요일)
	// next Wednesday (다음 주 수요일)
	// next Thursday (다음 주 목요일)
	// next Friday (다음 주 금요일)
	// next Saturday (다음 주 토요일)
	// next Sunday (다음 주 일요일)

다음 회는 몇 시에 합니까?	[공연 · 영화 · 연극] What time is the next show? ➡ At six thirty. (6시 반입니다.)
다음부터 그러지 않을 겁니다.	I won't do that again.
다음에 다시 오겠습니다.	① I'll be coming again. = I'll be here again. ② [다른 날] I'll come another day.
다음에 또 모이자.	Let's meet again.
다음에 또 오십시오!	[음식점] See you later! = Come again, please!
다음에 봐요!	See you later! = See ya! = See you around! = See you next time!
다이어트 중입니까?	Are you on a diet? ➡ Yes, I am. = Yes. (다이어트중입니다.)
다쳤어요?	① Who's hurt? (누가~) ➡ No one. (아니요.) ② Are you hurt? = Did you get hurt? ➡ ⓐ I'm OK. (괜찮아요.) ⓑ Yes, I got so hurt. (많이 다쳤어요.) ③ [넘어져서] Where did you get hurt? = Did you get hurt? (어디~) ➡ I'm OK. (괜찮아요.)
다행이네.	① [감탄] Good. = Good for you. ② [안심] Lucky for you. // Really lucky for you. (정말~)
다행입니다.	Lucky for you. // Real good luck. (정말~)

닥

닥쳐!	Shut up! = Hold your tongue! = Zip your mouth! ☞ 입 닥쳐!

닦

닦아요.	Wipe up the sink. = Clean up the sink. (싱크대를 깨끗이~)

단

단도직입적으로 말하겠습니다.	① Let me be straight with you. = Let me be direct with you. = I will speak to you straight. (당신에게~) ② [한참 말을 한 후에] Let me get to the point.
단맛 쓴맛 다 맛보다.	[속담] Taste the sweet and bitter of life. = Taste the sweetness and bitterness of life.
단무지 있습니까?	Do you have pickles?
단순하게 생각해!	Think simple!
단어는 어떻게 읽습니까?	How can I read the word? = How can I pronounce the word? // How can I pronounce this new word? (이 새~) ➡ Read it "dictionary." (이것은 'dictionary'로 읽습니다.)
단어의 발음은 무엇입니까?	How do you pronounce this word? = How is this word pronounced? (이~)
단짝하고 싸웠어.	I had a fight with my best friend.
단체로 갈 겁니까? 배낭여행으로 갈 겁니까?	Group touring or backpacking? ➡ Backpacking. (배낭여행이요.)
단추 채워!	Button up!
단풍이 정말 아름답습니다.	Leaves are so beautiful. // Leaves in the fall are so beautiful. (가을~)

달

달고 맛있습니다.	Sweet and delicious. // It's very sweet and delicious. (그거 아주~)
달러로 지불하겠습니다.	I'll pay in dollars. = I'd like to pay in dollars.
달러를 일본 돈으로 환전해 주세요.	Please change dollars to Yen. = I'd like to change dollars to Yen.
달리 방법이 없습니다. // 달리 선택이 없습니다.	① [선택] There is no choice. = No other choice. = Don't have any choice. // Except this, there is no choice. = This is the only choice. (이것 말고는~) ☞ 선택의 여지가 없습니다. ② [방법] There are no ways. ③ [대안] No alternatives.
달면 삼키고 쓰면 뱉는다.	To utilize a person when his service is needed, and keep him at a distance when he is no longer wanted.
달아나!	Run! = Run away! = Escape! // Run right away! (어서~)
달아나지 마!	Don't run away!

닭

닭살이야, 닭살.	Phew, goosebumps! = Goose pimples! = Goose flesh!

닮

닮았습니까?	Who do you resemble? = Who do you look like? (누굴~)

	➡ I look like my dad. (아빠를 닮았습니다.) // I look like my mom. (엄마를 닮았습니다.)

담

담배 끊었습니다.	I quit smoking. = I stopped smoking.
담배 피우면 안 됩니다.	[허가] You are not supposed to smoke. = You are not allowed to smoke.
담배 피우지 마세요.	① [완곡] Don't smoke, please. ② [금지] You shouldn't smoke. = You must not smoke. = Smoking is prohibited. ③ [경고문] No smoking!
담배 피워도 됩니까?	① Can I smoke? = May I smoke? = Is it OK to smoke? ➡ Go ahead. (편하실 대로요.) ② Can I smoke here? (여기에서~) ➡ ⓐ Yes, you can. (됩니다.) ⓑ No, you can't. (안 됩니다.)
담백한 걸로 주문할까요?	Can we order something light? = Can we have light food? ➡ Yes! (예!)
담요 한 장 갖다 주세요.	[기내] Can I get a blanket? = Would you get me a blanket?
담이 작습니다.	No courage. = Lack of courage. // He has no guts. (그는 ~)

답

답답하지 않습니까?	① [걱정] Aren't you frustrated? ② [사고방식] Isn't he narrow-minded? (그가 ~) ③ [장소 등이 비좁음] Isn't it small?

	④ [장소에 사람 등이 많아서] Isn't it crowded? ⑤ [옷 등이 꽉 껴서] Isn't it tight? ➡ ⓐ Somewhat. (약간이요.) ⓑ A bit. = A little. (조금이요.)
답답합니다!	I'm anxious! = I'm worried! // I'm very anxious! (정말~) ➡ Me, too. = I'm anxious, too. = So am I. (나도~)
답답해 죽겠어요!	① [마음이] I'm dying of frustration! ② [조급해서] I'm dying of concerns! = No news is killing me!

당

당신 거지요? // 당신 겁니까?	Yours? = Is it yours? = Does it belong to you? // Is this yours? = Does this belong to you? (이거~) ➡ ⓐ Yes, it's mine. Thank you. (제겁니다. 고맙습니다.) ⓑ No, it's not mine. (제 것 아닙니다.)
당신만 믿습니다.	① [신용] I trust you. = I believe you. // Everybody trusts you. = Everybody believes you. (전부 당신만~) ② [의지] I count on you. = I rely on you. = I lean on you.
당연하지.	Of course. ☞ 그럼(요)!
당일에 도착할 수 있습니다.	I'm arriving today.
당일코스 여행 있습니까?	Do you have a day tour? ➡ Yes. (있습니다.)
당장 나가!	① [재촉] Off now! ② [명령] Get out now! ③ 〈비속어〉 Get the hell out of here! = Get the fuck out of here!

당장 말씀드리기는 곤란합니다.	I can't tell you right now. = It's hard telling you right now.
당장 시작하겠습니다.	I'll get started right away. = I'll start right now.
당첨됐습니다.	① [복권] Won the lottery! (1등에~) ② [빙고] Bingo!
당황하지 마세요.	Don't be embarrassed, please. = Don't be perplexed, please. = Don't panic, please. ➡ How embarrassing! = I'm so embarrassed! (너무 당황스러워요!)

대

대금결제는 어떤 방식으로 할까요?	How would you like to pay? = How will you pay?
대단하긴 뭐가?	① [상대를 폄하] What's so special? = What's the big deal? ② How great?

대단하다! // 대단해!	① [놀람] How great! = Amazing! = Unbelievable!
	= I can't believe! = Incredible!
	// Really amazing! (정말~)
	// Pretty amazing! (아주~)
	➡ Not at all. (천만에요.)
	② [능력] Excellent! // Very excellent! (정말~)
	③ [담력 · 기개에 대한 칭찬] Great! ☞ 너답다!
	④ [쉽지 않은 일처리에 대해] Good job! = Well done!
	➡ Thank you. (감사합니다.)

대단하지?	Isn't it great? // Isn't it so great? (정말~) ➡ ⓐ Sure. (그럼요.) ⓑ Yes. (그래요.)
대단히 감사합니다.	Thank you very much. = Thanks a lot.

	= Thank you a great deal. = Thank you so much.
대략 몇 시간 걸립니까?	About how long does it take? = About how many hours does it take? ➡ About fifty minutes. (15분정도요.)
대략 몇 시입니까?	What time is it? ➡ It's about three thirty. (대략 3시 반이요.)
대사관은 어디에 있습니까?	Where is the embassy? // Where is the Korean embassy? (한국~) ➡ Around here. (부근에요.)
대접 받고 싶으면 먼저 대접하라.	[속담] Do to others as you would be done by others.
대접 잘 받았습니다.	[대접] Thank you so much for your entertaining. = Thank you for your hospitality.
대접하겠습니다.	I'd like to treat you. // I'll treat you next time. (다음에 제가~)
대충 때웁시다.	① [음식] Let's get a quick bite. = Let's have a small meal quickly. = Let's just grab a quick bite. ② [잠자리 등] Let's go easy.
대충 이런 걸로 알고 있습니다.	That's roughly what I know.
대충 지냅시다.	☞ 대충 때웁시다.
대학 나왔습니다.	I graduated from college. = I'm a college graduate.
대학교에 다니고 있습니다.	I am a college student. = I am attending college. = I go to college.
대학에 다닙니까?	① [학업] What college do you go to? = What college do you attend? = Where do you go to school? (무슨~)

	➡ I go to Harvard University. (하버드대학에 다닙니다.) ② [일] What college do you work for? (무슨~) ➡ I work for Harvard University. (하버드대학에 다닙니다.) 관련표현 freshman (대학교 1학년) // sophomore (대학교 2학년) // junior (대학교 3학년) // senior (대학교 4학년)
대학에 떨어질 뻔했습니다.	I almost failed the college.
대학원 시험에 떨어졌습니다.	I failed the graduate exam this time. (이번에~)
대학원에 다니고 싶습니다.	I'd like to go to a graduate school in China. (중국에서~)
대학을 졸업했습니다.	I graduated from college. = I graduated from university. = I am a college graduate. // I graduated from Seoul National University. (서울~)
대한항공 카운터는 어디에 있습니까?	Where are the Korean Airlines counters? ➡ They're inside. (안쪽에요.)
대화중에 끼어들어 죄송합니다.	I'm sorry to cut in on your conversation. = I'm sorry to cut you off during your conversation. = I'm sorry to interrupt.

더

더 기다려야 합니다.	You'll have to wait a little longer. = Please wait a little longer. // Wait one more day. (하루를~)
더 놀다가 가세요.	Please stay and enjoy yourself more here.

더 드세요.	Please have some more. = Why don't you have some more food? // Please have some more rice cake. (떡 좀 ~)
더 이상 괴로워하지 마세요.	Please don't be hard on yourself. // Please don't be hard on yourself about it. (그 일로~)
더 이상 긴말 할 것 없어!	No more words! = Stop saying any more words!
더 이상 드릴 말씀이 없네요.	I can't say a word. = I've got nothing to say.
더 이상 마음 쓰지 마세요.	Please don't think about it anymore. (그 일로~)
더 이상 말할 것 없습니다.	I don't have anything more to say. = Nothing more to say.
더 좋은 생각이 있습니까?	More ideas? ➡ No. (없습니다.)
더 크게 좀 말씀해주세요.	Please speak up! = Louder, please.
더는 못 참겠습니다.	I can't stand it anymore. = I can't bear it anymore. = I can't put up with it anymore.
더러운 놈아!	〈비속어〉 You, filthy! = You, disgusting pig!
더러운 성질하고는!	〈비속어〉 Fucking temperament! = Filthy temperament!
더러워!	[구역질나는 상황] Damn, disgusting! = Damn, filthy! = Shit, gross! (에이~)
더럽네.	It's dirty. // It's very dirty. (엄청~)
더워서 목말라 죽겠어요.	I am dying of thirst. = I'm so thirsty I could die.
더워요!	Hot! // So hot! = Sizzling hot! (너무~)

더워 죽겠어요.	I'm dying of heat. = This heat is killing me. = I can't stand this heat. = This heat is unbearable. = I'm burning up.
더위 먹었어요?	Is the heat getting to you? = Are you suffering from heatstroke? ➡ No. (아니요.)
더치페이로 합시다.	**Let's go Dutch!** = Let's split the bill! (우리~)

덕

덕분에 많은 도움이 됐습니다.	**I owe you much.** = You've helped me a lot. = Thanks to you. = I've got a great help from you.
덕분에 아주 잘 끝냈어요.	[행사를] Everything has been done well. Thanks to you. = Everything went well because of you.
덕분에 잘 지내고 있습니다.	I'm fine. Thanks to you. = I'm fine. I owe you a lot. // They're fine. Thanks to you. (그들은~)
덕분입니다.	① [안부인사] Thanks to you. (당신의~) ② Thanks to the doctor, the child has recovered. (아이의 병회복은 의사의 적절한 치료~) ➡ Yes. I don't know how to thank you. = I can't thank you enough. (그래요. 어떻게 감사해야 좋을지 모르겠습니다.)

덜

덜 떨어지긴!	Stupid! = Idiot! = Fool! = Retard! = Clumsy!
덜 떨어진 것들!	**Idiots!** = Fools!

덜렁대긴!	[건망증] So careless! = How reckless! // Oh my, how reckless! (이런~)
덜어줄게.	① [음식을 나눠줌] I'll share my food with you. = Please have some of my food. ② [상대방의 음식을 많아 덤] I'll take some of your food.

ㄷ

덥

덥습니다.	① It's hot. // It's very hot. (너무~) // It's really hot today. (오늘은 매우~) // It's a little hot. (좀~) // It's pretty hot today. (오늘 참~) ② [햇빛이 뜨거움] It's sizzling hot.

데

데굴데굴!	[물건이 구르는 소리] Rumble! Rumble!
데려다 주시겠습니까?	① [차로] Would you give me a ride to the school? (학교에~) ② Would you take me to school? (학교에~) ➡ Sure. (그래요.)
데려다 줄게요.	① [차로] I'll give you a ride. ② I'll take you to the park. (공원까지 ~) ➡ No, thanks. I'll take a bus. (아니에요, 버스 타고 갈게요.) ③ [같이 걸어서] I'll walk you to the park. (공원까지 ~)
데려다 줘서 고마워요, 조심히 가세요.	[차로] Thank you for the ride. Good-bye.
데려다 줘요.	① [차로] Please give me a ride. ② Please take me home. (집까지~)

데리고 가!	① [동반] Take him with you! (그를 ~) ② [끌어냄] Take him away! = Get him away! (저놈을~)
데었습니까?	[화상] Did you get burned? // How did you get burned? (어떻게~) ➡ Yes. I was careless. = I wasn't careful. (조심성이 없어서요.)
데워주세요.	① [음식을] Please warm it. = Please warm it up. // Would you warm it up? (좀~) ② 〈경어〉 Would you please warm it up again? (다시 한 번~)
데이트가 있습니다.	I have a date.
데이트합시다.	Let's go out. = Would you like to go out with me?
데이트했습니다.	They had a date. = They went out for a date. = They went out on a date.
데인 상처가 심합니까?	Is the burn severe? ➡ Yes. (상당히 심합니다.)

도

도깨비 같은 놈!	That fella is like a ghost!
도난당했습니다.	My wallet was stolen. = Somebody stole my wallet. (지갑을 ~)
도대체 무슨 난리야?	What the hell is going on? = What on earth is going on? ➡ Nothing. (아무 일도 아니야.)
도둑 잡아라!	Catch the thief!
도둑맞았습니다.	My bag was stolen. = Somebody stole my bag. (가방을~)

	// Many things were stolen. = Somebody stole many things of mine. (많은 물건을 ~) ☞ 도난당했습니다.
도둑이 제 발 저리다.	[속담] He that commits a fault thinks everyone speaks of it. = He that has a great nose thinks everybody is speaking of it.
도둑이야!	① Thief! ② [소매치기] Robber! = Robbery!
도망쳐!	Run! // Run away! (멀리~)
도서관은 어떻게 갑니까?	How can I get to the library? ➡ Just go straight. (앞으로 곧장 가면 됩니다.)
도서대출 기간은 얼마나 됩니까?	How long can I borrow a book? ➡ For a week. (일주일입니다.)
도시락 가지고 왔습니까?	Did you bring your lunch? = Do you have lunch with you? ➡ ⓐ Yes. (가지고 왔습니다.) ⓑ No. I forgot. (가지고 오는 걸 깜박했습니다.) ⓒ No. I couldn't. (못 가져왔습니다.)
도와드릴까요?	① Can I help you? = May I help you? = Do you need some help? ➡ Yes. Thank you. (예, 감사합니다.) ② [상대방이 도움을 원할 때] What can I do for you? ③ [상점 등에서 점원] Are you being helped? ④ [도우려는 의지] Is there anything I can do for you? = Is there anything you want?

도와주세요.	① [거들어줌] Help me, please.
	= Give me a hand, please.
	// Please help. (좀~)
	// Please help me. (저 좀~)
	// Would you help me once more. (다시 한 번만~)
	② 〈경어〉 Would you please help me?

	③ [간구] I'm begging you for your help. (좀~) ④ [물질적 도움] Can you lend me some money? = Can you help me out with money? ⑤ [지지 및 지원] I need your backup, please.
도와주셔서 감사합니다.	Thank you for helping me. // Thank you for spending your time for me. (바쁘신 데도~) ➡ Come on. It was nothing. (뭐 대단한 것도 아닌데요.)
도와줄래요?	① [직접적 요청] Can you help me? = Can you give me a hand? // Would you help me? (좀~) ➡ ⓐ Yes. (예.) ⓑ Of course. (그러지요.) ② [간접적 요청] I need help. ➡ Don't worry. I'm here for you. (걱정 마세요, 제가 있잖아요.) ➡ Wait a minute. I'll help you right away. (잠깐만요. 금방 도와드릴게요.) ➡ I'm sorry, but I can't help you. (이 일은 제가 돕기 힘들 것 같습니다.)
도움 많이 받았습니다.	Thank you so much for your help. (그동안~)
도움 필요하면 전화해요.	Please call me if you need my help.
도움을 드리지 못해 죄송합니다.	I'm sorry that I can't help you.
도움을 많이 받았습니다.	I appreciate your help. // I appreciate his help. (그 사람한테~)
도움이 못 되서 죄송합니다.	I'm sorry that I can't help you much.
도움이 필요하시면 부르세요.	Please let me know if you need help.
도움이 필요합니까?	Do you need help? = Would you like some help?

	➡ ⓐ I'm fine. Thank you. (감사합니다. 괜찮습니다.) ⓑ I'm OK. (괜찮아요.) ⓒ No. (아니요.)
도적에게 열쇠를 주다.	[속담] That's like setting the wolf to guard the sheep. = It's like having the fox guard the hen house. ☞ 고양이 보고 반찬 가게 지키라는 격.
도착하면 저한테 좀 알려 주실래요?	Would you let me know when you arrive? ➡ ⓐ Yes. (예.) ⓑ OK. (좋아요.) ⓒ Don't worry. (걱정 말아요.)

도착했습니까?	Did you get there? = Did you arrive there?
	// Did you get to the station? (역에~)
	// Did you get to Sinchon? (신촌에~)
	➡ ⓐ Yes. (예.) ⓑ Not yet. (아직요.)

도토리 키 재기.	They are the same level. = They are all alike.

독

독 안에 든 쥐.	Like a rat in a hole. = Rat in a pot.
독감에 걸렸습니다.	I've got a terrible cold. = I had a terrible cold.
독신입니까?	① Are you single? ➡ Yes. (예.) ② Why are you still single? (왜 아직도~) ➡ ⓐ Cause I haven't found my soul mate. (마음에 맞는 사람을 찾지 못해서요.) ⓑ Cause I haven't met my soul mate. (마음에 맞는 사람을 못 만나서요.)
독합니다.	Hard and strong. // So hard and strong. (참~)

돈

돈 가져왔습니까?	Did you bring money with you? ➡ ⓐ Yes, a little. (조금 가져왔습니다.) ⓑ No. (아니요.)
돈 갚으세요.	Pay back. // Pay my money back. (내~)
돈 냅니까?	[상점] Should I pay? // Where should I pay? = Where can I pay? (어디에 다~) ➡ At the cashier. (수납처로 가세요.)
돈 부치는데 수수료가 얼마입니까?	How much is the service fee for wiring? = How much should I pay for wiring? ➡ One percent of the total. (1%를 받습니다.)
돈 없어, 배 째!	I have no money! Cut my belly out!
돈 있으면 다야!	① [소용] What good is money? I'm not scared. (~겁 안 난다야!) ➡ Would have been better if you had had that courage before! (진작 이런 기개 있었으면 얼마나 좋았냐!) ② Money doesn't matter to me! I'm not scared. (겁 안 난다야!~)
돈 좀 빌려주세요.	Can I borrow some money? = Would you lend me some money?
돈만 있으면 귀신도 부릴 수 있다.	[속담] Money rules the world. = Money makes the world go round.
돈을 다 써버렸어요.	I've spent all my money. = All my money is gone. = I used up all my money.
돈을 다 잃었습니다.	[도박] I lost all my money. (전~)
돈을 입금하려고 합니다.	I'd like to deposit some money.

돈을 찾으려고 합니다.	I'd like to withdraw some money.
돈이 양반이다.	Money is power. = Money will do anything. = What will not money do? = With money, you can do anything.
돈이 없습니다.	① I have no money. = I don't have any money. = No money. ② [돈이 다 떨어짐] I'm broke. = I'm penniless.
돈이 없어졌습니다.	The money is gone. // My money is gone. (내~)

돌

돌다리도 두드려봐야 한다.	[속담] Look before you leap.
돌려드리겠습니다.	① [전화] I'll transfer you there. = I'll connect you there. // I'll transfer you to Room 201. (201호에 ~) ② [반납] I'll return tomorrow. (내일 바로~)
돌려서 말하지 마세요.	Please don't beat around the bush! = Please stop beating around the bush! = Please get to the point.
돌려주세요.	[반환] Please give it back to me. = Please return it. // Please return the bag. (어서 가방이나~)
돌아가 주세요.	① Please go back. ☞ 돌아가세요. ② [차] Please turn back.
돌아가!	Go back. // Go back right now. (어서~)
돌아가세요.	① [주인이 손님에게] Please leave. // Please leave now. We're closing. (그만~ 문 닫을 시간입니다.)

	② Please go back. = Please return. ③ [차량의 U턴] Make a U-turn, please.
돌아가셨습니다.	① [자리를 뜸] He's back. = He's gone. (그 사람은~) ② [사망] He's passed away. = He died. (그 분은~)
돌아가야겠습니다.	I should go back. = I should return. // I should go back right now. (바로~)
돌아다녀요.	① [배회] I'm just wandering. (그냥 ~) ② [도보로 돌아다님] **I'm just walking around here and there.** (그냥 여기 저기 ~) ③ [빈둥거림] I'm bumming around. // He's been just bumming around. (그 남자는 빈둥빈둥 ~)
돌아도 단단히 돌았구나!	You are so crazy! = You are such a freak!
돌아버리겠네.	**I'm going nuts.** = I'm going crazy. // I'm completely going crazy. (완전히~) ☞ 미치겠다!
돌아서!	Turn around! // About-turn! = About-face! (뒤로~)
돌아서 주세요.	Please turn around. = Please about-face. = Please about-turn.
돌아오세요.	Please come back. = Please return. (꼭~)
돌아오시면 전화주세요.	Please give me a call when you come back.
돌아오지 못할 길을 가다.	He / She's gone to the point of no return.
돌아오지 않을 겁니다.	Won't come back. // Won't come back again. (다시는~)
돌아옵니까?	Will you be back? = Are you coming back? // When will you be back? (언제~) ➡ Tomorrow. (내일 돌아옵니다.)
돌아와서 봅시다.	See you back. = See you then. = See you later.

돌아왔어요!	① I'm back! = I've come back! ② [집] I'm home!
돌았니?	Are you nuts? = Are you crazy? = Are you out of your mind? ➡ You are crazy! (너야말로 돌았구나.)
돌팔이!	[무면허의사] Quack! = Quack doctor! = Charlatan!

동

동감입니다.	① [일반적] I feel the same way. = Me, too. // I think so, too. (저도~) ② [의견일치] I agree with you.
동전으로 바꿀 수 있습니까?	Can you change it to coins? ➡ Sure. (그럼요.)
동전으로 좀 바꿔주세요.	Can you break this bill?
동전으로 주세요.	Give me small change, please. = Please give me coins.
동정하지 마세요.	Don't feel sympathetic for me. = I don't need your sympathy.
동창입니다.	He's my colleague. (그는 나의~)

돼

돼먹지 않았어!	Thumbs down! = Nonsense! = Boorish!
돼져버려라!	〈비속어〉 Fuck off! = Go to hell! = Drop dead!
돼지 같은 놈!	Pig! = Piggish! = Hog! = Hoggish!

돼지고기 한 덩어리에 얼마입니까?

How much is a loaf of pork?
➡ Five dollars and forty-five cents.
(5달러 45센트입니다.)

됐

됐습니다!

① [상대방의 행위를 제지] **That's enough!**
② [완성] It's done! =It's finished!
// It's all done! = It's all finished! (다~)
③ [거절] No, thanks! =That's OK!
④ [동의] That's it!
⑤ [양이 충분함 또는 상대방의 언행에 대해 짜증남]
That's good enough!
⑥ [불만의 말투] Fine! = OK! OK!
⑦ [제지] Stop it! That's enough!
⑧ [상처 등이 심하지 않음] I'm fine!
⑨ [승리] I won! = I got it!
⑩ [위안] It's all over!
⑪ [가망 있음] It's good! = It's OK!
⑫ [정중한 사양] No, thank you!
⑬ [간섭에 대해] I'm fine!

됐습니까?

① [완성] Are you done? = Did you finish?
➡ Yes. (예.)
② [만족] Do you like it?
➡ Yes. (예.)

되

되글을 가지고 말글로 써먹다.

To turn one's learning to best advantage.
= To make the most of meager education.

된

된장찌개 하나 주세요.	Please give me a miso soup. = Let me have a miso soup.

될

될 수 있으면 담배를 삼가세요.	Please refrain from smoking.
될 수 있으면 술을 삼가세요.	Please refrain from drinking.
될성부른 나무는 떡잎부터 안다.	[속담] Sandalwood is fragrant even in seed leaf. = Genius displays itself even in childhood. = As the twig is bent, so grows the tree.

됩

됩니까?	① Can you make it?
	// Can you make it at 9? (9시~)
	➡ Yes! (네!)
	② [완성] Will it be done?
	// When will it be done? (언제 다~)
	➡ Some time later. (좀 있으면 됩니다.)
	③ [주문] When will it be ready? (언제~)
	➡ Soon. (곧 됩니다.)
	④ How much more time will it take?
	= How much longer will it take?
	(얼마나 있어야 다~)
	➡ At least three days. (아무래도 3일은 걸립니다.)
	☞ 됐습니다!

ㄷ

두

두 귀로 똑똑히 들어!	Listen up! = All ears!
두 귀로 똑똑히 들었어.	I heard everything.
두 눈 똑바로 뜨고 다니란 말입니다.	Keep your eyes wide open.
두 눈으로 분명히 봤어요.	I saw it with my own two eyes!
두 다리 쭉 뻗고 자겠어요.	① I can sleep well. = I can sleep with no worries. (이제~) ② 〈직역〉 I can sleep with my legs straight. (이제~)
두 다리 쭉 뻗고 자다.	Sleep well.
두 마리 토끼를 다 잡을 수 없다.	[속담] If you run after two hares, you will catch neither.
두 번 읽어라.	Read it twice.
두 번째입니다.	Second time. // This is the second time. (이번이~)
두 분은 정말 잘 어울립니다.	① [젊은 부부] You look great together. ② [노부부] You are a well matched husband and wife. = You two are perfect for each other.
두 분이십니까?	[음식점] Are there two in your party? ➡ Yes. (예.)
두 사람	two people
두 손 다 들었다!	① [항복] I gave up. = I surrender to you. (너한테~) ② I totally gave up. (완전히~) ③ [감탄 · 감동] Two thumbs up!
두 시 괜찮습니까?	Is two OK with you? = Can you make it at two? = Does two work for you? ➡ OK with me. (괜찮습니다.)

두 시간이나 잤습니다.	I slept for two hours.
두 장 주세요.	[매표소] Two, please. = Two tickets, please. // Two tickets to Busan, please. (부산행표~)
두 팀의 실력이 비슷해 보입니다.	The two teams are equally great. = The two teams are well matched.

두고 보자!	① [협박] Just wait and see! = I'll see you again.
	// See you again! (우리~)
	② [보복] Watch your back! = I'll pay you back!
	// I'll pay you back later! (나중에~)

두고 봅시다.	① [일의 진행상태 대해] Let's wait and see. = Let's give it some time. ② [경기의 결과] Let's see. ③ [해 볼 기회를 줌] Let's give him another chance. (그 사람 좀~) ④ [협박] I'll see you again! ☞ 두고 보자!
두려워하지 마세요.	① Don't be afraid. = Don't be scared. ➡ No, I'm not. (무섭지 않아요.) ② [공포심] Don't be frightened.
두려워할 것 없습니다.	Nothing to be scared about. = Nothing scary.
두말 할 것 없어!	[단정] No more words! = Don't say any more words!
두말하게 하지 마세요.	I don't wanna say.
두부 한 모에 얼마입니까?	How much is a pack of tofu? ➡ Two dollars. (2달러입니다)
두통약 있습니까?	Do you have a painkiller? = Do you have medicine for headaches? = Do you have any headache medicine? ➡ Yes, I do. (있습니다.)
두통이 사라졌습니다.	My headache is gone. = No more headache. = My headache has disappeared.

둘

둘 다 원합니다.	I want both. (전~)
둘러대지 마세요.	Don't make up excuses. = Stop making excuses. (자꾸~)
둘러봅시다.	Let's look around. = Let's take a look around. // Let's look around some more. (우리 좀 더~)
둘은 많이 닮았어요.	[비슷한 데가 많다] They are alike. = They look like each other. = They resemble each other. = They look similar.
둘은 헤어졌습니다.	They broke up with each other. (그들은~) = They are not seeing each other anymore. // The two broke up after they had a fight. (다투고서~)
둘이 사귀는 거야?	Are they going out with each other? ➡ That's nonsense. They are here just to see a movie. (말도 안 돼. 그냥 영화 보러 온 거지.)
둘이 싸웠지요?	① [말싸움] They had an argument, didn't they? ➡ How did you know that? (어떻게 알았어요?) ② [주먹질] They had a fist fight, didn't they? ➡ Who told you so? (누가 그래요?)
둘이 잘 어울립니다.	They go well with each other. = The two look like a perfect match.
둘째 며느리 맞아보아야 맏며느리 착한 줄 안다.	[속담] You don't know what you've got until you've lost it. = You don't know what you've got until it's gone.

뒤

뒤돌아보지 마!	Don't look back!

뒤로 돌아서봐!	Turn around! ☞ 돌아서 주세요.
뒤로 물러서!	Step back!
뒤를 조심해!	Watch your back!
뒤통수 맞았어.	It was a big blow from behind. // He really stabbed me in the back. (그에게 완전~)
뒤풀이가 있어요.	There's a small party afterwards. = You're invited to a small party afterwards.

뒷

뒷간에 갈 적 마음 다르고 올 적 마음 다르다.	Danger past, God forgotten. = Once on shore, we pray no more.
뒷말 하지 마세요.	Don't speak ill of others behind their backs. // Stop saying bad stuff about me behind my back. (내~)
뒷맛이 독특해요.	It leaves a unique taste behind. = It has an interesting aftertaste. // It leaves a unique taste behind, not something sweet. (달지 않고, ~) ← What does it taste like? (어떻게 맛있습니까?)
뒷머리는 너무 짧게 깎지 마세요.	[머리] Don't trim too much on the back.
뒷문으로 아는 사람이 많습니다.	He has got a wide circle of acquaintances from an informal route. (그는~)
뒷북 치지 마세요.	Thanks for the history lesson. = Keep up with the program. = Wake up and smell the coffee. = Too little too late.

뒷일은 내게 맡기고 가세요.	Just go and leave the rest up to me. = Just go. I'll take care of the rest. = Just go. I'll cover you from here.

드

드디어 일어났구나.	That has happened after all. = That has finally come.
드라이기 좀 빌릴 수 있을까요?	Can I borrow a hair dryer? = Can I use your blow-dryer? ➡ Yes, here you are. (예, 가져가세요.)
드라이클리닝은 얼마입니까?	How much does it cost to get this dry-cleaned? = How much is the dry-cleaning? ➡ It is fifty dollars. (50달러요.)
드라이클리닝입니까, 물세탁입니까?	Is it for dry-cleaning or washing? ➡ It should be dry-cleaned. (드라이클리닝이요.)
드라이하실래요?	① [세탁] Is it for dry-cleaning? = Do you want to have it dry-cleaned? ② [두발] Do you want a blow-dry? ➡ No, not today. (아니오. 오늘은 안 합니다.)
드러누워요.	Lie down. // Lie down on the floor. = Lay yourself down on the floor. (바닥에~)
드릴 말씀이 있습니다.	① I have something to tell you. ☞ 할 말 있습니다. ② [보고] I have something to report.
드세요!	Have some! = Have seconds! // Help yourself! (마음껏~)
드셨네요.	[술을] You drank some alcohol. // You are drunk. (취하셨군요.)
드십시오.	Drink some tea. = Have some tea. (차~) ➡ Thank you. You have a seat, please. (감사합니다, 그만 앉으세요.)

듣

듣고 보니 그러네.	What you said seems to be right.
듣고 보니 일리가 있네요.	That makes sense now. = Now I can understand what you mean.
듣고 싶습니다.	I want your opinion. = I'd like to listen to what's on your mind. = I want to listen to what you think. = I'd like to hear what's on your mind. = I'd like to hear what you have to say. = I'd like to listen to what you have to say. (의견을~)
듣고 싶지 않아요.	I don't want to hear anything. (어떤 것도~) // I don't want to listen anymore. (더 이상~) ➡ You should, even though you don't want to. (듣고 싶지 않아도 들어야 해.)
듣고 있어요?	Are you listening to me? (내 말~) ➡ I'm listening. (듣고 있어.)
듣기 거북하네.	That's embarrassing to hear. = That's very uncomfortable to hear. = To listen to it makes me very uncomfortable.
듣기 싫어도 들어.	Listen even though you don't want to.

듣기 좋습니다.	[소리] That sounds good.
	// This music sounds pleasant to me.
	(이 음악은~)
	// This music is very tuneful.
	(이 음악은 곡조가 매우 좋군요.)

듣기 좋은 소리도 자꾸 들으면 싫증난다.	Even good words irritate me when you repeat them over and over again.
듣는데 문제가 있어요.	I can't hear well. = I have a problem with hearing. = I'm suffering from a hearing problem.

들

들려주셔서 감사합니다.	**Thank you for coming by.** = I'm glad you came by.
들리지 않아요?	Can't you hear something? = Don't you hear something? = Don't you hear that? ➡ Yes, I hear something. (들려요.)

들립니까?	① [가능] Can you hear me?
	➡ ⓐ Yes, I can hear you. (들립니다.)
	// I can hear you loud and clear. (잘 들립니다.)
	// No, I can't hear you. (안 들립니다.)
	ⓑ **I can't hear you well.**
	= I can barely hear you.
	(잘 안 들립니다. 조금만 크게 말씀해 주실래요?)
	➡ Can you speak up a little bit?
	② Do you hear me?

들어(요)!	① [음식] Help yourself! ☞ 드세요! ② [젓가락 사용] Try it with the chopsticks! ③ [올리기] Lift it up!
들어가 봐라.	Go home and take a rest. (집에~) // Go inside. (안에~)
들어가 쉬어라.	Go in and get some rest.
들어가도 됩니까?	Can I come in? ➡ ⓐ Sure, come in. (예, 들어오세요.) ⓑ No, you can't. (아니오, 들어오지 마세요.)
들어가세요.	① [작별인사] Good-bye. ② [안으로] Get in, please. ☞ 들어가 봐라. ③ [손님이 전송 나온 주인에게] You don't have to bother to come out and see me off. (그만~) ☞ 나오지 마세요.
들어가지 않아요.	It doesn't fit me. It's not big enough for me.

	= It doesn't fit me. It's too small for me. (옷이 작아서~)
들어본 적 없습니다.	① [경험] I've never heard of that. ② [소문] The rumor is new to me.

들어봐!	① [이야기] Let me tell you a story! (내 말을~)
	= Pay attention to me!
	= Listen to what I'm saying!
	// Please listen up!
	= Pay close attention to me! (내 말을 똑똑히~)
	② [소리] Check the sound, please!
	③ [물건을 손으로] Lift this up! (이걸 들어 올려봐!)
	// Hold this! (이걸 들고 있어봐.)

들어오든지 말든지 맘대로 하세요.	Come in or not, you choose. = Come in or not, it's up to you.
들어오세요! // 들어와!	Come in! = Get in!
들어오셔서 차 한 잔 하세요.	Come in and have some tea, please.
들어주셔야 합니다.	① [부탁] Please do me a favor. ② [간청] I'm begging you to do me a favor.
들어줘요.	① [물건] Can you help me with this? (이것 좀~) // Can you hold this for me? (들고 있어줘요.) ② [말] Hear me out, please.
들었습니까?	① Did you hear that? // Did you hear the news? (그 소식 ~) ➡ I heard it. (들었습니다.) ② From whom did you hear this? (이걸 누구한테서~) ➡ ⓐ He called me. (그한테서 전화가 왔어요.) ⓑ He e-mailed me. (그한테서 이메일이 왔어요.) ⓒ He text-messaged me. (그한테서 문자메시지가 왔어요.)
들었습니다.	I was told like that. (그렇게~)

	= That's what I was told.
	// At least, that's what I heard. (적어도 전 그렇게~)
	// I heard it on the radio. (라디오에서~)

들으면 병이고 안 들으면 약이다.	It would be better not to hear bad news.
들은 척도 안했어.	He turned a deaf ear on me. (그는 내말을~) = He wouldn't listen. = He refused to listen.
들켜버렸네.	[발각] It was found out. // He was caught red-handed. (그가 현장에서~)

듭

듭시다!	[건배] Cheers!

등

등 좀 긁어줘요.	[가려움] Can you scratch my back for me?
등 좀 두드려라.	Can you give me a back message?
등 떠밀렸어.	I was forced to do it. = I was dragged into doing it.
등기우편으로 보낼 수도 있습니다.	You can send it by registered mail.
등받이를 제 위치로 해주세요.	Please put the backrest back in place.
등산갑니다.	① We are going hiking this weekend. (주말에~) ② [산악등반] We are going mountain climbing this weekend. (주말에~)
등신!	① [상대방의 행위나 말에 대한 비난] Idiot! = It serves you right!

	② 〈속어〉 You suck! ☞ 꼬락서니하고는!
등을 돌렸습니다.	He turned his back on me. (그는 나에게~)
등이 가려워요.	My back itches. = I feel itchy in my back.
등이 고장 났습니다.	The lamp is broken in the room. (방의~)
등잔 밑이 어둡다.	① The beacon does not shine on its own base. = It's not easy to recognize what is right in front of you. = It's easy to miss what is under your nose. ② [가까울수록 소식을 늦게 안다.] The wife(husband) is always the last to know.
등쳐먹었어.	He conned me out of money. (그가 나를~) = He swindled me out of money.

디

디시(DC) 됩니까?	Can I get a discount on this? // What kind of discount can you give us on this? (얼마나~)
디시(DC)해서 얼마입니까?	How much is it if I get the discount? = How much is it with the discount?
디자인에 만족합니까?	Are you satisfied with this design? = Are you happy with that design? = Do you like the design?
디자인이 세련됐습니다.	The design is very stylish. // The design is so / very sophisticated. (너무~)
디자인이 좀 야합니다.	The design is a little bit loud. = The design is a little bit revealing. = The design is a little bit racy.

ㄷ

딜

딜레마에 빠졌어.	I'm in a bind. = I'm stuck in a bind. = I have a dilemma. = I'm in a dilemma.

딩

딩동!	[종소리] Ding dong!

따

따끔한 맛을 보여주지.	I'll show you what! = I'll teach you a lesson!
따 논 당상.	I'm sure about it. = There's no doubt about it.
따돌림을 당했어요.	I was always left out in the cold. (저는 언제나~) = I was always given the runaround. = I always got the short end of the stick.
따뜻합니다.	① [날씨] It's warm today. (오늘은 ~) ② [장소] It is warm in here. (여기는~) ③ [마음씨] She is a warm-hearted person. = She has a heart of gold. (그녀는~)
따뜻해졌습니다.	① [날씨] It's warmer than the other days. (전보다~) ② [방안] It's warmer than a few minutes ago. (몇 분 전보다~)
따뜻해질 것입니다.	It will get warmer and warmer as days go by. (날이 감에 따라 점점 더 ~)
따라오지 마세요.	Don't come with me. = Don't follow me.
따라 하지 마세요.	① Don't follow what I'm doing. ② [창작물 모방] Don't copy mine. ③ [말투 모방] Don't mimic my words.

따라오세요.	Please follow me. = Come along with me. // Come along this way. (여기로 ~)
따라잡을게요.	I'll catch up. // I'll catch up with you. (당신을 ~) // I'll catch up with the last class myself. (지난 수업을 알아서 ~)
따라하세요. // 따라서 해봐요.	① [말] Please repeat after me. = Say it after me, please. ② [행동] Please do just like me. = Please do just like what I'm doing.
따로따로 계산해요.	Let's go Dutch. = Let's pay separately.
따로따로 계산해 주세요.	Separate bills, please. = Separate checks, please.
따르릉!	Ring-ring!
따분할 때 전화해.	Call me when you're bored. = Give me a call when you've got nothing to do.
따분합니다.	I'm bored. // I'm bored to death. = I'm bored stiff. (정말~) ☞ 지루합니다.
따질 게 있습니다.	I have words with you. = I have a bone to pick with you. ☞ 짚고 넘어가야 할 것이 있어.

딴

딴 방법이 없습니다.	I have no other way (than this). = There's no other way (than this). (이 방법 외에는 ~)
딴 약속이 있습니다.	I have another appointment.
딴 여자가 생겼답니다.	I have another girl. = I'm seeing another girl. = I'm dating another girl.

딴말하기 없기다!	This is settled! No more talk about this!
딴전 피우지 마세요.	Please do not be unfocused. = Concentrate on your main duty! = Please focus on the matter at hand.

ㄷ

딸

딸깍 소리가 났어요.	I heard a rattling sound. = There was a rattling sound. = Something rattled, I heard.
딸꾹질이 나와요.	I have the hiccups. (자꾸~) = I can't stop hiccupping. = I keep hiccupping.
딸꾹질이 멈췄어요.	The hiccups have stopped. = I don't have the hiccups anymore.
딸랑딸랑!	Tinkle-tinkle!
딸은 출가외인.	A married daughter is no better than a stranger.
딸이 둘 있습니다.	I have two daughters.
딸이 참 예쁩니다.	① [어린 딸의 경우] Your daughter is adorable. // Your daughter looks like a doll. (인형처럼~) ② [성인 딸의 경우] Your daughter is very beautiful.
딸입니까? 아들입니까?	Is it a girl, or a boy? (아기가~)

땀

땀이 많이 납니다.	① [체질] I sweat a lot. ② [현재 상황] I'm sweating a lot.

땅

땅 짚고 헤엄치기.	[아주 쉬운 일] It's a piece of cake. = It's really easy.
땅에 엎드려!	Lie flat with your face down!
땅이 미끄럽습니다.	The ground is slippery.

때

때가 되면 올 겁니다.	He'll be back when it's time. (그는 ~)
때가 좋지 않아.	Now is not a good time. (지금은~) // We're not in a good time for it. = Timing is not good. (그것을 하기에~)
때리고 싶으시면 때리세요.	Hit me if you want.
때리는 시어미보다 말리는 시누이가 더 밉다.	There's always a person worse than a villain.
때문이야!	It's because of you! (너~) // This is all because of you! (이게 다 너~)

땡

땡 잡았네요.	You've really lucked out! = You are lucky! = What a stroke of luck!
땡땡!	Ding-dong!
땡그렁!	Clang! Clang!
땡땡이 쳤으면 벌을 받아야지.	You played hooky, so you deserve to be punished. // I will punish you for missing the classes. (수업~)

땡땡이 치자.	Let's play hooky. // Let's cut math. (수학 시간~)

떠

떠나고 싶으면 떠나.	Go if you want. // Leave me if you want. (나를~)
떠나기 섭섭합니다.	I feel so sad that I should go. // I'm so sad to leave here. (여기를~)
떠나지 말아요.	Don't go. = Don't leave, please. // Don't leave me, please. = Don't dump me, please. (나를~)
떠납니까?	Are you going? = Are you leaving? // When are you leaving? (언제~) ➡ I'm leaving this Saturday. (이번 토요일에요.)
떠들지 마세요.	Stop talking. = Don't make noise. = Stop making noise.

떡

떡 줄 사람은 생각도 않는데 김칫국부터 마신다.	[속담] Don't count your chickens before they are hatched.

떨

떨려 죽겠습니다.	I'm dead nervous. = I have so many butterflies in my stomach.
떨립니다.	① [마음] I'm nervous. ② [다리] My legs are trembling. ③ [이] My teeth are chattering.
떨어뜨렸습니다.	I dropped it.

떨어뜨린거지요?	① You dropped it, didn't you? ② [물건의 주인 확인] This is yours, isn't it? (당신이~)
떨어져!	[거리를 두도록] Get off! = Get off of me. // Get away from me. (나에게서~) ☞ 저리 가!
떨어져 있으면 더 애틋하다.	Absence makes the heart grow fonder.
떨어졌어요.	① [추락 및 낙상] I fell down. // I felt down the stairs. (계단에서 ~) ② [시험 등에 낙방] I failed it. // I failed the exam. = I messed up the exam. = I couldn't make it.
떨지 마세요.	Don't be nervous. = Take it easy. = Relax.

또

또	Again.
또 놀러오세요.	① Come again. ② [헤어지는 인사] I'll be looking forward to seeing you again. = I will see you again.
또 들러주세요.	Please come and visit me again. = I'd like to see you again. ☞ 또 놀러오세요.
또 만나게 되어 반갑습니다.	Nice to see you again. = I'm very pleased to see you again.
또 만나요.	See you again. // See you soon. (곧~) // I'll see you around. (이 근처에서~)
또 만났네!	We've met again!
또 뭐야?	Now what?
또 뭘 원하십니까?	What do you want this time?
또 뵙겠습니다.	I'll see you again.

또 사고 쳤어!	I caused trouble again! (나~) // You caused trouble again! (너~)
또 속았네.	I was fooled again. = I was deceived again.
또 오십시오.	Come again, please. = I'd like to see you again. ☞ 또 놀러오세요. // 또 들려주세요.
또라이야.	〈비속어〉 He's fucked up. (그는~)

똑

똑같습니까?	Are they the same? // Are these two the same ones? (이 둘이 ~)
똑같습니다.	They are the same ones.
똑같은 걸로 주세요.	I want the same one with this. (이것과 ~)
똑같은 걸로 하나 사줄게.	I'll buy you the same one.
똑같은 걸로 할래.	I'll take the same one.
똑같은 느낌입니다.	It feels the same.
똑딱똑딱!	① [시계소리] Tick-tock, tick-tock. ② [기계소리] Click-click, click-click.
똑똑!	① [노크소리] Knock! Knock! ② [나무 판 등에 부딪히는 소리] Tap! Tap!
똑똑하고 영리하게 생겼습니다.	He looks smart and bright. (그는 ~)
똑똑하네.	You are smart. = You are brilliant. = How brilliant!
똑똑합니다.	I'm smart. = I'm intelligent. (저는~)

똑똑히 기억하고 있습니다.	I remember clearly. = It's very clear in my memory.
똑똑히 들어!	Listen carefully to me! = Listen up. = Pay close attention to my words. = Listen carefully to what I'm saying! (내 말을~)
똑똑히 봐!	Look carefully at this! = Take a close look at this! (이것을~)
똑똑히 봤습니까?	Did you see it clearly?
똑바로 가세요.	Go straight. // Go straight down the street. (이 길을 따라~)
똑바로 서!	Stand straight! // Don't move and stand straight! (움직이지 말고 ~)
똑바로 앉아봐.	Sit up straight.
똑바로 쳐다봐!	Look straight at me! // Don't avoid my eyes! Look straight at me! (내 눈 피하지 말고~)

똘

똘똘하네.	You are so smart.

똥

똥 묻은 개가 겨 묻은 개 나무란다.	[속담] It's the pot calling the kettle black.
똥 마려워요.	① [직설적으로] I have a bowel movement. = I want to poo. ② [완곡하게] I want to go to the bathroom. = I have to go to the bathroom.

ㄷ

똥배가 나왔네.	① You have a big belly. ② [우스갯소리] You have love handles.
똥오줌을 가리다.	The baby is potty-trained. = The baby is toilet-trained. (그 아기는~)
똥이 무서워서 피하냐, 더러워서 피하지.	The reason I avoid it is not that I'm scared. I just don't want to get involved.

뚜

뚜껑 열린다!	① I'm really mad! = I'm about to blow my top! ② 〈비속어〉 I'm pissed off!
뚜껑을 열어!	Open the lid! = Take the lid off! = Uncover it! = Get rid of the cover!

뚝

뚝 그쳤다!	The sound stopped suddenly! (소리가~)
뚝 그쳐!	Stop crying!
뚝뚝 소리가 났어.	① [부러지는 소리] There was the sound of snaps. = There was the sound of something snapping. ② [떨어지는 소리] I heard the sound of something dropping. = I heard something drop.
뚝배기보다 장맛이 좋다.	Appearances are often deceptive.

뚱

뚱 돼지!	You are a hog! = How fat you are!

뚱딴지같다.	You are talking nonsense.

뛰

뛰는 놈 위에 나는 놈. // 뛰는 놈 위에 나는 놈 있다.	Diamonds cut diamonds. = There may be blue and better blue. = There is always a better person than you.
뛰어와!	Run here!
뛰어!	Run!

뜨

뜨거우니까 식혀서 드세요.	It's hot. Cool it before you eat it. = Let it cool before you eat it.
뜨거울 때 드세요.	Have this while it's hot.
뜨거워요.	It's hot.

뜸

뜸 너무 들이다 누룽지 된다.	① 〈직역〉 If you steam the rice too long, you can spoil it. ② Thinking too long before you do something can be not good.

뜻

뜻밖의 일입니다.	I didn't expect it to happen. = It is not expected. = Nobody expected it.

ㄷ

뜻이 있는 곳에 길이 있다.

Where there's a will, there's a way.

띠

ㄷ

띠가 무엇입니까?

What is your Chinese zodiac sign?

띠에 해당하는 동물

A cow. (소) A dog. (개) A mouse. (쥐)
A tiger. (호랑이) A dragon. (용) A sheep. (양)
A monkey. (원숭이) A pig. (돼지) A snake. (뱀)
A chicken. (닭) A rabbit. (토끼) A horse. (말)

라

라디오 좀 틀어.	Turn on the radio. // Turn up the radio. (크게~)
라면 먹을래요?	Would you like some ramen? ➡ No, I wouldn't. (먹고 싶지 않아요.)
라이터 팝니까?	Do you carry lighters here? // Do you have lighters here? ➡ ⓐ Yes, we do. (팝니다.) ⓑ Sure. Here you are. (예! 여기 있습니다.) ⓒ [마트에서] They are in aisle number three. = You can find them in aisle three. (예, 3번 복도에 있습니다.)

랩

랩을 씌워서 10분 동안 냉장고에 넣어두면 돼.	Wrap it and keep it in the refrigerator for 10 minutes. // Wrap it and keep it in the refrigerator for 10 minutes, like this. (이렇게~)

레

레스토랑 있습니까?	Is there a restaurant here? (여기~) ➡ ⓐ Yes, there is one. (예, 하나 있습니다.) ⓑ No, there's no restaurant here. (없습니다.)
레이디 퍼스트!	Ladies first! // After you! (먼저 하세요!)

렌

렌즈를 낍니다.	I wear contact lenses.

ㄹ

렌지에 물 끓이고 있습니다.	I have water boiling on the stove. = Water is boiling on the stove.
렌트하시겠습니까?	① [자동차] Do you want to rent a car? = Would you like to rent a car? ② [집] Would you like to rent an apartment? (아파트를~) // Would you like to rent a studio? (원룸을~)

로

로또 일등 당첨 축하합니다.	Congratulations on your winning the lottery!
로마는 하루아침에 이루어지지 않습니다.	Rome was not built in a day.
로마에 오면 로마의 법을 따라야 한다.	[속담] When in Rome, do as the romans do.

룸

룸메이트는 외국 사람입니까?	Is your roommate a foreigner? ➡ No, he(she) isn't (a foreigner). (아닙니다.)
룸서비스를 불러주세요.	Please call me room service. = Can I contact room service?
룸으로 배달해 주세요.	Please have it delivered to my room. = Send it to my room, please. // Send the breakfast to my room. (아침을~)
룸은 몇 호실입니까?	What is your room number? ➡ I'm in Room 101[one - o - one]. (101호실입니다.)

리

리모컨도 고장난 것 같습니다.	The remote control seems to be broken, too. = The remote control doesn't work, I guess.
리필 좀 해주시겠습니까?	[음료수] Can I get this refilled? = Can I get a refill?

링

링거를 맞았습니다.	I got an IV drip.

마

마구 지껄여라!	[주의 · 경고] You are talking too wild! Watch your tongue! = Watch your mouth!
마누라가 바람난 걸 모르고 있단 말이야?	You don't know that your wife is cheating on you? =You don't know that your wife is having an affair? ➡ To know that makes no difference! (알면 또 어떻게 하는데?)
마누라가 예쁘면 처갓집 말뚝에 대고 절한다.	Love me, love my dog.
마누라한테 꽉 잡혀 살고 있습니다.	He is under his wife's thumb. = He is whipped. (그 사람~)
마늘 냄새는 정말 못견디겠어요.	I can't stand the smell of garlic.
마늘이나 까요!	Just peel the garlic!
마른하늘에 날벼락.	The unexpected always happens.
마셔!	① [권유] Drink it! ② [건배] Bottoms up!
마셔 보세요.	Try it. // Try some. (좀~)
마시면서 이야기하자.	Let's talk over a drink.
마실 것 좀 줄래요?	Would you get me something to drink? = Do you have something to drink? // I'm thirsty. Can I have something to drink? (목이 마르네요. ~) ➡ Yes. I'll get you something. (예. 가져다 줄게요.)
마실래요?	Would you like something to drink?
마실 수 없음	① You shouldn't drink it. ② [간판] Unfit for drinking.

마음 아파하지 마세요.	Don't be so sad about it.
마음고생 하지 마세요.	Don't be too hurt about it. = Don't let it hurt you too much. = Don't be too torn up over it.
마음대로 생각해요.	Think as you, please.
마음대로 하세요.	① [편한 대로] Do whatever you want. = It's up to you. = Suit yourself. = Do it your way. ② [상황 봐가며] As you want. = As you like.
마음먹기 나름이야.	It's all in the mind. = It's a matter of mind. = It's up to your mind. = You just have to put your mind to it. = You just have to wish for it. = You just have to want it badly.
마음 먹었습니다.	I set my heart on that. = I have my mind set. = I made up my mind to do that. = I decided to do that. (그렇게 하기로~) // I have my mind set on going to college. (대학에 가기로~)
마음뿐 몸이 안 따라준다.	I'd really love to, but it's really hard to put into action. = It's easier said than done.
마음에 두고 있는 사람이 있습니다.	I have someone in my heart.
마음에 두지 마세요.	① [상처 주는 말에 대해] Don't take it harshly. = I'm sorry to hurt you. I didn't mean it. ➡ I'm okay. (괜찮아요.) ② I was sorry in the morning. It was not my intention. Don't take it seriously. (아침에 미안했습니다, 고의는 아니니, ~) ➡ No problem at all. I know you just wanted to show me that you care about me. (괜찮습니다. 저에게 관심 가져 주신 거 압니다.) ☞ 신경 쓰지 마세요.

	③ I was rude last night. Don't take it personally. (어젯밤 제 태도가 불손했습니다.~) ➡ I'm not you! (누가 당신 같은 줄 알아요!)

마음에 듭니까?	① [기호] Do you like it?
	// Do you like this? (이거~)
	➡ Yes, I like it very much. (아주 마음에 듭니다.)
	// The more I see it, the more I like it.
	= It's growing on me. (볼수록 점점 마음에 듭니다.)
	② [만족] Are you happy (with it)?
	= Are you satisfied (with it)?
	➡ Yes, it looks great. (예, 좋아 보입니다.)

마음에 없는 소리 하지 마세요.	Don't say things you don't mean.
마음은 굴뚝같다.	I'd really love to.
마음이 놓여요.	I feel relieved now. (이젠~) = I feel like a weight is off my shoulders. = Nothing gets on my nerves anymore. I feel much better.
마음이 불편해요.	It doesn't settle well with me. (그것 때문에~)
마음이 시키는 대로 하세요.	Do what's in your heart. = Follow your own heart.
마음이 잘 맞아요.	① We communicate well. (우린~) = We have good chemistry. = We have the right chemistry. ② [연인사이] We're a match made in heaven. ☞ 천생연분이다. 하늘이 맺어준 인연입니다.
마음이 편하겠어요?	Do you really think I am comfortable with this? (내가 지금~) // Do you think it makes me happy to do this? (누군 지금 마음이 편해서 이런지 알아요?)
마음을 굳혔어요.	I'm dead set on this. (이 문제에 대해~) // I already made up my mind. = I've already made up my mind. (이미~)

ㅁ

마음을 담은 것입니다.	I poured my heart into it. = I put my heart into it.
마이동풍.	All the words fell on deaf ears.
마중 나와서 감사합니다.	Thank you for coming to see me on arrival. = Thank you for coming out to meet me.
마침 잘 왔습니다.	You've come at the right moment. = You've come at just the right moment.
마침 잘 됐습니다.	[공교롭게 상황이 일치함] This is perfect timing.

ㅁ

막

막내입니다.	I am the youngest. (저는~)
막다른 골목이야.	[곤란한 상황] We're facing the dead end. = We're in hot water. = We're in bad shape. = We're in a difficult situation.
막상막하야!	They are neck and neck with each other. (그들은~)
막지 마세요.	Don't stop me.
막차는 몇 시에 도착합니까?	[버스] What time does the last bus arrive?
막차는 몇 시에 출발합니까?	What time does the last bus leaves/departs for Seoul? (서울행~) ➡ It leaves/departs at midnight. = It leaves/departs at twelve a.m. = It leaves/departs at twelve midnight. (심야 12시입니다.)
막차를 놓쳐버렸습니다.	[버스] I missed the last bus. = The last bus left already.
막히지 않으면 30분이면 갑니다.	It will take 30 minutes if there is no traffic.

만

만나 뵙게 되어 반갑습니다.	Nice to meet you. // I'm pleased to meet you. ➡ ⓐ Nice to meet you, too. (저도요.) ⓑ The pleasure is mine. (제가 오히려 기쁩니다.)

만나 뵙게 되어 영광입니다.	It's an honor to meet you.
	= I am so honored to meet you.
	// It's great to finally meet you. (드디어~)
	// I'm so glad to meet you in person. (직접~)

만나서 얘기합시다.	Let's meet and talk it over. (우리~)
만난 지 백일입니다.	It's been 100 days since we met. // Today is our one-hundred-day anniversary. (오늘이 ~)
만날 장소를 정합시다.	Let's decide where we are going to meet. = Where shall we meet? (우리~)
만날까요?	① Can we do something together some day? (언제 한번~) ② When and where shall we meet? (어떻게~) // When and where shall we meet tomorrow? (내일 어떻게~) ➡ You decide. (그쪽에서 말씀하세요.)
만납시다.	Let's get together tonight. (오늘 밤에~) = Let's spend time together tonight. // Let's meet at eight o'clock in the evening. (우리 저녁 8시에~)
만리 길도 한걸음부터.	A journey of a thousand miles begins with a single step. ☞ 천리 길도 한걸음부터.
만만치 않아.	You're just the same as me. (너도~)
만만하게 보지 마세요.	Don't think it is easy. = Don't think it is that easy. = Don't underestimate it. // Don't underestimate me. (나를~)

만만해 보여?	Do I look that easy? (내가~)
만사형통하세요.	Good luck with everything you do.
만수무강하세요.	Long life to you!
만인의 친구는 누구의 친구도 아니다.	A friend to all is a friend to none.
만족합니까?	① [만족] **Are you satisfied?** (그것에 ~) // Are you happy with that? ➡ ⓐ Yes, I am (happy / satisfied). (만족합니다.) ⓑ No, I'm not (happy / satisfied) (만족스럽지 않습니다.) ② [일이나 상황 등] How's that? (~, 어떻습니까?) ③ [미용실에서] Does that look all right? = How does that look? = Is that satisfactory? ➡ I like it. (마음에 듭니다.)
만지지 마세요!	**Hands off!** ① Don't touch it! (그것~) ② [경고문] Do not touch!

많

많은 지도 부탁합니다.	Please give me some advice and guidance.
많이 기다리셨지요?	You waited for a long time, didn't you? = I'm sorry to have you wait a long time. = I'm sorry to make you wait such a long time. ➡ No problem. (괜찮아요.)
많이 도와주세요.	I'd appreciate it if you helped me a lot. = I'd appreciate whatever help you could give me.
많이 드세요.	**Help yourself.**

많이 마셨습니다.	I've had enough to drink.
많이 먹었습니다.	① I had enough. ② [배가 터질 정도] I'm full.
많이 배웠습니다.	I learned a lot from you. = You taught me so much. = You've taught me so much.
많이 생각해봤어요.	I slept on it. = I thought about it for a long time.
많이 아파요.	It hurts a lot. // I still have pain. (여전히~) = It still hurts a lot.

많이 아픕니까?	① [고통의 정도] Do you feel a lot of pain?
	② [몸의 상태] Are you very sick?
	// Is he very sick? (그 사람~)
	// Is he in serious condition?
	(그 사람 상태가 심각합니까?)

많이 좋아졌습니까?	[몸의 상태] Are you feeling a lot better? ➡ I'm a lot better now. (많이 좋아졌습니다.)
많이 취했네요.	You are so drunk.
많이 컸구나!	[남자에게] You are a grown man now. // She has grown up! (그녀가 ~)
많지 않습니다.	① [수] There are not many. ② [양] There is not much.

말

말 타면 경마하고 싶다.	The more a man has, the more he desires.
말과 행동이 다르다.	His action doesn't match his words. = His actions aren't in line with his words. (그는~)
말꼬리 잡지 마.	Quit twisting my words around.

말은 심하게 해도 마음은 여리다.	He sometimes says bitter words, but he has a tender heart.
말이 말을 만든다.	Rumors lead to more rumors.
말 돌리지 마세요.	Do not try to lead me into a different topic. = Stick to the subject. = Don't try to change the subject.
말 되네요.	It makes sense.
말 들립니까?	Do you hear me? (제~) ➡ Yes, I hear you. (들려요.)
말 들어!	[주의 · 권고] Follow my advice! = Do what I'm telling you to do! = Give heed to what I say! = Take my word! = Take a tip from me! = Take my advice!
말 막하지 마세요.	Do not talk without thinking. // Please use decent language! (좋은 말을 사용 하세요!)
말 바꾸지 마세요.	Do not change the topic.
말보다 행동이 더 중요해.	Actions speak louder than words.
말 알아듣겠니?	Do you get it? // Do you understand what I'm saying? (내~) ➡ I got it. (알아들었어.)
말 잘 들어.	Listen up. = Listen carefully. = Mark my words.
말 잘했어!	[동의 · 동감] You can say that again! = I'm with you! = You're telling me!
말 좀 들어봐.	Open your ears to me!
말 좀 잘해 줘.	Put in a good word for me, please.
말 주의하세요.	Watch your mouth.

	= Be careful with your words. = Watch what you're saying.
말 참 많다!	You are so talkative! = You talk too much!
말 취소해.	Take it back. = Take back your words.
말 한마디에 천 냥 빚 갚는다.	A soft answer turns away wrath. = Good words are good cheap.
말 함부로 하지 마세요.	Don't speak thoughtlessly. // Think before you talk. (말하기 전 생각을 좀 하세요.)
말괄량이!	Tomboy!
말 나온 김에 좀 물어봅시다.	Since you mentioned it, let me ask you something. = Since you brought it up, let me ask you something. = While we're on the topic, let me ask you something.
말대꾸하지 마세요.	Don't talk back. // Do not talk back to your mother. (엄마한테~)
말대답하지 마세요.	Don't answer back. = Don't talk back.
말대로 하세요.	Follow my words. Do as I told you. (내~)
말도 꺼내지 마세요.	Don't even try to talk about that. = Don't bring that up. ☞ 말 마세요.
말도 안 돼! // 말도 안 되는 소리!	① [그런 일 없음 · 불가능] That's impossible! = That's out of the question! ② [황당한 말] That's nonsense! = What are you talking about? = Are you crazy? = Are you kidding? ③ [지시] No way! ④ [억지주장] That makes no sense! = That doesn't make any sense! = That doesn't figure! = Don't talk nonsense! = That's ridiculous!

말도 제대로 안 나옵니다.	I can't even talk.
말뜻이 뭔지 잘 모르겠습니다.	I don't get what you mean. = I don't understand what you are talking about.
말랐어요.	He is skinny. = He is thin. (그는 ~) // He is too skinny. (그는 너무~)

말로 합시다.	Let's talk it out. = Let's hash it out.
	// Let's work it out like adults. (성인들 이니까~)
	// Why don't you use words, not fists? (폭력 말고~)

말로만 하지 마라.	[실천을 요구] Put your words into action.
말로만 하는 얘기는 아니야.	I'm not just paying lip service. = It's not just lip service.
말마세요.	Don't say a word about it. = Don't even bring that up. = Don't even mention it. = Let's not talk about it. = I don't want to talk about it. ← How was your interview today? (오늘 면접 어떻게 됐어요?) ☞ 말도 꺼내지 마세요.
말만 하세요.	Anything you say. = I'll follow anything you say. = I'll go with whatever you say. = I'll do whatever you say.
말 시키지 마세요.	Don't make me talk anymore. (더 이상~) // I don't want to talk now. = I don't feel like talking now. (지금 말하고 싶지 않아요.)
말씀 계속하세요.	Keep talking. = Go on.
말씀 많이 들었습니다.	I heard a lot about you. (당신에 대해서~) = I've heard a lot of nice things about you.
말씀 좀 낮추세요.	[너무 정중한 표현을 쓰는 경우] Your words are too polite.

ㅁ

ㅁ

말씀 좀 들어보세요.	Listen to me, please. ➡ I don't want to see you anymore. Go! (더 이상 쳐다보기도 싫으니까, 가세요.)
말씀 좀 묻겠습니다. // 말씀 좀 여쭤보겠습니다.	Can I ask you something? = I have one thing to ask you.
말씀 함부로 하지 마세요.	Don't talk without thinking. // Think before you talk.
말씀대로 따르겠습니다.	I will follow your words. = I will do as I'm told. = I will follow your advice.
말씀드리겠습니다.	① Let me tell you about that later. (그것에 대해 다시~) ② [해명] Let me explain.
말씀드리기 곤란합니다.	I can't tell you here. (지금 여기서~) = It's hard to tell you here.
말씀드릴 수 없습니다.	I can't tell you. = It's hard to tell you. ☞ 말씀드리기 곤란합니다.
말씀들 나누세요.	Talk amongst yourselves, please. = Go ahead and have your discussion, please.
말씀을 잘 하십니다.	You are a good speaker. = You are good at speaking. = You are very eloquent. = You're a smooth talker. = You are so charming with words.
말씀이 일리가 있습니다.	What you say makes sense.
말씀이 좀 지나치십니다.	You are going too far.

말씀하세요.
// 말씀해 보세요.
	Go ahead and tell us/me. (어서~)
	// Can you say that again? (다시 한 번~)
	// Keep going with your conversation.
	= Continue your conversation. (계속~)

말씀해주세요.	① [말을] Can you say that again? (다시 한 번~) ② [알려줌] Tell me, please. (제발 저에게~) // Tell us, please. (제발 우리에게~) ③ [전달] Tell him what I say. (내 말을 그에게~)
말에 가시 있네.	Your words carry a sting.
말은 쉽지!	It's easy to say! = Talking about it is easy! = That's not as easy as it sounds! = That's easier said than done! = Talking about it is one thing, doing it is another!
말은 할수록 많아지고 돈은 쓸수록 적어진다.	The more you talk, the more talkative you will get. The more you spend, the poorer you will get.
말을 못하겠어요.	I can't put it into words.
말을 빙빙 돌리지 마세요.	Stop beating around the bush.
말을 했으면 실천에 옮겨야 합니다.	You have to put your words into action. = Practice what you preach. = Talk the talk, and walk the walk.
말이 그렇게 많아?	What is all this talking for? (왜~) ➡ I'm serious. (헛소리 아니야.)
말이 너무 많습니다.	You talk too much. // He is too talkative. = He talks too much. (그는~)
말이 너무 빠릅니다.	You speak too fast.
말이 맞습니다!	① You are right! = What you said is right! (당신~) ② [동의 표현] You can say that again! = I said it! ③ [정답] Bingo!
말이 심하네.	You are going too far. = That's too much.

ㅁ

말이 안 통합니다.	We can't communicate with each other. (우리는~) // My wife and I do not communicate well. (저와 아내는~)
말이 좋으니 하여도 달아 보아야 한다.	You cannot measure with your eyes. It's better check the weight.
말조심해.	① Watch your tongue. = Watch what you're saying. = Be careful with your words. ② [욕설에 대해] Watch your language. = Don't use bad language.
말주변이 없어요.	I'm not good with words. = I'm not good at expressing myself. = I can't word things well. = I'm not much of a talker. (저는~)
말짱해요.	I'm all right. = I'm not hurt. = I'm still in one piece. (저는~)
말참견하지 마세요.	Don't intervene while I'm talking. = Don't poke your nose into my affairs.
말하고 싶지 않아!	① [기분이 아님] I don't want to talk. = I don't feel like talking. ② [사실을 말해 주고 싶지 않음] I don't want to tell you.

말하기 곤란합니다.
// 말하기 난처합니다.
	It's hard to say.
	// It's hard to say right now. (지금~)
	// Let me tell you later. (나중에 말해 줄게요.)

말하기는 쉽지.	[행동으로 옮기기는 어렵다는 뜻] Easier said than done.
말하기에 이상한 일이지만!	It's strange to say, but...!
말하자면 길어요.	This is a long story. (이 일은 정말~)
말하지 마세요.	Don't say anything. = No more talking, please.

말하지 않겠습니다.	I won't tell you. = No comment. = I'll take the fifth. = I plead the fifth.
말한 대로 하지.	[동의] I will do as you say. = I will follow your words. (자네가~)
말할 수 없습니다.	I cannot tell you right now. (지금은 당신한테~)
말해!	① Tell me! // Tell me quickly! (빨리~) ② Go ahead! = Keep going! (계속해서~)
말해두지만!	[경고] Keep this in mind! (이것을~)
말해봐.	Tell me, please.

맑

맑다가 구름이 많이 낍니다.	It will be sunny at first and then it will get cloudy. = It will be sunny at first and then it will become cloudy.
맑다가 비옵니다.	It will be sunny at first and then it will start to rain.
맑습니다.	It will be sunny tomorrow. (내일 날씨가~)

맘

맘대로 해!	Do as you like! = Suit yourself! = Have it your way! // Don't worry about me! (난 상관 말고.) ☞ 좋을 대로 하세요.

맙

맙소사!	Oh, no!

맛

맛 좀 보세요.	Taste this, please. = Try this, please. // I made this for the first time, ~ (이거 오늘 처음 만들어 본건데. ~)
맛 좀 보십시오.	[시식 평가] Try some.
맛 좋다!	It tastes good! = It's delicious! = It is tasty!
맛없습니다.	① It doesn't taste good. = It's not tasty. = It's not delicious. ② [보통 아이들이 사용] It's yucky.
맛이 갔어!	① [음식] It's gone bad! (요리가~) ② [인사불성] He's dead! (그가 완전히~) ③ [모양새] You look trashed! (너~)
맛이 괜찮습니다.	It tastes good.
맛이 담백합니다.	It tastes plain.
맛이 싱겁습니다.	It tastes flat. = It's bland. = It's flavorless.
맛이 어떻습니까?	How does it taste? = What does it taste like? ➡ ⓐ Delicious. = Tastes good. (맛있습니다.) ⓑ Not good. (맛없습니다.) ⓒ Salty. (짭니다.) ⓓ A bit plain. = A bit bland. (약간 싱겁습니다.) ⓔ Not sour at all. (조금도 시지 않습니다.) ⓕ Sweet. (답니다.) ⓖ A little bitter. (약간 씁니다.) // It's very spicy. (매워 죽겠습니다.)
맛이 이상해요.	It tastes funny. = It tastes strange.
맛이 좋습니다.	It tastes good! = It's delicious. = It is tasty. ☞ 맛 좋다!
맛있게 드세요.	Enjoy your meal. = Bon appetite.

맛있게 잘 먹었습니다.	It was really delicious. // Thank you for the tasty food. I had a lot. (감사합니다. ~)
맛있게들 들어요.	Help yourself.
맛있습니까?	Is this tasty? = Is this delicious? (이거~) = Does this taste good? ➡ Good! Delicious! (괜찮아. 맛있어!)
맛있습니다.	It's delicious. // It's very tasty. = It's yummy. (참~)

망

망보고 있어.	[명령] Keep an eye out.
망설이지 말고 말해.	Don't hesitate to tell me. = Straighten it out without hesitation.
망신스럽네.	It's embarrassing. = It's a shame. = It's humiliating. = It's a dishonor.
망신을 당했어요.	I was put to shame. = I was humiliated. // I lost face in front of them. (그 사람들 앞에서~)

망쳤어!	① It was a disaster! // I ruined everything. (다~)
	② [일을] I ruined it. = I blew it.
	// [구어체] I goofed it up. = I screwed it up.
	// I ruined it this time. (이번 일은~)
	③ [시험을] I failed this exam.
	= I bombed this exam. (이번 시험~)
	④ [비난] You spoiled it. (네가~)
	// You spoiled the moment. (네가 분위기를~)

망할 놈!	Go to hell! = Damn boy!
망했어요.	He failed in his business. = He went bankrupt. = His business failed. = He filed for bankruptcy. (그의 사업이~) // He lost his shirt. (그는 쫄딱~)

맞

맞는 말씀입니다.	You are right.
	// Every single word you say is right.
	(당신 말이 모두~)
	// You've got a point. (잘 지적하셨어요.)

맞아(요)!	① [대답 · 동의] You're right! = I agree! = I couldn't agree more! = You can say that again! ② [긍정] Right! = Correct! // That's right! = You got it! (그 말~)
맞춰 봐!	Give me your guess! = Guess what! // Take a wild guess! = Take a stab at it! (대충~)

맡

맡겨! // 맡기세요.	① [보고만 있고] See what I'm going to do! (나한테~) ② [책임을 넘김] Let me take care of it! = Leave it up to me! (나한테~) ③ [물건 보관] Let me keep it for you! (나한테~)

매

매너가 없네요.	You have no manners. = You are bad-mannered.
매니아입니다.	I'm a movie buff. (영화~)
매도 먼저 맞는 놈이 낫다.	You had better face your difficulties as early as possible.
매력적입니다.	① You are charming. ② [여성에게] You are attractive. = You are so gorgeous. (당신은 정말~)

매를 아끼면 애를 버립니다.	[속담] Spare the rod, spoil the child.
매우 기쁩니다.	I'm so happy. = I'm very glad. // I'm very glad, too. (저도~)
매우 똑똑합니다.	He is very smart. = He is so smart. (그가~)
매우 좋습니다.	Very good.
매운 것, 짠 것, 단 것 다 피하세요.	Avoid anything spicy, salty, and sweet.
매일 몇 시에 일어납니까?	What time do you get up every morning? ➡ At six thirty. (6시 반이요.)
매정합니다.	You are hard on me. = You are harsh on me. // You are too harsh on me. (너무~)
매진되었습니다.	Sold out. // The tickets are all sold out. (표가~) // The tickets for today are all sold out. (오늘 표는 다~)

맥

맥도날드를 무척 좋아합니다.	I like McDonald's very much. // Many kids are crazy about McDonald's. (많은 아이들은~)
맥주 한 병 주세요.	A bottle of beer, please. // A bottle of beer first. (먼저~)
맥주 한 잔 주세요.	A glass of beer please.

맵

맵습니다.	It's hot and spicy. // It's too spicy. (너무~) // It's really spicy. (정말~)

맹

맹세합니다.	I swear to God. (하늘에 대고~)
맹세코 사실입니다.	That's true. Cross my heart!

머

머리 드라이 해드리겠습니다.	Let me blow-dry your hair.
머리 들지 마세요.	Don't raise your head.
머리 빗으려고 합니다.	I'm going to comb my hair.
머리 숙여요.	Lower your head.
머리 조심하세요.	Watch your head!
머리 좀 써라.	Use your brain. = Use your head. = Put your thinking cap on.
머리 좀 자르겠습니까?	You want to have your hair trimmed a little? ➡ Trim a little, please. (좀 잘라주세요.)
머리가 나쁩니다.	① He is not smart. = He is dull. (그는~) ② [비하] He is stupid. = He is dumb.
머리가 많이 아픕니다.	I have a bad headache.
머리가 아픕니다.	I have a headache.
머리가 약간 어지럽습니다.	I feel a little bit dizzy.
머리가 어지러워서 토하고 싶습니다.	My head reels and I feel like throwing up.
머리가 총명합니다.	He is clever. = He is bright.

	= He is intelligent. (그는~) // He is a real egg-headed person. = He is egg-headed. (정말~)

머리는 어떤 모양으로 /스타일로 할까요?	① What style do you have in mind?
	➡ Just a trim, please. (그냥 다듬어 주세요.)
	// I'd like a perm. (파마 하겠습니다.)
	// I'd like it dyed. (염색해 주세요.)
	// I want a part in the middle.
	= I want a centerpart. (중간 가르마로 해주세요.)
	② [자를 경우] How would you like to have your hair cut?
	➡ I want it shoulder length. (어깨 길이로 잘라 주세요.)
	// I want to have my head shaved. (대머리로 쳐주세요.)
	③ [길이] Would you have your hair cut long or short?
	➡ [손동작과 함께] This short, please. (이만큼 잘라 주세요.)

머리를 약간만 손질해 주세요.	I want to have it trimmed a little.
머리부터 감으세요.	Wash your hair first.
머리에 피도 안 마른 것이!	You are still wet behind your ears!
머물 겁니까?	① [숙박] Until when would you like to stay here? (언제까지~) ② [체류] How long are you going to stay in New York? (뉴욕에 얼마나~) ➡ For ten days. (10일이요.)

먹

먹고가!	Eat this before you go!
먹고 싶어요.	I want to eat this. (이것~) // I want to have it, too. (저도~)

먹고 있어요.	I'm eating.
먹는 양이 적습니다.	He is a not big eater. = He is a light eater. = He doesn't eat that much. = He doesn't have a big appetite. = He eats like a bird. (그는~)
먹던 것도 괜찮아요.	Leftovers are okay with me.
먹보!	You are such a pig!
먹어!	Eat! = Grab a bite!
먹어도 될까요?	Can I eat this? (이거~) ➡ No, you should not eat this. (이거 먹으면 안 됩니다.) // That is not for eating. = That is not edible. (그건 먹는 용이 아닙니다.)
먹어보세요. // 먹어봐!	Try this! (이것을~) // Try one! (하나~) // Try a piece! (한 조각~)
먹어보지 않았습니다.	I didn't have it yet.
먹어본 적이 없습니다.	I haven't had it before. // I haven't had Greek food before. (그리스 음식은~)
먹었어요.	I already had it. (벌써~) // I just ate it. (방금 전에~)
먹여주고 재워줍니다.	We provide room and board.
먹으러 가자.	Let's go out to eat.
먹으면 먹을수록 맛있네.	The more I eat it, the better it tastes.
먹을 때는 개도 안 건드린다.	〈직역〉 Even a dog cannot be bothered while eating.
먹을 복이 없습니다.	I'm not lucky with regard to food.
먹을 수 없습니다.	① I can't eat it. ② [건강에 해로워서] I have to be careful with my diet.

	③ [습관이 안 돼서] I've never had that kind of food before. ④ [양이 많아서] It's too much for me to eat. = It's too much for me to finish. ⑤ [비싸서] It costs me a lot of money. ⑥ [시간이 없어서] I don't have time for it. ⑦ [배가 불러서] I have had enough. = I'm full. ⑧ [식용이 아니라서] It's not edible.
먹읍시다. // 먹자!	Let's eat.

ㅁ

먼

먼 길 오시느라 힘드셨지요.	Thank you for your trouble in coming all this way. = Thank you for trouble in coming all the way over here.
먼 친척보다 이웃사촌이 낫다.	[속담] A good neighbor is better than a brother /relative far off.
먼저 가세요!	You go first! = After you!
먼저 갑니다!	① [작별인사] I must be going first. = I have to go now. ② [순서] Let me go first!
먼저 내리고 나중에 타세요.	Get off first, get in later.
먼저 본 사람이 임자다.	Finders keepers!
먼저 일어나겠습니다.	[작별인사] I must be going. = I have to leave now.
먼저 주무세요.	You go to bed first.
먼저 하세요.	① [동작을 권유] After you. = I'll go after you. = You first. ② Be my guest.

멀

멀리 못나갑니다.	[전송 나온 주인이 손님에게] I must say good-bye here. = Let's say good-bye here.
멀리 해라.	You should avoid him. = You should stay away from him. = You should keep him at arm's length. (그를~)
멀미가 나서 토하고 싶습니다.	I feel carsick and feel like vomiting.
멀었습니까?	① [준비] Do we still have many things to get ready? (준비가 아직도~) ➡ No, we're done. (됐어요.) ② [주문] Do we have to wait more to be served? ➡ Here you go. (자, 나갑니다.) ③ [거리] Do we still have a long way to go? ➡ ⓐ We'll arrive soon. = We'll arrive shortly. (곧 도착합니다.) ⓑ We're almost there. (거의 다 왔어요.) ⓒ We'll arrive in a few minutes. (몇 분 안에 도착합니다.) ⓓ We still have a long way to go. (아직 멀었습니다.) ④ [기다리는 시간] Do we still have to wait more? (아직~)

멀었습니다.	① [시간] We still have many hours to go. (아직~)
	② [실력 · 수준] This is a lot of room for improvement. (아직~)
	// Compared to you, I have a long way to go. (당신에게 비하면~)
	// I have a long way to go if I want to beat you. (당신을 이기려면~)
	③ [거리] We still have a long way to go. (아직~)
	// We're still far away from Yongsan here. (여기서 용산까지는 아직~)
	④ [시기상조] The time is not ripe yet.

	= It's not time yet. = The time is not right yet. ⑤ [연습을 더 요구함] I'm still far behind. I need to practice more.
멀쩡해요.	[별 문제 없음] No problem at all. // Everything is all right. (모든 것이~)
멀쩡했는데.	[물건 등이] It was all right till yesterday. = There was no problem till yesterday. (어제까지~)

멈

멈춰(요)!	Stop!

멉

멉니까?	① Is it far from here? (여기서~) ➡ ⓐ Not so far. (별로요.) ⓑ A little bit. (좀 멀어요.) ② How far is it from here? (여기서 얼마나~) ➡ It's eighteen kilometers from here. (18킬로미터입니다.)

멉니다.	It is far from here. (여기서~)
	// It's really far from here. (정말~)
	// It's too far from here. (너무~)

멋

멋대로 짐작하지 마세요.	Don't make wild guesses.
멋있다! // 멋지다!	① [남자의 외모] He looks great! = He is so attractive! = He is cute! // He still looks good! (지금도~)

② [여자의 외모] **She is gorgeous!**
= She is beautiful! = She looks great!
③ [감탄] Wow! That's great!
④ [행위에 대한 칭찬] Good job! = Excellent!
// You did a wonderful job today. (오늘 정말~)
☞ 대단하다! // 훌륭합니다!
⑤ [차림새 · 모습] Look at you!
= How fabulous you look!
= You look great!
= You look like a million dollars!
// You look great in these clothes!
(너 이 옷 참~)
⑥ [상황 · 멋진 행위] It's cool!
⑦ [경치] It's beautiful! = It's breathtaking!
// This river is beautiful! (이 강은 정말~)
☞ 아름답습니다.

멍

멍멍!	Bowwow!
멍석 깔 때는 안하더니.	You didn't show it in public.
멍석 펴놓으면 못한다.	It's easy to do in private, but not in public.
멍청이!	Idiot! = 〈비속어〉 **What an ass!** = What a pigeon!
멍청한 놈! // 멍청한 자식!	Stupid! = Fool! = You are as stupid as a donkey.

메

메뉴 좀 보여주세요.	I'd like to see the menu. = Can I take a look at the menu? = Will you show me the menu? = May I have a menu, please?
메리 크리스마스!	Merry Christmas!

메모 남기세요.	Leave a message, please.
메모 남기시겠어요?	Can I take your message? // Will you leave a message for him? (그에게~) ➡ No, thank you. I'll call him back tonight. (됐고요. 저녁에 전화 드리겠습니다.)
메모리 용량은 좀 커야 합니다.	We need a large memory capacity.
메스껍다!	I feel nauseous. = I feel sick to my stomach. // I feel sick after I eat greasy food. (기름기 있는 것을 먹기만 하면 속이~) ☞ 구역질난다!
메시지 받으면 전화 해줘.	Call me back when you get/hear this message.
메시지를 남겨주시면, 연락을 드리겠습니다.	[전화녹음] Hello. This is Hyeyoung. I can't get to the phone now. If you leave me a message, I will call you back. (안녕하세요. 전혜영입니다. 지금은 전화를 받을 수 없습니다.~)
메시지를 남기고 우물 정자 버튼을 누르세요.	Leave your message and press the pound button.
메일은 잘 받았습니다.	I've got your e-mail. // I got the e-mail you sent me the other day. (지난번~)

며

며칠 쉬면 괜찮아질 겁니다.	If I take a few days off, I will get better.
며칠만 더 기다려주세요.	Give me a few more days.
며칠입니까?	What is the date today? (오늘은~) ➡ It's October tenth. (10월 10일입니다.)
며칠 정도 걸릴까요?	How many days will it take? ➡ (It will take) Three days. (사흘이요.)

면

면도 좀 해주세요.	Can I have my face shaved?
면도하시겠습니까?	Would you like a face-shave? = Do you want to have your face shaved?
면목 없습니다.	① [체면] I'm so ashamed of myself. = That is a shame on myself. ② [미안함] I'm so sorry. = I owe you an apology. // Sorry, I have no excuse. (변명할 여지가 없습니다.)
면세로 살 수 있나요?	Can I buy it tax-free? = Is it tax-free?
면이나 끓여 먹읍시다.	Let's make some noodle soup and eat it.
면접 결과는 어떻습니까?	How did the interview go? ➡ ⓐ I passed the first round. (1차에 합격했습니다.) ⓑ I failed. (떨어졌습니다.) ⓒ I don't know how it went. (모르겠습니다.)
면허증 있습니까?	[허가증] Do you have a license? ➡ ⓐ Yes, I do. (있습니다.) ⓑ No, I don't. (아직 없습니다.)

명

명령하지 마세요.	Stop bossing me around. = Stop being so bossy. = Stop giving me orders. (명령조로 말하지 마세요.)
명성 그대로군.	It is worth the name. = I see why it has a name. = I see why it is famous. (과연~)
명심하세요. // 명심해!	Take it to heart. = Keep it in mind.
명절을 축하합니다.	Happy holidays!

	// Happy Thanksgiving day! (추수감사절을 축하합니다.)
명함을 가지고 계십니까?	Do you have your business card with you? = Do you have your business card on you? ➡ Yes, I have it here. (가지고 있지요.) = Yes, I have it with me.

몇

몇 가지 물어 볼게요.	Let me ask you a few things. = I'd like to ask you a few things. ➡ Sure. Go ahead. (그러세요.)
몇 개 드릴까요?	How many do you want? = How many would you like? ➡ Give me six first. (먼저 6개 주세요.)
몇 년 되었습니까?	How long have you been learning English? (영어를 배운지~) ➡ Just a year. (겨우 1년 됐습니다.)
몇 년도였습니까?	What year was it? (그것이~) ➡ It was nineteen eighty-eight(1998). (1998년이었습니다.) **연도와 관련한 표현** Three years ago. (재재작년) Two years ago. (재작년) Last year. (작년) This year. (올해) Next year. (내년) Two years later. (내후년) Three years later. (내내후년)
몇 대 몇으로 이겼습니까?	How much did you win by? = How many points did you win by? ➡ ⓐ We won by a score of two to one. (우리가 2대 1로 이겼습니다.) ⓑ We lost by a score of one to zero. (우리가 0대 1로 졌습니다.) ⓒ We won by three points. (우리가 3점차로 이겼습니다.)

몇 대 몇입니까?	What is the score? ➡ We're winning by a score of two to one. (우리가 지금 2대 1로 이기고 있습니다.)
몇 도입니까?	① [기온] What is the temperature today? (오늘은~) ➡ It's twelve degrees Celsius. (섭씨 12도요.) ② What proof is this bottle? (이 술은~) ➡ It's ninety(90) proof. (45도입니다.) ※ two proof = 1% alcohol
몇 등 했습니까?	What was your ranking in your class? ➡ Of course, I was first in my class. (당연히 1등이죠.)
몇 번 버스를 타야합니까?	Which number bus do I have to take? ➡ Take number ten. (10번 버스를 타세요.)
몇 번으로 거셨습니까?	[전화] What number did you dial? ➡ Sorry, I think I've got the wrong number. (전화 잘못 걸었습니다.)
몇 번을 말했니?	How many times have I told you? = How many times have you been told? (내가~) ➡ I have had enough. (충분히 들었어요.)
몇 분 남았습니까?	How many minutes do I have? = How many minutes are left? ➡ You have ten minutes. = Ten minutes are left. (10분이요.)

몇 분간입니까?	How many minutes do we have?
	➡ We have fifteen minutes. (15분)
	// We have thirty minutes. (30분)
	// We have forty-five minutes.(45분)
	// We have sixty minutes.
	= We have an hour. (60분)
	// We have seventy minutes.
	= We have an hour and ten minutes. (70분)
	// We have ninety minutes.

	= We have an hour and thirty minutes. (90분)
몇 분입니까?	① [사람] How many people are there in your party? ➡ There are eight people. = There are eight people in our party. (8명입니다.) ② [시간] What time is it now? ➡ It's two o'clock now. (지금 두 시입니다.) // It's two fifteen now. (두시 15분입니다.)
몇 살이니?	How old are you? ☞ 나이가 몇 살이니?
몇 시 되었습니까?	What time is it now? = Do you have the time? = Could you tell me the time? = May I ask you the time? (지금~) ➡ It's one o'clock. (1시입니다.) // What is the time in London? (런던시간으로는~) ➡ It's midnight in London. (현지시간은 자정입니다.)
몇 시 비행기입니까?	What time is your flight going to leave? ➡ It's going to leave at eleven twenty-five. (11시 25분입니다.)
몇 시 표가 있습니까?	What time do you have tickets for?
몇 시간 걸립니까?	How many hours does it take? = How long does it take? // How many hours does it take from Seoul to New York? (서울에서 뉴욕까지~) ➡ It takes about thirteen hours. (열세 시간 정도 걸립니다.)

몇 시간입니까?	How many hours? = How long?
	➡ An hour and fifteen minutes. (한 시간 15분.)
	// An hour and a half. (한 시간 반.)
	= An hour and thirty minutes.
	// Two hours. (두 시간.)

// Three hours. (세 시간.) // Four hours.(네 시간.)
// Five hours. (다섯 시간.)

몇 시입니까?	What is the time? = What time is it? ☞ 몇 시나 되었습니까?
몇 식구입니까?	How many people are there in your family? ➡ There are eight people. (8명입니다.) ☞ 식구는 몇입니까?
몇 월 며칠입니까?	What is the date? ➡ It's October the second. (10월 2일입니다.) = It's the second day of October. **월 표현** What month is it? (몇 월?) ➡ January (1월) February (2월) March (3월) April (4월) May (5월) June (6월) July (7월) August (8월) September (9월) October (10월) November (11월) December (12월) **일 표현** What date is it? (며칠?) the first day (1일) the second day (2일) the third day (3일) **개월 수 표현** How many months? (몇 개월?) one month (1개월, 한 달) two months (2개월, 두 달) three months (3개월, 세 달) four months (4개월, 네 달) five months (5개월, 다섯 달) **날짜 수 표현** How many days? (며칠?) one day (하루) two days (이틀) three days (사흘) four days (나흘) five days (닷새)
몇 입니까?	[숫자] What number is this? (이것은~) ➡ This is seven. (이것은 7입니다.) **수사** one (1) two (2) three (3) four (4) five (5) six (6)

seven (7) eight (8) nine (9) ten (10) eleven (11)
twelve (12) thirteen (13) fourteen (14)
fifteen (15) sixteen (16) seventeen (17)
eighteen (18) nineteen (19) twenty (20)
thirty (30) forty (40) fifty (50) sixty (60)
seventy (70) eighty (80) ninety (90)
one hundred (100)
one hundred and four (104)
one hundred and ten (110)
one hundred eleven (111)
one hundred nineteen (119)
one hundred twenty (120)
two hundred (200) two hundred twenty (220)
two hundred and two (202)
one thousand and four (1,004)
one thousand and forty (1,040)
one thousand and four hundred
= fourteen hundred (1,400)
two thousand (2,000)
two thousand and two hundred
= twenty two hundred (2,200)
ten thousand (10,000) twenty thousand (20,000)
twenty thousand and two hundred two (20,202)
a million (백만) two million (2백만)
a billion (10억) two billion (20억)

몇 점입니까?

What is your grade?
// What is your grade for English?
(영어 성적은~)

➡ I got eighty-five. (85점입니다.)

몇 째세요?

Where do you come?
= Where do you come in your family?
= Where do you fall in your family?
(형제 중~)

➡ ⓐ I'm the eldest. (첫째입니다.)
ⓑ I'm the second oldest. (둘째입니다.)
ⓒ I'm in the middle. (가운데입니다.)
ⓓ I'm the youngest.
= I'm the baby. (막내입니다.)
ⓔ I'm the only child. (독자입니다.)

몇 초입니까?	How many seconds? ➡ Ten seconds. (10초.) // Twenty seconds? (20초~?)
몇 학년에 다닙니까? // 몇 학년입니까?	What grade are you in? = What year are you in? ➡ ⓐ I'm in the second year of junior high. (중학교 2학년이요.) ⓑ I'm in the second year of high school. (고등학교 2학년이요.)
몇 호실입니까?	What is your room number? ➡ I'm in Room 102[one-o-two]. (102호실이요.)

모

모기 보고 칼 빼든다.	Breaking a butterfly on the wheel. = Killing a fly with a long spear.
모닝콜 해주세요.	I'd like a wake-up call.
모두 // 모두들	Everyone. = Everybody. = All people. // All people concerned. (관련된 모든 이들)
모든 것이 잘 되길 빕니다.	I wish you good luck with everything you do. = I wish you good luck in everything you do.
모든 길은 로마로 통한다.	[속담] All roads lead to Rome.
모든 일이 뜻대로 되길 빕니다.	I hope everything will turn out as you wish.
모든 일은 마음먹기에 달려있다.	Everything depends on your resolve. = Everything is up to what you think.
모든 준비가 끝났습니다.	Everything is ready. = We're done with all the preparations.
모레 만나는 게 어때요?	Why don't we meet the day after tomorrow? = Shall we meet the day after tomorrow?

	➡ That sounds good. = That's a good idea. = Sure, no problem. (좋아요.)
모로 가도 서울만 가면 된다.	The end justifies the means.
모르겠습니까?	① [이해] Don't you understand? = **Don't you get it?** ➡ I don't understand. = I don't get it. (모르겠어요.) ② [어떤 사실을] Don't you know it? = You don't know it? ③ [면식] You don't know me? = You don't know who I am? (날~) // You don't know the person? = You don't know him/her? (그 사람을~) ➡ No, I don't. (예.)
모르겠습니다.	① [이해] I don't understand. = **I don't get it.** = I'm not really following you. ② [눈으로 봐서] I can't measure it with my eyes. ③ [어떤 사실을] I don't know. = I have no idea. = **I have no clue.** = I know nothing. // **I don't have the slightest idea.** (정말~) ④ [면식] I don't know him. = He is a stranger to me. (그를~)
모르는 게 약입니다.	Ignorance is bliss.
모르는 게 없군요.	[칭찬] You know everything. (당신은~) // You must be a walking encyclopedia. (걸어다니는 백과사전 같군요.)
모르는 소리!	You don't know anything! = **You are talking nonsense!** = That's nonsense! ☞ 헛소리!

모셔다 드리겠습니다.	① Let me take you home. (집까지~)
	// Let me take you home to the airport.
	(공항까지~)
	② [자동차로~] **I'll give you a ride.**
	// Let me give you a ride home.

	= Let me take you home in my car. (집까지~) ☞ 바래다줄게요.
모습이 예전 그대로네.	You look the same as you did before. = You look exactly the same as you did before. ➡ You, too. You haven't changed at all. (너는 안 그래? 하나도 변한 게 없어.)
모시고 같이 가겠습니다.	I will accompany you there. = Let me go with you there. (거기까지~)
모임이 있어서 일찍 나갔습니다.	[퇴근] He left early because he has an appointment. (그는~)
모입니까?	① Where shall we meet tomorrow? (내일 어디서~) ➡ At the main entrance. (정문에서요.) ② When shall we meet? (언제~) ➡ A year later. = In one year. (1년 후에요.)
모처럼 한자리에 모였으니 거국적으로 건배!	We are all here after a long time, so cheers!
모처럼만에 만났는데.	We've finally met each other after a long time.

목

목구멍이 포도청.	The hungry belly has no ears. = Poverty is an enemy to good manners.
목마른 사람이 우물판다.	A man with thirst digs a well.
목말라요?	Are you thirsty? ➡ Yes, I'm thirsty. (목말라요.) // No, I'm not thirsty. (목마르지 않습니다.)
목소리 들으니 반갑습니다.	I'm happy to hear from you.

목소리 들으니 알겠습니다.	I recognize your voice.
목이 아픕니다.	① I have a pain in my neck. ② [감기증상] I have a sore throat.
목이 마릅니다.	I'm thirsty. = I have a dry throat. // I'm parched. (몹시~)
목이 쉬었구나.	**You have a frog in your throat.** = Your voice got hoarse/husky.

ㅁ

몰

몰라 뵈었습니다.	Sorry. I didn't recognize you.
몰라, 몰라!	① [짜증내며] I don't know. Let's stop it here. ☞ 관두세요. ② [관련성 부정] I have nothing to do with it. = I'm not concerned with it.
몰라도 돼.	You don't have to know. // None of your business. (너와 상관없는 일이야.) ☞ 상관하지 마.
몰라서 물어.	[알면서] You know that. = You are absolutely aware of that.
몰라서 물어?	① You really don't know? ➡ No, I don't. (모르겠는데요.) ② [시치미] Aren't you asking me pretending that you don't know? ➡ No, I'm not. I really don't know. (누가 시치미 뗐다고!)
몰라요.	① I don't know. = **I have no idea.** (난~) // I know nothing. = I can't make heads or tails of it. = I don't have the faintest idea.

= I don't know the first thing about it. (전혀~)

② [상관 안함] I don't care.
// I don't care. I was late but it was not my fault. (난~, 약속에 늦었다고 제 탓하지 마세요.)
☞ 모르겠습니다.

몰래 빠져나갔어요.

He snuck out. = He slipped off.
= He went out secretly. (그가~)

몰상식하네!

① What a lack of common sense!
② [버릇없음] So rude! = Mannerless!
// He has no manners! = He is ill-mannered!
= He is rude! (그는 정말~)

몰카에 찍혔어!

My picture was taken by a hidden carmera.
= I was captured by a hidden camera.

몸

몸 건강하시길 빕니다.

I wish you good health.

몸만 와!

Just bring yourself!
= You don't have to bring anything!

몸매가 멋지십니다.

① You have a nice figure.
= You are in good shape.
② [여자에게] You've got great curves.
③ [남자에게] You are really well-built.

몸무게는 얼마입니까?

How much do you weigh?
= What is your body weight? (당신의~)
➡ ⓐ I weigh fifty kilograms. (50킬로그램입니다.)
ⓑ My body weight is about sixty kilograms. (60킬로그램 정도입니다.)

몸살 났어요.

My whole body aches.
= My whole body is suffering from fatigue.

몸에 손대지 마세요.	Don't touch my body. = Hands off my body. (내~)
몸에 안 좋습니다.	It's not good for your health. = It's not helpful for your body. // It will make you unhealthy. (그러면~)
몸에 힘이 하나도 없습니다.	I feel very weak.
몸은 어떻습니까?	How do you feel? = How's it going? // How are you doing these days? (요즘~) = How are you feeling lately? ➡ Not so bad. (그런대로요.)
몸이 나셨네요.	Looks like you have gained some weight. = Looks like you have put on some weight.
몸이 멀어지면 마음도 멀어진다.	[속담] Out of sight, out of mind.
몸이 불편한 것 같습니다.	I'm not feeling myself. = I'm feeling under the weather. = I feel heavy. = I think I'm coming down with something.
몸이 불편합니까?	Aren't you feeling good? ➡ No, I'm not feeling good. (약간 불편해요.)
몸이 좋아졌습니다.	① [건강상태] He feels better now. = He is in a better condition now. (그는~) ② [살이 찜] He has put on some weight lately. (그는~)
몸조리 잘하세요.	Please take good care of your health.
몸조심하세요.	① [작별인사] Take care! // Have a safe trip! (여행길~) ➡ You, too. (너도.) ② [주의 · 당부] Please take care of yourself.
몸짱!	[주로 여자에게] She has a knockout body. = She has a killer body. (그녀는~)

몹

몹쓸 사람들!	They are wicked! = How wicked they are!

못

못 가봤습니다.	I have never been there. = Never been there.
못 견디겠습니다.	I can't stand it. // I cannot stand this place. (여긴 정말~)
못 들은 걸로 할게.	I never heard that. = You never said that.
못 떠나겠어요.	I can't leave here. (여길~)
못 만났어요.	I haven't seen him for ten days. (벌써 10일이나 그를~)
못 말리겠군요.	There's no stopping you. = There's no way to stop you. = You just can't be stopped. = You just don't give up. (정말 당신은~)
못 먹겠습니다.	I cannot eat this. = I cannot have this. (이 음식은~)
못 먹는 음식이 있습니까?	Is there any food you cannot eat? ➡ I can't stand the fishy smell. = I can't stand the smell of fish. (생선 비린내를 못 견딥니다.)
못 먹었습니다.	① I couldn't eat it. (그것을~) ② I haven't eaten anything for three days. (3일 동안~)
못 믿겠습니다.	① [의심] I can't believe it. = I doubt it. ➡ I can't tell a lie. (전 거짓말을 못합니다.) ② [신뢰할 수 없음] I can't trust him.

ㅁ

	= I don't have confidence in him. = He's not reliable. (그는~) ③ [확신할 수 없음] I'm not sure of it. = I'm not confident of it.
못 봤습니다.	① I didn't see it. ② I couldn't see it.
못 알아들었습니다.	[이해가 안 됨] I don't get it. = I don't understand.
못 올라갈 나무는 쳐다보지도 마라.	Don't even start something that you cannot go through with.
못 올지도 모릅니다.	It's possible that I cannot come. = I might not be able to come.
못 옵니다.	I can't come again. (저는 다시~)
못 일어납니다.	I can't get up at eight in the morning. = I can't wake up at eight a.m. (아침 8시에는~)
못 읽겠습니다.	[많아서] I can't read through it all.
못 입겠습니다.	[옷이 작아서] I can't wear it. It's too small for me.

못 참겠어!	[화나서] I can't stand/take it!
	= It's beyond my patience!
	// I can't stand his behavior! (그 사람 행패를~)
	// I can't stand it anymore!
	= I can't bear it anymore! (더 이상은~)
	// This is too much for me! (도저히~)
	// I can't be here anymore!
	= I can't stand this place anymore!
	(여기는 도저히~)

못 챙겨왔습니다.	I didn't bring it. // I forgot to bring it, too. (저도~)
못갑니다.	① [의지] I can't go. = I won't go. ② [제지] You cannot enter.
못나갑니다.	[허가] You can't go out.

못난 놈!	① [바보 같음] You are so foolish! = How stupid you are! ② [장래성이 없음] You are impossible! ③ [무능] You are a no-good! = You are a good-for-nothing! ④ [찍소리 못하는 놈] You are a coward! = What a chicken!
못난이!	① [무능] You are a no-good! = You are a good-for-nothing! = You are a jerk! ② [외모] How ugly you are!
못됐다!	① [말투가] You are talking really mean! = You sound really wicked! (정말~) // You sound too wicked! (너무~) ② [의리가 없음] You have no sense of honor! (정말~) ③ [마음씨] You are so mean! = You are so bad!
못된 송아지 엉덩이에 뿔난다.	A no-good person is acting up.
못들은 척 했지.	I pretended that I didn't hear.
못살게 구는구나.	You are being hard on me.
못살게 군단 말이야!	My classmates are always bullying me! (학교 친구들이 만날~)
못살게 굴지 마세요.	Stop bullying me. = Don't be hard on me.
못살면 조상 탓.	Blaming ancestors for one's poverty.
못살아!	① [짜증] I can't stand it! ② [원망] I can't stand you any more! = You are a pain in the neck! (너 때문에~)
못살아요.	① [죽음이 임박함] He cannot live long. = He will not live long. = He doesn't have long to live.

	= His days are numbered. (그는 얼마~) ② [가난] He is poor. = He is badly off. = He doesn't have a penny to his name. (그는~)
못생겨서 죄송합니다.	Sorry, I'm ugly. = Sorry that I'm not good-looking.
못생겼습니다.	He is ugly. = He is not good-looking. = He is bad-looking. (그는~)
못생긴 게!	How ugly you are!
못쓰겠습니다.	① [사용불가] I cannot use it. ② [약 등] I cannot take it. ③ [글씨가 많아서] I cannot write it all. = I cannot copy it all. (다~)
못하겠습니다.	① [하기 싫어서] I don't feel like doing it. ② [일이 많아서] It's impossible for me to do it. = It's too much work for me. ③ [능력이 안 되어] I can't do it. = It's beyond my ability. = I can't do it. = It's beyond what I'm capable of. ④ [계속해서] I can't go on with it. ⑤ [포기] I'm out. = I want to give up.
못하는 게 없군요.	[칭찬] Is there anything you can't do? = What is it that you can't do? = You are excellent at anything you do! = You are multi-talented!
못합니다.	① [가능 · 능력] I'm not able to do it. = I can't do it. = I can't handle it. ② [수준] I'm not good at it. (잘~) ③ [경제력] I can't afford to do it. ④ [금지] You can't do it. = You shouldn't do it. ⑤ [상황판단] I can't do such a thing. (그런 일은 난~) ⑥ [야구 · 테니스 · 포커 등을 할 줄 모름] I don't know how to do it.

묘

묘하네요!	It's weird!

무

무거워 죽겠어요.	This is really heavy. = The weight is killing me.
무겁습니까?	How much does it weigh? (얼마나~) ➡ It weighs seventy kilograms. (70킬로그램입니다.) ☞ 몸무게는 얼마입니까?
무게가 초과되었습니까?	Is my baggage over the weight limit? = Are my bags over the weight limit? = Are my bags too heavy? (제 짐~) ➡ It's five kilograms over the limit. (5킬로 초과입니다.)
무능한 인간!	You are a good-for-nothing! = You are useless! = You are impossible! ☞ 못난이!, 밥통!
무단횡단은 위험합니다.	Jaywalking is dangerous.
무더워 죽을 지경입니다.	The heat is killing me.
무덥습니다.	It's really muggy. = The weather is scorching hot.
무례하군요.	You are so rude. = You don't have manners. // You are too rude. (너무~)
무례함을 용서하세요.	Forgive my rudeness, please.
무료로 증정합니다.	It's offered free. = It's free of charge. = It's a free gift. ☞ 서비스입니다.
무료 배송은 몇 킬로그램까지입니까?	Up to how many kilograms can be delivered free?

➡ Twenty kilograms is the maximum. (20킬로그램입니다.)

무리야!

① [억지 부림에 대해] That is an unreasonable demand! = You are going too far!

② [실현 불가능] That's impossible to do. // It's beyond my ability. (내 능력으론~)

무리하지 마세요.

① [불가능한 일 시도] Don't try to do the impossible.

② [지나침] Don't go too far. = Don't try too hard. = Don't go overboard. (너무~)

무사히 잘 다녀오세요.

① Have a safe trip.

② [비행기 여행] Have a safe flight.

무서워 죽겠어요.

I'm scared to death. = I'm terrified to death.

무서워요!

① [감정 상태] I'm so scared! (너무~)

➡ What is so scary? (뭐가 무서워!) // I'm afraid of my father! (아버지가 ~)

② [사물에 대한 두려움] The scene is frightening! = The scene is horrible! (그 장면은 정말~)

③ [얼굴] He looks scary! = He looks horrible! (그는~)

무서워하지 마세요.

Don't be afraid. = Don't be scared. = Don't be frightened. = Don't panic.

무섭긴! // 무섭긴 뭐가!

What is so scary?

무소식이 희소식입니다.

No news is good news.

무슨 날입니까?

What is the occasion? = Is it a special day today?

무슨 뜻이야?

① What do you mean? = What are you talking about? // What do you mean by that? (그게~)

② [의도 · 속뜻] What are you implying?

③ 〈비속어〉 [불만] What the shit are you talking about? (너 이게 무슨~)

ㅁ

	➡ I don't mean anything special. (별 뜻 아니야.)
무슨 말부터 해야 할지 모르겠습니다.	I don't know how to start the conversation. = I don't know where to start. = I don't know what to say.
무슨 말씀을요!	[칭찬에 대해] Don't mention it!
무슨 말씀인지요?	What do you mean by that? = What are you talking about? = I don't know what you mean.
무슨 말이야?	① [반문] What's that again? ② 〈비속어〉 [헛소리] What the shit are you talking about? (그게~) ③ [자세한 설명을 요구] What are you talking about? = Give me the specifics. = Give me the specific details.
무슨 말인지 알겠습니다.	I see your point. = I understand what you mean.
무슨 상관이야!	That's none of your business! = Mind your own business! = You have nothing to do with this!
무슨 소리야?	① [반문] What's that again? ☞ 무슨 말이야? ② [말뜻이] What do you mean? // What do you mean by that? = What's your point? (그게~) ☞ 무슨 말씀인지요? ③ 〈비속어〉 [허튼소리에] What the shit are you talking about? ☞ 무슨 말이야? ④ [바깥 소리에] What is that sound? Can't you hear something? ⑤ [엉뚱한 말에] What nonsense are you talking about?
무슨 요일입니까?	What day is it today? 요일 It's Monday. (월요일입니다.) It's Tuesday. (화요일입니다.)

	It's Wednesday. (수요일입니다.) It's Thursday. (목요일입니다.) It's Friday. (금요일입니다.) It's Saturday. (토요일입니다.) It's Sunday. (일요일입니다.)
무슨 일 생겼습니까?	① Is there anything wrong with you? = Is anything the matter? ② [사고] What happened? ➡ I hit the car. (차에 부딪쳤습니다.) ③ What happened to him? (그한테~) ➡ He had a car accident. (차사고 났어요.) ☞ 왜 그래?
무슨 일이 있어도 하겠습니다.	I will do whatever happens. = I will stick with it whatsoever. = I won't give up doing it whatsoever. = I will do it no matter what.
무슨 일입니까?	① [갑자기 나타난 상대방에게] What's up? ② [표정이나 상태가 좋지 않은 상대방에게] What's wrong with you? = What's the matter? = What's the trouble with you? = What's troubling you? ➡ I'm not feeling well. (몸이 좋지 않아요.) ③ [전화상에서] What are you calling about? ④ [시비] What's going on here?
무슨 일인지 말해봐!	Tell me what's going on!
무슨 짓이야?	What do you think you are doing? // What do you think you are doing now? (지금~) ➡ Nothing. (아무것도 아니에요.)
무승부로 끝났습니다.	It ended in a tie. // The game ended in a draw. = It was a tie game. (그 경기가~)
무승부입니다.	It's a tie score. // We are in a tie game. (우리는~) // The two teams are playing a tie game now. (양 팀은 지금~)

무시하지 마세요.	① [과소평가] Don't underestimate me. (날~)
	= Don't look down on me.
	// Don't underestimate him. (그를~)
	② [상대해 주지 않음] Stop ignoring me. (날~)
	= Don't belittle me. = Don't put me down.
	= Stop walking all over me.
	// Do not ignore him.
	= Treat him well. (그를~)

무시해.	Just ignore it. It's not a big deal. (별일 아니니까~)
무식하면 용감한 법이야.	Fools rush in where angels fear to tread. = Ignorance makes people bold.
무식한 놈!	You are an ignorant man!
무심코 던진 돌에 개구리는 맞아죽는다.	A stone carelessly flung can kill a frog.
무엇 때문이야?	[이유] Why? // Why are you learning English? (영어를 배우는 게~) ➡ Because it's interesting. (재미있어서요.)
무엇 좀 드시겠습니까?	① [음식] Would you like something to eat? ➡ No, thank you. Don't bother to prepare anything. (아니요. 신경 쓰지 마세요.) ② [음료] Would you like something to drink? ➡ ⓐ I'd like a green tea, please. (녹차 한잔 주세요.) ⓑ Anything is okay. (아무거나, 뭐든 괜찮습니다.) ③ [주문] What would you like to order? ➡ A cup of tea, please. (차 마실래요.)
무엇 좀 살까요?	What about buying something? ➡ Some fruits would be okay, I guess. (과일 좀 사면 되겠지요.)
무엇을 도와 드릴까요?	① Can I help you? = May I help you? = Is there anything I can help you with? ② [상점 등에서] What can I help you? ➡ Thank you. I'll call you when I need something. (고맙습니다, 필요할 때 부르겠습니다.)

무엇을 드실래요?	① [음식] What would you like to eat? // What would you like for dinner? (저녁은~) ➡ I'd like fried rice. (볶음밥이요.) ② [음료] What would you like to drink? ➡ I'd like a tea. (차 마실래요.)
무엇을 원합니까?	[주문] What would you like? ➡ A bottle of wine, please. (포도주 한 병요.)
무엇을 잘 먹습니까?	What kind of food do you enjoy eating?
무엇을 좋아합니까?	[음식] What is your favorite food? ➡ My favorite food is Korean-style barbecue. (한국 불고기요.)
무엇을 주문하시겠습니까?	[음식] Can I take your order? = Are you ready to order? ➡ Every kind of *gimchi*, please. (김치를 종류대로 주세요.)
무엇을 하고 있습니까?	What are you doing? ➡ [포커] Let's play bridge. (브리지를 하자.)
무엇을 하려고요?	What are you going to do? ➡ I'm going to a hot spring and taking a hot bath. (온천에 몸을 좀 담그려고.)

무엇을 합니까?	① [직업을 물을 때] What do you do?
	= What do you do for a living?
	② What do you usually do in your free time?
	= What do you usually do in your spare time? (남는 시간에~)
	// What do you usually do when you take a break? (쉴 때~)
	// What do you usually do when you have nothing to do? (한가할 때~)
	// What do you usually do on weekends? (주말에~)
	➡ ⓐ I usually play tennis. (항상 테니스 칩니다.)
	ⓑ I go to my part-time job. (아르바이트하러 갑니다.)

무엇입니까?	What is it? (그것은~) // What is this? (이것은~) ➡ This is a book. (이것은 책입니다.)
무자식이 상팔자.	Love of children is an eternal encumbrance.
무정합니다.	You are so heartless. // He has no heart. (그는~)
무지 쉬워요.	It's so easy. = It's a piece of cake. = It's a breeze.
무척	Very much.

문

문 닫아요!	[명령] Close the door! = Shut the door!
문 닫을 시간입니다.	[영업 종료] It's time to close. = It's about closing time.
문 좀 열어주세요.	Would you open the door, please?
문단속 잘하세요.	Be sure to lock the door.
문병 가겠습니다.	I will visit you in the hospital. // I will visit and see you in the hospital when I have time. (시간 나면~)
문안 인사를 가야지요.	We have to go and see him. (그에게~)
문은 열려있어요.	① The door is open. ② [상점] It is open now. = It is in business now. (지금~)
문을 닫습니까?	What time do you close? = When is the closing time? (상점은 몇 시에~) ➡ We close at ten o'clock. (10시에 문을 닫습니다.)
문을 엽니까?	[영업] When/What time do you open? (몇 시에~) // Until when are you open?

	= What are your hours of operation? = What are your hours of business? (몇 시까지~) ➡ We're open till one o'clock in the afternoon. (오후 1시까지 문을 엽니다.)
문자 보낼게.	[핸드폰] I will send a text-message to you. // I will text-message you.
문자 왔어.	[핸드폰에] You've got a text message. = You've got texts. (네~)
문자도 씹어.	He ignores my texts. (그가~)
문제 있습니까?	① [질문] Have you got a question? (무슨~) ➡ No, I don't. (없습니다.) ② [곤란] Is there any problem? = Is there anything wrong? = Is there any trouble? (무슨~) ➡ No, I'm okay. (괜찮아요.)
문제없습니다.	① [안심] Nothing to worry about. ② [쉽게 처리할 수 있음] No problem. It's easy. = Nothing is easier. ③ [심각하지 않음] Not a serious problem at all. ④ [완벽함] It's perfect. = It's flawless. = Nothing to be desired. ⑤ [위안] Not a problem at all. = I'm okay. = I'm all right.
문제 일으키지 마.	Don't rock the boat. (공연히~) = Don't disturb the situation. // Don't cause a scene. (공공장소에서~)

묻

묻지 마세요.	Don't ask. // Don't ask me. (저에게~)
	// Don't ask anything. (어떤 것도~)
	// Don't ask too many questions. (너무 많이~)

물

물 끓이는 중이에요.	I'm boiling water.
물 내려!	[화장실] Flush the toilet!
물 만난 고기다.	It's like a fish in water.
물 있습니까?	Have you got some water?
물 좀 더 주세요.	① Please get me some more water. = Can I have some more water? ② [빈 찻잔에] Can you fill this up with more water? ③ [화단] Please water them more. // Please water the plants more in the garden. (정원 식물에~)
물 한 병 갖다 주세요.	Please get me a bottle of water.

물 한 잔 주세요.	Can I have a glass of water, please?
	// Can I have a glass of hot water? (뜨거운 물~)
	// Can I have a glass of cold water with ice? (얼음물~)

물건 올리는 것 좀 도와주세요.	[기차나 비행기에서] Would you help me with lifting these things up? // Would you help me with these?
물건을 잃어 버렸습니다.	I lost my belongings.
물건을 찾아주셔서 감사합니다.	Thank you for finding me my belongings.
물고기와 곰발바닥을 함께 얻을 수 없다.	You can't have your cake and eat it, too.
물러나세요.	① Back off. (뒤로~) ② [자리나 직위에서] You'd better retire from your post.

	// It's time to leave. Give up. (이쯤에서 깨끗하게~)
물러주세요.	① [반품] I'd like to return this. (이것을~) ② [환불] Can I get a refund on this?
물론 아니지요.	Of course not.
물론이지요.	[확신] By all means. // Of course, it is. = Definitely yes. = Sure thing. = No doubt about it. = You bet. = You can bet your life. = Needless to say. (그야~) // It goes without saying. = It is as clear as day. ☞ 당연하지.
물어보겠습니다.	① [질문] I will ask him. (그에게~) ② Excuse me, can I ask you something? (좀~)
물어줄게!	[변상] Let me pay for it! = I will make up for your loss! = I will pay for the damage!
물어줘!	[변상] Pay for it! = Pay for the damage!
물에 물탄 듯 술에 술탄 듯하다.	① [성격] He is so wishy-washy. = He is so indecisive. = He is a man of indecision. (그는~) ② [사태관망] He is sitting on the fence. He hasn't made any decision yet. (그는~)
물에 빠진 사람 지푸라기 잡는 심정이다.	I feel like a drowning man catching at a straw.
물은 건너보아야 알고 사람은 지내보아야 안다.	If you want to get to know a person, you should spend time with him.
물을 많이 드세요.	Drink a lot of water.
물이 끓어요.	The water is boiling.
물이 나오지 않습니다.	The water doesn't come out from the tap. = The water is shut off.

ㅁ

	// Hot water doesn't come out of the shower. (샤워기에서 더운~) ➡ I'll take care of it in a minute. (곧 조치해 드리겠습니다.)
물이 뜨겁네요.	The water is hot.
물이 샙니다.	The roof leaks. (지붕에~) // This cup leaks. (이 컵은~)
물이 올랐어요.	He is riding high. = He is on top of the world. = He is number one these days. (그는~)

뭉

뭉치면 산다.	In unity there is strength.

뭐

뭐 그런 놈이 다 있냐?	What a creature! = What an odd person! = What kind of person is that?
뭐 대단한 것도 아닙니다.	That is nothing great. = That is nothing special.
뭐 마실래?	What would you like to drink? = Would you like something to drink? ➡ I'd like a beer. (맥주 한 잔 할래.)
뭐 먹고 싶니, 만들어 줄게.	What would you like to eat? I'll make it for you. ➡ I feel like some noodles. (국수 먹고 싶어.)
뭐 먹을래요?	What do you want to have? = Would you like something to eat? // What would you like for dinner? (저녁으로~) ☞ 무엇을 드실래요?
뭐 묻은 개가 겨 묻은 개를 나무란다.	The pot calls the kettle black.

뭐 어때서!	What is wrong with it? = What is the big deal? = What is the big deal about it? (그게~) // What seems to be the problem with this? (이게~)
뭐 이따위가 다 있어!	What a damn thing this is!
뭐 잘못 됐냐?	Did I do anything wrong?
뭐 잘못 먹었냐?	[비난] Are you out of your mind? // What do you think you are doing? ➡ I don't know. (모르겠어요.)
뭐 좀 드실래요?	Would you like something to eat? ☞ 뭐 먹을래요?, 무엇을 드실래요?
뭐가 급해?	What is so urgent? = Why are you in such a hurry? ➡ The class will start in just a minute. (수업시작해요.)
뭐가 달라요?	What is so different? ➡ They are absolutely different. (당연히 틀리지요.)
뭐가 대단해!	[폄하] That is not so great! = I can't see anything great in it.
뭐가 되고 싶니?	What do you want to be in the future? ➡ I want to be a scientist. (과학자가 되고 싶습니다.)
뭐든지 괜찮습니다.	Anything is okay.
뭐든지 다 잘 먹습니다.	I can eat any kind of food. = I'm not picky about food.
뭐든지 다 좋아요.	[주문] Anything is good.
뭐든지 말씀만 하십시오.	Just name it. = Just tell me what you want. // We've got everything from A to Z. = We've got everything under the sun. (~ 다 있습니다.)

ㅁ

뭐든지 먹을 수 있습니다.	You can eat whatever you want. // I'm so hungry that I could eat even a horse. (배고파서~)
뭐라고요?	① [잘못들음] What? = What did you say? = Huh? = You said what? = Pardon me? = Excuse me? = Can you repeat that? = Could you say that again? ② [어이없음] What? = What the hell are you talking about?
뭐라고 말해야 할지 모르겠어요.	I don't know what to say. = I have no idea what I have to say.
뭐랄까?	What do I have to say?
뭐랬어?	[사실 확인] What did I say to you? (내가~)
뭐로 드릴까요?	What would you like to order? ➡ I'd like a bowl of tomato soup. (토마토 수프 한 그릇 주세요.)
뭐로 만들었습니까?	What is this made of? (이것은~) ➡ It's made of flour. (밀가루요.)
뭐야?	① [행위] What are you doing now? ② [사고] What is it? ➡ Nothing. (아니야.) ③ [경멸] What are you? ④ What are you talking about? ☞ 무슨 소리야? // 무슨 말이야?
뭐야 그놈?	What is wrong with him? = What's his problem?
뭐야 또?	[불평] What is the matter this time?
뭐야 이게!	What is all this? = What is all this about? (다~)
뭐하는 거야?	① [꿍꿍이 속] What do you think you are doing? = What are you thinking? (대체~) ② [행위에 대한 비난] What are you doing? Give it back to me! (뭐하는 거야? 돌려줘!)

뭐하는 사람이요?	[직업] ① What do you do for a living? = What is your job? = What's your occupation? ➡ I am a shopkeeper. (저는 상인입니다.) ② What does that person do? (저 사람은~) = What's that person's job? ➡ He is a merchant. (그는 장사꾼입니다.)
뭐하려고?	What are you going to do? = What are you up to? ➡ Nothing. (아무것도 아니에요.)
뭐해?	① What are you doing? // What are you doing today? = What are you up to today? (오늘~) ② [멍하니 한눈 팔 때] What's up?

뭔

뭔 일 있어?	Do you have any problem? // Do you have any problem with her? (그 여자와~) ➡ There can't be any problem between she and I. (무슨 일이 있을 게 뭐있어!)
뭔 일인데?	What's the matter? = What's the problem? = What happened? ☞ 무슨 일입니까?
뭔데?	① [확인] What do you mean? = What are you talking about? ② [사물에 대해] What is it?
뭔데 그래?	① [끼어드는 상대에게] What do you think you are? (네가~) ② [심상치 않은 분위기] What's the matter here? = What's the problem here? = What's going on here? ➡ Nothing. (아무것도 아니에요.)

뭘

뭘?	What?
뭘 드릴까요?	[상점] What would you like? = What are you looking for? = Is there anything you are looking for? ➡ A bottle of whiskey, please. (위스키 한 병이요.)
뭘 드실래요?	What would you like to eat? = Would you like something to eat? ☞ 무엇 좀 드시겠습니까?
뭘 모르는군.	You know nothing about it.
뭘 봐?	What are you looking at?
뭘 시킬까요?	[주문] Would you like me to order something? = What would you like to order? ➡ Order anything. (아무거나 시켜요.)
뭘 안다고 그래!	What do you think you know about it? ➡ [빈정대며] Yeah, you know everything. (너 잘났다!)
뭘 안다고?	① [무시 · 빈정대며] Do you know anything? ② [관여할 수 없음] What do you know about it? (네가~)
뭘 원하십니까?	What do you want? ☞ 무엇을 원합니까?
뭘 입지?	What am I going to wear?
뭘 찾는 거야?	What are you looking for?
뭘 하고 있어!	[망설임] What are you doing? Go ahead! (~. 어서해!) = What are you hesitating for? Go ahead!
뭘까?	[추측] What do you think it is?
뭘요!	[감사 · 수고 · 실례에 대한 대답] Not at all.

= Don’t mention it.
// It was nothing. (~ 아무것도 아니었어요.)
⬅ Thank you. (고마워!) // Good job. (잘했습니다.)

뭘

뭘 하러 갔어요?	Why did you go there? = What took you there? = What were you doing there? (거기에~) // What took you there yesterday? (어제~) ➡ I was shopping. (물건 사러 갔었어요.)

미

미국 어디 어디를 가봤습니까?	Which parts of the United States have you been to? ➡ I have been to many places. (많은 곳을 가봤어요.)
미국 대사관은 어디에 있습니까?	Where is the American Embassy? ➡ It’s on Jong-ro. (종로에 있습니다.)
미국 사람입니까?	Are you American? = Are you from the Untied States? = Are you from the States? (당신은~) ➡ Yes, I’m American. = I’m from the States. (예, 미국 사람입니다.)
미국 생활에 익숙합니까?	Are you familiar with living here in the States? = Are you adjusting well here in the States? (여기~) ➡ Yes, I feel a lot more familiar living here. = Yes, I think I’m adjusting well. (익숙해졌어요.)
미국 선생님께 배웠습니다.	I learned it from my American teacher.

미국에 언제까지 머뭅니까?	How long are you going to stay in the States? = Until when are you going to stay in the United States? ➡ Until September next year. (내년 9월이요.) // For about a month. (약 한 달입니다.)
미국에 온지 얼마나 되었습니까?	How long have you been here in the United States? ➡ Just a week. (미국에 온지 일주일밖에 안됐어요.)
미국에 처음 왔습니다.	This is the first time in the States. = I've never been here in the States before.
미국에서 얼마나 머뭅니까?	How long are you going to stay in the United States? ☞ 미국에 언제까지 머뭅니까?
미국 영화도 좋아합니까?	Do you like American movies? = Do you enjoy watching American films?
미국 요리가 좋아집니다.	I'm getting fond of American food. = I'm getting to like American food more and more. (점점~) // I'm getting into American food these days. (요즘~)
미국 요리를 잘 먹습니다.	I eat American food well.

미국 요리를 좋아합니다.	I like American food.
	// I love American food. (매우~)
	// My favorite is American food. (가장~)

미국인입니다.	I am American. = I'm from America. = I'm from the United States. (저는~)
미꾸라지 한 마리가 흙탕물을 만든다.	One rotten apple spoils the barrel.
미끄럼 조심하세요.	Watch out! It's slippery. = Watch your step. The floor is slippery.
미끄럼주의!	[경고문] Caution! Wet floor!

미루자.	Let's put it off. = Let's put it on the back burner. = Let's put it on hold. (그걸 좀~)
미리 생일을 축하합니다.	I want to congratulate you on your birthday in advance. = Happy early birthday!
미리 알려주세요.	Please give me advance notice. = Please let me know in advance. = Please give me notice in advance.
미리 알아서 처리해주세요.	Please take care of that beforehand.
미리 좀 깨우지?	You should have woken me up earlier. = Why didn't you wake me up earlier? ➡ I wanted you to have more sleep. (좀 더 주무시라고요.)
미스 리입니다.	I am Miss I. (저는~)
미스입니다.	I am single. = I'm not married. // She is not married yet. = She is single. (그녀는 아직~)
미스터 김이군요.	You are Mr. Gim. (당신이~)
미안!	I'm sorry. ☞ 미안합니다. // 죄송합니다.
미안하게 생각합니다.	I am so sorry. = I apologize with all my heart. (마음으로 정말이지~)

미안합니다.	① [실례를 범하는 경우] Please excuse me.
	// Excuse me, can I smoke? (~, 담배 피우겠습니다.)
	// Please excuse me. I must be going. I've got a work to take care of.
	(~, 일이 좀 있어서 가 보겠습니다.)
	② [실수를 한 경우] I am sorry. It's my fault.
	// I'm so sorry. It's my fault. (정말~)
	➡ That's no problem. = That's all right.
	= Never mind. (괜찮습니다.) ☞ 죄송합니다.

ㅁ

	③ [방해하는 경우] Sorry to interrupt you. = Sorry for bothering you. = I'm sorry for troubling you.
미안해하지 마세요.	Don't be so sorry about it. = There's nothing to be sorry about it.
미운 일곱 살.	He is in his naughty childhood. (그는 ~)
미워!	I hate you! = I dislike you! = You are the last person I want to see. (네가~) ☞ 싫어요!
미정입니다.	It's up in the air. = It's not decided yet. (아직~)
미쳐버리겠다!	① I feel like I'm losing my mind! = I feel like I'm going insane! // It is driving me crazy! (그것 때문에~) = It drives me up the wall! ② [화가 나서] I'm going to explode! = I'm freaking out!
미쳤냐?	① Are you crazy? ➡ ⓐ I'm crazy. So what? (미쳤다. 왜?) ⓑ I'm not crazy at all. (안 미쳤어.) ② [약을 잘못 먹고] Do you think I'm crazy? (내가~)
미쳤어!	[단정] You are crazy! = You are out of mind! = You are not yourself! (너~)
미치겠다!	① [정신이] I feel like I'm losing my mind! ② [화가 나서] I'm going mad! = I'm going to explode! = I'm freaking out! ③ [스트레스] It is driving me crazy! = It's driving me insane! = It drives me up the wall! (그것 때문에~) ☞ 미쳐버리겠다. ☞ 돌아버리겠네. ④ [초조 · 원망] I'm getting anxious! = I'm growing anxious! (정말~) ⑤ [귀찮음 · 짜증] I hate this!

미친년!	① Crazy girl! ② 〈비속어〉 Bitch!
미친놈!	What a crazy duck!
미친놈들!	Nuts!

민

민망해!	It's so embarrassing!
민심이 천심.	The voice of people, the voice of God.

믿

믿거나 말거나!	[방임] Believe it or not!
믿는 도끼에 발등 찍힌다.	In trust is treason.
믿습니다.	① I believe you. = I trust you. (당신을~) ② [부탁이나 희망을 기탁함] My trust is on you. = I have full confidence in you. (그럼 당신만~) ③ [확신] I believe it. = I am so sure of it. (그것을~)
믿어요!	① [일 처리] Trust me! (나만~) ② Believe my words! (내말을~) // Take my word for it! = You've got my word!
믿어주세요.	[부탁] Believe me, please. = Trust me, please.
믿을 만한 사람입니다.	He is trustworthy. (그는~) = He is a reliable person. = He is the person you can rely on.
믿을 수 없습니다.	① [사실 · 정보] I cannot believe it. (그것을~) // I can't believe my eyes. (내 눈을~)

	② [사람] I can't believe him. (그는~) = He is not reliable. = He's not trustworthy. = He is not to be relied on. ③ [놀람 · 당황] Unbelievable! = Incredible! ④ [의심] I doubt it. = I have a doubt about it.
믿지 않아요.	① [사실] I don't believe it. (그것을~) ② [사람에 대한 신뢰] I don't trust him. (그를~) = I don't have confidence in him.

밀

밀지 마세요.	[차 안에서] Don't push. There are so many people in here. (~안에도 사람이 많습니다.)
밀어봐.	Give it a push. (한번~) // Push it hard. (힘껏~)

밉

밉살스러운 인간!	How obnoxious you are! =You are an eyesore.

밑

밑 빠진 독에 물 붓기.	It's like shoveling sand against the tide
밑져야 본전입니다.	Trying wouldn't do any harm. = It wouldn't hurt to try. (성사가 안 되도~)
밑지는 장사입니다.	I'm losing money as it is.
밑천도 못 찾아요.	① You can't take back your original funds. ② [이중으로 손해 봄] You can double your damage.

바

바가지 그만 긁어!	Stop nagging, please. = Don't nag me. = Stop pestering me. = Enough with your nagging.
바가지 씌우지 말아요!	[가격을] Don't rip me off! = You shouldn't rip me off!
바가지요금이네!	It's a real rip-off!
바겐세일입니다.	We're having a bargain sale. // We're having a great winter bargain sale. (겨울 대~)
바깥에 나가서 바람 좀 쐬자.	Let's go outside and get some fresh air.
바꿔드리겠습니다.	① [교환] I will definitely give you an exchange. = I can definitely exchange this for you. (꼭~) // I will exchange the clothes for other ones. (그 옷을~) ② [전화] Let me put you on with him. (그를~)
바꿔주세요.	① [전화] Can/May I speak to Mr. Gim? = I'd like to speak to Mr. Gim. = Is Mr. Gim there? = Is Mr. Gim available? (김선생님을 ~) ② [물건 교환] Can I exchange this with another one? (다른 것과~)
바늘 가는데 실 간다.	They always go with each other. // They are inseparable. (뗄 수 없는 사이이다.)
바늘 도둑이 소도둑 된다.	He that will steal a pin will steal an ox. = He that will steal an egg will steal an ox.
바늘로 찔러도 피 한 방울 안 난다.	He is as cold as stone.

ㅂ

바늘방석에 앉은 것 같다.	I'm so uneasy that I feel like I'm sitting on a bed of thorns. = I feel like I'm on pins and needles.
바다는 메워도 사람의 욕심은 채우지 못한다.	You can fill up the ocean, but you cannot fill up a man's avarice.
바다에 바늘 찾기.	It's like looking for a needle in a haystack.
바닥을 쓸어라.	Sweep the floor.
바람 맞았어요.	I got stood up. // He stood me up. (그에게~)
바람 불어요.	It's windy. // It's windy outside. (밖에~)
바람 쐬러 갑시다.	Let's go and get some air.
바람 쐬러 나왔어요.	We are here to get some air. = We are here for some fresh air. (우리는~)
바람 앞의 등불.	It's like a candle flickering in the wind.
바람났어요.	My husband cheated on me. (내 남편이~) // My wife cheated on me. (내 아내가~)
바람둥이입니다.	① [남자] He is a playboy. = He is a womanizer. = He is a lady killer. = He is a skirt chaser. (그는~) ② [여자] She is a playgirl. = She is a flirt. (그녀는~) ③ [비속] She is a slut.
바람을 넣어야 합니다.	[타이어에 바람이 빠져서~] The tire has to be filled up with air. = The tire has to be filled with air.
바람이 불어서 왔어?	What brought you here? = What brings you here? (무슨~)
바람이 붑니다.	① The wind is blowing outside now. (밖에 지금~) ② [일기예보] It's windy today. (오늘은~)

바람이 세찹니다.	The wind is blowing hard. // We have strong wind today. (오늘~)
바람이 약해졌어요.	The wind has died down.
바람 피웁니까?	Are you having an affair? = Are you cheating on me? (다른 여자와 ~) ➡ No, I'm not. That'll never happen. (그런 일 없어요.)
바래다줄게.	① Let me take you home. = I'll get you home. (집까지~) ② [차로] Let me take you home in my car. = Let me give you a ride home.
바로!	Right away! = Immediately!
바로 갈게요.	① [장소로 감] I'll be there right away. = I'll be there in no time. ② [도착] I will arrive there soon. ③ [가는 중] I'm going. = I'm on my way. ④ [전화통화] I will be over to you right away.
바로 돌아올 거야.	I'll be back right away.
바로 됩니다.	It will be done right away. = It will be ready in a minute.
바로 말해!	Give it to me straight! // Tell me the truth! ☞ 바른대로 말해!
바로 저 사람입니다.	That is the person I talked to you about. (제가 말한 사람이~)
바른대로 말해!	① Tell me the truth! = Be frank! = Tell me honestly! = Be honest! ☞ 바로 말해! ② Call a spade a spade! (바로 불지 그래!)
바보 같은 놈!	Fool! = Idiot! = How stupid!

ㅂ

ㅂ

바보 같은 소리!	① That's nonsense! ② 〈비속〉 You are talking bullshit!
바보 같은 짓 그만해!	Stop screwing around! = Stop fooling around! = Stop messing around!
바보 아니야!	[비난] Are you an idiot? = You're such an idiot! = You stupid!
바보 취급하는구나!	You are making a fool of me! (날~)
바보 같이 굴지 마!	Don't play the fool! = Don't be a fool! = Don't be a chicken! = Don't be silly!

바빠서 죽을 지경입니다.	I'm so busy that I'm not myself.
	= I'm as busy as a bee.
	// I live in a whirl of business.
	= I'm always on the go. (날마다~)
	// I'm up to my ears in work. (일이 많아~)
	☞ 바쁩니다.

바쁘다고 바늘허리에 실 매어 쓰랴.	(The) more haste, (the) less speed. ☞ 급할수록 돌아간다.
바쁘기는요.	I'm not busy at all.
바쁘지 않나요?	① Aren't you busy? ② [급히 처리할 일에] Do you have time, or are you busy? ➡ I am very busy. (아주 바빠요.)
바쁜 것 없습니다.	I don't have any urgent business. = I have some time. = I have a light schedule. = I have an easy schedule.
바쁜데 온 거 아니야?	Is it a bad time? = Did I come at a bad time? (내가~)
바쁩니까?	Are you busy now? (지금~) ➡ ⓐ Yes, a little bit. (약간 바쁩니다.) ⓑ Yes, I'm so busy. (바빠 죽을 지경입니다.)

	ⓒ No, I'm not busy at all. (바쁘긴요! 바쁘지 않습니다.) ⓓ I have a lot of time now. (지금 매우 한가합니다.)

바쁩니다.	① I'm busy. = I've got no time at all.
	= I'm tied up. = My schedule is full.
	= My hands are full. // I'm a bit busy. (약간~)
	// Today is a bit busier than yesterday.
	= It's a bit busier than yesterday.
	(오늘은 어제보다 좀~)
	// I've been busy lately. (요즘 참~)
	➡ You look lively and cheerful.
	(힘이 넘쳐 보이는걸요.)
	② [할일이 많음] I'm up to my ears in work.
	☞ 바빠서 죽을 지경입니다.

바지 좀 추켜올려.	Pull your pants up!
바지를 벗어봐!	Take off your pants!
바짝 따라와!	Follow close behind me! = Catch up with me! = Don't fall behind!

박

박수로 격려해주세요.	Cheer him up with some applause. = Applaud him, please. = Give him a big hand. (그를~)
박수치세요.	Clap your hands.

밖

밖에 나가 바람 좀 쐬고 와라.	Go out and get some fresh air.
밖으로 나갑시다.	[적당한 자리를 찾아] Let's go out and look for a place.

ㅂ

반

반갑습니다.	① [처음 만나는 인사] Nice to meet you. = I'm very glad to meet you. = I'm pleased to meet you. = Happy to meet you. ② [일상] Nice to see you. = Happy to see you. = Pleased to see you. ③ [예기치 못한 만남] What a nice surprise!
반값으로 해줘요.	Let me take it at half-price.
반납해 주세요.	Please return it before six the day after tomorrow. (이틀 후 저녁 6시 전에~)
반대방향으로 왔습니다.	You have come in the opposite direction.
반대합니다.	I have an objection. // I'm opposed to it. = I'm against it. (그것에~)
반드시	Surely. = Certainly.
반반이야!	It's half and half!
반씩 나눠!	Let's go fifty-fifty! // You half, and me half! (나 반, 너 반, ~)
반칙입니다.	It's against the rules. = It's a violation of the rules. = You are cheating. = You went against the rules. = You violated the rules.
반품해 주세요.	I want to return it.

반했습니다.	I fell in love with her.
	= I was fascinated by her. (그녀에게~)
	// I fell in love with her at first sight. (그녀에게 첫눈에~)
	// I've got a crush on her.
	= I have a crush on her.

	= I'm crazy about her. = I fell for her. (그녀에게 홀딱 ~)

받

받겠습니다.	① [물건] I'll take it. = Let me take it. ② [전화] I'll get it. = Let me answer it.
받아두세요.	[물건 · 금전 등] Take it, please = Keep it, please. // Take it first. (우선~)
받아주세요.	① [선물 등] Please take this. = Please accept this. ② [사람을] Accept me, please. (절~)
받으세요.	Take it, please. ☞ 받아두세요. ① [공짜로 줌] Take this, please. It's free of charge. (이거~) ② [선물로 줌] Take this, please. It's a gift for you. (이거~) ③ [돌려 줌] I'd like to return this. (이거~) ④ [물건을 건네줌] Here you are. (이거~)
받을 수 없어요.	① [선물] I can't take this. = I can't accept this. ➡ Take it. It's okay. (받아, 괜찮아.) ② [남이 주는 물건] I'm not taking any (from others). (어떤 것도~)

발

발 들어!	Hold your feet up!
발 디딜 틈이 없습니다.	[사람들로 가득 차서~] It's crowded with people.
발 없는 말이 천리 간다.	Bad news travels fast.
발등에 떨어진 불이나 끄세요.	It's an emergency. Take care of this situation prior to anything else.

ㅂ

발등에 불이 떨어지다.	I am in a very urgent situation. = I am pressed by urgent business. = I am pressed by an urgent matter of business.
발목이 삐었어요.	I sprained my ankle.
발밑을 조심하세요.	Watch your step.
발에 쥐가 났어요.	I've got a cramp in my leg.
발을 다쳤습니다.	I've hurt my foot.
발을 밟아서 미안합니다.	I'm sorry. I stepped on your foot.
발음이 매우 좋습니다.	Your pronunciation is very good. = Your pronunciation is excellent.
발음이 원어민 같습니다.	You sound like a native speaker. = Your pronunciation is similar to that of a native speaker.
발이 넓다.	He knows a lot of people. = He has a wide range of acquaintances. = He is well-connected. = He has got a lot of connections. = He has so many friends in various fields. (그는~)
발이 붓습니다.	My feet swell up. // My feet swell up very often. = My feet get swollen very often. (자주~)
발이 아파요.	I have a pain in my feet. = I feel pain in my feet. = My feet hurt.

밤

밤 말은 쥐가 듣고 낮 말은 새가 듣는다.	[속담] The walls have ears.

밤 자고나서 문안하게.	Visit me after you get up tomorrow morning.
밤새도록 울었어요.	I cried all night. = I cried the night through.
밤새웠어요.	① [자발적으로] I stayed up all night. // I stayed up last night. = I didn't sleep at all last night. (어제~) ② [할 수 없이] I pulled an all-nighter last night. (어젯밤~)
밤새지 마세요.	Don't stay up all night. = Don't do an all-nighter. // Don't stay up many nights. = Don't stay up all night often. (자주~)

ㅂ

밥

밥 값 좀 해라.	[뭔가 유용한 일을 하라는 뜻] You need to earn your keep. = You need to contribute, too. = You need to do your part, too. = You need to pitch in, too.
밥 먹고 가!	Have a meal before you go!
밥 먹고 출근해.	Wake up! Have a meal before you go to work. (빨리 일어나. ~)
밥 먹으러 가자.	Let's go to eat. = Let's go for a meal. = Let's go and grab something to eat.
밥 먹자!	① Let's have a meal! ② [식탁에서] Let's eat! = Let's start! = Let's dig in!
밥 생각 없습니다.	① I don't feel like eating. ② [입맛이 없음] I don't have any appetite today. (오늘~)
밥 차려!	Prepare a meal! = Set the table!
밥맛 없습니다.	I have no appetite at all.

밥맛이야!	① I'm allergic to you. = You really turn me off. = I'm tired of you. ② 〈비속〉 You suck!
밥벌레!	You are a useless person. = You are good for nothing. ☞ 못난이
밥이 보약이다.	Not skipping a meal saves you from an illness.
밥이나 먹겠니?	Do you think you can make a living doing that? (그렇게 해서~) // Do you think you can bring home the bacon with that type of job? = You'll starve doing that type of work! (그런 일 해서~)
밥통!	You are a jerk! = How stupid you are! ☞ 얼간이 // 못난이

방

방 열쇠 여기 있습니다.	Here is a key to the room.
방 열쇠 주세요.	Give me the room key, please.
방 열쇠입니다.	This is the key for my room. (이게 제~)
방 있습니까?	[숙박] Do you have any rooms available? = Are there any vacancies here? ➡ No, there are no vacancies for about two days. (없습니다. 요 이틀 모두 빈방이 없습니다.)
방 좀 치워주세요.	Clean up the room, please.
방 카드를 반납하세요.	Return the room card, please.
방 카드를 잃어버렸습니다.	I lost my room card.

방귀 뀌는 소리하고 있네!	① What nonsense! = What a bunch of nonsense! = You are talking rubbish. ② 〈비속어〉 What bullshit! = What a bunch of bullshit!
방귀 뀌었지?	Did you fart? = Did you cut the cheese? = Did you break wind? // Who farted? = Who cut the cheese? = Who broke wind? (누가~)
방금 나갔습니다.	He has just gone out. (그는~)
방금 뭐라고 했어요?	What did you say just before? ➡ No, nothing. (아무것도 아니에요.)
방문객은 사절합니다.	① We do not accept visitors here. ② [간판] No visitors allowed.
방문이 잠겨버렸습니다.	I'm locked out of my room. Can you give me a hand? (~ 도와주시겠습니까?)
방법을 생각 좀 해봐!	① [수단] Think about how to deal with this. ② [난관 통과] Think about how we should go through this.

방법이 없습니다.	① There's no way.
	// There's no way this time. (이번에는 정말~)
	// There's no way to settle this. (해결~)
	② [불가능] There's no way out. (빠져나갈~)
	// I don't see the end of this. (이 상황에 대한~)

방심했어요.	I was careless. = I was caught off my guard.
방으로 드시죠.	Get into the room, please.
방을 예약했습니다.	I made a reservation for a room. // I booked a room for two nights. (이틀 밤 묵을~)
방이 없습니다.	There are no vacancies. = All rooms are occupied.

방이 지저분합니다.	The room is messy. // The room is a wreck. = The room is in total disorder. = The room is in total disarray. (매우~)
방학에 어디 가고 싶어?	Where do you want to go on your vacation? ➡ I want to travel Europe. (유럽에 여행 가고 싶어.)
방학은 언제부터 시작입니까?	When does your vacation start? ➡ ⓐ The vacation starts in mid-December. (방학은 12월 중순입니다.) ⓑ It starts on the twenty-second. (22일부터 시작합니다.)
방학을 뭘 하며 보낼까?	How will I spend the long vacation? = How am I going to spend the long vacation? (긴~) ➡ Call me when you are bored. (심심할 때 전화해.)
방학을 했습니다.	① My vacation has started. ② [방학중] I'm having a vacation. = I'm on vacation.
방해가 되었나요?	Am I interrupting you? = Am I bothering you?

배

배 터지겠어! // 배 터지겠습니다.	[과식] I'm so full I could burst. = I'm so full I could explode. = I'm so full I'm about to burst. = I'm so full I'm about to explode.
배 째!	Sue me!
배가 아픕니다.!	I have a pain in my stomach! = I have a stomachache!
배가 좀 고픕니다.	I'm a little bit hungry.
배고파요.	I'm hungry. = My stomach is growling.

배고파 죽겠어요.	I'm starving. = I'm dying of hunger. = I'm so hungry that I could eat a horse.
배고픕니까?	Are you hungry? ☞ 시장합니까?
배꼽 빠지겠어요.	I'm laughing so hard that my sides hurt. = I'm in stitches. = I could die laughing. (너무 웃어서~)
배달됩니까?	Do you deliver? ➡ ⓐ Yes, we do. (됩니다.) ⓑ No, we don't. (안 됩니다.)
배달서비스가 있습니까?	Do you have delivery options? ➡ ⓐ Yes, we deliver. = Yes, we have a delivery option. = Yes, we have some delivery options. (배달합니다.) ⓑ Sorry, we don't have any delivery service. (미안합니다. 배달은 안 합니다.)
배달해 주세요.	I want it delivered.
배보다 배꼽이 더 크다.	It is the tail wagging the dog. = The postage costs more than the goods.
배부르게 먹었습니다.	I have had enough. = I ate my fill.
배불러 죽겠네.	I'm stuffed to death.
배불러요.	I'm full. = I'm stuffed. = I have a full stomach. // I can't eat another bite. (더 이상 못 먹겠어요.)
배상해 드릴게요.	I'll pay for the damages. (피해에 대해~)
배신을 때리다니!	You traitor! = How could you betray me? = How could you stab my back?
배우고 싶습니다.	I want to learn English. (영어를~)
배우는데 늦은 나이란 없다.	Never too old to learn.

ㅂ

ㅂ

배운 게 없습니다.	I haven't learned anything. // I don't have a good educational background. (얼마~) ☞ 가방 끈이 짧습니다.
배운지 반년 됐습니다.	It has been half a year since I started to learn it.
배웁니까?	① What do you learn? (뭘~) ➡ I'm learning how to use computers. (컴퓨터를 배웁니다.) ② How many hours do you learn it every day? (매일 몇 시간~) ➡ Four hours. (4시간이요.)
배웅 나오지 마세요.	You don't have to come and see me off. ➡ See you and take care! (살펴가세요.)
배웅해 드리겠습니다.	I'll go with you and see you off. ➡ I'm okay. You don't have to. (괜찮아요. 나오지 마세요.)
배웠습니까?	① Where did you learn English? (영어를 어디서~) ➡ I learned it at Michigan University. (미시건대학에서 배웠습니다.) ② Where did you learn it? (어디서~) ➡ I learned it at a private institute. (학원에서 배웠습니다.) ③ How did you learn English? (영어를 어떻게~) ➡ ⓐ I learned it by myself. = I learned it on my own. (혼자 배웠습니다.) ⓑ I learned it while watching English TV. (TV방송으로 배웠습니다.) ⓒ I learned it at a private institute. (학원에서 배웠습니다.) ④ How long have you been learning it? (몇 년간~) ➡ For three years. (3년이요.)
배은망덕도 유분수지.	How could you bite the hand that feeds you?

배짱이 두둑해요.	She's not afraid of anything. = She's fearless. = She's gutsy. = She has guts. (그녀는~)
배탈납니다.	Cold food can upset your stomach. (찬 것 먹으면~)
배탈났습니다.	① [증상] My stomach is upset now. = I have an upset stomach. ② [설사] I've got the runs. = I have the runs. = I've got diarrhea. = I have a diarrhea.

ㅂ

백

백 달러를 오십 달러짜리 두 장으로 바꿔주세요.	Can I exchange a 100 dollar bill for two 50 dollar bills? = Can I exchange a 100 dollar bill for two fifties?
백년해로하시길 바랍니다.	[결혼] I hope you guys are happy forever. (두 분이~)
백문이 불여일견.	Seeing is believing. = A picture is worth a thousand words.
백수라서 돈이 없습니다.	I'm unemployed now, so I'm broke.
백지장도 맞들면 낫다.	[속담] Two heads are better than one. = Many hands make light work.
백화점이 있습니까?	Is there a department store near here? (이 근처에~) ➡ Yes, there is one. (있습니다.)

밸

밸런타인데이 축하해!	Happy Valentine's Day, honey! (자기야, ~)

뱁

뱁새가 황새 따라가려다 가랑이 찢어진다.	① 〈직역〉 If a crow-tit tries to walk like a stork, he will break his legs. ② Tailor your ambitions to the measure of your abilities.

버

버렸습니다.	① [쓰레기 등] I threw it away. ② [이별] He dumped me. = He turned his back on me. (그가 나를~)
버스 왔어요!	The bus is here! = The bus has arrived! = The bus has come!
버스 지난 다음에 손 흔들어 봐야 소용없다.	[속담] It's no use crying over spilt milk. = It's too late for regrets. ☞ 엎질러진 물이야.
버스를 타고 갑니다.	I take a bus there. = I go there by bus. (거기에~)
버스를 타고 출퇴근합니다.	I go to work by bus every day. (매일~)
버스정거장은 어디에 있습니까?	Where is the bus stop? ➡ Go ahead one hundred meters. (앞쪽으로 100미터 가세요.)
버스표는 어디에서 사야 합니까?	Where can I get the bus ticket? ➡ At a bus stop. (정거장요.)

번

번갯불에 콩 볶아 먹듯 했어.	You have finished it too quickly. (너~)

번거롭게 해드려 죄송합니다.	I'm sorry for troubling you. = I'm so sorry to bother you. = I'm sorry for getting you into such a mess.
번데기 앞에서 주름잡네.	[속담] You are teaching a dog to bark. = Are you teaching a fish how to swim? ☞ 공자 앞에서 문자 쓴다.
번쩍	① [번개] The lightning flashed. ② [가볍게] lightly // He lifted it up lightly. (그는 그것을 번쩍 들어올렸다.)

ㅂ

벌

(몇) 벌	One piece of clothing. (한 벌의 옷) // Two pieces of clothing. (두 벌의 옷)
벌써 8시입니다.	It's already 8 o'clock.
벌써 일어났어.	He has already got up. (그는 ~)
벌컥벌컥!	Gulp, gulp! // He gulped it down. (그는 그것을 ~ 마셨다.)
벌통을 쑤셔 놓은 듯.	It's crowded like a beehive.

법

법은 멀고 주먹은 가깝다.	Where drums beat, laws are silent.

벙

벙어리 냉가슴 앓듯 한다.	It's like suffering in silence.

베

베풀어주신 은혜에 감사드립니다.	Thank you for your mercy.

벨

벨소리가 납니다.	I hear a bell ring. // I hear the doorbell ring. (문~)

벼

벼는 익을수록 고개를 숙인다.	① 〈직역〉 The boughs that bear the most hang the lowest. = The more noble, the more humble. ② The more modest you should be, the more you learn.
벼락출세했다.	He is an upstart. = He is a parvenu. (그는~) // He has made a rapid rise in this business. (이 분야에서 그는 ~)
벼락치기했어.	I crammed for the exam. (그 시험~)
벼룩의 간을 빼먹어라.	[착취가 심함] You are skinning a flea for its hide. // This is all. (It's like) you are trying to get blood from a turnip. (이게 다야, ~)

변

변덕이 죽 끓듯 한다.	He's full of whims. = He's really capricious. = He blows hot and cold. (그는~)
변명이라도 해봐.	Say something for yourself.

변명하지 마세요.	Don't make excuses. = Don't try to explain. = Don't give me any ifs, ands, or buts. // I don't need your excuses. = There are no ifs, ands, buts about it. (변명 따위는 필요 없어.)
변상해!	Pay for the damage! = Compensate for the damage! ☞ 물어줘!
변태 아니야?	What a pervert!
변한 게 하나도 없네.	[모습] You haven't changed at all.
변환할 수 있나요?	Can you change this document into a pdf file? (이 문서를 pdf 파일로~)

ㅂ

별

별 차이 없습니다.	There's not much difference. // They are not so different. (그것들은~)
별개의 것입니다.	① They are separated ones. // The winter in Seoul is not so different from that of Tokyo. (서울의 겨울과 도쿄의 겨울은~) ② [영향 관계] It won't make much of a difference. = It won't have any strong influence. = It won't affect a lot.
별거 아닙니다.	① [큰 일] Not a big deal. = Nothing to worry about. ② [별다른 일] Nothing special.
별거 중입니다.	They are living separately. = They are living apart from each other.
별꼴이군!	What a spectacle! = I never thought I'd live to see this happen.

별로	① Not so much. (~없어) ② Not so good. (~좋지 않아.)
별로 멀지 않습니다.	It's not so far from here. (여기서~)
별로 바쁘지 않습니다.	I'm not so busy.
별로 비싸지 않습니다.	It's not so expensive. = The price is not so high.
별로 좋아하지 않습니다.	I don't like it much. = I'm not into it that much.
별로 좋지 않습니다.	① [몸상태] I'm not feeling good. = I'm a bit under the weather. = I'm not in good condition. ② [생활 · 상태 · 수준] I'm not doing good. = I'm not doing well. ③ [수준 · 평가] This place is not high class. (여긴~)
별로 춥지 않습니다.	I'm not that cold.
별말씀을!	① [감사] My pleasure! = The pleasure is mine! = You're welcome! ☞ 천만에요. ② [칭찬] Don't mention it! = Not at all!
별문제 없습니다.	There's no problem. = Not a problem at all. = There's nothing to worry about.
별일 다 있네.	Now I've seen everything.
별표(*) 버튼을 누르세요.	[전화] Push the asterisk button.

병

병세가 많이 호전되었습니다.	He is a lot better now. = He is in a lot better condition. = His illness has taken a turn for the better. (그의~)

병세가 어떻습니까?	How's his condition? (그의~) ➡ He is in serious condition. = He is in critical condition. (병이 꽤 심각합니다.)
병신 같은 놈! // 병신!	You stupid! = You stupid jerk! = You stupid idiot! = You loser! = You sucker! = You piece of garbage!
병신 자식이 효도한다.	[속담] Crooked logs make straight fires.
병원에 갑시다.	Let's go to (the) hospital. = Let's go to see a doctor.
병원에 빨리 갑시다.	Let's go to (the) hospital quickly. = Let's hurry to (the) hospital.
병은 나았습니까?	Did you recover from your illness? ➡ I almost recovered. Thank you for caring about me. (거의 다 나았습니다. 신경 써주셔서 감사합니다.)

보

보고 싶어 미치겠어!	I'm dying to see you! = I really miss you! = I can't wait to see you! (너를~) // I'm dying to see the movie! = I want to see the movie so badly! (그 영화를~)
보관됩니까?	[물건] Can you take this in custody? ➡ Sure, I can. (그럼요.)
보기 좋습니다.	You look so good. = You look great. (너무~) ☞ 예쁩니다.
보긴 뭘 봐?	What are you trying to look at? ➡ ⓐ What's wrong with that? (보면 어쨌다고?) ⓑ I'm not allowed to look at it? (보면 안 돼?) ⓒ I don't lose anything by not seeing it. = I'm not missing anything by not seeing it.

	= I'm not missing out by not seeing it. (안 보면 그만이지 뭐.)
보릿고개.	The barley hump. // The spring farm hardship period.
보살펴주셔서 정말 감사합니다.	Thank you for taking care of me.
보상해줄게.	Let me make it up to you.
보세요!	Look here! (여기 좀~) // Look again! = Take another look! (다시 한 번~)
보여주세요!	Can you show it to me? (저에게 좀~)
보입니다.	① [목표물] It's within my sight. = I see it now. ② [시각] I see it. ③ [가능] I can see it now. (이제~)
보자고 했습니까?	① [찾아옴] What brought you here? (무슨 일로~) ➡ I'm here to borrow some money from you. (돈 좀 빌리려고.) ② [약속해서] Why did you want to see me? (왜 저를~) ➡ I have something to tell you. (할 말이 있어서.)
보조개가 예쁘군요.	You have pretty dimples.
보증합니다.	I guarantee. // I guarantee the quality. (품질은~) // I can vouch for him. (그를~)
보채지 마세요.	Don't rush me. // Stop rushing me like that. (그렇게~)
보충수업 받으러 갑니다.	I'm going to take a supplementary course.
보통 인연이 아니네!	This is not just an accident. // This must be an act of Providence. (이건~)
보통이 아니네!	He is beyond expectations! (그는 ~)

ㅂ

보통입니다.	① [수준] I'm just average. (나는~) ② [특이하지 않음] It's not unusual. = It's common. (그것은~)
보험 드실래요?	Would you like to apply for insurance?
보험에 들고 싶습니다.	I want to apply for insurance.
보험에 들었습니다.	I'm insured. (저는~) // My house is insured. = I have my house insured. = I have home insurance. (우리 집은~)

복

복 많이 받으시고 오래오래 사세요.	Mercy on you and live a long life!
복도 많아요.	You are blessed.
복도 청소하러 갈게.	I'm going to clean up the hallway.
복사 좀 부탁합니다.	Can you photocopy this? ➜ Okay. No problem. (예, 알았습니다.)
복수하고 말 거야.	I will revenge on him. = I will get even with him. = I will pay him back. = I will get it back at him. = I will return him what I got. (그에게~) // I will fix him for it. (그것에 대해 그에게~)
복습하세요.	You should review what you learned. = You'd better brush up on what you learned today. (오늘 배운 것을~)
복잡하게 생각하지 마세요.	Don't think complicatedly. = Don't take it complex. Take it simple.
복잡하네요.	① [일 등이] It's complicated. = It's a complex thing to do.

② [음식점에 손님이 많음] This place is a little crowded. (여기는 좀~)

본

본 기억이 있습니다.	I have seen it before. I remember it.
본 듯합니다.	I think I saw it before. = Seems like I've seen it before. (어디서~)
본 적이 있습니다.	I have seen it before. // I saw it when I was in the U.S. (미국에서~)
본론으로 돌아갑시다.	[대화 중] Let's get back to the point. = Let's get back to the main topic.
본론으로 들어갑시다.	Let's take up the main issue. = Let's get down to brass tacks. = Let's get down to business.
본색을 드러내시지.	Show me your true colors. = Show your true identity.
본인 부담입니까?	Are you paying on your own? (당신~) ➡ Yes, I am. (본인 부담입니다.)
본인입니까?	Are you this person? ➡ Yes, I am. (본인입니다.)
본전도 못 건졌다.	It was a total loss. = Even the principal was lost. = I lost everything. = I couldn't get my money's worth. // I lost both capital and interest. (이자는 물론~)
본전도 안 남아요.	We sell at the original price. // If you insist on the price, we have to sell it at a loss. (이러시면~)

볼

볼 것도 없네, 뭐!	It isn't worth looking!
볼일 보세요.	Do your own business. = Do your own work. // Go and do your own business on hand. (가서 각자~)
볼만합니다.	It's worth looking. (한번~)

봄

봄에 씨를 뿌려야 가을에 거둔다.	You have to sow the fields in the spring to reap them in the fall.
봄을 좋아합니다.	I like spring.
봄은 따뜻합니다.	It's warm in the spring.

봅

봅시다.	① [관찰] Let me take a look. (저 좀~) ② [대화] Please come here and see me. (이리 와서 저 좀~) ③ [만남] See you tomorrow. (내일~) // See you again. (또~) // See you next week. (다음주에~) // See you next year. (내년에~)

봉

봉사료가 포함된 건가요?	Is the service charge included? ➡ ⓐ Yes, it is. (네. 그렇습니다.) ⓑ No, it's not. (아니오. 그렇지 않습니다.)

ㅂ

봐

봐!	Look! // Look at me! (날~)
봐도 될까요?	Can I take a look at it? ➡ Sure, you can. (그러세요.)
봐드리겠습니다.	I will let you off this time. (이번에는 ~)

봐주세요.	① [관찰] Please keep an eye on this.
	= Watch this, please. (이것 좀~)
	② [부탁] Please help me with this. (이것 좀~)
	➡ Sure, let's see. (그래요. 봅시다.)
	③ [용서] Please give me a break.
	= Please forgive me.
	// Please let me off this time. (이번에는~)
	// Please will you ignore just one time? (한 번만~)
	④ [목숨] Please let me go.
	= Spare me, please. (좀~)
	⑤ [짐 등을] Please keep an eye on my bag. (내 가방 좀~)
	// I'm going to get some food. Please keep an eye on this. (먹을 것 좀 사러갈 테니, 좀~)

봤지?	See? // It turned out as I said. (내가 말한 대로 되었지?)

뵌

뵌 적 있지요?	We've met before, haven't we? (우리~)

뵙

뵙게 되다니 정말 우연이네요.	It's a coincidence that we met each other. // What a coincidence to meet you here!

	= What a coincidence to run into you here! = What a coincidence to bump into you here! (여기서~) ➡ Where are you heading now? (지금 어디 가시는 길이세요?)
뵙고 싶었습니다.	I wanted to see you.

부

부끄러워하긴! // 부끄러워하지 마세요.	Don't be shy!
부끄럽습니다.	① [창피함] I'm so embarrassed. = It's so embarrassing. ☞ 창피해! ② [기대에 못 미침] I'm a lot short of the expectations. ③ [입장 난처함] I feel awkward. ④ [부족한 작품이나 재주 등에] I'm not that good. = It's not so good.
부끄럽지도 않냐!	Shame on you! = It's a disgrace! = You should be ashamed!
부담 갖지 마세요.	① [걱정] Don't worry about it. // Don't worry too much about it. (너무~) ② [스트레스] Don't get stressed. = Don't feel any pressure. ③ [초대 · 선물] Don't take it as a burden.
부담스럽습니다.	It weighs on my mind. = It worries me so much.
부러질지언정 굽히지 않는다.	I'd rather break than bend.
부럽습니다.	I envy you. = I am envious of you. = I'm jealous of you. // I really envy you. (정말~)

ㅂ

ㅂ

부모 마음은 다 똑같습니다.	All parents feel the same for their own kids.
부모님, 안녕하셨어요.	Father. Mother. How are you?
부부 싸움했어요?	Did you have a fight with your wife? = Did you have an argument with your wife? (아내와~) // Did you have a fight with your husband? (남편과~)
부부싸움은 칼로 물베기.	Nothing is so unpalatable as a lovers' quarrel.
부자되세요!	Make a big fortune! = Make big money! = I hope you make a fortune. = I hope you become a billionaire.
부자입니다.	① He is rich. = He is a rich man. = He is a man of wealth. (그는~) // He is rich with a capital R. = He's got much to burn. (그는 정말~) ② [억만장자] He is a billionaire. (그는~)
부자 집 자손입니다.	He was born with a silver spoon in his mouth. (그는~)
부재중입니다.	① [자동응답기 녹음] I'm not in right now. (저는 지금~) ② He is not here now. (그는~)
부전자전이네.	**Like father, like son.** = It's handed down from father to son. ☞ 그 아버지에 그 자식이네.
부주의했습니다.	**I was careless.** = I was not careful enough. = I was heedless. = I was not attentive enough. (제가~)
부탁 좀 들어주세요.	Do me a favor, please. = I have a favor to ask of you.
부탁하나 해도 될까요?	May/Can I ask you a favor? = Will you do me a favor?

	= Could you help me? = Would you give me a hand? ☞ 도와줄래요?
부탁드립니다.	I'd like to ask you to help me. (~, 저 좀 도와주세요.) ➡ ⓐ Sure. I'm glad to help you. (좋습니다, 기꺼이 도와드리죠.) ⓑ Sorry, I don't have time right now. (미안합니다, 저도 바쁩니다.)
부탁합니다.	① [사정] Please help me with this. (이 일을 ~) ② [간청] I'm imploring you to help me. = I implore you to help me. ③ [전화] Can you put me on to Miss I? (미스 리 좀~) ④ [물건 요청] Can you get me some water, please? (물 좀~) ⑤ [행선지] Can you take me to Sinchon, please? (신촌~)
부탁했습니다.	Somebody asked me to do it. (누가 저한테~)

북

북아메리카에서 쓰는 말투입니다.	That is how people speak in North America.
북적북적한 분위기를 좋아합니다.	I like a place crowded with people. = I like a place busy with many people.

분

분명히 말해주지.	Let me straighten it out. = Let me put it clearly.
분발하겠습니다.	I'll try my best. = I'll try harder. = I'll try to go the extra mile.

분발해!	Try your best! = Try harder! = Muster your energy! = **Boost up your energy!**
분수에 맞게 살어!	Live within your means! = Cut your coat according to your cloth! = Stay within your budget!
분위기 깨네.	He is spoiling the atmosphere. (그가~) = He is destroying the atmosphere.
분위기 깨지마.	Keep the ball rolling. = Don't spoil the mood.
분위기 살벌하다.	The atmosphere is very hostile. // The environment here is very heavy. (여기~)
분위기 좀 살려보자.	Let's liven things up.
분위기 파악 좀 해!	Consider your surroundings!
분통이 터진다!	That makes me angry. = That freaks me out. (그것 때문에~)

불

불가능합니다.	① It's impossible. = It's out of the question.
	= **Not a chance.** (그것은~)
	// Not in a million years. (절대~)
	// This is impossible. (이건~)
	// This situation is impossible.
	(이런 일이 일어난다는 것은~)
	② [치료가] This is a terminal disease. (이건~)
	= There is no cure for this disease.
	= This is an incurable disease.
	= This is beyond medical treatment.

불고기 2인분 주세요.	Two portions of Korean barbecue, please.
불공평해요.	It's not fair. (그건~) = It's unfair. // It's really unfair. (정말~)

불난 집에 부채질이야!	You are pouring oil on the fire. = Don't add fuel to my anger.
불러줘서 고마워요.	Thank you for inviting me.
불만 있으면 말씀하세요.	If you have some complaints, don't hesitate to tell me.
불 좀 붙여주세요.	① [램프] Light a lamp. ② [담배] Light a cigarette. = Can you light my cigarette?
불쌍하네요.	What a pity! // He is so poor. (그는 참~) = He is so miserable.
불 좀 켜주세요.	Can you turn the light on?
불이야!	Fire!
불편합니까?	Are you not feeling well? = Are you sick or something? (어디가~) ➡ ⓐ I have a headache. (머리가 좀 아파요.) ⓑ I have a stomachache. (위가 불편합니다.) ☞아픕니까?
불행 중 다행입니다.	It is a blessing in disguise.

붕

붕!	① [자동차 소리] Zoom! // The car zoomed off! (그 차는 ~ 출발했다.) ② [방귀소리] Prrrt! // He broke wind. = He let out a fart. = He farted. = He broke wind. = He passed gas. (그는 ~ 방귀를 뀌었다.)
붕붕!	[벌이 나는 소리] Bzz! // The bee made a buzzing sound. = The bee buzzed. (그 벌은 ~ 소리를 냈다.)

ㅂ

붕어빵이네.	[부자 두 사람을 보고] You two look exactly like each other. = You take after each other. (영락없는~)

블

블랙커피 한 잔이요.	Can I have a cup of black coffee? = A cup of black coffee, please. = I'd like to go for black. ⓐ [연한 것] A black coffee, mild one, please. ⓑ [진한 것] A black coffee, strong one, please.

비

비 온 뒤에 땅이 더 굳는다.	① Ground packs after a rain. = After a storm comes a calm. ② [격려] If you overcome the difficulties now, a good thing will come to you someday.
비가 내리기 시작합니다.	It has started to rain.
비가 오네.	It's raining.
비가 오락가락 해.	The rain is on and off.
비가 올 것 같습니다.	① [임박] It's about to rain soon. = It's going to rain in a minute. (곧~) ② [상태] It looks like raining. // It looks like it's going to rain tomorrow. = It's likely to rain tomorrow. (내일~)
비가 자주 옵니까?	Do you have a lot of rain here? (여기~) ➡ We have some occasionally. (가끔 옵니다.)
비겁한 놈!	You are a coward!

비겼어요.	We ended the game in a tie. = It was a tie game. (그 경기를~)
비꼬지마!	Don't be sarcastic! = Don't speak cynically!
비누 좀 빌려 쓸까요?	Can I use your soap? = Can I borrow your soap? ➡ Sure. Go ahead and use it. (쓰세요.)
비닐봉지 하나 주세요.	Can I get a plastic bag?
비밀 지켜.	Keep it a secret. = Keep it to yourself. = Keep it under your hat. = Don't tell anyone. // This is between us. = This is between (just) you and me. = Don't spill the beans to anyone. = Don't tell anyone. (아무에게도 말하지 마.) ➡ I will keep it a secret. = My lips are sealed. = Your secret is safe with me. (비밀 지키겠습니다.)
비밀번호 네 자리를 입력해주세요.	① Enter the four-digit password, please. ② [현금지급기 등] Enter your four-digit PIN number. = Enter your four-digit personal identification number.

비밀입니다.	It's a secret.
	= Let's keep it under wraps. (그건~)
	// This is a secret. (이건~)
	// It's between you and me. (당신과 나 사이의~)
	// It's a secret from her.
	= Don't tell her about it. (그녀에게는~)

비상구는 어디입니까?	Where is the emergency exit? = Where is the fire escape?
비슷합니다.	① They are all similar. (다~) ② [유사] There are some similarities between the two. = They are like each other.

ㅂ

= They are similar to each other. (그 둘은 약간~)
// It is similar to me. (그는 저와~)
// It is similar to mine. (그것은 제 것과~)
③ [퀴즈의 답] You are very close.

비싼 것 같습니다.

① [보아서] Seems expensive.
= It looks quite expensive.
= It looks like they are overcharging us.
② [생각에] I think it's expensive.

비쌉니까?

Is it expensive?
➡ ⓐ Yes, it's expensive. (비쌉니다.)
ⓑ No, it's not expensive. It's cheap. (쌉니다.)

비쌉니다.

It's expensive.
// That's too much expensive.(너무~)
= That's unreasonable. = Too steep.
= The price is unreasonably high.
= The price is out of line.

비열한 놈!

You are so mean!

비용이 얼마나 듭니까?

① [경비] How much does it cost?
// How much does it cost to get there? (거기에 가려면 ~)
➡ It costs fifty dollars. (50 달러 듭니다.)
② [서비스를 받는데] How much do you charge for that? ☞ 얼마나 합니까?

비웃지 마세요.

Don't laugh at me. (저를~)
= Don't make fun of me.

비위가 좋아요.

① [용감하게 시도함] She has some nerve. (그 여자는~)
② [뻔뻔스러움] She is impudent.
③ [음식] I can eat any kind of food.
= My stomach is for any kind of food.

비위에 맞지 않아요.

① [취향] It doesn't suit my taste.
= It's against my taste.

	② [성향] Such a thing goes against the grain with me. (그런 일은~) ③ [음식] The food goes against my stomach.
비자가 한 달이군요.	Your visa is valid for a month. (당신의 ~)
비자를 못 받았습니다.	I couldn't get my visa issued.
비자를 연기했습니까?	Did you extend your visa expiration date? = Did you get an extension on your visa? ➡ I got it extended once. (비자를 한 번 연기했습니다.)
비켜!	① Step aside! (한쪽으로~) ② [길을 막고 있음] Get out! = Get out of my way! = Clear the way! = Make way for me!
비켜주세요.	[길 양보] Can you get out of my way? = Can you clear the way? = Can you make way for me?
비행기 태우지 마세요.	Don't flatter me. = Don't put me on. = Don't butter me up.
비행기 태워주니까 하늘 높은 줄 몰라요.	My compliments gave you a big head.
비행기는 몇 시 것입니까?	What time is your flight? ➡ It's supposed to leave at three in the afternoon. (비행기는 오후 세 시입니다.)
비행기는 몇시에 떠납니까?	What time does the flight leave?
비행기는 몇 시에 탑니까?	When is your boarding time?
비행기는 언제 착륙합니까?	When are we landing?
비행기는 정시에 출발합니까?	Is the plane going to leave on time? ➡ The flight will take off as scheduled. (비행기는 정시에 이륙합니다.)

ㅂ

ㅂ

비행기는 탑승을 시작했습니까?	Has this flight started boarding? = Has the boarding for this flight started? (이~)
비행기를 갈아타야 합니다.	We have to transfer to another flight.
비행기입니까?	What is your flight number? = What flight are you going to take? (어느~) ➡ The flight number is OZ 707[seven-o-seven]. (OZ 707편입니다.)
비행기표 좀 확인하고 싶습니다.	I'd like to confirm my flight schedule.
비행기표는 얼마입니까?	How much is the ticket? // How much is the ticket to New York? = How much does it cost to fly to New York? (뉴욕에 가는~) ➡ It's one thousand and five hundred dollars. = It will cost/be one thousand and five hundred dollars. (1,500달러입니다.)
비행기표를 보여주세요.	Show me your ticket. = Can I see your ticket?
비행기표를 예약하고 싶습니다.	I want to make a reservation for an airline ticket. // I want to book a flight to L.A. (L.A.행~)
비행기표를 예약하시겠습니까?	What day would you like to reserve a ticket for? (어느 날~) ➡ The sixth, please. (6일 날이요.)
비행기표 좌석을 확인하고 싶은데요.	I'd like to confirm my seat on the flight.

빅

빅 세일!	It's on big sale! = They're having a big sale!

빈

빈 수레가 소리만 요란하다.	Empty vessels make the most sound. = Great talkers are little doers.
빈 좌석이 있습니까?	Do you have a seat available? = Do you have any seats available? ➡ Yes, we do. (있습니다.)
빈둥거리는 거 보기 싫다.	I don't want to see you idle about. = I don't want you to be a couch potato. (네가~)
빈말이라면 안하는 것이 낫다.	It would be better not to say anything than an empty talk.
빈방 있습니까?	Do you have a room available? = Do you have any rooms available? = Do you have vacancies here? // Do you have vacancies tonight? (오늘밤~)
빈방이 나면 바로 연락해주세요.	When you get a vacancy, please call me right away.
빈자리가 없습니다.	① We're full today. = All seats are fully booked. = All seats are occupied. ② There are no vacancies at the moment. (현재로는~) // We're fully booked up till next Sunday. (다음 주 일요일까지~)
빈자리가 있습니까?	Do you have a seat available? = Do you have any seats available?
빈틈이 없군요.	[일처리] You have done a perfect job. = You have covered your bases.

빌

빌려주세요.	Please lend it to me. = Can I borrow it?

빌려줄래?	Can you lend it to me? // Can I borrow your textbook? (교과서 좀~) ➡ Here you go. (가져가.)
빌어먹을!	〈비속어〉 Damn it!

빙

빙빙 돌리지 말고 말해.	Don't beat around the bush. = Get to the point. = Give me the bottom line. = Give it to me straight. = Stop skirting around the issue. = Don't avoid the issue.

ㅂ

빚

빚이 많아.	I am heavily in debt. = I am deep in debt. = I owe a lot of money.
빚졌습니다.	I'm indebted to you. = I owe you one. (이번에는 당신에게~)

빛

빛 좋은 개살구.	Appearances can be deceptive.

빠

빠른 걸로 주세요.	① [음식주문] Anything that you can serve quickly, please. = Anything that can be served quickly, please.

	② [기차표] Earlier one, please.
빠른 길로 가주세요.	Take the shortest way, please. (가장~)
빠른 길로 갑시다.	Let's take the shortcut. (우리~)
빠를수록 좋습니다.	① [시기가] The sooner, the better. ② [시간이] The earlier, the better. // ~. Make a quick decision. (~어서 결정하세요.) ③ [속도] The faster, the better.
빠삭해.	He is an expert in the field. = He is an expert on the subject. = He knows everything about it. = He's been down that road before. (그는 그런 쪽으로~)
빠져! // 빠져있어!	① [말참견] Keep out of this! = Stay out of this! = Attend to your own business! (넌~) ② [끼지 말고] Don't poke your nose into this! = Don't get nosy! (좀~)
빠지면 안 돼!	① You shouldn't skip it! ② [꼭 필요함] Please don't bail out of this! = Please stay! We need you. (넌~) // Please stick with us! We really need you. (우리한테는 네가~)
빠진 도끼자루.	An ax without a handle.

빨

빨대가 없습니다.	There are no straws.
빨래판으로 빨래를 합니다.	I use a washboard for washing my clothes.
빨리 가서 문 열어주세요.	Go and answer the door right away.

빨리 가봐!	Go right away!
빨리 가자!	Let's hurry!
빨리 갔다 와!	Go and come back quickly!
빨리 나와.	Come out quickly!
빨리 뛰어!	Run fast!
빨리 문 열어!	Open the door right away! = Open the door promptly!
빨리 와!	Come quickly! = Don't be long! = Hurry back! = Be right back!
빨리 자라.	Go to bed early. = Go to sleep early.
빨리 좀 가주세요.	① [속도] Speed up, please. = Faster, please. ② [운전] Step on it, please. = Pick it up, please. ③ [걸음] Walk faster, please.
빨리 좀 해!	[재촉] Hurry up! = Make haste! = Quick, please! = Step on it! // We have no time to lose. = We are short on time! = We are short of time! (시간 없어!) ☞ 서둘러!
빨리 준비하겠습니다.	Let me whip it up.
빨리 치워!	[정리] Clean it up quickly!
빨리 타!	Get in! Quick!
빨리요, 빨리!	Hurry up! Hurry!

빵

빵 좀 드실래요?	Would you like some bread?

빼

빼 닮았네요.	You look exactly like him. (그를 쏙~) = You are the spitting image of him.
빼도 박도 못하다.	I'm caught in the middle.
빼주세요.	① Let me be out. ② [명단에서] Take me off the list, please. (날~) ➡ Okay. (알았습니다.)

뺏

뺏는 사람이 임자다.	Takers are keepers.

뺑

뺑소니 사고야.	① It's a hit-and-run. = It's a hit-and-run accident. ② [이미 벌어진 사고에 대해] It was a hit-and-run. = It was a hit-and-run accident.

뻔

뻔뻔하구나!	[부끄러움을 모름] You are brazen-faced! = You have no shame! = You are so impudent! = You are so cheeky. = What a cheek! = You are shameless! = You got some nerve! = How blatant you are!
뻔뻔한 놈!	He has a lot of neck.

뻥

뻥 까지마!	① [거짓말] Don't tell a lie! ② [과장] Stop trying a bluff! = That's baloney!
뻥 치네!	You are lying! = That is baloney!
뻥이 세구나!	You are exaggerating too much! = You are a boaster!

뼈

뼈가 부러졌어요.	I have a broken bone. = My bone is broken. = I broke my bone. // I broke my wrist bone. (손목~)
뼈 빠지게 일합니다.	He works his tail off. (그는~)

뽀

뽀뽀!	Kiss!
뽀뽀하네.	They are kissing. (저 사람들~)
뽀뽀해줘!	Give me a kiss!
뽀뽀해줄게.	Let me give you a kiss.

뽑

뽑혔어요.	I was selected. (제가~) // I was voted. (투표로~) // I was chosen to be the representative. (대표로~)

뽕

뽕 갔었어요.	I was stuck on him. (그에게~)

뿌

뿌드득!	[이갈이] She grinds her teeth when she sleeps. = She gnashes her teeth when she sleeps. (그녀는 ~소리를 내며 잔다.)
뿌린 대로 거둔다.	① [속담] You reap what you sow. ② You are responsible for what you did. (한 일에 대해 책임을 져야 한다.)

삐

삐걱삐걱 소리가 났어.	There was a creaking sound. = I heard a creaking sound. = I heard something creaking.
삐딱하게 생각하지 마!	Don't think awry of it!
삐었어요.	I've sprained my ankle. (발목을~)

삐졌니?	Are you pissed off? (너~)
	// Are you mad at me? (너 나에게~)
	// Are you put out again? (또~)

ㅂ

사

사겠습니다.	① [구입] I will take this. = Let me take this. (이것으로~) ② [접대] It's on me. ☞ 내겠습니다.
사계절 모두 아름답습니다.	The four seasons are all beautiful.
사계절이 분명합니다.	The four seasons are distinct.
사고났어요!	There was an accident!
사고는 생기기 마련인거야.	Accidents happen. = Accidents will happen.
사고쳤니?	① What trouble did you make again? = What trouble did you cause again? (너 또 무슨~) ➡ What trouble! I did nothing. (무슨 사고를 쳤다고! 아무 짓도 안했어.) ② What is it this time? (이번엔 무슨~) ➡ Nothing special. (별일 아니에요.)
사공이 많으면 배가 산으로 간다.	[속담] Too many cooks spoil the broth.
사과드립니다.	I apologize. = I owe you an apology. ➡ ⓐ That's all right. = It doesn't matter. (괜찮아요.) ⓑ Forget it. = Don't worry about it. (신경 쓰지 마세요.)
사귀고 있습니다.	① [데이트 중] I'm going out with him. = I'm seeing him. = I'm dating him. (그 남자하고~) ② [교제 중] He is my boyfriend. = I'm in a relationship with him. (그 남자하고~)
사귀는 사람 있나요?	Are you in a relationship?

	= Are you spoken for? = Are you seeing anyone?
사귀는 사람 있습니다.	I'm in a relationship. = I have a girlfriend/boyfriend.
사귑시다.	① [연애] Why don't we start dating? = Why don't you go out with me? = Can I ask you out? ② [친구] Why don't we become friends?
사기당했습니다.	I got swindled. = I got cheated. = I got defrauded. = I got screwed.
사기치네!	You are cheating! = You are lying! ☞ 뻥 치네!
사기 치지 마세요.	Don't cheat on me, please. = Don't screw me, please. = Stop swindling, please.
사기꾼!	① Swindler! = Crook! ② [거짓말] Liar!
사는 게 재미없습니다.	My life is dry and dull. = There's not so much fun in my life. ➡ You have to stick with it even though it's not fun. (재미없어도 살아야 해.)
사는 게 죽느니만 못합니다.	I can't find my life worth living.
사돈 남 말 하네!	It takes one to know one!
사라져!	Go away! = Get out of my sight! = Get away from me! // [속어] Get the hell out of here! ☞ 꺼져!
사람 살려!	Help!
사람 싱겁긴!	Don't be so dull!
사람 죽어요!	Here is a person dying! = Someone is dying!

사람 팔자 알 수 없다더니!	Nobody knows what destiny one is led to!
사람은 외모로 판단하는 것이 아니다.	You cannot judge a book by its cover. = Don't judge people by their looks/ appearance.
사람은 죽어서 이름을 남기고, 호랑이는 죽어서 가죽을 남긴다.	Tigers leave only their skins when they die, but through his achievements a man's name lives on.
사람을 뭐로 보고 그래!	[무시하지 말라는 의미] Who do you think you're talking to? I'm not that kind of person!
사람이 참 좋으시네요.	How nice you are! = You are a good person. = You are so good-natured. = You must have good credit.

사랑에 빠졌어요.	I fell in love with him. (그와~)
	// I fell in love with her. (그녀와~)
	// I'm head over heels in love with her. (그녀와 푹~)

사랑에는 국경이 없다.	Love has no frontiers. = Love knows no borders. = Nationality doesn't matter in love.
사랑은 원래 유치한 겁니다.	Love makes people childish.
사랑은 원래 눈멀고 귀먹는 것입니다.	To love a thing makes the eye blind, the ear deaf.
사랑이 밥 먹여 주나요?	Love cannot pay the bills. = Love doesn't pay the rent.
사랑하게 해주세요.	Let us love each other. (우리 그냥~)
사랑하는 사람 있습니까?	Do you have someone in your life? ➡ Yes, I have. (사랑하는 사람 있습니다.)
사랑하지 않아요.	I don't love you. (당신을~)

	// I don't love you anymore. = My love is over. (더 이상~)
사랑한 적 없어요.	I have never loved you. (당신을~)
'사랑한다'라고 말한 적이 없어.	In three years' time, you have never said "I love you" to me. = In three years, you have never told me that you loved me. (3년 동안, 넌 한 번도~)
사랑해!	I love you! ➡ I love you, too. (나도.)
사랑해?	① Do you love me? (날~) ➡ Yes, I do. (사랑해.) ② How much do you love me? (날 얼마나~) ➡ I love you more than anything. = I love you more than I can say. = I love you as much as a hundred and a thousand. = My love for you is as deep as the ocean and as high as the sky. = There is no limit to my love to you. (하늘만큼 땅만큼, 죽는 날까지 사랑해.)
사 먹습니다.	I eat out every day. (날마다~)
사면초가입니다.	I'm stuck. = I'm between the devils and the deep blue sea.
사무실이 찾기 쉬워요.	The office is easy to find.
사부님!	Master!
사서 고생이다.	You chose all these troubles. (넌~) // Why all the troubles? (왜 사서 고생이니?)
사세요.	[구입] Take it. // Go ahead and get it. (어서~)
사시겠습니까?	① Do you want to buy this? (이거~) ➡ Sorry, I'm not interested in it. (죄송합니다, 관심 없습니다.) ② Are you sure you will take it? = Are you sure you want to take it?

ㅅ

	= Are you sure you would like to take it? (확실히~) ➡ Yes, I'll take it. (예.)
사실대로 말해!	Speak the truth! = Tell me the truth! = Come clean! = Tell it as it is! = Give it to me straight!
사실입니다.	It's true. = I'm speaking the truth. // I'm telling you it's true. (정말~)
사십니까?	[거주지] Where do you live? (어디서~) ➡ I live in Seoul. (서울에서 삽니다.)
사양하지 마세요!	① [겸손] Don't hesitate! ② [거절] No more refusals, please. (더는~)
사양합니다.	No, thanks. = I'll have to take a pass. // I'll pass this time. (이번에는 ~)
사업이 날로 번창하길 바랍니다.	I hope your business will thrive.
사업이 성공하길 바랍니다.	I wish you success with your business. = I hope you will go ahead in the game with your business.
사연이 있어.	He has his say. (그는~) // Everyone has his or her say. (누구에게나~)
사용법을 가르쳐주세요.	Tell me how to use it, please.
사용합니까?	① For what do you use this? = What is the usage of this? (이것은 어디에~) ➡ It is for containing boiled rice. (밥을 담아두는데요.) ② How do you use this? (이거 어떻게~) ➡ ⓐ You should open it first. (먼저 열면 됩니다.) ⓑ Let me show it to you. (제가 보여드릴게요.)
사이가 좋지 않습니다.	We're not doing well with each other.

	= We're not on good terms with each other. = We're not getting along well. (우리 둘~)
사이다 한 잔 주세요.	A glass of soda, please. = A glass of Sprite, please.
사이로 좀 지나가겠습니다.	Let me pass through between you two. ☞ 가운데로 좀 지나가겠습니다.
사이즈와 디자인이 다양합니다.	We have various sizes and designs. (우리 제품의~)
사이트를 찾습니까?	Are you looking for a web site?
사이트에 자주 들어갑니까?	Do you visit the web site often?
사인 좀 해주세요.	Can I get your signature here? = Can I get your autograph here?
사인하고 받아주세요.	Sign here and take this, please.
사인해주세요.	Please sign here. (여기~) // I've got a package for you. Could you sign for it? (택배입니다.~)
사정 좀 봐주세요.	① [용서] I have some good personal reasons. Please let me go this time. (이번에는~) ② [형편 이해] Please understand my circumstances.
사직하셨습니다.	He resigned. = He stepped out. = He quit office. = He quit the job.
사진 같이 찍을까요?	Shall we take a picture together?
사진보다 실물이 낫네요.	[여성에게 칭찬] You are more beautiful than your pictures. = You look better in person.
사진을 현상해주세요.	Please develop this film.
사진이 실물보다 낫네요.	He looks better in pictures than he does in person. (그는~)

사진이 잘 나왔네요.	You came out beautiful in this picture. = You are really photogenic.
사진 좀 찍어주세요.	Please take a picture of me.
사진 좀 찍어줄래요?	Can you take a picture of me?
사진 찍어도 됩니까?	Can I take a picture here? (여기서~) ➡ Sure. (됩니다.)
사진 찾으러 왔습니다.	I am here to pick up my pictures.
사진촬영 금지입니다.	You cannot take pictures here. = You are not allowed to take pictures here. (여기는~)
사촌이 땅을 사면 배가 아프다.	[속담] An envious man waxes with the fatness of his neighbor.
사후약방문.	It's like calling the doctor after somebody has died.

산

산 입에 거미줄 치랴.	We won't starve.
산만합니다.	He is not attentive. = He is a real space cadet. (그는 주의가~)
산을 잘 타시네요.	You are a good hiker. = You hike well.
산전수전 다 겪었어요.	① I've been through a lot of things. = You can't imagine what I've gone through. ② [고생] **I've been through hell.**
산책하러 갑시다.	Let's go for a walk. = Why don't you go out and take a walk?

살

살 거면 사고 안 살 거면 관둬요.	Take it if you're okay with the price. If not, go.
살 겁니까?	Are you going to buy it? = Are you going to get it? // Are you really going to buy this? (정말~) ➡ I am. (정말 삽니다.)
살 빠졌다!	You've lost some weight! (너~)
살 수가 없어요.	① I can't buy it. ② [경제적 능력 없음] **I can't afford that.** = I can't get it because it's too expensive.
살 좀 빼라.	Lose some weight! = You need to lose some weight.
살 좀 쪘습니까?	Have you gained some weight? = Have you put on some weight? ➡ Yes, I put on a lot of weight. = Yes, I got chunky. (그럼요, 많이 쪘어요.)
살고 싶지 않냐!	You don't want to live anymore, do you? ☞ 죽고 싶냐!
살고 싶지 않아요.	I don't want to live anymore.
살게!	① [식사 전] Let me treat you. (내가~) // I will buy you dinner. (내가 저녁~) ② [식사 후] I will pay the bill. = **It's on me.** (내가~) ③ [물건] I'll get it. = I'll buy it. (그것을 ~)
살까?	Do you think I have to buy/get it? ➡ ⓐ Sure. It looks good. (그래, 물건 좋아 보인다.) ⓑ No. Don't. (아니야, 사지마.)

ㅅ

ㅅ

살려주세요.	① [구조요청] Help! Help me, please! ② [용서] Forgive me, please. = Please have mercy on me. = Please save me. ③ [석방] Please let me go.
살살 다루세요.	Treat it gently. = Handle it gently. = Handle it with special care.
살살 좀 해!	① [상처부위를 만짐] Softly, please! = Gently, please! ② [일을 쉬어가며] Take it easy! = Do it slowly! ③ [물건 운반] Gently, please!
살살해주세요.	[선처] This is the first time, so please don't be too harsh. (이번이 처음이니, ~)
살았다.	[안도] What a relief!
살얼음판을 걷는 기분이야.	I feel like I'm skating on thin ice. = I don't feel safe at all. = I'm feeling so insecure.
살짝 알려줘.	Whisper it in my ear. (나에게만~)
살쪘다!	You've gained some weight! (너~) // He/She is too fat. = He/She is too overweight. (저 사람 너무~)
살찝니다.	① I'm growing fat. = I'm putting on weight continuously. (계속~) ② (그런 음식은) Such food makes you fat.
살코기 주세요.	I want some meat.
살펴가세요.	[작별인사] Bye. = Take care. // Take care of yourself! (잘~)

삼

삼가 조의를 표합니다.	I'd like to offer my condolences. = Please accept my deepest condolences.
삼가세요.	Refrain yourself from it. = Quit drinking. = You must be on your guard against drinking. = You have to keep from drinking. (술을~)
삼세판으로 합시다.	Let's make it the best of three games. = To win, you must beat me two out of three times.
삼십 분이나 늦었어요.	You are thirty minutes late.

삽

삽니까?	① [동네] Where do you live? (어디에~) ➡ I live in Mok-dong. (목동에요.) ② [주소] What is your address? ➡ My address is 107[one-o-seven], Saemaeul Road, Seoul. = I live at 107[one-o-seven], Saemaeul Road, Seoul. (서울 새마을길 107호요.)
삽시간에 퍼졌어요.	The rumor spread like wildfire. (소문이~)

샀

샀습니까?	Where did you buy it? (어디서~) ➡ I bought it at a shop. (상점에서 샀습니다.)
샀습니다.	I bought it.

상

상관없는 일입니다.	It has nothing to do with me. (이건 저와~)

상관없습니다.	① [선택] **I don't care.** = It doesn't matter.
	= Anything is okay.
	= It doesn't make any difference.
	= I have no preference. (어느 쪽도~)
	② [장애물] That is nothing to be concerned about. = That is no obstacle at all.
	= I don't care about it.
	= That is okay to me.
	= I don't mind it at all. (그런 것이 있어도~)
	☞ 괜찮습니다.
	③ [관계없음] **It has nothing to do with me.** (그건 나와~)
	// This has nothing to do with me. (이건 나와~)
	// This has nothing to do with you.
	= This is none of your business. (이건 당신과~)

상관하지 마! // 상관하지 마세요.	[간섭 · 참견] **Keep your hands off!** = None of your business. = Stop poking your nose into my business.
상다리가 부러지다.	All kinds of delicacies are on the table.
상대가 안 됩니다.	[적수] He is no match for me. = I do not consider him a rival. = He is not a rival for me. = I am a lot more than a match for him. (그는 나한테~)
상대가 되겠냐?	Do you think you can be a match for me? (네가 내~) ➡ Sure, I can. (물론이죠.)
상대하지 마세요.	Don't deal with him. = He is not the person to deal with. (그를~)
상사병에 걸렸어요.	The love bug has bitten me. = I'm lovesick.

상상도 못했습니다.	I couldn't even imagine it. = It's beyond my imagination.
상상에 맡길게.	I will leave it up to your imagination. // I will let you imagine the rest. = The rest is up to your imagination. (나머지는~)
상세히 좀 말씀해보세요.	① Elaborate on it. = Elaborate. = Give me more explanations. (더~) ② Give me the details. = Be more specific. (자세히~)
상심하지 마세요.	[위로] Don't be so sad. = Don't be so broken-hearted. = Don't take it too hard/harsh on yourself.
상영은 몇 시에 합니까?	What time does the movie start? (그 영화~) ➡ It starts at seven in the evening. (저녁 7시요.)
상의합시다.	Let's talk it over. = Let's discuss it together.(우리~) // Let's talk it over later. (다음에 다시~)
상전벽해.	〈직역〉 Mulberry plantations have changed into a sea. ☞ 세상은 돌고 돈다.
상점 좀 둘러보자!	Let's look around some shops! = Let's go window-shopping!
상점은 몇 시에 문을 닫습니까?	What time does the shop close? ➡ ⓐ We never close. (이 상점은 문을 닫지 않습니다.) ⓑ We're open twenty-four hours. = We're open around the clock. (24시간 영업합니다.)
상처 받지 마세요.	Don't get yourself hurt. // Don't be offended. I didn't mean to hurt you. (내 말에~. 상처주려는 의도는 아니었어요.)
상점은 어디에 있습니까?	Where is the shop? = Where can I find the shop? (그~)

ㅅ

	➡ It's across this street to the north. (이 도로 북쪽입니다.)
상점을 돌아다닙니다.	I go around some shops when I get bored. = I go window-shopping when I have nothing to do. (심심할 때~)
상점이 있습니까?	Is there a shop near here? (이 근처에~)
상황을 봐서요.	It depends on the situation. = Let's see what happens. (그건~)
상황이 이렇게 된 겁니다.	That's the way things have worked out.

새

새 가슴이구나!	You are a coward! = What a chicken! = You are as timid as a rabbit!
새 발의 피야.	It is a drop in the bucket. (그건~)
새것으로 교환해 주시면 됩니다.	I'd just like to exchange it for a new one.
새끼야!	〈비속어〉 You the brat! = Hey, jackass!
새로 산 옷입니다.	These are newly bought clothes. = I bought these clothes today. (이거 오늘~)
새로운 마음으로 시작해 봅시다.	Let's turn over a new leaf. = Let's start over.
새벽에 잠들었어요.	① [잠자리에 듦] I went to bed at dawn. ② [잠에 빠져 듦] I fell asleep at dawn. // I couldn't sleep until dawn. (내내 못자다가~)
새빨간 거짓말!	That's a downright lie! = That's an absolute lie! = That's absolutely not true. = You are an out-and-out liar!

새옹지마.	Inscrutable are the ways of Heaven.
새집으로 이사한 거 축하합니다.	Congratulations on your new house!
새치기하지 마세요.	Don't cut in. = Don't butt in (line)!
새파랗게 어린것이!	How could a young kid like you do such a thing! = How dare you! You were just born yesterday!
새해 복 많이 받으세요.	Happy New Year. = I wish you a happy new year.
새해에 건강하세요.	I wish you a healthy new year.
새해에 무슨 계획 있습니까?	What are your new year's resolutions? = Have you made any vows for the new year? ➡ I have nothing like that. (새 계획 같은 거 없습니다.)
새해에는 무슨 소망 있습니까?	Do you have any new year's wishes? ➡ I just wish to be healthy. = I just hope I will be healthy. (몸만 건강하길 바랍니다.)
새해에는 좋은 일만 생기길 바랍니다.	I wish you good luck with everything in the new year.

색

색깔을 가장 좋아합니까?	What color do you like the most? = What is your favorite color? (어떤~) ➡ I like red the most. = Red is my favorite. (빨간색을 가장 좋아합니다.) **색깔의 종류** black (검은색) white (흰색) gray (회색) purple (자주색) blue (푸른색) pink (분홍색) yellow (노란색) green (녹색)

색깔이 너무 어둡습니다.	The color is too dark.
색깔이 너무 진합니다.	The color is too dark.
색깔이 너무 화려합니다.	The color is too loud.
색깔이 더 어울립니까?	① What color goes better with it? (어느~) ➡ I think the red. (빨간색이요.) ② [옷을 고를 때] What color looks better on me?
색시가 고우면 처가집 말뚝보고 절을 한다.	Love me, love my dog.

샌

샌드위치 만들어 왔어요.	Here are some homemade sandwiches. = I made sandwiches and brought them here. = Here are sandwiches that I made on my own.

샘

샘플 있습니까?	[견본품] Do you have a sample? ☞ 견본 있습니까?

생

생각 안 납니까?	You don't remember me? (저~) ➡ Ah, now I remember. (아, 이제 생각납니다.)
생각 없습니다.	[식사] I don't feel like eating. (밥~) ➡ You have to eat! (밥 먹어야지!)
생각 잘했다!	[선택에 대한 칭찬] That sounds like a good idea!

	= You made the right decision! = Excellent choice!
생각 중입니까?	What are you thinking? = What's on your mind now? (무슨~) ➡ I'm thinking about how to improve our company. (회사발전이요.)
생각 중입니다.	① I'm thinking. ② I'm still thinking. I'm not decided. (결정 못하고, 아직~) ③ [선택 고려 중] That's one possibility. (그것을~)
생각나는 대로 말해봐.	Speak your thoughts to me.
생각났어요.	① [기억남] I remember it. (그것이~) // Now I remember it. (이제~) ② [아이디어] A good idea hit on/upon me. = A good idea came to me. = A good idea dawned on me. (좋은 생각이~)
생각도 그렇습니다.	[동의] My thoughts exactly. = That is what I was thinking. = I totally agree with you. = You took the words right out of my mouth. = I see eye to eye with you on it. = I have the same opinion with you. = We think the same way. (내~) ☞ 생각이 똑같네요. // 생각이 저와 똑같습니다.
생각도 못한 일입니다.	This is beyond my thoughts. = This is beyond my imagination. = I never expected this. (이건 정말~)
생각만 해도 소름끼쳐.	The very thought turns me pale. = The very thought grosses me out. = Just thinking about it gives me the creeps.
생각보다 별로야.	It's not as good as I thought. = It's not as good as I expected. (내~)
생각에 변함이 없습니까?	Haven't you changed your opinion? ➡ Do I have to? (왜 바꿔야 하죠?)

생각에 빠져 있었어요.	① I was lost in thought. = I was lost in my thoughts. ② [몽상] I was daydreaming.
생각을 바꿨습니다.	I changed my mind.
생각이 너무 짧았습니다.	I didn't think fully about that.
생각이 똑같네요.	You have the same opinion as me. = I have the same opinion as you. = I see eye to eye with you. = Great minds think alike. ☞ 생각도 그렇습니다.
생각이 삐딱해!	① Your thoughts are defiant! ② [비난] You have a very negative way of thinking! = You don't see things straight!
생각이 있습니다.	[방법] I have an idea.
생각이 저와 똑같습니다.	We think the same way. = We speak the same language. ☞ 생각도 그렇습니다.
생각이 틀렸습니다.	Your opinion is wrong. = Your way of thinking is wrong. = You've got it wrong. (당신의~) // I was wrong. (내~)
생각하는 대로 말하세요.	Say what's on your mind. = Give me the bottom line. = Come out with it. = Tell me straight out. (숨기지 말고~)
생각한 대로야.	[예상이 빗나가지 않음] It's exactly what I thought. = It's exactly as I thought. = It's exactly what I predicted. = It's exactly as I predicted. (내가~)
생각할수록 혼란스럽습니다.	The more I think, the more confused I am.
생각할 일이 너무 많아.	① I have so many things to think about. ② [고민이 많음] I have a lot of things on my mind.

	= Many things are weighing heavily on my mind. = I've got so many worries.
생각해 볼 시간 좀 주세요.	Give me some time to think about it.
생각해보겠습니다.	① I will think about it. = Let me think about it. = I'll give it a thought. // I'll think about it, so go back and wait. (~돌아가서 좀 기다리세요.) ② [심사숙고] Let me sleep on it. (좀더~)
생각해보세요.	① Think about it. = Give it some thought. (좀~) ② Give it a second look. (다시 좀~) ③ [심사숙고] Sleep on it. ④ [권유] Look at it this way. (이렇게 한번~)
생각해봐야겠습니다.	① I think I have to think about it. = I think that's food for thought. ② I need to think about it more. (좀더~) ➡ What? Do you still need to think about it more? (뭐라고, 아직도 좀 더 생각해봐야한다고?)
생각해봤습니다.	① I thought about it. ② [심사숙고] I gave it a long thought. = I slept on it a long time. ③ [고려] I gave it some consideration.
생겼습니까?	[생김새] How does she look? = What does she look like? (그녀는 어떻게~) ➡ ⓐ She looks just average. = She is just average. = She is just an average girl. (보통입니다.) ⓑ Pretty good. (그런대로요.)
생겼습니다.	① [없던 것이] It just came out of nowhere. (그냥~) ② [임신] She's pregnant. (그녀에게 아이가~) ③ [여자] She looks beautiful. = She is pretty. (예쁘게 ~)

ㅅ

	④ [남자] He's good-looking.= He is handsome. = He's attractive. (잘 ~)
생긴 꼬락서니하고는!	[모욕] Look at you! How dreadful you are! = How ugly!
생긴 대로 논다니까!	His actions match his appearance! (그는~)

생김새가 어떻습니까?	What does he look like? (그 사람~)
	// How does she look? (그녀~)
	➡ ⓐ Just average. (보통입니다.)
	ⓑ Looks good. (괜찮습니다.)
	ⓒ He is handsome. (잘생겼습니다.) (그는~)
	// She is beautiful. (예쁩니다.) (그녀는~)

생리 중입니다.	I'm on my period. = I have my period.
생리대 좀 사다주세요.	Can you buy me some (maxi) pads?
생사람 잡다.	You are doing an innocent person an injury.
생선이 싱싱합니까?	Are the fish fresh? ➡ They are newly caught, so very fresh. (방금 잡아 올려서, 당연히 싱싱하죠.)
생수 있습니까?	① Have you got mineral water? ② Do you have bottled water? (병에 들어있는~)
생일 축하합니다.	Happy birthday! = Congratulations on your birthday!
생일선물입니다.	This is a birthday gift for you.
생일은 언제입니까?	When is your birthday? ➡ My birthday is the twenty-ninth of April. = April twenty-ninth. (내 생일은 4월 29일입니다.)
생일파티를 엽시다.	Let's have a birthday party. // Let's have a birthday party tonight. (오늘저녁에~)

생트집 잡지 마세요.	Stop giving me a hard time. = Stop picking fault with me.
생활에 익숙합니까?	[적응] Are you adjusting well here? (여기~) ➡ Not so bad. (그런대로요.)

샤

샤워 중입니다.	He is in the shower. (그는~)
샤프(#) 버튼을 누르세요.	Press the pound button. ☞ 우물정자(#) 버튼을 누르세요.

서

서늘해졌습니다.	It got cooler. (날씨가~) // It is cooler these days. (요즘~)
서당 개 3년이면 풍월을 읊는다.	The sparrows near the school sing the primer.
서두르자!	① [동작] Let's go fast! ② [준비] Let's hurry up!
서두르지 마세요.	Don't hurry. = Don't be in a hurry. = Take your time. = Don't rush. = No need to rush. = Don't jump the gun.
서두르지 말고, 천천히 해!	Do not hurry! Slow down!
서둘러!	Hurry up! = Shake a leg! = Make it snappy! = Step on it! = Get a move on! ☞ 빨리 좀 해!
서둘러주세요.	Will you please hurry up a little? = Will you please do it a little quicker? = Please hurry. (조금만~)

ㅅ

서로 인사 나누세요.	① Why don't you greet each other? ② [소개] Introduce yourself to each other.
서류가 필요합니까?	What documents do I need? (어떤~) ➡ A copy of your identification card. (신분증 복사본 하나요.)
서류는 이력서와 신분증 복사본 한 부입니다.	All you need is a resume and a copy of your identification card.
서리가 내립니다.	We've got frost here this time of the year. (이 맘 때쯤~)
서먹서먹하네요.	It feels like we are apart from each other. // It feels very awkward to be here. (여기 있는 게~)
서명해주세요.	I need your signature here. (여기~)
서비스는 너무 엉망입니다.	The service is terrible here. = The service sucks here. (여기~)
서비스입니다.	This is on the house. = This is a free gift. = This is free of charge. (이것은~) ☞ 공짜입니다. 무료로 증정합니다.
서슬이 퍼렇다.	① 〈직역〉 The knife has a sharp edge. (그 칼은~) ② [기세 등등] He has a threatening attitude. (그는~)
서울에 살고 있습니다.	I live in Seoul.
서울 가서 김 서방 찾기 하는 거야.	[정말 찾기 힘든 것] You are looking for a needle in a haystack.
서투른 장인이 연장 탓 한다.	[속담] A bad workman always blames his tools.
서툴러요.	I'm not good at it. = I'm clumsy with it. = I'm very awkward with it. // I'm all thumbs when it comes to typing. (전 타이핑이~)

선

선곡할게요.	[노래방] I will choose a song. = Let me choose a song.
선량합니다.	He is a clean sheet. = He is a good-natured person. (그는 매우~)
선무당이 사람 잡는다.	A little knowledge is a dangerous thing.
선물을 하나 하고 싶습니다.	I want to give you a present today. (오늘 당신에게~)
선생님, 안녕하세요?	① [남자 선생님께] Hello, sir! // [연배 있는 여자 선생님께] Hello, ma'am. ② [남자 선생님께] Hello, Mr. Jang! (장~) // [여자 선생님께] Hello, Ms. Jang. (장~)
선생님이 되려고 합니다.	① [계획] I am going to become a teacher. ② [바람] I want to be a teacher.
선약이 있습니다.	① [지인과의 약속] I have a plan. ② [병원이나 미용실 등의 예약된 약속] I have another appointment. // I'm sorry, but I have another appointment. (미안하지만~)
선착순.	First come, first served. // It is for the first twenty people to come. (~20명입니다.)
선착순입니다.	It's on a first-come-first-served basis. = It's first-come-first-served.
선택 잘 했어요.	You made the right choice. = Good choice!

선택의 여지가 없습니다.	I have no other choice. (달리~)
	// I don't have any other choice than this.
	(이것외에는~)
	// We have no choice. (저희들은~)

선택해!	Choose! // Pick one! (하나~)

ㅅ

선풍기를 씁시다.	Let's turn on the fan first. (우선~)

설

설 // 설날	New Year's Day ☞ 구정
설거지 내가 할게.	Let me wash the dishes. = Let me do the dishes.
설교하지 마세요.	Stop preaching. = Stop lecturing.
설마!	That cannot be! = Impossible! = Unbelievable! = No kidding! = You must be kidding!
설마가 사람 잡아.	Never say never. = You think it is impossible, but it really happens. = Saying never can ruin a man.
설사합니다.	I have diarrhea. = I've got the runs. = I have the runs. = I've got diarrhea.
설상가상.	It's making matters worse. = It's adding insult to injury. ☞ 엎친 데 덮친 격이군!
설탕 넣을까요?	Would you like some sugar in it? ➡ Just a little bit. (조금 만요.)

섭

섭섭합니다.	① [실망] I'm disappointed. // You disappointed me. (당신에게~) ② [유감] I'm so sorry that I've got to be going. (일찍 가게 되어~)
섭섭하지 않게 해드릴게요.	You won't get disappointed.

성

성가시게 하네.	You're really bothering me. (정말 사람~) // It's a real nuisance. = It's a pain in the neck. (그것 참~)
성격이 너무 좋습니다.	① He has a good personality. = He is a very nice person. = He is very friendly. (그는~) ② [시원시원한 성격] He has an easy-going and cool personality. (그는~)
성격이 좀 화끈합니다.	① [정열적] He is enthusiastic. = He is very passionate. = He is full of enthusiasm. (그는~) ② [뒤끝 없는] He doesn't hold a grudge. = He is open-hearted. (그는~)
성공적이었습니다.	It was successful. = It was a success. = We came through with flying colors.
성공하시길 빕니다.	① I wish you success. = I hope you will succeed. // I hope you will succeed abroad, too. (외국에서도~) ② [공연이나 연주] Break a leg!
성공할 겁니다.	You will succeed. = You are going to pull it off.
성공해서 돌아오세요.	Come back with success. // Come back with success soon. (하루 빨리~)
성급하게 결론 내지 마세요.	Don't jump to any conclusions. = Don't jump the gun.
성급하면 손해입니다.	Haste makes waste.
성내지 마세요.	Don't be mad. = Don't be angry. = Don't freak out.

ㅅ

성씨가 어떻게 되십니까?	What is your last name? = What is your family name?
성의 표시니 받아주세요.	This is a token of my gratitude, so take it, please. ➡ ⓐ Thank you. You didn't have to bother to prepare this. (뭘 이런 걸 다.) ⓑ No, thank you. I'm not taking anything. (관두세요.)
성적표가 나왔어요.	I got my report card today. = I got my grades today. (오늘~)
성질 건드리지 마!	Don't get on my nerves! = Stop hitting my nerves! = Don't get up my nose!
성질 머리하고는! // 성질 한 번 더럽네!	You are so hot-tempered. = You are so quick to get angry.
성질이 급합니다.	I'm short-tempered.
성질이 좀 더러워요.	He is a little ill-natured. (그는~)
성질이야!	He is so quick to pick a fight! = He is always ready to fight! (그는 툭하면~)
성탄을 축하합니다.	Merry Christmas! ☞ 메리 크리스마스!
성함을 여쭤 봐도 될까요?	Excuse me, may I ask your name? = Excuse me, can I have your name, please? (실례지만~) ➡ Sure. I'm Gim Daemyeong. (물론이지요, 저는 김대명 입니다.)
성함이 어떻게 되십니까?	What is your name? ➡ ⓐ My name is Gim Myeong. (제 이름은 김명입니다.) ⓑ My first name is Myeong, and my last name is Gim. (성은 김이고, 이름은 명입니다.)

성형 수술했어요?	Have you gotten a face-lift? = Did you get a face-lift? = Did you go under the knife for plastic surgery? ➡ Never. I was born with this. = I'm all-natural. = I'm 100% natural. (100% 자연산이요.)

섶

섶을 지고 불 속으로 뛰어들다.	Jump into flames with an oil barrel.

세

세관신고서를 작성했습니다.	I filled out the declaration form.

세부적인 것은 생략해.	Cut out all the details.
	// Don't be too specific. (너무 자세히 말하지 마.)
	// Make it simple. = Cut it short. (간단히 말해.)

세 살 버릇 여든까지 간다.	[속담] Old habits die hard. = A leopard cannot change his spots.
세상 말세다, 말세야!	This world is going to the dogs!
세상 물정을 몰라.	You don't know much about the world. = You're out of touch with society. (너는~)
세상 일이 다 그렇죠 뭐.	That's life.
세상 참 좁다!	What a small world! = What a small world we live in!
세상에!	[감탄] What on earth! = My god!
세상에 공짜는 없다.	There's no such thing as a free lunch.

ㅅ

세상에는 별별 사람이 다 있다.	There are all sorts of people in all sorts of conditions in the world.
세상은 돌고 돈다.	The wheel is come full circle.
세상을 떠났습니다.	① He died. (그는 ~) ② [정중한 표현] He passed away. (그 분은~) ③ [비유적 표현] He left the world. = He went to his eternal home. = He went back to Mother Earth. (그는 ~) ④ 〈구어〉 He kicked the bucket. = He sank to the grave.
세상이 다 네 거야.	The world is yours. = The world is at your doorstep. = The world is your oyster.
세수하고 싶은데.	I want to wash my face.
세숫비누는 어디에 있습니까?	Where is the facial soap? = Can you see the facial soap? ➡ Isn't it that one? (그거 아니냐?)
세어보세요.	Count them.
세워주세요.	[자동차] Pull over, please. (옆쪽에~) // Stop here for a second, please. = Hold it up for a moment, please. (여기서 잠깐~)
세월은 사람을 기다려주지 않는다.	Time and tide wait for no man.
세월이 약이다.	Time heals everything. = Time cures everything.
세월이 참 빠르다.	Time flies. = Time flies like an arrow.
세일됩니까?	Can I get a discount on it? ➡ You can get a twenty percent discount. (20% 할인됩니다.)
세일합니까?	Is it on sale? ➡ It's on sale. (세일합니다.)

ㅅ

	// You can take this product forty percent off the regular price. (이 상품은 40% 세일합니다.)
세제를 다 썼습니다.	We ran out of detergent. // We ran out of laundry powder. (세탁용~)
세차는 얼마입니까?	How much does it cost to have my car washed? ➡ It's ten dollars. (10달러입니다.)
세탁서비스를 부탁합니다.	I'd like a laundry service.
세탁소는 어디에 있습니까?	Where is the drycleaner's? = Where is the drycleaner? ➡ It's on the main street outside. (바로 바깥 큰길에 있습니다.)
세탁소에 맡기세요.	Take it to a drycleaner's
세탁소에 맡기려고 합니다.	I'm going to take it to a drycleaner's.
세트메뉴에 커피는 들어갑니까?	Does the value meal include coffee? = Does the combo meal include coffee?

섹

섹시하다!	Sexy! = Foxy! = Hot!
	// She's so sexy! (그녀는 정말~)
	// The clothes look so sexy! (옷이 너무~)

센

센 개 꼬리 시궁창에 삼 년 묻었다 보아도 센 개 꼬리다. // 개 꼬리 삼 년 두어도 황모 못 된다.	[속담] You can't make a silk purse out of a sow's ear. = A crow is never the white for washing herself.

셋

셋째입니다.	The third one. // I'm the third one. (저는~)

셔

셔츠를 사고 싶은데요.	I'd like to buy the shirt. = I want to buy the shirt.
셔터를 누르면 됩니다.	[카메라] Just press the button.

ㅅ

소

소 잃고 외양간 고치기네.	① [속담] To lock the stable door after the horse is stolen. = After death, the doctor. = To cover the well after the child has been drowned in it. ② After death comes a doctor. = Prescription after death. = While men go after a leech, the body is buried. ☞ 사후약방문.
소개하겠습니다.	I'd like to introduce myself first. (제가 먼저~) // I'd like to introduce my family. (우리 가족을 ~)
소개해 줄래요?	Would you introduce that person to me? (저 분을 저에게~)
소경 문고리 잡은 듯.	[속담] A blind man may sometimes catch the hare.
소고기요리를 주세요.	Would you give me beef. = Let me have beef. // Would you please give me beef? (정말이지~)
소금을 건네주세요.	Please pass me the salt.

소란 피우지 마!	Don't make a fuss! = Don't make trouble! = Don't cause troubles!
소리 내지 마!	Don't make a sound! = **Hush!** = Quiet!
소리 좀 높여주세요.	[라디오 등] Would you turn up the volume?
소리 좀 크게 해주세요.	Speak louder, please. = Louder, please. = Raise your voice, please.
소리치지 마!	① Don't shout! = Don't yell! ② [공포 등에 질려 내는 소리를 금지] Don't scream!
소매치기 당했어요.	I got pickpocketed. = I had a pickpocket take my money. // I got pickpocketed in the bus. (버스에서~)
소매치기 조심하세요.	Beware of pickpockets.
소문난 잔치에 먹을 것 없다.	[속담] Great boast and small roast.
소문 내지 마세요.	Don't start rumors. = Don't spread rumors. // Don't spread rumors anymore. (더는~)
소변보러 갔어요.	He went to the restroom. (그는~)
소식이 있으면 바로 연락해주세요.	Please let me know if you have any news.
소심하구나!	① [소심하고 마음이 좁음] How timid! ② [겁 등이 많음] Coward! ☞ 겁이 많구나!
소용없습니다.	[효과 · 용도] It's useless. = It doesn't work out. = It's hopeless.
소원 빌어요!	**Make a wish!** ➡ I am doing it. (빌고 있습니다.)
(소주) 한 병 주세요.	Give me a bottle of wine. = Let me have a bottle of wine.
소지품을 맡기는 곳이 있습니까?	Is there any place where I can leave my stuff? ➡ Yes. (예.)

ㅅ

소질이 있어요.	You've got what it takes. = You've got talent. // My sister has musical talent. = My sister has a very good ear for music. (제 동생은 음악에 ~)
소탐대실.	To incur a great loss by pursuing a small profit. = To suffer a big loss in going after a small gain.
소파에 앉으세요.	Please sit on the sofa. // Please sit on this sofa. (이쪽~) ➡ I can sit on the chair. (의자에 앉으면 돼요.)
소화불량 같습니다.	I have indigestion.
소화불량에 듣는 약을 주세요.	Please give me medicine for indigestion. = Would you give me medicine for indigestion?

속

속 보인다!	① I can read your mind! ② You're revealing yourself!
속단하지 마세요.	Don't make a hasty decision. = Don't jump to a conclusion. = Don't jump to conclusions.
속상해요.	① [분노] I'm upset. ② [슬픔] I'm not in a good mood. = I feel down. = I'm sad. // I'm so sad. (정말~)
속셈이야?	What the hell are you thinking now? (무슨~) ➡ What? (무슨 속셈은?)
속이 다 시원하다!	I feel so relieved!
속이 불편합니다.	I don't feel OK. = I don't feel good. = I feel uncomfortable.

속이냐?	Are you deceiving me? = Are you cheating me? (날~) ➡ ⓐ I don't know that kind of thing. (난 사람 속일 줄 몰라요.) ⓑ No, I'm not! (속이지 않았어요!)
속지 마세요.	Please don't get deceived. = Please don't be tricked.
속히 연락주세요.	Please contact me as soon as possible.

손

손 내보세요.	Give me your hand. = Hand forward.
손 놓으세요.	① [일반적인 경우] Let go of my hand. ② [상대방이 손으로 잡고 있음] Hands off!
손 놔요!	① [손을 잡고 있는 경우] Don't hold my hand! = Let go of my hand! ② [몸이 잡고 있는 경우] Let me go! = Don't hold me! = Get off me!
손 뗄래요.	I'm off now.
손 씻고 와라.	Wash your hands.
손 씻었어요.	I washed my hands.
손 이리 내!	Give me your hands!
손재주가 좋아요.	I'm good with my hands. // She's quite good with her hands. (그녀는 참 ~)
손 좀 봐줘라.	[혼내줌] Take care of this bastard! (이놈~)
손 좀 줘봐!	Give me your hand. = Let me see your hand.
손 치워!	Take your hands off! = Hands off! // Hands off now! (얼른~)

ㅅ

손 펴봐!	Open up your hands!
손가락 걸어!	[약속] Pinky swear! = Pinky promise!
손가락이 따끔 거립니다.	My fingers feel itchy.
손님 오셨습니다.	You've got a visitor. = Someone wants to see you.
손님이 찾습니다.	Someone has been waiting for you. // Someone has been waiting for you there. (저쪽에~)
손님 접대중입니다.	She's waiting on her visitor. (그녀는~)

손대지 마세요.	① [사물에] Don't touch! = Hands off!
	= Keep your hands off.
	// Keep your hands off it. (그것에~)
	// Keep your hands off the artifacts here. (여기 작품에~)
	② [쓸데없는 짓을 더하는 경우] Don't be disruptive anymore! (더 이상~)
	③ 〈경고문〉 Don't touch!

손도 굳었어요.	My hands got stiff. // My hands got frozen stiff. (너무 추워서~)
손도 대지 않았어요.	I didn't even touch. // I didn't even touch at all. (전혀~)
손들어!	Hands up! = Put your hands up! = Raise your hands.
손들었다!	① [항복] I surrender! = I give up! // You win! = I surrender to you. (너한테~) ☞ 졌다! ② [손을 올림] I raised my hands!
손목을 삐었어요.	I've got a sprained wrist. = My wrist is sprained. = I sprained my wrist.
손바닥 뒤집듯 쉽다.	It's a piece of cake. ☞ 누워서 떡먹기야.

손으로 더듬어봐.	Fumble for it.
손을 데었습니다.	My hand got burned. = I got a burn on my hand. = I burned my hand.

솔

솔직히 말해(봐)!	Be honest! = Speak honestly! = Give it straight to me! = Give it to me straight! = Open up to me!

송

송구스럽게 생각합니다.	I'm so impressed. = I'm so honored.
송별회를 해드리겠습니다.	I'll throw a farewell party.

쏼

쏼라쏼라!	[외국인 떠드는 소리] Blah, blah, blah!

쇠

쇠귀에 경 읽기.	[속담] To sing psalms to a dead horse. = To whistle psalms to the taffrail. = To knock at a deaf man's door.
쇠뿔도 단김에 빼라.	[속담] Strike the iron while it is hot. = Hoist your sail when the wind is fair. = What's worth doing is worth doing promptly.

쇼

쇼 하니?	[시침 떼기] Are you doing this for show? ➡ Sort of. (조금은요.)
쇼크입니다.	It's a shock! = It's totally a surprise!
쇼킹했어요.	It's shocking! = It's astonishingly surprising.
쇼핑백이 필요하십니까?	Do you need a bag? ➡ Yes, please. (예.)
쇼핑하고 싶습니다.	I wanna go shopping. // I wanna go shopping in other department stores. (다른 백화점에 가서~)
쇼핑해요.	Let's go shopping. = Let's go to shop! // Let's go shopping together. (우리 같이~)

ㅅ

수

수건으로 얼굴 닦으세요.	Wipe your face with the towel. // Wipe your face with this towel. (이~)
수고 많았습니다.	I appreciate what you have done. Well done. = Thank you for your work. You've done a good job. = Thank you for your work. Good job. // I appreciate what you have done so far. (그동안~) ➡ Sure. = No problem. (천만에요.)
수고들했습니다. // 수고하셨습니다!	Thank you for your trouble. = Thank you so much for your hard work. = Thanks for a job well done.
수고해!	Thanks for your work! = Thanks for your job! = Thanks for your trouble!
수고해주세요.	Thank you for your trouble.

	➡ ⓐ You're welcome. (천만에요.) ⓑ This is my work. = This is my job. = This is my responsibility. (제가 할 일인데요.)
수고해주셔서 감사합니다.	① Thank you so much for your hard work. ② [국가나 회사 등에] We appreciate what you have done for us. ➡ Don't mention it. (그런 말씀 마세요.)
수고했습니다!	Well done! = Good job! = You've done well! ➡ ⓐ Sure. = You're welcome. = No problem. = Not at all. = It's nothing. (천만에요.) ⓑ Don't mention it. (별말씀을요.)
수다 좀 그만 떨어!	Stop chatting! // Stop talking to me! (나한테~) // Stop talking to your father. (네 아버지에게~)
수리 좀 해주세요.	Would you repair it?
수리 중입니까?	Under construction? // Is the street ahead under construction? (앞쪽에는 길을~) ➡ ⓐ The street is under construction. (길을 수리 중입니다.) ⓑ The road is under construction. (도로를 수리중입니다.)
수박 겉핥기지요.	It's shallow. = It's superficial.
수속 서류가 부족합니다.	Not enough documents for processing. // You don't have enough documents for processing. (당신의~)
수속은 다 끝났습니다.	Your processing is all done.
수수료는 4% 받습니다.	The fee is 4 percent.
수수합니다.	[옷이] The clothing is plain. = The clothing is humble.

ㅅ

ㅅ

수술해야 합니다.	You need an operation. // You need an operation right now. (즉시~)
수신인의 주소는 아래쪽에 쓰세요.	Please write the recipient's address at the bottom.
수신자 부담입니다.	① [개인전화] It's a collect call. ② [회사 등에 거는 전화] It's toll-free.
수업은 몇 시에 시작해요?	When does the class begin? = When does the class start? ➡ At eight-thirty. (오전 8시 반요.)
수업을 마칩니다.	The class is over. = The class is finished. // The class is over now. (지금~)
수업을 몇 교시합니까?	How many classes do you have? ➡ Four classes. (4교시합니다.)
수업을 빼먹었습니다.	I skipped a class. = I didn't go to class.
수업하러 가니?	[인사] Are you going to class? = Are you heading to class?
수염이 석자라도 먹어야 양반이다.	[속담] Pudding rather than praise. = The belly has no ears.
수영을 못합니다.	I can't swim. = I don't know how to swim. = I'm not good at swimming.
수영을 잘합니까?	Are you good at swimming? = Can you swim well? ➡ ⓐ Yes. (잘합니다.) ⓑ Just so so. (보통입니다.) ⓒ Not well. (잘 못합니다.) ⓓ Not at all. (못합니다.)
수영을 잘합니다.	I'm good at swimming. = I can swim well.
수영을 할 줄 모릅니다.	I can't swim well. = I'm not good at swimming. = I don't know how to swim.

수입은 어떻습니까?	How's your salary? = How's your pay? // How much money do you make a month? (한 달 봉급은~) ➡ About three thousand dollars a month. (한 달에 삼천달러 정도요.)
수작 부리지 마!	① Don't play dirty! = Stop the nonsense! = Don't be silly! = Stop being silly! ② Don't screw around! ③ [아첨] Don't flatter her! (그 여자한테 ~) = Don't butter her up! (그녀한테~)
수작이야?	What the hell is going on? = What the hell are you doing? (무슨~) // What the hell is going on again? = What the hell are you doing again? (또 무슨~) ➡ Cut the crap! (쓸데없는 소리 그만해!)
수줍어하지 마!	① [미안해함] Don't be ashamed! ② [부끄러움] Don't be shy! = Don't be timid!
수표를 현금으로 바꿔주실래요?	Would you exchange this check to cash, please? = Would you change this check to cash, please? = May I cash this check, please? = May I change this check to cash, please? = May I exchange this check for cash, please? ➡ OK. (알겠습니다.)
수프를 먹을래요.	I'd like to have soup.

숙

숙박카드를 작성해주세요.	Please fill out the registration form.
숙제 먼저 하고 놀아라.	Do your homework, and you can play. = Play after you do your homework.

숙제는 다 끝냈습니다.	I have finished my homework. // I've finished the homework assigned by the teacher. = I'm done with the homework from the teacher. (선생님이 내준~)

순

순진한 척 하기는!	Stop pretending you're innocent. = Don't pretend you're naive. = Don't play innocent.

ㅅ

술

술 가져와!	① Give me drinks! = Get me alcohol! = Bring me wine! = Let me have liquor! ② 〈속어〉 Get me booze!
술 끊었어요.	I quit drinking.
술 냄새나!	I can smell the booze on your breath! = You smell like booze!
술 너무 많이 마셨어요.	You've had too much to drink. = You're drunk.
술 따라드리겠습니다.	Let me fill your cup.
술 따르지 마세요.	Don't fill my cup. = I don't want you to fill my cup.
술 마셔도 됩니까?	Can I drink it? ➡ Sure. (물론이지요.)
술 마시면 안 됩니다.	Can't drink. // I can't drink. (저는~)
술 못 마십니다.	I can't drink much. = I'm not into drinking.
술 잘 마십니다.	I like drinking. = I'm into drinking.

술 취했어요.	Got drunk. // He's drunk. (그는 ~)
술 한 잔 사겠습니다.	I'd like to buy you a drink.
술 할 줄 압니다.	I can drink.
술래잡기하자!	Let's play hide and seek! // Let's play hide and seek together! (우리~)
술맛 떨어지네!	I don't wanna drink! // Damn it. I don't wanna drink! (젠장~)
술버릇이 없습니다.	No manners of drinking.
술안주는 뭐로 할까요?	What appetizer would you like to have for wine? = What appetizer do you want for wine? = What do you want to have for wine appetizers? ➡ Let's have some nuts. (마른안주로 하지 뭐.)
술에 약합니다.	I can't drink much.
술이 너무 독합니다.	The drink is too strong.
술잔이 비었다.	My cup is empty.
술주정합니다.	He took too much. (그는~)

숨

숨 막혀요.	I'm chocking. = I can't breathe. = I'm suffocating.
숨 쉬어!	Take a breath! = Breathe! // Take a breath while running! = Breathe while running! (달리다가 ~)
숨 좀 돌리고.	Let me get my breath back.

ㅅ

숨을 깊이 들이쉬세요.	Take a deep breath.
숨이 막힙니다.	I'm chocking. = I'm suffocating. = I can't breathe well.

숭

숭배합니다.	① [존경] I admire you! ② [지나친 사랑] He adores his daughter. (그는 딸을 ~)

ㅅ

쉬

쉬고 싶습니다.	I want to rest. = I need a break.
	// I want to rest for a while.
	= I need a short break. (잠시~)
	// I will rest this week.
	= I will have a break this week. (이번 주에는~)

쉬세요.	① [저녁 취침인사] Rest now.
	② Take a break. = Take a rest. (좀~)
	// Have a short break.
	= Take a rest for a while. (잠시~)
	// Rest well. = Get fully relaxed. (푹 ~)

쉬엄쉬엄 해!	① [일반적인 경우] Take it easy! ② [일 등] Don't work too hard! = Don't work so hard!

쉽

쉽게 믿지 마세요.	Don't be gullible. ☞ 함부로 믿지 마세요.
쉽지 않습니다.	No easy. // This isn't that easy. (이 일은 그리~)

쉿

쉿!	① [의성어] Hush! ② Be quiet! = Silence! ③ [명령] Shut up! ☞ 입 닥쳐!

슈

슈퍼에 가자.	Let's go to the market.

슛

슛!	Shoot!

스

스승의 날을 축하드립니다.	Happy Teacher's Day.
스위치는 어디에 있습니까?	Where's the switch? // Where's the light switch? (등의~) ➡ It's on the left side of the porch. (현관 왼쪽에 있습니다.)
스케이트 좋아합니까?	Do you like skating? = Do you like to go skating? ➡ Yes, I do. (좋아해요.)
스케줄이 빡빡합니다.	My schedule is tight. = I have a tight schedule.
스키를 잘 탑니까?	Can you ski well? // Can he ski well? = Is he a good skier? (그는~) ➡ ⓐ Yes, very well. (잘 탑니다.)

	ⓑ Just average. (보통입니다.) ⓒ Not well. (잘 못 탑니다.) ⓓ Not at all. (못 탑니다.)
스테이크 하나 주세요.	I'd like to have a steak. = Let me have a steak.
스톱!	① [동작] Stop! = Don't move! ② [차] Stop the car!
스트레스가 너무 심합니다.	It's so stressful. = I have too much stress. = I'm stressed out.

습

습관이 됐습니다.	It became a habit. = I'm so used to it.

승

승낙했어요.	① Agreed. ② He said, "Yes." (그가~)
승진을 축하합니다.	Congratulations on your promotion. = I celebrate your promotion. = Good for you. You've got the promotion. ➡ I got promoted. (승진했어요!)
승패를 가리기가 어렵습니다.	① [막상막하] It's difficult to decide who's winning and who's losing. = They're equally great. = They can't compete with each other. ② [결과를 예측 불허] The result is in doubt. = The result is uncertain.

시

시간 다 됐습니다.	Time's up. = It's time.

시간 됐습니다.	[종료] Time is over.
시간 없습니다.	① [여유] I have no time. = I don't have time. = I don't have much time. ② [차 시간에 댈] I'm running short on time. = I don't have enough time. ☞ 시간이 없습니다.
시간 있습니까?	Do you have time? = Are you free? // Do you have time tomorrow? (내일~) ➡ Sorry, but I have something else important planned. = Sorry, but I have something else important going on. (미안합니다, 중요한 일이 있어서요.)

시간 있습니다.	I have time. = I'm free.
	// I will be free tomorrow. (내일은~)
	// I'm free anytime. (언제든지~)

시간 좀 내주세요.	Please spare me some time. = Please spend some time with me. = Please give me a little bit of your time.
시간 지켜라.	① [약속시간] Keep in time. = Be punctual. = Try to be on time. ② [정해진 시간] Keep the time.
시간나면 꼭 연락주세요.	Please contact me when you're free. = Please contact me when you have some time.
시간나면 놀러오세요.	Please stop by when you're free. = Please visit me when you're free. = Please visit me when you have time. = Please come and see me when you have time.
시간나면 또 놀러오세요.	Please come again when you're free. = Please come again when you have time.
시간나면 자주 들르세요.	Please make frequent visits when you're free. = Please make frequent visits when you have time.

ㅅ

ㅅ

시간나면 자주 연락합시다.	Let's get in touch when we are free. = Let's get in touch when we have time.
시간나면 전화주세요.	Please call me when you're free. = Please give me a call when you have a minute.
시간내주세요.	Please make some time for me. = Please set aside a minute for me. = Please give me some time. // Please make sure to make some time for me. (다음에 꼭~)
시간에 늦겠어.	I'm late. = I'm not gonna make it.
시간은 금이다.	Time is gold. = Time is precious. = Time is money.

시간은 얼마나 걸립니까?	How long does it take?
	// How long does it take by train? (기차를 타면~)
	➡ Three hours. (3시간 걸립니다.)
	// How long does it take from Seoul to Daejeon by train?
	(서울에서 대전까지 기차를 타면~)
	➡ About two hours. (2시간 정도 걸립니다.)

시간을 낭비하지 마세요.	Don't waste your time. = Don't squander your time.
시간을 어떻게 보냅니까?	How do you spend your time? ➡ Reading online books. (인터넷으로 소설을 읽습니다.)
시간을 지체하지 마세요.	Don't delay. = Don't be late. = Don't slow down.
시간이 늦었으니 빨리 주무세요.	It's already late. Go to bed. ➡ OK. (알았어요.)
시간이 됩니까?	[기차나 비행기 시간에 댈] ① Can you make it on time? ➡ No, I can't. (제시간에 안 됩니다.)

	② Can you make it now? (지금~) ➡ No, I can't. (제시간에 안 됩니다.)
시간이 많습니다.	I have much time. = I'm so free. // I have much time now. (지금~)
시간이 맞지 않아요.	The time is not correct.
시간이 언제 납니까?	When are you free? = When do you have time? ➡ Tomorrow evening. (내일 저녁이요.)
시간이 없습니다.	① [시간이 임박] Time's up. = It's time. ② [시간이 촉박] We don't have enough time. = We don't have much time. (우리~) ③ [시간이 부족함] We have no time to lose.
시간이 지났습니다.	Time's over. = Time's passed.
시간이 참 빠르네요.	Time is so fast. = Time flies. = Time is as fast as an arrow.
시간이 충분합니다.	[시간적 여유] I have much time. = I have enough time. = I have sufficient time.
시계는 5분 느립니다.	It is running 5 minutes behind. = It is 5 minutes behind. // That watch is running 5 minutes behind. (저~)
시계는 5분 빠릅니다.	It is running 5 minutes fast. = It is 5 minutes fast. // That watch is running 5 minutes fast. (저~)
시끄러워 죽겠네.	I can't stand the noise!
시끄러워!	① [소란스러워서] Quiet! = Be quiet! ② [헛소리] Shut up! = Cut the crap! ③ [잔소리] Cut it out! = Stop lecturing! ④ [짜증남] So noisy!

ㅅ

	⑤ [말을 못하게 함] Don't say a word! = Stop saying! = No more words!

시끄럽다!	① Really noisy! (정말~) // Very noisy!
	= So noisy! (너무~)
	// This place is really noisy! (이곳은 정말~!)
	② Shut up! ☞ 입 닥쳐!

시끌벅적한 것을 좋아합니다.	I like noisy places.
시내 나가세요?	[인사] Are you going downtown?
시내구경 갑시다.	Let's go downtown.
시내구경하고 싶어요.	I'd like to go downtown.
시내에 갑니다.	I'm going downtown. = I'm heading downtown.

시네요.	[맛이] Sour. // This is very sour. (이거 참~)
	// This is so sour. (이거 너무~)
	// This is really sour. (이거 정말~)

시도해 봐!	Give it a try! = Give it a shot! = Try!
시력이 좋지 않습니다.	I have bad sight. = I can't see well.
시무룩합니까?	Are you down? // Why are you so blue? = Why do you have such a long face? (왜 ~)
시범 좀 보여주세요.	Show me first. // Show him first. (걔한테~) ➡ OK. (그래.)
시부모님과 지내기가 힘이 듭니다.	It's difficult to get along with my parents-in-law. = I'm having difficulties getting along with my parents-in-law.
시비 걸지 마세요.	Don't pick quarrels. = Don't cause quarrels. = Don't pick fights. = Don't start arguments.

시시해!	Flat! = Boring! = Not interesting! = Dull!
	= Silly! = Stupid!
	// This book is boring. (이 책은~)
	// This game is boring. (이 게임은 정말~)

시외전화는 어떻게 겁니까?	How can I make a long distance call? ➡ Press the area code first off. (먼저 지역번호를 누르세요.)
시원섭섭해요.	It feels bittersweet. = It's a bittersweet feeling. = My feeling's volleying down between joy and disappointment. = I feel relieved but sorry.
시원한 걸로 마시고 싶습니다.	I'd like something cold. = Let me have something cold. = I want something cold.
시원합니다.	① [기분이] I feel cool. = I feel good. = I feel relieved. ② [날씨가] It's cool. // It's very cool today. (오늘 날씨가 정말~)
시원해!	I feel relieved. = I feel better. // Phew whew, I feel relieved. (어휴~)
시작!	Begin! = Start! = Go!
시작도 안했습니다.	I didn't even start. // I haven't started yet. (아직~)
시작이 반이다.	A good beginning is half the battle. = Well begun is half done.
시작하세요.	Start now. = Begin now.
시작합니까?	Are you starting? // When do you get started? = When will you begin? (몇 시부터~) // When will you start your breakfast? = When will your breakfast get started? (아침 식사는~)

ㅅ

	➡ Are you starting now? (바로~)

시작합니다.	It's starting. = It's ready. = Time to start.
	// It'll get started right now. (바로~)
	// I will start right now. (제가 바로~)
	// I'll start now. (제가 지금~)

시장가세요?	[인사] Are you going to shop? = Are you going shopping?
시장에 사람들이 많습니다.	There are many people in the marketplace.
시장이 반찬이다.	[속담] Hunger is the best sauce.
시장합니까?	Are you hungry? ➡ ⓐ Yes! (예!) ⓑ I'm OK. I can stand it. (그런대로 견딜만합니다.) ⓒ I'm fine now. (괜찮습니다.) ☞ 배고픕니까?
시집 안갑니다.	① I'm not marrying. = I don't wanna get married. ② [고집] I wouldn't get married.
시집가고 싶습니다.	① [소망] I'd like to get married. = I wanna get married. = I hope to get married. ② [간절함] I'm desperate to get married. = I desperately want to get married.
시집갔습니까?	Married? ➡ She's married. = She's taken. (그녀는 시집갔습니다.)
시차적응이 안됩니다.	I'm suffering from jet lag. = I'm jet-lagged. // I'm still suffering from jet lag. (저는 아직~)
시청까지 얼마입니까?	How much is it to the city hall? ➡ One dollar. (1달러입니다.)
시치미 떼지 마세요.	① Don't pretend you don't know it.

	② Don't put on a poker face. ③ Don't hide your true feelings.
시키는 대로 하겠습니다.	① [지시나 배치에 따름] I will do what you want me to do. = I will do whatever you want. ② [명령에 따름] I will do as you said. (그럼~)
시키는 대로 해!	① Do as you're told! // Do as I told you! (내가~) ② Do what you're told!
시팔!	〈비속어〉Fuck! = Shit! = Fuck off! ☞ 씹! // 씹할!
시험 망쳤어!	I messed up on the test. = I failed the test. = I screwed up on the test. = I blewed the test.
시험에 떨어졌어요.	I failed the test. = I messed up on the test.
시험에 통과했습니까?	Did you pass the test? ➡ Yes. (예.)
시험에 합격했어요.	I passed the test.
시험은 어떻게 봤어?	How was the test? ➡ It was OK. (그럭저럭.)
시험은 완전히 망쳤어요.	I totally messed up on the test. = I bombed the test. = I totally failed the test. // I totally messed up on this test. (이번~)
시험이 끝났습니다.	The tests were finished. = I'm done with the tests. // I'm so happy to finish the tests. (기쁘게도~)
시험이 내일입니다.	I have a test tomorrow.

식

식구는 누구누구 있습니까?	Who are there in your family? // Who do you have in your family? (집에는~) ➡ There are Father, Mother and me. (아버님, 어머님 그리고 저입니다.)

ㅅ

식구는 몇입니까?	How many are there in your family? ➡ Dad, Mom, a sister and me. (아빠, 엄마, 누나와 저입니다.)
식기 전에 드세요.	Please eat the food before it becomes cold.
식당에 갑니다.	I'm going to a restaurant.
식당은 몇 시에 문을 엽니까?	When will the restaurant be open? = When is the restaurant open? ➡ At 6 in the morning. (아침 6시요.)
식당이 있습니까?	Any restaurants? // Any restaurants here? (근처에~) ➡ Yes. (있습니다.)
식사 중에 죄송합니다.	I'm sorry to interrupt your meal. = Sorry to bother your meal.
식사 중입니다.	I'm on my meal. = I'm eating now.
식사 후에 디저트도 있습니까?	Do you serve dessert? = Do you have a dessert menu? ➡ Yes. (있습니다.)
식사는 언제합니까?	When will you have a meal? = What time is the meal? ➡ ⓐ Right now. (바로요.) ⓑ Some time later. (더 있다가요.)
식사는 잘합니까?	How's your eating? = Do you eat well? ➡ I hardly eat. (밥을 거의 못 먹어요.)
식사 예약하고 싶습니다.	① [식당 등에 예약] I'd like to make a reservation. = I'd like to reserve some seats. ② I'd like to make a reservation for tonight. (오늘 저녁~)
식사 주문이요.	Order for the meal.
식사 준비 좀 도와줄래요?	Can you help me prepare for the meal? ➡ OK. (그러죠.)

식사 초대는 언제 합니까?	When will you invite us for the meal? ➡ Some time later.
식사하러 갑시다.	Let's go to eat.
식사하러 갈까요?	Shall we go for something to eat? = Why don't we go for something to eat. // Shall we go for something to eat together? (같이~) ➡ OK. Let's go. (가죠.)
식사하면서 얘기 나눕시다.	Let's enjoy some conversation while we eat. = Let's chat while we eat. // Let's take some time to chat while we eat. (우리 천천히~)

식사했습니까?	Did you have a meal? = Did you eat something?
	➡ ⓐ Yes, I did. (먹었습니다.)
	// Yes, I had it already. (벌써 먹었습니다.)
	ⓑ Yes, I just had it. (방금 먹었습니다.)
	ⓒ No, I didn't. (아니요.) // Not yet. (아직 아닙니다.)

식상했습니다.	I've had enough of it. = I'm fed up with it. = I'm sick and tired of it. // I'm sick and tired of this program. = This program is not interesting at all. (이 프로는 너무~)
식언하지 마세요.	Don't break your words.
식었는데 따뜻하게 데워줄래요?	It's cold. Would you warm it up? = It's cold. Would you warm it up? // The rice became cold. Would you warm it up? (밥이~)
식욕이 없습니다.	I don't have an appetite. = I have no appetite. = I've lost my appetite. // I have no appetite these days. = I've lost my appetite these days. (요즘~)
식욕이 왕성합니다.	I have a good appetite. // Youth have a good appetite. (젊은이는~)

식은 죽 먹기야.	It's a piece of cake. = It's a snap. = It's a cinch. ☞ 누워서 떡먹기야.
식자우환.	[속담] Ignorance is bliss.
식중독에 걸렸습니다.	I have food poisoning.
식후에 하나씩 드세요.	[포장 약] Take one after a meal. = Take one after eating food.

신

신경 꺼!	① [간섭] None of your business! = Never mind! = No concern of yours! ② [걱정] Don't worry about it!

신경 끄세요!	① [쓸데없는 간섭에] None of your business.
	= Don't bother! = Never mind!
	= Never think of it! = Ignore it!
	// Never mind me! (저한테~)
	// Never mind him! (그 사람~)
	② [쓸데없는 참견에] Cut it out! = Stop bothering!
	= Don't care about me!
	③ [멋대로 추측하는 것에] Don't take it seriously!
	④ [번거로움을 피함] Don't bother!
	⑤ [걱정] Don't worry!

신경 많이 써주세요.	Please pay attention to this thing. = Please take this thing seriously. // Everybody, please pay attention to it. (모두들~)
신경 써주세요.	Please take it seriously. = Please pay attention to it. // Please take this thing seriously. (이 일을~)
신경 쓰세요.	Mind your business. (당신 일이나~) // Mind your own fiancé. (당신 약혼녀나~)

ㅅ

신경 쓰지 마세요.	① [걱정] Don't worry. ☞ 걱정하지 마세요.
	// 마음에 두지 마세요.
	② [간섭] Never mind. = Don't care.
	= Don't mind. = Don't bother.
	// Don't bother much. (너무~)
	③ [말] Don't take my words seriously. (내 말을~)
	④ [심려] Don't worry about it.
	⑤ [차나 다과 준비] I'm fine. Don't bother.
	(괜찮습니다, ~)
	// Don't bother. I will leave soon.
	(~, 좀 앉았다가 가겠습니다.)
	⑥ [제3자의 간섭에] Never mind it.
	// Never mind him. (그 사람~) ☞ 냅둬요!
	// 상관하지 마세요.

신경 쓰지 않아요.	Don't mind. = Don't care. = Don't bother.
	// I don't mind. (전~)
	// I don't mind at all. (저야~)
	// I don't care about your past. (전 당신의 과거를~)
	➡ Don't lie. I know you do care.
	(속이지 말아요. 신경 쓰는 거 알아요.)

신경 쓸 것 없어요.	① [일반적] Don't bother.
	// Don't bother. Do your business.
	(~일보세요.)
	② [관여] Don't care about it.
	// Don't care about it that much. (그렇게~)
	③ [걱정] Don't worry. = Never mind.
	= Never think of it.
	= Don't take it personally.
	// Don't take my words personally. (내 말~)
	④ [쓸데없는 일에] Never mind.

신경과민이야!	All nerves! = Oversensitive. // He's all nerves. = He's oversensitive. (그는~)
신경 써주셔서 감사합니다.	I'm thankful that you bothered to help me. // I'm thankful that you bothered to help me so far. (그동안~)

ㅅ

신경질 나 죽겠네.	I'm so upset. = I'm so angry. = I'm so mad.
신고했습니까?	Did you report it? // Did you report it to the police? (경찰에~) ➡ ⓐ Yes, I did. (신고했습니다.) ⓑ No. Not yet. (아직 안 했습니다.)
신나게 놀아보자.	**Let's have fun!** = Let's play! = Let's enjoy. // Let's have fun, everybody. (모두~)

신나게 마셔보자.	[술을] Let's drink and have fun.
	// Let's drink and have fun together. (우리 둘~)
	// Let's drink and have fun tonight. (오늘 밤~)

신난다!	Exciting! = Cool! = Awesome! = Hooray! = Fantastic!
신랑, 신부가 내빈들께 인사를 올리겠습니다.	Bride and groom will bow to the guests.
신랑, 신부를 위한 건배!	Toast to the bride and groom. = Let's drink a toast to the bride and groom.
신랑, 신부의 앞날을 축복합니다.	Bride and groom, may god bless you.
신문 좀 갖다 주세요.	Bring me newspapers, please. = Get me newspapers, please.
신발 벗지 마세요.	Don't take off your shoes.
신사 숙녀 여러분!	Ladies and gentlemen!

신세를 많이 졌습니다.	**I owe you a lot.** (제가~) // I owe you a lot.
	= I appreciate what you've done so far. (그동안~)
	// I owe him a lot. (그에게~)

신세를 졌습니다.	[인정 빚] I owe you a lot.

	= I appreciate you so much. // I owe him a lot. = I appreciate him so much. (그에게~)
신어보세요.	[양말, 신발] Try these on. = Wear these. = Put these on.
신호등에서 오른쪽으로 도세요.	Turn right at the traffic light. // Turn right at the traffic light ahead. (저 앞~)
신혼대길하고 백년해로 하십시오.	May you have good luck with your marriage and grow old together.
신혼여행은 어디로 갑니까?	Where are you going for your honeymoon? ➡ To Hawaii. (하와이로요.)

ㅅ

실

실력이 아직 녹슬지 않았어.	Not rusty yet. // I'm not rusty yet. (내~)
실례 좀 하겠습니다.	[잠시 볼 일로 자리를 뜨면서] Excuse me. = Pardon me.
실례지만, 혹시···	Excuse me, but··· = I'm sorry, but···
실례합니다, 좀 지나가겠습니다.	Excuse me. Let me go through here. ➡ Go this way, please. (이리로 지나가시죠.)

실례합니다.	① [폐를 끼치는 경우] Excuse me. = Sorry.
	= I'm sorry. = I beg your pardon.
	= Pardon. = Pardon me.
	= Beg your pardon.
	② [(잠시) 자리를 뜰 때] Excuse me. = I'm sorry.
	// Excuse me, but I should leave now.
	(~, 먼저 가보겠습니다.)
	③ [길 양보를 구함] Excuse me. = I'm sorry.
	// Excuse me, but I am going this way.
	(~, 좀 지나가겠습니다.)

	// Excuse me, but let me go through here. (~. 좀 지나가게 해주세요.)
실례했습니다.	① Excuse me. ② Sorry. // Very sorry. (정말~) ➡ ⓐ That's alright. (천만에요.) ⓑ Don't mention it. (그런 말씀 마세요.) ③ [말실수에 대한 사과] I'm so sorry.
실망스럽습니다.	① I was very disappointed. (사람 정말~) ② My kid is very disappointing. = I'm disappointed with my kid. = My kid let me down. (우리 아이 정말~)
실망시키지 마세요.	Don't disappoint me. = Don't let me down. (날~)
실망하지 마세요.	Don't be disappointed. = Don't be downhearted. = Keep your head up.

실망했습니다.	I'm disappointed.
	// I'm really disappointed. (정말~)
	// I'm so disappointed. (너무~)
	// I'm a little disappointed. (좀~)
	// I'm so disappointed in you. (당신에게 너무~)

실수 없도록 해!	Don't make any mistakes. = Don't make a mess of it.
실수를 한 적이 있습니다.	I've made a mistake. // I've made the same mistake. (저도 같은~)
실수입니다.	It was a mistake. // I made a mistake. = My mistake. = My bad. (제~) // This is my mistake. (이건 제~)
실수했습니다.	① [행위를] I made a mistake. = My mistake. = It was a mistake. // I made a big mistake. = My big mistake. = It was a big mistake. (큰~) ② [예의가 벗어나는 경우] I screwed. (제가~) ③ [말을] I made a slip of the tongue.

실언했습니다.	I made a mistake of words. = It was a slip of the tongue.
실연당했습니까?	Were you dumped? ➡ Never. (그런 일 없습니다.)
실컷 먹었어요.	I indulged in chocolate. (초콜릿을 ~)
실패는 성공의 어머니이다.	Failure is but the threshold of success. = Failure teaches success.
실패했어요.	I failed.

싫

싫어요!	① [원치 않음] I hate it! // I hate it so much! = I don't like it so much! = I really hate it! (정말~) ② [물건이 마음에 안 듦] I don't like it! ③ [간절하지 않음] No! ④ [미움] I hate it! = I don't like it! = I dislike it! // I hate you! (당신이~) // I really hate it! (정말~) ⑤ [거절] No way! ⑥ [약속] No, thanks! ⑦ [귀찮아함] No!
싫증납니다.	I'm tired of it. // I'm tired of this work. (이 일은 정말~)

심

심각하게 생각하지 마세요.	① [판단] Don't take it seriously. = Don't take it hard. ② [사실로 받아들임] Don't take it seriously. = Don't take it hard.

	// Don't take it too seriously. = Don't take it too hard. (너무~)
심각하지 않습니다.	It's not that serious. ☞ 괜찮습니다.
심각합니다.	① [병이나 사태가] It's serious. ② I'm serious. (전~)
심각해 하지 마세요.	Don't take it serious. = Don't take it hard.

심려를 끼쳐드려 정말 죄송합니다.	I'm so sorry for the troubles.
	= I'm so sorry to bother you.
	// I'm so sorry for the big troubles.
	= I'm so sorry to bother you much. (너무~)
	// I'm so sorry that I have bothered you so far. (그동안~)

심부름 좀 해줄래요?	Would you run an errand for me? = Will you do me a favor?
심심해!	Boring! = I'm bored! // So boring! = I'm so bored! (정말~) // I'm bored because I'm not with Dad! (아빠 없으니까, ~)
심은 대로 거둔다는 걸 잊지마세요.	You will reap what you sow. = Remember you'll reap what you sow.

심하잖아요.	[불만] It's too much. = It's not fair.
	// This is too much.
	= This is not fair. (이러는 게~)
	// It's really unfair. (~정말이지!)

심했습니다.	① [행위가 지나침] It was too much.
	= It was terribly bad. (너무~)
	// It was really too much. (정말~)
	// It was really over. (정말 너무~)
	// It was too much to him.
	= You have done terribly bad to him.
	(그에게 너무~)
	② [상식에서 벗어남] This was unfair. (이건 너무~)
	③ [정도] I went too far. (제가 ~)
	// It went over. (그것은 좀~)

ㅅ

	④ [지나친 언사] It was excessive. // It was really excessive. (정말~)
심호흡하세요.	Take a deep breath.

십

십년공부 도로 아미타불.	[속담] Failing to reap the fruits of one's long exertion by grudging a little effort at the last stage.
십 년이면 강산도 변한다.	[속담] Ten years is an epoch.
십 분 남았습니다.	You have ten minutes left. = Ten minutes left. // You still have ten minutes left. (아직~)
십 분 전 두시입니다.	Ten to two. = Ten before two.

싱

싱거워요, 간을 좀 더해요.	Add some more salt.
싱겁긴!	You, dull! ☞ 사람 싱겁긴!
싱글 룸으로 주세요.	Give me a single room.
싱글벙글하시네요.	You have a big smile. = You are very smiley.
싱싱하다!	[과일 · 야채 등이] Fresh!
싱싱해 보입니다.	[생선이나 야채가] They look fresh.
싱크대가 막혔습니다.	The sink is clogged.
싱크대를 깨끗이 닦아요.	Wipe up the sink. = Wipe the sink. = Clean up the sink.

ㅅ

싸

싸가지 없는 새끼!	〈비속어〉 Hopeless bastard!
싸가지! // 싸가지 없군!	① [예의 없음] No manners. = Ill-mannerd. // Really ill mannered. (정말~) ② [양심 없음] Hopeless freak!
싸가지고 갈 겁니까?	Is it to go? ➡ ⓐ Yes, to go, please. (가지고 갑니다.) ⓑ No, for here. (아니요, 여기서 먹을 겁니다.)
싸게 좀 안됩니까?	① Can't you lower the price? = Can't you make it cheaper? = Would you cut down the price? = Please give me a discount. // Can't you ever lower the price? (정말~) ➡ Not anymore. (더는 안 됩니다.) ② [할인] Can't you give me a discount? ➡ Ten percent off. (10% 싸게 드릴게요.)
싸게 좀 해주세요.	Please lower the price. = Please make it cheaper. = Please cut down the price. = Please reduce the price.
싸구려!	Cheap thing!
싸구려는 역시 표가 나!	It looks so cheap! = Everybody knows it's cheap!
싸다!	Cheap! ☞ 쌉니다.
싸우지 말고 잘 지내요.	Please don't fight. Let's get along well with each other.
싸웁니다.	① [말다툼] We often argue. (우린 자주~) ② [주먹다짐] We often fight. (우린 자주~)
싸웠어요?	① [말다툼] Did you guys have an argument? (두 사람~)

	// Did you have an argument with her? (그녀와~)
	// Did you have an argument with your brother-in-law? (형부랑~)
	➡ ⓐ No. (아니야.) ⓑ Why did I? (그럴 리가요?)
	② [주먹질] Did you guys have a fight? (두 사람~)

싸주세요.	[음식 등을 포장] Let me have it in a bag. = Wrap my food up. = Put my food in a bag. // Let me have this in a bag. (이거~)

싹

싹수없는 놈!	〈비속어〉 Hopeless bastard! = Hopeless scumbag! = Hopeless asshole! = Despicable scoundrel!

싼

싼 게 비지떡이다.	Cheap and inferior. = Buy cheap and waste your money. = Penny-wise and pound-foolish.
싼 방 있습니까?	Do you have cheap rooms? // Do you have cheaper rooms? (좀 더~) ➡ No, all gone. (다 나가고 없습니다.)

쌀

쌀쌀합니다.	It's chilly. // It's chilly today. (오늘은~)
쌀 있나요?	① [소유] Do you have rice? ② [판매] Do you sell rice?

쌉

쌉니다.	Cheap. // Very cheap. (아주~) // Really cheap. (정말~)

쌍

쌍꺼풀을 수술했어요.	I had double eyelid surgery. = I had plastic surgery on my eyes. // She had double eyelid surgery. (그 여자는~)
쌍년!	〈비속어〉 ① Bitch! ② Whore! = Slut!
쌍놈!	〈비속어〉 Bastard! = Son of a bitch! = Scumbag! = Asshole!
쌍수를 들어 찬성합니다.	I give my hearty support. = I agree with all my heart.

쌕

쌕쌕!	[코고는 소리] Snore, snore!

쌤

쌤통이다!	① You deserve it! ② [자업자득] It serves you right! ③ [인과응보] You reap what you sow! = That's just justice! = That's fair! ☞ 고소하다!

쌩

쌩!	[바람 소리, 달려가는 소리] Whistling!

써

써 봐도 됩니까?	Can I use it? = Can I test it? = Can I try it? ➡ Of course. (그럼요.)
써 보세요.	① [글씨] Try to write again. (다시 한 번~) ② [용도] Try it again. (다시 한 번~)
써 봐!	① [글씨] Write it! ② [모자] Try it on! = Put it on! ☞ 차 봐! ③ [물건] Try it!

썩

썩 나가!	① [밖으로] Get out! = Go out! ② [명령형] Out! = Go away!
썩 꺼져!	Get the hell out of here! = Go away!

썰

썰렁하다!	① [온도] It's chilly! // It's really chilly! (진짜~) ② [사람 등이 없음] It's empty! ③ [유머 등] It's not interesting!
썰렁한 자식!	Empty-headed fellow! = Silly fellow!
썰렁해!	Flat and dull! ☞ 유치해!
썰어주세요.	[고기 등을 얇게] Slice it, please.

ㅅ

썼

썼습니다.	① [글씨] I finished writing. (글씨를 다~) ② [사용] I'm all done. = I used it up. (다~) // I spent all my money. = I used up all my money. (돈을 다~)

싹

싹!	[빗소리, 물소리] Splash!
싹싹!	[비 내리는 소리] Splash, splash!

쓰

쓰세요.	① [글씨] Please write it. // Please write it here. (여기에~) ② [사용] Please use it.

쓸

쓸데없는 걱정 마세요.	① [고민] It's of no use worrying. = It's useless worrying. = It's not worth worrying. ② [걱정] Don't trouble yourself with useless worries.
쓸데없는 말 작작해!	Cut the crap! = Stop babbling!

쓸데없는 소리!
// 쓸데없는 소리 그만해!
// 쓸데없는 소리 작작해!
	① Cut it out! = Cut the crap!
	= Stop babbling! = Don't say useless words!
	② [남에 일에 간섭] Stop!

쓸데없는 소리 하지마!	Stop the useless words! = No more silly words! = Cut the crap! = Stop it!

쓸데없는 짓 하지마!	Don't do useless things! = Don't do such useless things!
쓸데없는 짓이야!	It's useless! = It's not worthy!
쓸데없이 굴지 마라!	It's of no use doing it!
쓸데없이!	① Useless! = Of no use! ② Not worthy!
쓸모없는 놈!	Useless bastard! = Useless scumbag!
쓸모없어!	Useless! = Hopeless! // You're worthless! = You're useless! = You suck! (넌 정말~) ☞ 형편없어!
쓸쓸합니다.	① [사람] I'm lonely. ② [장소 등이] I'm very lonely. (너무~)

씹

씹! // 씹할!	〈비속어〉 Sucks! = Fuck! = Damn! = Fuck off! = Shit! = Got damn it! // It sucks! (이런~)
씹할 년!	〈비속어〉 Bitch! = Fucking whore! = Slut!
씹할 놈!	〈비속어〉 Bastard! = Scumbag! // You, bastard! (이~)
씹할 새끼!	〈비속어〉 Fucking bastard! = Fucking scumbag! = Fucking asshole! // You, fucking bastard! (이~)

씻

씻고 자!	Wash and then go to bed! // Wash quickly and then go to bed! (어서 가서~)

ㅅ

씽

씽씽! [바람소리] Shriek!

ㅅ

아

아!	① [놀람 · 감탄] Ah! = Oh! = Oh, dear! = Dear me! = Oh, boy! = My goodness! = Goodness gracious! = (Good) Heaven! ② [실망 · 슬픔] Ah! = Alas! = Why! = Well! ③ [동조] Oh! = Oh, yes! = Well! ④ [말을 걸 때] I say! = Say! = Look! = Listen! ⑤ [호격] Hey! ☞ 야!
아가리 닥쳐!	〈비속어〉 Shut the fuck up! = Knock the shit off! // Shut the fuck up before I cut it up! (아가리 찢어버리기 전에, ~)
아가씨	Ms. // Ms. I (미즈 리)
아가야!	Baby! = Sweetie! = Honey! = My dear!

아깝다!	① [아쉬움] It's a pity! // What a pity! (정말~) // What a pity! = That's too bad! (너무~)
	② Too good to eat! (먹기에~) // Too precious to spend! (돈 쓰기가~)
	③ What a pity! = Unfortunate! // Unfortunate! I narrowly missed it. = What a pity! I missed it by a hair. (간발의 차이로~)

아내가 귀여우면 처갓집 말뚝보고 절한다.	[속담] Love me, love my dog.
아내가 바람났습니다.	My wife's cheating on me. = My wife is having an affair. = My wife loves someone else.
아내가 임신했습니다.	My wife is pregnant. = My wife is expecting a baby. = My wife has conceived.
아는 것이 힘이다, 배워야 산다.	Knowledge is power. You should learn.
아는 사이입니까?	① [면식] You guys know each other? (둘이~) ➡ ⓐ Of course. (물론 알죠.)

ㅇ

	ⓑ We met once. (딱 한 번 뵙어요.) ⓒ Yes, but not that close. (알지만, 친하지는 않아요.) ② Did you guys meet before? (서로 전에~) // Do you know her? (그녀와~) ➡ ⓐ Yes, I know her. But I'm not that close to her. (그녀를 알지만, 친한 사이는 아닙니다.) ⓑ Yes. I have known her for a long time. (예, 오래 전에 알던 사이입니다.)
아니 땐 굴뚝에 연기 나랴.	[속담] No smoke without fire. = No smoke, no fire. = Where there's smoke, there's fire. = There's no smoke without fire.
아니, 아니요!	[거절] No, no!
아니라고 생각합니다.	① I'd say no. ② [상황 설명] I think not.
아니면 말고!	① [단념] Yes, or no! ② [거절하는 경우] No? Fine!
아니야!	① [직접 대답을 회피] No! = Nay! // It's nothing! (아무것도~) ② [거절] No, no! (~, 아니야!) ③ Never! (난 절대~) ☞ 아니요!
아니요!	① [부정] No! = Not at all! = Nay! = Nope! = Never! ② [과거 행위나 완료의 부정] Did not! ☞ 안했습니다. ③ [예상 · 추측에 대해] No way! ④ [감사에 대해] Not at all! ☞ 천만에요! ⑤ [사과나 위로] That's OK! = That's alright! // That's OK! I'm fine now. (~이제 됐어요.) ☞ 괜찮아요! ⑥ [만족해하며 거절] It's fine! ⑦ [거절] No, thanks! = Enough! ⑧ [단념] Fine! I don't wanna say anymore. (~, 말 안할래.)

아니지!	① [추측] No way! ② [바람] What! ③ [부정] No!
아닌 밤중에 홍두깨.	A great surprise. = A bolt out of the blue. = That's out of the blue! = That's out of left field! = That was out of the blue! = That was out of left field!
아닌 척 하지 마!	Don't pretend you don't know it!
아닙니까?	① [반문] Isn't it? ② [강한 긍정] It's yours, isn't it? (이건 당신 것~) ➡ Yes. (예.)
아닙니다.	No. ☞ 아니요!
아드님을 빨리 낳으시길 바랍니다.	I hope you'll have a son soon.
아들 나신 것 축하합니다.	Congratulations on having a baby son.
아들과 딸 둘입니다.	I have a son and two daughters.

아르바이트합니까?	① Do you work part-time?
	// Do you work part-time while going to school? (학교 다니면서~)
	// Do you work part-time in your free time? (남는 시간에~)
	// Do you work part-time while you're off? (쉴 때~)
	➡ ⓐ Yes! (예!)
	ⓑ Not yet. (아직 안 합니다.)
	ⓒ Twice a week. (일주일에 두 번 합니다.)
	② What part-time job do you have? (어떤~)
	➡ ⓐ I am a tutor. = I tutor kids. (가정교사입니다.)
	ⓑ I teach high school students. (고등학생을 가르칩니다.)

아름답습니다!	① [얼굴] Beautiful! = Pretty! = You're beautiful! = You're pretty!

	// So beautiful! (참~)
	// You're the most beautiful person that I've ever seen. (제가 봤던 사람 중에 당신이 가장~)
	② [옷 · 꽃 등의 색깔] Beautiful!
	// Really beautiful! (참~)
	③ [음악] Beautiful!
	④ [경치] Beautiful! =Pretty! = Quite a view!
	// Very beautiful! (참~)
	// The leaves are very beautiful! (단풍이 정말~)
	// The Han river is very beautiful! (한강은 정말~)
	⑤ [감탄] Beautiful! // Very beautiful! (참~)
	// Really beautiful! = So beautiful!
	= What a beauty! (너무~) ☞ 예쁩니다!

아마 그럴 겁니다.	Maybe.
아마 모를 겁니다.	You may not know it. = Maybe you don't know it.
아무거나 잘 먹습니다.	I eat everything. = I eat anything well.
아무것도 모릅니다.	① [사실을] I don't know anything. = I know nothing. // Except these, I know nothing! (이것들 말고는~) ② [철이 없어서] Don't know! = Unaware! = Don't understand! // He doesn't know! = Unaware! = He doesn't understand! (걔는~) ③ [기능 · 학문] Don't understand! = Don't get it!

아무것도 아닙니다.	① [사태] It's nothing. = Nothing at all. = It's fine.
	= It's OK. ☞ 괜찮습니다.
	② [대단치 않음] It's not serious. = Nothing.
	// This is nothing. = This isn't serious. (이건~)
	// This is nothing. (이 정도 성적은~)
	③ [일 처리가] It's an easy thing.
	= It's a piece of cake. = It's a breeze.
	= It's a walk in the park. = It's a snap!
	☞ 식은 죽 먹기야!

	④ [선물을 건네면서] It's nothing. = It's very small.
	// It's nothing. Please take this. (~받아주세요.)
	⑤ [일반적인 수준] Nothing.
	// This is nothing. (이건~)
	⑥ [정상적임] Nothing special. ☞ 별거 아닙니다.

아무거나!	[음식 주문] Anything! = Whatever!
아무거나 다 먹습니다.	I eat anything. = I eat everything.
아무거나 다 좋습니다.	Anything is fine. = Anything is OK. = Anything is good to me.
아무거나 시키세요.	① [음식] Anything you like. ② [분부] Whatever you want.
아무래도 좋습니다.	[동의] Anything is fine. = What so ever. = Whatever. = Anything is OK. = Anything is good.
아버지는 어디서 근무하십니까?	Where does your father work? ➡ At a school. (학교에서요.)
아뿔싸!	① [감탄] Dear me! = Oh my! ② [놀람] Oh my! ③ [실수] Darn it! = Gosh! = Damn! = Oops! ☞ 아차!
아삭아삭!	Crunch, crunch!
아쉬운 거 없습니다.	Nothing to regret. = Nothing to sigh about.
아쉽네요.	① I'm sorry. = That's too bad. = That's not good. = It's a pity. = What a pity. = Too bad. // I'm so sorry. (정말~) ☞ 유감입니다. ② [헤어지기] I don't want to let you go. = I don't want to say goodbye to you. ☞ 섭섭합니다.
아시아나 항공카운터는 어디에 있습니까?	Where are the check-in counters for Asiana Airlines?

	= Where are the Asiana Airlines counters? ➡ Inside. (안쪽에 있습니다.)
아시죠?	Don't you know? // Don't you know me? (절~) ➡ ⓐ Yes. You are Mr. Smith. (알지요. 스미스씨이시죠.) ⓑ Sorry, but I don't know you. (모르겠는데요.)
아십니까?	Do you know? // Do you know me? (저를~) ➡ Sorry. I don't know you. (모르겠는데요.)
아아!	[대화 중 깜박한 일이 생각이 남] Oops!
아야!	① [감탄] Ouch! ② [고통을 호소] Oh, god!
아우!	[늑대 울음소리] Awoo!
아웅, 까꿍!	[3세 전후 아이와 숨래잡기 놀이] Peekaboo!
아이 있습니까?	Do you have children? ➡ ⓐ Yes, I do. (있습니다.) ⓑ No, not yet. (아직 없습니다.)
아이가 없습니다.	We have no children. (우리는~) // I have no children yet. (아직~)
아이고!	① [놀람] Oh! = Ah! = Oh my! = My goodness! ② [고통] Ouch!
아이스크림 사줘요.	Buy me an ice cream.
아이스티 한 잔 주세요.	Let me have an ice tea. = Get me an ice tea, please.
아이참!	① [감탄] Oh! = Ah! = Oh my! = My goodness! ② [불평] Shit! = Shoot! ☞ 이런! // 웃기네!
아이쿠!	[감탄] Oh, my god! = My goodness! = Oh, Jesus! ☞ 아이고!

아저씨, 안녕하세요.	Hello, Mr. // Hello, Mr. Baker. (베이커씨~)
아주 좋아요.	Very good. = Great. =Terrific. = Awesome.
아주 좋았어!	Excellent!
아차!	① [감탄] Dear me! = Oh my! ② [어떤 일이 갑자기 생각이 남] Darn it! = Gosh! = Damn! = Oops!
아첨하지 마세요.	Don't flatter me. = Do not butter me up.
아침 드세요.	Have breakfast. = Time for breakfast.
아침 몇 시에 출발합니까?	What time will you leave? ➡ Seven. (7시예요.)
아침식사는 어디서 합니까?	Where will you have breakfast? ➡ The restaurant on the first floor. (1층 레스토랑에서요.)
아침식사는 언제 합니까?	When will you have breakfast? = What time will you have breakfast? ➡ At eight. (8시예요.)
아침식사는 포함됩니까?	Does it include breakfast? ➡ Yes. (포함됩니다.)
아침잠이 많습니다.	I'm not a morning person. = I get up late.
아파요!	[고통 호소] It hurts me! // It hurts me a lot! (너무~)
아파죽겠어요.	It's killing me. = It's so painful.
아픈 데는 찌르고 그래요.	I poke where it hurts.
아픈 만큼 성숙한다.	The more pain you have, the more you grow.
아픕니까?	① [진찰] Does it hurt? // Where does it hurt? (어디~) ➡ My shoulder. (어깨요.) ② [단정] Aren't you sick? (어디~)

ㅇ

	③ [고통] Are you sick? = What's wrong? = Something wrong? (어디~) ➡ ⓐ I'm fine. (괜찮습니다.) ⓑ I'm not sick. = I'm OK. (안 아파요.)

악

악랄하다!	Vicious! = Cruel! = Evil!
악수해요.	Let's shake hands. (우리~)

안

안 갑니까?	Aren't you going now? ➡ Some time later. (좀 있다가 바로 가요.)
안 갑니다.	① [자리를 비키지 않음] I'm not going. ② [어떤 장소에] I'm not going there.

안됐습니다.	① [나이] Not yet. // Not thirty yet. (서른 살이~)
	② [시간] Not yet.
	// Not one o'clock yet. (아직 1시가~)
	③ [곤경에 빠짐] Too bad. // He's too bad. (그 사람~)
	④ [동정] I'm sorry. // That's too bad.
	= I'm so sorry. (정말~)
	⑤ [유감] It's a pity. // What a pity. (정말~)
	// So sorry. (너무~)
	⑥ [불행] Too bad. // I heard you got fired. Too bad. (실직하셨다고 들었는데, 너무~)
	⑦ [위로] I feel sorry. = I'm sorry to hear that.
	// I feel so sorry. (참~)
	⑧ [운수 나쁨] That was unfortunate.
	// That was so unfortunate. (너무~)

안 된다면 안 됩니다.	I said no. That's it. // I said no about this. That's it. (이거~)

안 될 것 같습니다.	Seems like a no. = Seems unlikely. = Can't be. = It can't be. = Not possible.
안 됩니다.	① [반대] No. = I disagree. = I object. = No way. // That's a no. (그건~) ② [금지] No way. = Must not. ③ [좋지 않음] Not good. ④ [불가능함을 나타냄] Impossible.= Zero chance. ⑤ [바람직하지 않음을 권고] Don't. ⑥ [협상의 여지가 없음] Out of the question. = Don't even think about it.
안 보면 마음도 멀어진다.	[속담] Out of sight, out of mind.
안 봐도 알아요.	① [확신] I know it without seeing. ② [짐작] Maybe I know it without seeing.
안 삽니다.	I won't buy.
안 속아!	I won't be deceived! = I won't be fooled! = I won't be tricked!
안 왔습니다.	① Not here. // John hasn't been here yet. (존이 아직~) ② [귀가] My son hasn't come home yet. (아들이 아직 집에 ~)
안개가 낍니다.	It's foggy. = There is a bad fog. // It will be foggy 3 days later. (글피에는~)
안경을 낍니다.	I wear glasses.
안내해 드리겠습니다.	① Let me show you the way. = Follow me, please. = Come this way. ② 〈경어〉 It's my honor to show you the way. (제가~)
안녕!	① [만났을 때] Hi! = Hello! ☞ 안녕하세요! ② [헤어질 때] Bye! = Good bye! = So long! = See ya! ☞ 안녕히 가세요! // 잘 가!

ㅇ

안녕하세요! // 안녕하십니까!	① [때와 상관없이 연하나 동년배에게 하는 인사] **What's up!** = **Howdy?** = How are you doing? ☞ 안녕! ② [때와 상관없이 연장자에게 하는 인사] Hi! = Hello! ➡ Hi. (안녕!) ③ [아침 인사] Good morning! ➡ Good morning! (안녕하세요!) ④ [오후 인사] Good afternoon! ➡ Good afternoon! (안녕하세요!) ⑤ [저녁 인사] Good evening! ➡ Good evening! (안녕하세요!) ⑥ [아는 사이의 안부 인사] How are you? = How have you been? // How are you? Long time no see. (~오랜만에 뵙네요.)
안녕하셨습니까?	[서로 아는 사이의 인사] How have you been? ➡ Fine. = Good. (안녕하지요.)
안녕히 가세요!	① [작별 인사] Bye! = Good bye! = Bye for now! ☞ 잘 가! ② [주인이 손님에게 하는 작별 인사] Bye! Have a good day. ☞ 살펴가세요.
안녕히 계세요!	① Bye for now! ☞ 안녕히 가세요! ② [손님이 주인에게 하는 작별 인사] Bye! Thank you. ☞ 나오지 마세요.
안녕히 주무세요.	[일반적으로 가정에서만 사용함] ① Good night. ② Sweet dreams. ☞ 잘 주무세요!
안마해 드릴게요.	I'll give you a massage.
안방 먼저 청소하세요.	Please clean up the master room first off.
안부 전해주세요.	Say hello to your mother, please. = My best regards to your mother. = My best wishes to your mother. (당신 어머니께~)

	// Say hello to your mother for me. (제 대신 당신 어머니께~) ➡ OK, I will. Thank you. (예, 감사합니다.)
안색이 안 좋아 보입니다.	You don't look good. = You look bad.
안성맞춤입니다.	It's the right thing. = It's perfect. (그게 ~) // You're the right person for the job. = You're perfect for the job. (당신이 그 일에 ~)

안심하세요.	① Don't worry. = No worries. = Feel at home.
	= Feel at ease.
	// Don't worry. Nothing will happen. (~별일 없을 거야.)
	② Relax now. (이제~)
	// Relax. There's nothing wrong. (~문제없어요.)
	☞ 괜찮습니다.
	③ [겸양] Please don't worry.

안아줘!	Please hug me. = Please give me a hug. // Please give me a big hug. = Please hug me tight. (꼭~)
안에 뭐가 있습니까?	What's inside? = What's in it? ➡ ⓐ A credit card. (신용 카드 하나요.) ⓑ Nothing. (뭐 없습니다.)
안으로 드십시오.	① [안내] Please go inside. // Mr. Johnson, please go inside. (존슨씨, 자, ~) ➡ Not necessary. (그럴 필요 없습니다.) ② [집안으로 안내] Please come inside. = Please come in. ☞ 들어오세요.
안전벨트 매주세요.	Please fasten your seat belt.
안전을 위해서 안전벨트를 매주세요.	Please fasten your belt for safety.
안쪽으로 드시죠.	① Come inside, please. ② 〈겸양〉 Would you please come on over?

	= Would you please come in? = Would you please come inside?
안타깝습니다.	It's a pity. // What a pity. (너무~) // That's too bad. (정말~) ☞ 애석합니다. // 안됐습니다.
안하는 게 좋겠어요.	I'd better not do it.
안합니다.	Not anymore. // Not anymore now. (이제~)
안했습니다.	I didn't do it. // I didn't do it yet. (아직~)

앉

앉아계세요.	Please sit. // Please sit for a minute. (잠시~)
앉아도 됩니까?	May I sit? = Can I have a seat? // May I sit here? (여기에~) ➡ Go ahead. (그러세요.)
앉아서 기다리세요.	Please sit and wait. // Please sit and wait here. (여기~)
앉아서 말해요.	Please tell me from your seat.
앉아서 쉬세요.	Please sit and rest.
앉아서 얘기합시다.	Let's sit and talk.
앉아서 좀 기다리세요.	〈겸양〉 Would you please take a seat and wait?
앉아요!	① Grab a seat! = Sit down! = Take a seat! = Have a seat! ➡ I'm fine. = I'm OK. (괜찮습니다.) ② [명령] You, sit! (거기 좀~) ③ Come here and sit. (이리 와서~)
앉아주세요.	Please sit down. // Please have a seat quickly. (어서~)

앉았다 가세요.	Please sit down for a minute.
	// Please come to my house and sit down for a minute. (집에 와서 잠시~)
	// Please come in and sit down for a minute. (들어와서 잠시~)

앉으세요.	Grab a seat, please. = Sit down, please.
	= Take a seat, please. = Have a seat, please.
	// Grab this seat, please. (여기~)
	// Grab a seat here, please. (이쪽에~)
	// Come here and grab a seat, please. (이쪽으로 와서~)
	➡ Thank you. (네, 감사합니다.)

알

알게 뭐야!	① [방임] None of my business! = I don't care! = I don't mind! // I don't care about him! (그놈~) ② [무시] What about it? ③ [상관 없음] Leave me alone! ☞ 냅둬요!
알게 되어 반갑습니다.	Good to see you. = Nice to see you. = Happy to meet you. = Glad to meet you. ☞ 만나 뵙게 되어 반갑습니다.
알고 있습니까?	Do you know it? ➡ ⓐ Yes, I do. (알고 있습니다.) ⓑ No, I don't. (모릅니다.) ⓒ I know it well enough. (충분히 알고 있습니다.)
알레르기가 있습니다.	I'm allergic. // I'm allergic to beef. (소고기에~)

알려주세요.	① Let me know it. (저에게~)
	// Let me know it when we arrive at the train station. (기차역에 도착하면 좀~)
	// Let him know what I said. (내 말을 그에게~)
	② [통보] Please inform me of it. (꼭~)

알려줘서 고맙습니다.	Thank you for the information.

알림!	[안내문] News! = Announcements!
알면 병이고 모르면 약이야.	[속담] Where ignorance is bliss, it is folly to be wise. = Ignorance is the peace of life.
알아둘게 있어.	[경각심] You should know this. (너~)
알아둬!	Keep it in mind!
알아듣게 좀 얘기해봐!	Please help me understand what you're saying!
알아들었습니까?	① [확인] Do you understand it? = Do you get it? = Do you follow me? ➡ ⓐ Yes, I do. (알아들었습니다.) ⓑ No, I don't. (못 알아들었는데요.) ➡ ⓐ I understand. = I get it. (알아들었어요.) // I understand this time. (이번엔~) ⓑ I don't understand. (알아듣지 못했어요.) ② [확실히] Got it? = Is everything clear to you? ➡ Yes, I got it. (알아들었습니다.) ③ [부탁 · 당부] Does it make sense? = Do you get it? ➡ I get it. = I see. (알았어요.) ☞ 알았습니까?
알아들을 수 있습니까?	[가능] Can you understand it? = Can you see it? ➡ ⓐ Yes, I can. (알아들을 수 있습니다.) ⓑ No, I can't. (알아들을 수 없습니다.)
알아맞혀봐!	Guess!
알아보시겠습니까?	① [면식] Can't you recognize? = Can't you tell? // Can't you recognize me? (저를 아직~) ➡ No, I can't. (못 알아보겠는데요.) ② [반문] Do you know? // Do you know me? (절 아직~) ➡ ⓐ I don't know anybody. (난 누구도 모릅니다.) ⓑ I really don't know. (정말 모르겠어요.) ③ [시력] Can you see? // Can you see me? (절~) ➡ Yes, I can. (알아보겠어요.)

알아봐 주세요.	[조사] Please investigate it. = Please inquire into it. // Please investigate it right away. (즉시 좀~)
알아봤습니까?	① [조사] Did you investigate it? = Did you inquire into it? ➡ ⓐ Yes. (알아봤어요.) ⓑ Not yet. (아직요.) ② [수소문] Did you find it out? ➡ ⓐ Yes, I did. (알아봤습니다.) ⓑ I found out everything. (다 알아봤습니다.) ⓒ No, I didn't. (아니요.)
알아서 결정해!	Decide for yourself! = Make a choice yourself! // Decide for yourself keeping the situation in mind! (실제 상황에 맞게~) ☞ 결정해!
알아서 해!	① [모든 것을 내맡김] All yours! ② [결정] Do what you want! ③ [편할 대로] Do as you please! ④ [상황을 봐가며] You may do as you think is right! = You may do what you think is right! ⑤ [책임지고] Do it at your own risk! (이번엔 네가~) ⑥ [처신] Make a choice yourself! ☞ 결정해!
알았습니까?	① [어떤 사실을] Did you get it? = Did you know it? ➡ Yes. = Yeah. (알았습니다.) ② [이해] Did you understand it? = Did you get it? = Did you follow me? = Are you with me? ③ [기억] Did you remember it? = Did you recognize it? ➡ Yes. (알았습니다.) ④ [듣고 이해] Did you see it? ➡ Yes. (네.) ⑤ [명령조] Understand? ➡ Yes. (알았어요.) ⑥ [부탁 · 당부] Can you see it?

ㅇ

= Can you get it? ☞ 알아들었습니까?
⑦ [무전 송신 등에서] Do you copy?

알았습니다.

① I understand.
② [동의] I see. = I get it. = OK.
③ [마지못해 하는 동의] OK.
④ [체념 · 결단 · 승낙] Got it.
⑤ [명령 복종] [남자] Yes, sir. [여자] Yes, ma'am.
⑥ [무전 송신 등에서] Copy that.
⑦ [지시에 따름] Sure. = You got it.
⬅ I'll clean up the master bedroom. You get the living room.
(난 안방을 청소할 테니 넌 거실을 맡아.)

암

암에 걸렸습니다.

I was diagnosed with cancer.
= I've got cancer. (제가~)
➡ Can you be healed? (치료할 수 있답니까?)
➡ I don't know. (모르겠어요.)

암탉이 울면 집안이 망한다.

[속담] It goes ill with the house where the hen sings and the cock is silent.
= It is a sad house where the hen crows louder than the cock.

압

압니까?

① [어떤 사실을] Do you know?
➡ Yes. = Sure. (알아요.)
// Do you know he's married?
(그가 결혼한 일을~)
➡ I don't even know him. How could I know if he's married?
(그 사람을 모르는데, 어떻게 알겠습니까?)
② [이해] Do you understand? = Do you get it?

➡ Yes, I understand. = Yes, I get it.
(이해합니다.)

➡ Yes, I do. (압니다.) ☞ 알았습니까?

③ [사람을 이해] Can you understand?

④ [면식] Do you know?
// Do you know him? (그를 ~)

➡ Yes, I do. (압니다.)

앗

앗!	[감탄] Jesus! = Dear! = Oh, my! = Oh, my god! = Oh, my goodness!

앙

앙심 품지 마세요.	Don't take it personally. = Don't hold grudges. // Please don't take it personally. = Please don't hold grudges. (제발~)
앙코르!	[노래] Encore! = One more time! = Once more again! = Again!

앞

앞으로 가!	① Go forward! // Go straight forward! (곧장~) ② [계속 진행] Move on!
앞으로 가다가 우회전하면 됩니다.	Go straight and turn right.
앞으로 나오세요.	[실내] Come to the front. = Come on over.
앞장서요!	[길 안내] You go first! = After you! = You go ahead!

애

애석합니다.	It's a pity. = I feel sorry. // What a pity! (정말~)
애인 있습니까?	① [남자 애인] Do you have a boyfriend? ② [여자 애인] Do you have a girlfriend? ③ [남녀 공용] Are you seeing someone?
애인이 생겼습니다.	① [남자] I have a girlfriend. ② [여자] I have a boyfriend.

야

야!	① [사람을 부름] Hey! = Hey you! = Hey there! ② [감탄 · 칭찬] Hooray! = Oh! = Oh dear! = Good heavens! = Dear me! = Oh my! = Good gracious! ③ [헛소리] Ah! ☞ 아!
야구 잘하네.	Good baseball player! // You are a good baseball player. = You play baseball well. = You're good at baseball. (너~)
야근해야 합니다.	I'll have to work till late. // I'll have to work till late today. (오늘~)
야근했습니다.	I worked till late.
야단났어!	① I'm in big trouble! = This is terrible! = It's a disaster! = What's wrong with me! ② A terrible thing happened to me! ☞ 큰일 났어요!
야비한 짓이야.	It's a cheap shot. = It's mean.
야옹!	[고양이 울음소리] Meow!

야하다!	① [옷의 노출이] Hot! // Very hot! (너무~) // The clothes look so hot. (옷이 너무~) ② Sexy! = Saucy! // A little sexy! (약간~)

약

약 먹고 자.	Go to bed after taking medicine.
약 타러왔습니다.	I'm here to get my medicine. = Can I get my medicine?
약소하지만 받아주세요.	It's nothing. Please take it. = Please accept my small gift to you. = I'd like to give you a little present.
약소합니다.	It's nothing. = It's a small thing. = It's a little thing. // I have a small thing for you. (준비한 것이 너무~)
약속!	[새끼손가락 걸어서] Promise! = Pinky swear! = Pinky promise!
약속 어기지 마!	Don't break the promise!

약속 있습니다.	① [약속] I have an appointment.
	// I have an appointment for tonight. (오늘 저녁에~)
	// I have an appointment with someone else.
	= I'll have to meet someone else. (다른 사람과~)
	// I have an appointment with him. (그와~)
	// I have an appointment today. (오늘은~)
	② [데이트] I have a date.
	// I have a date tomorrow. (내일은~)
	③ [회식] I have a party. ☞ 회식이 있습니다.
	④ [개인적인 만남] I have a plan.

약속 잡을게요.	I'll make an appointment. // I'll make an appointment next time. (다음엔 제가~)

약속시간과 약속장소 잡아요.	Decide on the time and place. = Set up the time and place. // Let's decide on the time and place. (우리~)
약속을 어겼습니다.	I broke the promise. // She broke the promise. (그녀가~)
약속을 지킬 겁니다.	I'll keep the promise.
약속해주세요.	[승낙] Please make a promise. = Please promise.
약속했어!	[다짐] You made a promise! = You promised!
약은 식후에 드세요.	Take the medicine after eating food. // Take this medicine after eating food. (이~)
약은 하루에 세 번 먹습니다.	You should take the medicine three times a day. // You should take this medicine three times a day. (이~)
약점만 꼬집지 마세요.	Don't just focus on my weak points. // Don't just focus on others' weak points. (남의~)
약혼을 축하합니다.	Congratulations on your engagement.
약혼했습니다.	I got engaged. = I'm engaged. // We got engaged. (우리~)

얄

얄미워!	① [반감] I hate you! = I don't like you! ② [원망] I hate you! = I dislike you! ☞ 미워!

얇

얇습니다.	It's thin.
	// This fabric is very thin. (이 원단은 참~)
	// This cloth is very thin. (이 천은 참~)

얌

얌전하게 굴어!	Play nice! = Be nice! ☞ 가만있어!

양

양다리 걸치고 있어.	[연애] ① [남자] I'm seeing two women at the same time. ② [여자] I'm seeing two men at the same time.
양보해주세요.	Please yield. // Please yield to me. (저한테~)
양심도 없는 놈!	Bastard with no conscience! // You, bastard with no conscience. (이~)
양아치(들)!	① [거지의 속어] Beggar! = Rag and bone man! = Panhandler! = Ragman! = Ragpicker! ② [건달] Bum!
양약은 입에 쓰다.	Medicine tastes bitter.
양의 탈을 쓴 늑대입니다.	A wolf in sheep's clothing. // He's a wolf in sheep's clothing. (그놈은~)
양자택일하세요.	Please choose one between the two. = Please choose one alternative.
양치질하고 세수해.	Brush your teeth and wash your face.
양해바랍니다.	Please understand me. = I'm asking for your understanding. = Please excuse me. // I'm asking for your generous understanding. (너그러이~)

애

얘기 나누고 있습니다.	① [용무] I'm having a talk.

ㅇ

	② [이야기하는 중] I'm talking.
얘기 똑똑히 들어!	[명령] Listen up! // Listen to me! (내~)

얘기 좀 나눕시다.	① [한담] Why don't we have a talk?
	// Why don't you have a talk with me? (나하고~)
	// Why don't we have a talk together?
	= Let's have a talk. (우리~)
	= Let's talk together. (우리 ~)
	② [용무] Can you talk? = Do you have a minute?
	// Can you talk with me?
	= Can you give me a minute? (나하고~)

얘기 좀 들어봐요.	① [해명] Please listen. // Please listen to me. (내~) ➡ I don't want to hear any excuse. (어떤 변명도 듣고 싶지 않아요.) ② [알려주고 싶음] You gotta listen to this.

얘기해주세요.	① [단순한 말] Please tell.
	// Please tell me. (저에게~)
	② Let me know.
	// Let me know at the train station.
	(기차역에 도착하면~)

얘야!	① Hey, you! ② [어린아이] Hey, kid! = Kid!

어

어깨 좀 두드려라.	Rub my shoulders. = Massage my shoulders. = Give me a shoulder massage. ➡ Do you feel better? (시원하세요?) ➡ Yes. (시원하다.)
어깨가 욱신거립니다.	My shoulders are aching.
어느 것을 원합니까?	Which do you want? ➡ ⓐ This one. (이거요.) ⓑ That one. (저거요.)

어느 것을 좋아합니까?	Which do you like better? // Which do you like better, coffee or tea? (커피와 차 중에~) ➡ I like tea better. (차를 좋아합니다.)
어느 나라 사람입니까?	What is your nationality? = Where are you from? ➡ I'm Korean. (나는 한국 사람입니다.)
어느 분입니까?	① Who's that? ☞ 누구십니까? ② [말하는 대상] Who are you talking about? (말씀하신 분이~) ➡ That person. (저분입니다.)
어디 가서 얘기 좀 합시다.	Let's go somewhere and have a talk.
어디 갑니까?	① [인사형식] Are you going somewhere? ➡ ⓐ Just for some fresh air. (바람 쐬러갑니다.) ⓑ I'm going to work. (출근합니다.) ⓒ I'm going out for a while. (잠시 나갑니다.) ② [장소 확인] Where are you going? ➡ I'm going out for a while. (잠깐 나갑니다.)
어디 갔었습니까?	① Where did you go? = Did you go somewhere? // Where did you go yesterday? = Did you go somewhere yesterday? (어제~) ➡ ⓐ I went downtown. (시내에요.) ⓑ I went to my aunt's home. (이모 집에 갔었어.) ② [말 안하고 나간 경우] Where were you? ➡ I met my friend. (친구 만나러 갔어요.)
어디 사람입니까?	Where are you from? ➡ I'm from Seoul. (서울 사람입니다.)
어디 아프냐?	[경멸] Are you crazy? = Are you nuts?
어디 좀 보자.	[관찰] Let's see. = Let me see. = Let me take a look.

어디?	[불가능함] Where?
어디가려고 합니까?	① Where are you going? = Are you going somewhere? ➡ ⓐ Just for shopping. (물건 하나 사려고.) ⓑ To New York. (뉴욕에요.) ⓒ None of your business! (신경 끄셔!) ② [계획] Where will you go? ➡ I will go to New York. (뉴욕에 갑니다.)
어디로 갈까요?	① Where do you wanna go? ② [택시] Where would you like to go? = What's your destination? ➡ Gangnam, please. (강남이요.)
어디서 뵌 것 같습니다.	I think we met before.
어디서 왔습니까?	Where are you from? ➡ ⓐ I'm from Korea. (한국에서 왔습니다.) ⓑ I'm from L.A. (LA에서 왔습니다.)
어디십니까?	① [전화] Who's calling, please? ➡ This is Minsu Gim. (김민수라고 합니다.) ② Who are you? ☞ 누구십니까?
어디야?	[위치확인] Where are you now?
어디어디를 가봤습니까?	Where have you visited? = Where have you been? // Where have you visited in America? = What places in America have you visited? (미국의~) ➡ Almost everywhere. (거의 다 가봤습니다.)

어디에 있습니까?	[위치확인] Where are you now?
	// Where are we now? (우리가 ~)
	// Where am I on the map? (지도에서 제가~)
	➡ Here. (이 위치요.)

어디입니까?	What's the next station? (다음 역은~)

	// What was the previous station? (전역은~) ➡ Dongdaemun. (동대문이요.)
어땠습니까?	How was it? // How was it today? (오늘~) ➡ It was good. (좋았어요.)
어떤 남자입니까?	What kind of man is he? ➡ I don't know. (모르겠어요.)
어떤 여자입니까?	What kind of woman is she? ➡ I don't know. (모릅니다.)
어떻게 가는지 가르쳐주세요.	Would you tell me how to get there? ➡ Take the subway. (지하철을 타세요.)

어떻게 갑니까?	How can I go there? = How can I get there?
	// How can I go to Ihwa Woman's University? (이대는 ~)
	// How can I get to City Hall? (시청은~)
	➡ You see the way ahead of you. Go straight after turning right. It's almost one stop away. (앞쪽 저 길 입구 보이지요? 우측으로 꺾어진 다음에 방향을 바꾸지 말고 쭉 가세요. 거의 한 정거장 정도 가면 도착합니다.)

어떻게 그럴 수 있죠?	① [능력] How could you do that? ➡ I don't know. (잘 모르겠어요.) ② [이유] Why did you do that? // Why did he do that? (그 사람이~) ➡ He's narrow-minded. (그 사람 속이 아주 좁아요.) ③ [의외의 상황이 발생] How could it happen? ➡ ⓐ That's the way it goes. (일이란 게 그런 거야.) ⓑ But it turned out to be true. (하지만 사실로 확인했습니다.)
어떻게 됐습니까?	① How's it going? // How's it going now? (지금~) ➡ Everything is OK. (모든 것이 다 정상입니다.) ② How did it go after that? (후에~)

	➡ After that, ... (나중에는 말이야…) ③ How did it turn out? (결과가~) ➡ Normal. (정상입니다.) ④ [사태나 상태가] What's going on? = How'd it go? // What's going on with him? (그 사람~) ➡ ⓐ Good. (좋아요.) ⓑ Fine. (괜찮아요.)

어떻게 된 거야?	① [사태] What happened?
	// What happened to you? (너 이거~)
	// What happened to him? (그 사람은 도대체~)
	➡ He ran away from home. (그녀석이 가출했어요.)
	➡ Because of whom? (누구 때문이래?)
	➡ I don't know yet. (아직 몰라요.)
	② [질책 · 불만] What's wrong?
	= What's the matter?
	// What's the matter with this? (이게~)
	// What's the matter with your face? (얼굴은~)
	➡ I don't know. (모릅니다.)
	③ [해명요구] How would that be possible?
	// Would this be possible? (이게~)
	➡ I don't know. (모르겠어요.)
	④ [사고] What happened?
	// What the hell happened? (도대체~)
	➡ I don't know. (모르겠어요.)

어떻게 생각합니까?	① [판단] What do you think?
	// What do you think about me? (나를~)
	// What do you think of China? (중국을~)
	// What do you think of it? (그것~)
	// What do you think of this matter? (이 일을~)
	// What do you think of this? (이것에 대해~)
	// What do you think of the person? (그 사람을~)
	➡ ⓐ He seems very nice. (참 좋은 사람 같습니다.)
	ⓑ I don't think he has a very good personality.
	② [추측] How do you think it goes?
	③ [의견을 구함] What do you think?
	// What do you think about her? (그녀를~)

	// What do you think about the new teacher? (새로 오신 선생님을~)
어떻게 알겠어!	① ['난 모른다'의 의미] How would I know? (내가~) ② ['아무도 모른다'의 의미] Nobody knows. = Only god knows. ③ ['넌 모른다.'의 의미] How could you possibly know? (네가~)
어떻게 여길(왔어요)?	① [예상치 못한 만남] How come? ➡ Looking for someone. (사람 찾으려고요.) ② [간만에 연락도 없이] What brings you here? ➡ Because I missed you. (보고 싶어서요.)
어떻게 오셨습니까?	① [교통수단] How did you get here? ➡ By bus. (버스로요) ② [용무] What can I do for you? = How can I help you? ➡ I'd like to meet Mr. Murray. (머리씨를 찾는데요.) ③ [안내] May I help you?
어떻게 이런 일이!	Why did that happen? = How could that possibly happen?
어떻게 좀 해봐!	[해결방법] Do something!
어떻게 지냅니까?	How are you? = What's going on these days? // How have you been these days? = What have you been up to? (요즘~) ➡ ⓐ Fine. (잘 지냅니다.) ⓑ So so. (그런대로요.)
어떻게 지냈습니까?	☞ 어떻게 지냅니까?
어떻게 하기로 했습니까?	① [계획] What are the plans? = What are you planning? = What are you planning to do? ② [결정] What did you decide?
어떻게 하면 좋을까요?	What should I do? ➡ Never mind him. (그 사람 신경 쓰지 마세요.)

	// What should I do with this? (이 일을~) ➡ Calm down. You'll figure it out. (조급해하지 마세요. 방법이 있을 겁니다.)
어떻게 한 거야?	① [방법 확인] How did you do that? // How did you do this? (이거~) ➡ I don't know. (몰라요.) ② [수작] What did you do?
어떻게 할 건데?	① What are you going to do? = What will you do? // What on earth are you going to do? (도대체~) ② What is he going to do to me? (그 사람이 날~) ➡ Nothing at all. (어떻게 하지 못할 거야!) ③ [상대의 위협에 대해] So what will you do to me? (그러면~)
어떻게 해야 좋을까요?	☞ 어떻게 하면 좋을까요? ➡ Do as you usually do. = Do as you normally do. (하던 대로 해요.)
어떻게 해야 좋을지 모르겠어요.	I don't know what to do. // I really don't know what to do. (정말~) ➡ There's a way. (한 가지 방법이 있는데요.)
어떻게 해야 할까요?	☞ 어떻게 하면 좋을까요?
어떻게 해야 할지 모르겠어요.	☞ 어떻게 해야 좋을 지 모르겠어요.

어떻습니까?	① [의견을 구함] What do you think?
	= How do you think? = What about you?
	= How about you?
	// What do you think about this vase?
	(이 꽃병은~)
	// What do you think about the beer?
	(맥주 맛이~)
	➡ It tastes very good. (아주 좋습니다.)
	// What do you think about tomorrow?
	= How does tomorrow sound? (그럼 내일은~)

	➡ ⓐ I will be free tomorrow. (내일은 시간이 있습니다.) ⓑ I won't be free tomorrow, either. (내일도 시간이 없습니다.) ② [상황 · 사태] How is he? (그 사람~) ➡ He's fine. (괜찮습니다.) ③ [상황 · 건강 · 형편] How's it going? // How's it going now? = Are you doing well? (~잘 지내세요?) ➡ ⓐ Doing well. (잘 지냅니다.) ⓑ So so. (그런대로요.) ④ [생각] What do you think? ➡ Very good. (매우 좋습니다.)
어렵습니다.	① It's difficult. // It's a little difficult. (약간~) ② [육체적] It's hard. // It's a little hard. (약간~) ③ [곤란함] It's tough. // It's a little tough. (약간~)
어른 둘, 아이 하나요.	[입장표] Two adults and one child.
어른 말을 안 들으면 손해를 본다.	You'll suffer if you don't listen to adults.
어리광 부리기는!	What a baby! = You're acting like a baby!
어리바리합니다.	I'm kinda dumb. (제가 ~)
어리석었어요.	You were stupid. = You were an idiot. // I was stupid. (제가~)
어린애가 아닙니다.	I'm not a kid. // I'm not a kid any longer. (난 이제~)
어림없는 소리! // 어림도 없는 소리하지마! // 어림도없지!	① [안 통함] I don't buy it! ② [반대] I don't think so! ③ [대화 거절] Cut the crap! ④ [헛된 생각이나 말] That's nonsense!
어머(나)!	① Oh, my! ② Geez! = Oh, no! ☞ 맙소사!

어머니날을 축하합니다.	Happy Mother's Day! // Happy Mother's Day to all mothers! (세상 모든 어머님들, ~)
어머니는 주부입니다.	My mother is a housewife. = My mother is a homemaker.
어색해요.	Awkward. // Very awkward. (너무~)
어서 들어갑시다.	Let's enter. = Let's go in.
어서 들어오세요.	Please come in. = Please come inside.
어서 들어요.	[식사] Help yourself.
어서 말해!	Say it!
어서 먹어!	Eat now! = Eat it!
어서 앉으세요.	Please sit. = Have a seat, please.
어서 오십시오!	① [손님을 맞을 때] Welcome! ② [손님을 안으로 모실 때] This way, please. ③ [음식점] Hi. // Hi. What would you like to have? (~주문하시겠어요?) ➡ Let me have a cafe latte. (카페라떼 한잔 주세요.)
어서 일어나!	Get up! = Get up now! = Stand up now!
어서 자!	Go to bed! = Go to bed now! = Go to sleep!
어수룩하긴!	So naive!
어울리는 것 같습니다.	Looks like it's going well. = Looks like the things are going well. // Looks like things are going well for them. (둘이 잘~) = They look so compatible.
어울리지 않아요.	① We're mismatched. (우린~) // Actually, they're mismatched.

	= They are not compatible, as a matter of fact. (사실 그들은~)
	② [배필 · 자격] I'm not good enough for you. (난 너한테~)
	// You're not good enough for him. (넌 그 사람과~)
	// You are mismatched. (너희들은~)

어울린다.	① The dress looks really good on you.
	= The dress suits you very well. (원피스가 정말~)
	② [말이나 직업이] It's just perfect for you.
	// I'm fit for the job. (그 일은 나한테~)
	③ [배필 · 자격] A good match!
	// You are a good match for each other.
	= You look great with each other.
	= You are a well-matched husband and wife.
	= You are so compatible for each other. (너희 둘 잘~)

어이가 없어서!	① [이해가 안 됨] That beats everything!
	// That really beats everything! (정말~)
	② [할 말이 없음] I'm dumb-founded.
	= I'm dumbstruck!
	// I'm so dumbstruck! (정말~)

어제 다르고 오늘 다르다.	Yesterday is one thing, and today is another. = Yesterday and today are different.
어제 무엇을 했습니까?	What did you do yesterday? ➡ I met my friend. (친구를 만났어요.)
어제 밤에 잘 잤습니까?	Did you sleep well last night? = Did you have a sound sleep last night? ➡ Yes, I did. (잘 잤어요.)
어제 일 같다.	It's just like yesterday.
어쩌려고?	What do you want? // What do you want then? (그럼~)

	// What do you want from me then? (그럼 나보고~) ➡ Do as you did before. (하던 대로 해.)
어쩐지!	I already knew it! ☞ 그랬었구나!

어쩔 수 없습니다.	① [대책이 없음] I have no alternatives.
	② [방법이 없음] **I can't help it.** = I have no choice.
	// I really can't help it. (정말~)
	③ [불가피함] It's necessary. = It's inevitable.
	// This is necessary. (이건~)

어지러워요.	I feel dizzy. = I'm kind of light-headed.
어차피 가는 길입니다.	It's on my way anyway.
어차피 같은 방향입니다.	We're going the same direction anyway.
어학연수 왔습니다.	I'm here to learn the language. // I'm here to learn English. (영어~)
어학연수를 가려고 합니다.	I'm planning to go abroad to study the language. // I'm planning to go to America to study English. (미국에~)

억

억울합니다!	[누명] **I feel victimized!** = I feel like I'm a victim! = I'm innocent! // I really feel like I'm a victim! (정말~)
억울해 죽겠어요.	① [섭섭해서] ☞ 억울합니다! ② [누명] I'm innocent of the charge.
억지 춘향이.	It's like doing against my will.
억지로 마시지 마세요.	Shouldn't drink against your will. // Shouldn't drink alcohol against your will. = You shouldn't force yourself to drink.

	= You shouldn't drink if you don't want to. (술을~)
억지로 하지 마세요.	You shouldn't do it against your will. // You really shouldn't do it against your will. (정말~)

언

언니는 미국에 있습니까?	Is your elder sister in America?

언제 갑니까?
// 언제 떠납니까?
	When are you leaving?
	= When will you leave?
	➡ Tomorrow. (내일이요.)
	관련표현
	the day after tomorrow (모레)
	// three days from now (글피)
	// this morning (오늘 아침)
	// this afternoon (오늘 오후)
	// this evening (오늘 저녁)
	// three tomorrow afternoon (내일 오후 세시)

언제 갔습니까?	When did you leave?
	// When did she leave? (그녀는~)
	➡ Just now. (방금 갔습니다.)
	관련표현
	three days ago (그끄저께) // two days ago
	= the day before yesterday (그저께)
	// yesterday (어제) // today (오늘)
	// morning (아침) // evening (저녁)
	// a.m. (오전) // noon (정오) // p.m. (오후)

언제 겁니까?	① [전화] When will you call? ➡ Tomorrow. (내일이요.) ② [날짜] When was it? ➡ On the twentieth. (20일이요.) ③ [시간] When was it? ➡ Ten in the morning. (오전 10시요.)

언제 한 번 만납시다.	Let's meet some time. // Let's meet together. = Let's get together. (우리~)
언제입니까?	① [날] When is it? ➡ Tomorrow. (내일이요.) ② [날짜] When is it? ➡ On the second. (2일이요.) ③ [시간] When is it? ➡ At two. (2시요.)
언제든지.	[부탁에 대한 동의] Anytime. ⬅ Buy me some books. (책 좀 사다줘.)
언제든지 다 좋습니다.	Anytime is fine with me. = It works out for me anytime. = Whenever you want.
언짢아하지 말아요.	Don't feel bad about it. = Don't feel unhappy.

얼

얼간이!	Moron! = Nerd! = Bonehead!
얼굴도 못봤어요.	I haven't seen his face. (그이 ~) // I went there everyday, but I haven't seen his face. (만날 갔으면서~)
얼굴만 예쁘다고 여자냐!	A pretty face isn't everything!
얼굴보다 마음이 예쁩니다.	She is more beautiful on the inside than she is on the outside.
얼굴에 손댔어요?	① [성형수술] Did you have plastic surgery? ☞ 성형 수술했어요? ② [만짐] Did you touch the face?
얼굴에 철판 깔았구나!	You have no shame! = You are so shameless!
얼굴을 이쪽으로 돌려봐요.	Please turn your head this way.
얼굴이 많이 익어요.	You look so familiar to me. // She looks so familiar to me. (그 여자는~)

얼굴이 무서워요.	The face is scary. // Her face is scary. (그 여자는~)
얼굴이 반쪽이 됐네.	Your face looks so small because you lost lots of weight.
얼굴이 부었습니다.	My face is swollen. = I have a swollen face.
얼굴이 빨개졌네.	My face got red. = It made me blush. = I blushed.
얼굴이 빨개집니다.	I blush. = My face gets red. // I blush whenever I meet new people. (낯선 사람을 만나면~)
얼굴이 왜 우거지상이냐!	① Why the frown? = Why are you frowning? = Why the scowl? = Why are you scowling? ➡ Nothing. (아무 일도 아닙니다.) ② Why the frown about the little thing? (그깟 일에~) ➡ What frown? (누가 우거지상을 했다고요.)
얼른 가!	Go quickly!
얼른 나가!	Out quickly!
얼른 앉으세요.	Please sit quickly!
얼마나 걸립니까?	How long does it take? // How long does it take here to City Hall? (여기서 시청까지~) ➡ Twenty minutes on foot. (걸어가면 약 20분 걸립니다.)
얼마나 살 수 있습니까?	① [물건] How much can I buy? ➡ To the extent you want. (원하는 만큼이요.) ② [생명] How long can I live? // How long can she live? (그녀는 얼마나~) ➡ She could die anytime. (언제든지 돌아가실 수 있습니다.)
얼마나 합니까?	① [물건의 값어치] How much is it?

	// How much is this? (이거~)
	➡ About three dollars. (3달러 정도요.)
	// How much are the cucumbers? (오이는~)
	➡ Two dollars and fifty cents per pound. (1파운드에 2달러 50센트입니다.)
	② [경비나 비용] How much does it cost?
	③ [서비스] How much do you charge for that?

얼마든지 쓰세요.	Please use it as much as you want.
얼마든지 있습니다.	I have plenty of it. = I have lots of it. // I have plenty of friends. = I have lots of friends. (친구는~)
얼마짜리로 드릴까요?	① [지폐] What kinds of bills do you want? ➡ Ten dollar bills all. (전부 10달러짜리요.) ② [물건의 가격] Which do you want? ➡ One of five dollars. (5달러 정도로요.)
얼어 죽겠다!	You look like you're freezing to death!
얼어 죽는 줄 알았습니다.	I thought I'd freeze to death. = I felt like I was going to freeze to death. // I thought I'd freeze to death. (꽁꽁~)
얼음 좀 주세요.	Give me some ice, please.
얼음이 꽁꽁 얼었습니다.	It's frozen hard.
얼음이 얼었습니다.	It's frozen.
얼음장 같다.	You're like ice. = You're so cold.
얼짱!	Beautiful face! = So pretty! = Such a pretty face!

얽

얽히고 설키다.	Very complicated.

엄

엄마를 닮았습니다.	You look just like your mother. = You resemble your mom.
엄마야!	[감탄] Oh, dear! = Oh, my goodness! = Oh, boy!
엄살떨지 말아요.	Don't exaggerate.
엄지손가락을 치켜세우다.	He's giving the thumbs up. (그는 ~)
엄합니다.	Strict! // He's very strict with me. (그분은 저한테 매우~)

업

업혀요!	On my back! ➡ No. (아니에요.)

없

없는 것 없이 다 있습니다.	① [상품] I have everything. = I have all. ② [보잘 것 없는 작은 것이지만] I have but small things. = I have but meaningless things. = I only have small things. = I only have meaningless things.
없는 것보다 낫습니다.	It's better than nothing. // It's better than nothing anyway. (어쨌든~)
없던 걸로 합시다.	Let's just act as if it did not happen. = Let's pretend it didn't happen. = Let's say it didn't happen.
없습니다.	① [외출 중] Not here. // He's not here. (그는~) ② [물건이] I don't have it. ③ [재고가 없음] Nothing left. = Sold out.

없어졌습니다.	① [물건] Gone. // The bag is gone. (가방이~) ② [사람] Gone. // She's gone. = She's disappeared. (그녀가~)

엉

엉뚱한 생각하지 마세요.	Stop thinking of nonsense. = Don't think of nonsense.
엉뚱한 소리 마세요.	Stop talking about nonsense. = Cut the crap, please.
엉망이군!	It's a mess! = What a mess! // It's a total mess! (완전히~)
엉엉!	[우는 소리] Bawling!
엉큼해!	So wily! = So crafty! ➡ Bitch! You are wily! (이년아, 네가 더 엉큼해!)
엉터리야!	① [상황이] It's a sham! = What a sham! = What a fake! ② [속임] It's a fake! (그건~) ③ [말이] It's completely nonsense! (그건 완전히~) ④ [꼴 같지 않음] Crap!

엎

엎드려!	Lie on the ground! // Lie on the ground quickly! (빨리~)
엎어지면 코 닿을 데.	So near. = So close. = It's in spitting distance. = It's just a stone's throw away.
엎지른 물은 다시 담지 못한다.	[속담] It's no use crying over spilt milk.

ㅇ

엎지른 물은 주워 담지 못한다.	☞ 엎지른 물은 다시 담지 못한다.
엎질러진 물이야.	It's like spilt milk.
엎친 데 덮친 격이군!	① It made things worse! ② [속담] It never rains but it pours. ☞ 가난한 집 제사 돌아오듯 한다. // 설상가상.

에

~에, (어디)에	① [장소] to // I'm going to Incheon. (인천에 갑니다.)
	// I'd like to go to Incheon.
	(인천에 가고 싶습니다.)
	// Is this train for New York?
	(이것은 뉴욕에 가는 기차입니까?)
	// Is this for City Hall? (시청에 가는 버스입니까?)
	➡ Yes! (예!)
	② [비행기로] to // I'm going to L.A. (LA에 갑니다.)
	③ [존재] in // He's in Texas. (그는 텍사스에 있습니다.)
	// I live in Seoul. (서울에 살고 있습니다.)
	// I'd like to study at a university in Boston.
	(보스톤에 있는 대학교에서 공부했으면 좋겠어요.)
	④ [도착] at // Please let me know at Seoul Station. (서울역에 도착하면 좀 알려주세요.)

~에게, (누구)에게	① [수여] to // I'll give you a ring later. = I'll give you a call later. (이따가 너에게 전화할게.) ② [사역] to // Tell him to eat. (그에게 밥 먹으라고 해라.) ③ [학습] from // I learned English from him. (제 영어는 그에게 배웠습니다.) ④ [보고나 경례] to // I'm reporting to you. (선생님께 보고 드립니다.)
~에서, (어디)에서	① [거리] from // Is your home far from the school? (집은 학교에서 멉니까?) ➡ Not so far. (별로 안 멉니다.)

	② [장소] in // at
	// I grew up in Seoul. (서울에서 자랐습니다.)
	// I have lived in Seoul. (서울에서 쭉 살았습니다.)
	// I work at a travel agency. (여행사에서 일합니다.)
	// I work at a company now. (저는 현재 한 회사에 출근하고 있습니다.)
	// We met at a park for the first time. (우리는 공원에서 처음 만났습니다.)
	③ [기점] from
	// I'm from Arizona. (애리조나에서 왔습니다.)
	// I'm from Korea. (한국에서 왔습니다.)
	④ [도달] at // Please get off at Seoul Station. (서울역에서 하차하면 됩니다.)

에어컨을 켜주세요.	Please turn on the AC.
에어컨이 고장 났습니다.	The AC is out of order. = The AC is not working.
에어컨이 너무 셉니다.	The AC is too cold. // The AC in the office is too cold. (사무실의~)
에어컨이 안 됩니다.	☞ 에어컨이 고장 났습니다.
에이 씨!	〈속어〉 Shit!
에취!	① [재치기 소리] Achoo! = Ahchoo! ② [기침 소리] Cough!

엘

엘리베이터는 올라갑니까, 내려갑니까?	Is the elevator going up or down? ➡ ⓐ Going up. (올라갑니다.) ⓑ Going down. (내려갑니다.)
엘리베이터를 이용하세요.	Use the elevator. // Use the next elevator. (다음~)

엘리베이터를 타십시오.	① ☞ 엘리베이터를이용하세요. ② Get in the elevator, please.

여

여권수속을 밟으려 왔는데요.	I'm here to go through the passport processing.
여권을 보여주세요.	Show me your passport. = Can I see your passport?
여권을 잃어버렸습니다.	I lost my passport.
여권을 재발급 받아야 합니까?	Should I have to make my new passport? // Where can I get a new passport? = Where can I go to make a new passport? (어디 가서~) ➡ You'll have to go to the consulate. (영사관에 가야 합니다.)
여기 어떻게 왔습니까?	Why are you here? = Why did you come here? ➡ For business. (일이 있어서요.)
여기 있습니다.	① [영수증 · 잔돈 · 물건 등을 건네줄 때] Here it is. = Here we go. ② [물건이 있는 곳] Here they are. ③ [존재] Here. // I'm here. (저~) ④ [물건을 찾음] Here it is. = Here we go.
여기가 어디입니까?	Where am I? ➡ Here's Gwanghwamun. (여기 광화문이야.)
여기까지 합시다.	[논의] Let's call it a day. = Let's finish here. = Let's wrap things up now. // That's all for today. (오늘은 ~)
여기는 웬일이야? // 여기 웬일이세요?	① What brings you here? = What are you doing here? = What brought you here?

	➡ I have something to do. (일이 좀 있어서요.) ② [우연한 만남] ☞ 이게 누구야?
여기를 봐주세요.	Look here.
여기서 가깝습니다.	It's close from here. // My home is close from here. (우리 집은~)
여기서 거기까지 얼마나 걸립니까?	How long does it take from here to there? ➡ ⓐ Not so long. (멀지 않습니다.) ⓑ About one hour. (1시간이요.)
여기서 끝내자.	① [수업] Let's close now. = Let's call it a day. = Let's wrap it up now. (우리~) ② [대화] Let's finish now. (우리~) ③ [회의] Let's finish now. = Let's wrap it up now. (우리~) ④ [이별] Let's break up now. (우리~)
여기서 드실 겁니까, 가지고 가실 겁니까?	[패스트푸드점] Here or to go? ➡ ⓐ Here. (여기서 먹을 겁니다.) ⓑ To go. (가지고 갑니다.)
여기서 말씀하세요.	Please talk to me here. ➡ OK. (그러죠.)
여기서 뭐하세요?	What are you doing here? // What are you doing here now? (지금~) ➡ ⓐ I'm drinking tea. (차 마셔요.) ⓑ I'm waiting for someone. (사람 기다려요.) ⓒ I've got something to tell you. (너한테 할 말이 있어.)
여기서 일합니까?	Do you work here? ➡ Yes. (예.)
여러 가지로 감사했습니다.	Thank you so much for many things.
여러 말할 필요 없습니다.	Don't need to say in detail.

여러분 안녕하세요!	① [전체] Hi, everyone / guys! = Hello, everyone / guys! ② [수업] Hi, class! = Hello, class! = Hi, everyone! = Hello, guys! (학생~)
여름방학은 언제 시작합니까?	When will summer vacation begin? ➡ It will begin in mid-July. (여름방학은 7월 중순입니다.)
여름에는 좀 덥습니다.	It's a little hot in summer.
여름은 후덥지근합니다.	It's sticky hot in summer. // Summer in New York is sticky hot. (뉴욕의~)
여보!	① [남편의 호칭] Honey! = Darling! = Sweetheart! ② [아내의 호칭] Honey! = Darling! = Sweetheart!
여보세요!	[전화] Hello! = Hullo!
여우를 피해서 호랑이를 만나다.	[속담] Out of the frying pan and into the fire.
여유 있습니까?	[시간적으로] ① Do you have time? ➡ ⓐ Yes. (여유 있습니다.) ⓑ No. (그럼요.) ② Are you free? ➡ Yes, I'm free. (여유 있습니다.)
여자는 정말 골치 아파요.	Women are a big headache. = Women are troublemakers.
여자는 질투가 많아요.	Women are more likely to be jealous. = Women are likely to be more jealous.
여자들은 다 똑같아.	[폄하] Women are women! = All women are the same.
여자를 밝힙니다.	Likes women. // He likes women. = He's a womanizer. (그는~)

ㅇ

여자복도 많다니까.	So lucky with women. // This dude is so lucky with women. (이 자식은~)
여자의 마음을 모르겠습니다.	I don't know what women think. // I really don't know what women think. (정말~)
여자입니다.	Woman. = Female. // I'm a woman. (저는~)
여쭤보겠습니다.	[존칭표현] May I ask you a question? (한 가지~) ➡ Feel free to ask me anything, please. (사양마시고, 말씀하세요.)
여행갈까요?	Shall we travel? = How about taking a trip? // Shall we travel together? (우리 같이~) ➡ Sounds good. = Great. (좋아요.)
여행 왔습니다.	Here for traveling. = For sightseeing.

역

역겹다!	① Disgusting! = Nauseating! ② Sickening! // You're really sickening! (너 정말~) ③ [냄새] It smells disgusting! = It smells nauseating!
역사의 수레바퀴는 되돌릴 수 없다.	You can't stop the wheels of history. = History repeats itself.
역시 너답다!	[능력 · 기백] It's just like you!
역에 도착하면 알려주세요.	Please let me know at the station.
역을 지나쳤습니다.	I passed by the station. // I passed by the station again today. (오늘 또~)

연

연결해드리겠습니다.	I'll call you. // I'll call you at extension number 113. (내선 113번으로~) ➡ Please connect me to extension number 222. (내선 222번 좀 연결해주세요.)
연극하지 마, 가증스러워!	Don't act. I hate it! // Don't act again. I hate it! (다신~)

연락드릴게요.	① I'll contact you.
	② [전화로] I'll give you a call.
	= I'll call you.
	// I'll give you a call again. (또~)
	// I'll give you a call again later.
	= I'll call you back. (나중에 다시~)
	// I'll give you a call right away. (바로~)

연락받았습니다.	[통보] I have been informed. = I have been told.
연락이 안 됩니다.	I can't contact him. = I can't get a hold of him. (그와~)
연락주세요.	① Please contact me. ➡ Yes. (예.) ② [전화] Please call me. = Please give me a call. = Please give me a ring. ③ [통보] Please inform me.
연락처입니다.	My contact information. // This is my contact information. (이건 저의~)
연락하고 지내자.	Let's keep in touch. = Let's keep in contact. // Let's keep in touch with each other. (우리~)
연락합니까?	How can I contact you? (제가 당신한테 어떻게~) ➡ By cell phone. (핸드폰으로 해요.)
연세가 어떻게 되십니까?	How old are you? ➡ I'm fifty-five. (55세입니다.)

연습해!	Practice! // Keep practicing! (계속~)
연애 따로, 결혼 따로야.	Love is one thing and marriage is another.
연애 중입니다.	I'm in love. // They're in love. (그들 둘은 지금~)
연체됐습니다.	① Overdue. // Your book is overdue. (당신 책이~) ② Your loan payment is overdue this month. (이번 달 대출금이~)
연휴인데 야외로 놀러 갑시다.	It's a holiday. Let's go out. // It's a holiday next week. Let's go out. (다음 주가~)

열

열 받네!	I'm so mad! = I'm losing my temper!
열 번 찍어 안 넘어가는 나무 없다.	[속담] Little strokes fell great oaks.
열 길 물속은 알아도 한 길 사람 속은 몰라!	[속담] You can sound water ten fathoms deep, but you cannot sound the human heart a single fathom!
열나고 목도 아픕니다.	I have a fever and a sore throat.
열려라 참깨!	Open, sesame!
열 손가락을 깨물어 안 아픈 손가락 없다.	All the ten fingers will feel the same pain when you bite them.
열쇠 주세요.	① Give me keys, please. ② [겸양표현] Would you please give me room keys? (방~)
열쇠를 방에 두고 깜박했습니다.	I left the keys behind in the room.
열심히 공부할게요.	I will study hard.

열심히 하자!	① Try hard! ② [공부] Study hard!
열심히 할게요.	① [맡은 바 책임] I'll do my best. = I'll try my best. ② [노력] I'll try hard. // I'll try harder. (더~)
열심히 해!	① [일을] Work hard! ② [노력] Try harder next time! (다음번에 더~)
열심히 해보겠습니다.	☞ 열심히 할게요.

열어(봐)!	[가방 · 문 등을] Open up!
	// Open up quickly! (빨리~)
	// Open the door quickly. (문을~)

열은 없습니다.	You have no fever.
열이 내렸습니다.	Your body temperature went down.
열이 있습니까?	Do you have a fever? ➡ Yes, I do. (열이 납니다.)
열중 쉬어!	Attention!

염

염병할!	Damn it! = Fuck! ☞ 제기랄!
염색하시겠습니까?	① [젊은이] Would you like to color your hair? = Would you like to get your hair colored? = Would you like to have your hair colored? ➡ ⓐ Yes. (염색해주세요.) ⓑ Please color it blonde. (금발로 염색해주세요.) ② [노인] Would you like to dye your hair? = Would you like to get your hair dyed? = Would you like to have your hair dyed?
염치없는 놈.	〈비속어〉 Such a shameless bastard!

엿

엿 먹어라!	〈비속어〉 Fuck you! = Fuck off!
엿듣고 있습니다.	Someone is eavesdropping on the conversation. (누군가~)

영

영(0) 번을 누르고나서, 지역번호를 누르세요.	Press zero and then press the area code. // Press zero first off and then press the area code. (먼저~)
영광입니다.	It's an honor. // This is an honor. (이건~)
영수증 가져왔습니다.	I've got the receipt. = I brought the receipt.
영수증주세요.	① [건네주기를 요청] Let me have a receipt. = Give me a receipt, please. ② [발행을 요청] Make out a receipt, please. = Issue me a receipt, please.
영어가 어렵습니다.	English is difficult. = It's difficult to learn English.
영어가 전공입니다.	My major is English. = I major in English. = I'm majoring in English.
영어공부를 합시다.	Let's study English. // Let's study English for an hour everyday. (매일 한 시간~) ➡ ⓐ That sounds good. = That's a good idea. = Great. (좋은 생각이네요.) ⓑ I'd like to, but I have to study Chinese. (그러고 싶지만, 중국어를 공부해야 합니다.)
영어과 학생입니까?	Are you a student in the English Department? ➡ Yes. (그래요.)

영어능력시험을 봤습니다.	I took an English proficiency test. // I took an English proficiency test. It was too difficult. (~ 시험이 너무 어려웠어요.)
영어노래 부를 줄압니까?	Can you sing English songs? ➡ Yes. I can sing two songs. (네. 두 곡 할줄 압니다.)
영어로 어떻게 말하는지 가르쳐주세요.	Would you tell me how to say it in English? // Would you tell me how to say this in English. (이 말을~)
영어로 어떻게 말합니까?	How do you say it in English? // How do you say this in English? (이거~)
영어로 어떻게 말하는지 모릅니다.	I don't know how to say it in English. // I don't know how to say this in English. (이 말을 ~)
영어를 가르쳐주세요.	Please teach me English. = Would you please teach me English?
영어를 모릅니다.	① [영어에 대한 전반적인 능력] I don't know English. ② [말하기] I can't speak English.
영어를 아는 사람 있습니까?	[대화 가능] Can anybody speak English? // Can anybody speak English here? (이 부근에 누구~) ➡ I have no idea. Ask it to others. (잘 몰라요, 다른 사람에게 물어봐주세요.)
영어를 알아듣겠습니까?	Can you understand English? // Can you understand my English? (제~) ➡ ⓐ Yeah. Well enough. (그런대로 알아들어요.) ⓑ Just a little. (많이는 못 알아들어요.)
영어를 어디서 배웠습니까?	Where did you learn English? ➡ In America. (미국에서요.)
영어를 얼마나 배웠습니까?	How long have you studied English? ➡ ⓐ About a year. (약 1년 배웠어요.)

	ⓑ I've studied English for six months. (영어를 6개월 정도 배웠어요.) ⓒ It's been a year. (1년 되었어요.)
영어를 잘 못하니, 이해해주세요.	I'm not good at English. Please understand that.
영어를 잘 못합니다.	① [전반적 능력] I'm not good at English. = My English is not so good. ② [말하기] I can't speak English well. = I'm not a fluent English speaker.
영어를 잘합니까?	① [전반적 능력] Are you good at English? ② [말하기] Do you speak English well? = Can you speak English fluently? = Are you a fluent English speaker? ➡ No. Just a little. (아니오. 몇 마디만 합니다.)
영어를 전공합니다.	I major in English. = I'm majoring in English. = I am an English major. = My major is English. ☞ 영어가 전공입니다.
영어를 할 줄 모릅니다.	I can't speak English. ☞ 영어를 잘못합니다.
영어를 할 줄 아는 가이드를 부탁합니다.	I'd like to have a guide who can speak English. = I need a guide who's able to speak in English. = I'd like to have an English-speaking guide.
영어를 할 줄 압니까? // 영어로 말 할 줄 압니까?	Can you speak English? = Can you speak in English? ➡ ⓐ Yes! (예!) ⓑ Just a little. (조금 할 줄 압니다.) ⓒ No, I can't. (할 줄 모릅니다.) ⓓ Not at all. (조금도 못합니다.)
영어를 참 잘합니다.	You speak English very well. = You speak in English so fluently. = Your English is so good. = You're a fluent English speaker.

영어 메뉴판이 있습니까?	Do you have a menu in English? ➡ Yes. (있습니다.)
영어 배우고 싶습니다.	I'd like to learn English.
영어 배우고 있습니다.	I've been learning English.
영어 배우기 어렵습니까?	Is it difficult to learn English? ➡ It's not so easy. (쉬운 편은 아닙니다.)
영어 선생님께 배웠습니다.	I learned from the English teacher. // I learned the song from the English teacher, Mr. Baker. (그 노래를 베이커 ~)
영업이 끝났습니다.	The hours of business are over. = Our hours of business are over. = The store is closed.
영웅도 미인엔 약하다더니!	Who says even Ceasar couldn't refuse Cleopatra?
영원히 행복하세요.	I hope you will be happy forever.
영전하신 것을 축하합니다.	Congratulations on your promotion.
영화 보러 갈까요?	Would you like to go to a movie? = Wanna go to a movie? ➡ ⓐ OK, let's go. (봅시다.) // Good. (좋아요.) ⓑ I can't. (못갑니다.) ⓒ I'm not interested. (관심 없습니다.)
영화는 몇 시부터 상영합니까?	When will the movie start? ➡ Five in the afternoon. (오후 5시입니다.)
영화는 어떻습니까?	How was the movie? = How do you like the movie? // How do you like this movie? (이~) ➡ It's fine. (그런대로 볼만해요.)
영화는 재미있습니까?	Is the movie interesting?

➡ ⓐ It's interesting. (재미있습니다.)
ⓑ Not interesting. (재미없습니다.)

옆

옆에 앉아도 될까요?	Can I sit next to you? ➡ Sure. (물론이죠.)
옆자리에 사람 있습니까?	Is the seat next to you taken? ➡ No. (없습니다.)

예

예!	① [대답 또는 확인] Yes! = Yeah!
	② [동의] OK. // OK, I see. (~알았습니다.)
	// OK. I'll be right there. (~곧바로 가겠습니다.)
	// Yes. That's right. (~맞습니다.)
	// Yes. It's me. (~접니다.)
	⬅ Excuse me, but are you Mr. Gim?
	(실례합니다만, 당신이 김 선생이십니까?)
	③ [부름의 대답] Yes. ☞ 갑니다!
	④ [전화] Hello! ☞ 여보세요!
	⑤ [출석대답] Yes. = I'm here. = Here.

예금하려고 합니다. // 예금해주세요.	I'd like to deposit the money. = Please deposit the money. // I'd like to deposit 100 dollars. (100달러를~)
예매해야 합니까?	Should I purchase a ticket in advance? ➡ Yes. (예.)

예쁩니다. // 예쁘시네요.	① [얼굴] Pretty. = You're pretty.
	// Really pretty. (참~)
	// Miss, you're really pretty. (아가씨 참~)
	② [색깔 · 모양 등이] It's pretty. ☞ 아름답습니다!

예약할 수 있습니까?	① Can I make a reservation? ➡ Sure. (예.) ② Can I reserve a seat? = Can I make a reservation?

	// What airlines can I reserve? (어느 항공사의 항공편을~) ➡ ⓐ Korean Airlines. (대한항공이요.) ⓑ Asiana Airlines. (아시아나항공이요.)
예약했습니까?	Did you make a reservation? ➡ Yes, I did. (예약했습니다.)
예외로 할 수 없습니다.	There's no exception. // There's no exception because of you. (당신 때문에~)
예외로 해주세요.	Please take it as an exception. // Please take it as an exception. Only once. (한번만~)
예의 없이 굴지 마라.	Stop acting like you have no manners.
예의 좀 지키세요.	Please have some manners.
예의가 없네요.	You have no manners. // You really have no manners. (정말~)
예측불허야!	Unpredictable! // 〈비속어〉 [종잡을 수 없는 경우] That bastard is unpredictable! (저 녀석은 ~)

옛

옛날 그대로야!	It's just like the old days.
옛말 그른 데없다. // 옛말이 틀린 게 하나 없다.	Old sayings are always true.

오

오 분 남았어요.	Five minutes left. = I have five minutes left.

	// Five minutes left still. (아직~)
오겠습니다.	① I'll be there. // I'll be right there. (곧~) ② [귀가] I'm returning home. // I'm going home soon. (곧~)
오금이 저리다.	I feel numbed.
오는 정이 고와야 가는 정도 곱다.	Give as you get.
오늘은 당신 생일입니까?	Is it your birthday today? = Is today your birthday? = Is your birthday today? ➡ Yes. (예.)
오늘은 몇 월 며칠입니까?	What's the date today? ☞ 몇 월 며칠입니까?
오늘은 무슨 요일입니까?	What day is it today? ☞ 무슨 요일입니까?
오라는 데는 없어도 갈 곳은 많다.	There is no place to invite, but many places to visit.
오락게임 그만 해라!	Stop playing computer games now!
오래 기다렸습니다.	I've been waiting for a long time.
오래 기다리게 해서 죄송합니다.	I'm sorry for making you wait for a long time.
오래 기다리셨습니까?	Have you waited for a long time? ➡ ⓐ Yes, but it's fine. (괜찮습니다.) ⓑ No. I'm just here. (저도 방금 도착했습니다.)
오래 기다리셨습니다.	① [말하는 사람] I've been waiting for a long time. ☞ 오래 기다렸습니다. ② [상대방] You've been waiting for a long time. // Guys, you've been waiting for a long time. (여러분~)
오래 살고 싶습니다.	I hope to live long. = I want to live long.

오래오래 사세요.	[생신 축하] May you live long. // May you be blessed and live long. (복 많이 받으시고~)
오랜만입니다!	It's long time no see. = Long time no see. = I haven't seen you for a long time.
오른쪽으로 가세요.	Go to the right, please.

오른쪽으로 도세요.	Turn right, please. = Make a right turn, please.
	// Go out and turn right, please. (나가서~)
	// Turn right at the first traffic lights. (첫 번째 신호등에서~)

오른쪽으로 붙어서 가세요.	Close to the right, please.
오리무중.	① [심리] I'm in a fog. ② [이해불능] I'm at sea.
오바이트할 것 같아요.	I think I'm going to throw up. = I think I'm going to puke.
오버하는 거 아니야!	That's too much!
오버하지 마!	① [소란 · 성질] Don't go too far! ② [잘난 체] Stop acting like that!
오빠!	[친오빠] Brother!
오셨어요!	You are here! = You've come here!
오순도순 행복하게 사시길 바랍니다.	[결혼 인사] May you live happily ever after.
오시느라 고생했습니다. // 오시느라 수고하셨습니다.	Thank you for bothering to come. // Thank you for bothering to come here. (여기까지~) ➡ No problem. (별말씀을요.)
오신 걸 환영합니다.	Welcome. // Welcome to Korea. (한국에~)
오십 보 백 보입니다.	[속담] A miss is as good as a mile.

오전 내내 바빴어요.	I was busy all morning.
오전 시간은 다 괜찮습니다.	I'm fine anytime in the morning.
오줌 누고 올게요.	I should pee. = I should go to the restroom.

오지 않았습니까?	Not here?
	// Why hasn't he come here? (그는 왜~)
	// Why hasn't he come here yet? (그는 왜 아직~)
	➡ Maybe he's sick. (아마 병났나 봅니다.)

오지랖이 넓다.	Such a meddler.
오징어에 땅콩 주세요.	Give me a squid and nuts, please.
오해받기 싫어요.	I don't wanna be misunderstood. // I don't wanna be uselessly misunderstood. (괜한~)
오해하지 마세요.	① Don't misunderstand. = Don't take it wrong. = Don't take it the wrong way. ② 〈경어〉 Don't misunderstand, please.
오후 내내 바빴어요.	I was busy all afternoon.
오후 시간은 다 좋습니다.	I'm fine anytime in the afternoon.

옥

옥동자 보신 걸 축하합니다.	Congratulations on having a son!
옥동자를 빨리 낳기를 바랍니다.	I hope you'll have a son soon.
옥에 티야!	① It's like a spot in the sun! ② [속담] No silver/gold without its dross!

온

온가족이 편안하기를 기원합니다.	My best wishes for your family. = I wish you all peace.
온가족이 화목하고 단란하게 지내길 기원합니다.	I hope you have peace and harmony in your family. = I wish you peace and harmony in your family.
온라인 게임 합시다.	Let's play online games. // Let's go to play online games. (우리 나가서~)
온라인 신청을 하고 싶습니다.	I'd like an online application.
온몸이 나른해요.	I feel tired. = I am weary.
온몸이 땀으로 젖었습니다.	I'm all wet with sweat.
온지는 얼마나 됐습니까?	① How long have you been? ② How long have you been here? // How long have you been in Korea? (한국에~) ➡ I've been here for a half year already. (벌써 반 년 넘었습니다.)

올

올거야?	Will you come? // When will you come? (언제~) ➡ I don't know. (나도 몰라.)
올 수 있습니까?	Can you come? // What time can you come? = When can you come? (몇 시에~)
올라가!	Go upstairs! = Up!
올라가세요.	Go upstairs, please. = Up, please.

올라와!	Come on up! = Up here!
올라오세요.	Come on up, please. = Up here, please.
올해는 몇 년도입니까?	What year is this year?

옳

옳은 말씀입니다!	① That's right! = You're right! ② [발언에 대해] You can say that again!

옷

옷 갈아입어!	Change your clothes!
	// Hurry to change your clothes!
	= Change your clothes quickly! (빨리~)
	// Here, change your clothes! (자, ~)

옷 벗지 마세요.	Don't take off your clothes, please.
옷 좀 세탁해주세요.	Would you clean the clothes? = Clean the clothes, please? // Would you clean these clothes? = Clean these clothes, please. (이~)
옷을 더 껴입고 나가세요.	Put some more clothes on when you go out.
옷을 세탁하려고 합니다.	I'm going to do the laundry.
옷을 입는 것을 도와주세요.	Please help me put the clothes on.
옷이 날개다.	[속담] Fine feathers make fine birds. = Apparel makes the men. = Clothes make the man. = The tailor makes the man. = Good clothes open all doors.

와

와!	[감탄] Wow!
와글와글!	[떠드는 소리] Hurly-burly!

와본 적이 있습니까?	Have you ever been?
	// Have you ever been here? (이곳에~)
	➡ ⓐ Yes, I have. (와본 적이 있습니다.)
	// No. It's my first time. (처음 왔습니다.)
	ⓑ No, I haven't. (와본 적이 없습니다.)
	ⓒ Never. (한 번도 와본 적이 없습니다.)

와서 도와줘요!	Help me! // Somebody help me! (누가 좀~) ➡ ⓐ I'm coming. (갑니다, 가요.) ⓑ Wait. I'll be right there. (잠깐만요, 바로 갑니다.)
와주시겠어요?	Will you come? ➡ ⓐ Sure. (그러죠.) ⓑ No, I can't. = Sorry I can't. (안됩니다.)
와주시길 바랍니다.	I wish you come. = I'd like you to come.
와주셔서 감사합니다.	Thank you for coming. // Thank you for coming here. (여기~)

왁

왁자지껄!	[떠드는 소리] Uproar! = Clamour!

완

완벽한 사람은 없다.	No one perfect. = There's no such things as a perfect man.

완벽합니다.	① It's perfect. ② [나무랄 데가 없음] It's perfect. = It's flawless. = It's impeccable.
완전하지 않습니다.	① [완전성] It's not perfect. ② [완결성] It's not complete.

왔

왔구나!	Here! // Here you are! (너~) // Here you are, too! (너도~)
왔다 갔어요.	Here before. // He was here before. (그가 이곳에~) ➡ Really? (그래?)
왔습니까?	Did you come? // When did you come? (언제~) // When did you come to Korea? (언제 한국에~) ➡ ⓐ Yesterday afternoon. (어제 오후요.) ⓑ Last month. (지난달말에요.)
왔어요!	① Here! // I'm here! (저~) ② [상대에게] You're here! = You've come here! ③ Spring has come! (봄이~)

왕

왕림해 주신 걸 환영합니다.	Thank you so much for coming. // Thank you so much for coming, everyone. (여러분께서~) ➡ I came here to see you. It's been a long time since I saw you last time. (며칠 못 봐서 자네 얼굴 좀 보려고 왔네.)
왕복표 하나주세요.	Give me a round trip ticket, please. = Let me have a round trip ticket.

왜

왜 그래?	① [행위에 대해] What's the matter? = Why did you do that? ② [말에 대해] What's the matter? = Why did you say that? ③ [당혹감] Why? = How come? // Why? What's wrong? (~도대체 무슨 일인데?) ➡ Nothing. (아무것도 아니에요.) ④ [상황파악] What happened? ➡ I had a car accident. (차사고 났어요.)
왜 나야?	① [사태] Why me? ➡ Who else then? (그럼 누굴?) ② [이유] Why is it me? ➡ Who else then? (그럼 누굴?) ③ [추측] Why me? ➡ I didn't know, either. (나도 생각 못했어!)
왜 또 그래?	Why are you doing this again? = What's the problem again? ➡ You know why! (왜 그러냐고, 알잖아.)
왜 안 되는데?	① [이유] Why not? ➡ Because it's not possible. (안 되면 안 되는 거지.) ② [사태] Why not? ➡ Because there's a problem with your proof. (네 증명서가 문제래.)

왜 안 오는거야?	① [이유] Why not come?
	// Why has he not come?
	= Why hasn't he come? (그 사람~)
	② [불만] How come ~?
	// How come he's not here? (그 사람~)
	➡ He has something else to do. (일이 있어요.)

왜 울어?	① Why are you crying? ② [사태] What's the matter? Why are you crying?

	➡ I messed up the test. (시험 망쳤어요.)
왜 웃어?	Why are you laughing? = What's so funny?
왜 이러는 거야?	① [시비] Why are you doing this? = Why is that? ② [사태] What's wrong? = What's the matter? = What's the problem? // What's wrong today? (오늘~)
왜 이렇게 했어?	Why did you do that? ➡ I don't know, either. (나도 모르겠어.)
왜요?	① [이유] Why? = How come? = For what? ② [사태] How? ③ [시비] What's it for?

외

외국에 유학가려고 합니다.	I'm going to study abroad. // He's going to study abroad. (그는~)
외국인입니다.	You're a foreigner. // I'm a foreigner. (저는~)
외로운 거 빼곤 다른 건 다 괜찮아요.	Everything is fine except my loneliness. // Everything is fine but I'm a little lonely. (약간~)
외로워하지 마세요.	Don't feel lonely. // Don't feel lonely anymore. (더는~)
외롭게 하지 마세요.	Don't make yourself feel lonely. // Don't make me feel lonely. (날~)
외롭습니다.	I'm lonely. // I'm too lonely. (너무~)
외모가 다가 아닙니다.	Appearances are not everything. = Beauty is but skin deep.
외모로 판단하지 마세요.	① Don't judge a person by his/ her looks.

	= You shouldn't judge people by the way they look. (사람을~) ② [속담] Don't judge a book by its cover.
외상 됩니까?	Can I pay it later? ➡ No. = No way. (안됩니다.)
외식합시다.	Let's eat out.
외출금지다.	You're grounded. // You're grounded from now on. (오늘부터~)
외출중입니다.	I'm out. // He's out. = He's not here. (그는 잠시~)
외출하고 싶지 않습니다.	I don't want to go out. // I don't want to go out today. (오늘~)
외출하세요.	[인사표현] Please go out for a change.

왼

왼쪽으로 가세요.	Go to the left, please. = Go left, please.
왼쪽으로 도세요.	Please turn left. = Please make a left turn. // Go out and turn left, please. (나가서~)
왼쪽으로 붙어서 가세요.	Close to the left, please.

요

요구르트를 좋아합니다.	I like yogurt.
요리 주문할래요?	Would you like to order? = Are you ready to order? ➡ Yes! (예!)
요리가 너무 짭니다.	It's too salty. // This is too salty. (이~)

요리가 매운가요?	Is it hot and spicy? ➡ ⓐ No. (아니요.) ⓑ Not so hot and spicy. (별로요.)
요리가 식었습니다.	It's become cold.
요리를 드십시오.	Please eat it.
요리를 시키지 않았는데요.	I didn't order the food. // I didn't order this food. (이~)
요일입니까?	What day is it? ☞ 무슨 요일입니까?
요점만 말해!	Get to the point! = Only main points! // Get to the point quickly! (어서~)
요즘 뭐하십니까?	What's up? = What are you up to? ➡ Nothing special. (별일 없습니다.)
요즘 바쁩니까?	Are you busy? ➡ ⓐ Yes, I am. (바쁩니다.) // Just a little bit. (조금 바쁩니다.) ⓑ Not at all. (하나도 안 바쁩니다.)
요즘 어떻게 지내십니까?	How have you been these days? ➡ ⓐ I'm fine. Thanks to you. (덕분에 잘 지냅니다. 당신은요?) ⓑ Fine. How about you? (덕분에요, 당신은요?)
요즘 어떻습니까?	[안부인사] How have you been? = How are you? = How are you? = How are you doing? = How's it going on? ➡ ⓐ Very good. (아주 좋습니다.) ⓑ Fine. (괜찮습니다. 잘 지냅니다.) ⓒ I'm OK. (그런대로.) ⓓ So so. (보통이야.)
요통이 있습니다.	I have a backache. ☞ 허리가 아픕니다.

욕

욕심은 한이 없다.	[속담] Avarice knows no bounds. = Greed has no limits. = The more one has, the more one wants.
욕심이 많다!	You're too greedy! = You want too much!
욕하지 마세요.	① Don't say four-letter words. = Don't use bad language. = Don't say bad words. ② [심한 욕설] Don't swear.

용

용건만 간단히 말씀하세요.	Say it in brief. ➡ OK. (그러죠.)
용기내세요.	Have courage. = Be courageous. // Have courage again. (다시~)
용돈주세요.	Give me some pocket money, please. = Allowance, please.
용두사미가 되어서는 안됩니다.	Don't end it in an anticlimax. = It shouldn't be an anticlimax.
용두사미로 하지 마세요.	You shouldn't make it an anticlimax.
용변 후 물 내릴 것.	① [화장실] Flush! ② [공고문] Please flush after use!
용서 안 할 거야.	I won't forgive. // I won't forgive you. (널~)
용서를 빕니다.	I feel so sorry. // I feel so sorry with all my heart. (진심으로~)

용서해주세요.	① [용서를 구함] Please forgive me.
	// Please forgive me. Only once. (한번만~)
	// Please forgive my fault. (제 잘못을~)

	➡ I won't forgive you this time. (이번엔 용서하지 않을 거야.) ② [관용을 바람] I ask you for your generosity. = I beg you for your generosity.
용장 밑에 약졸 없다.	[속담] A good general will make good men. = As is the master, so will his men be. = Like master, like men.
용지에 기입해주세요.	Please fill out the form. // Please fill out this form. (이~)

우

우거지상이야?	Why the frown? // Why the frown? You should be happy! (그럼 당연히 기뻐해야 맞지!~) ➡ Yeah, I'm happy, too. (그래요. 저도 기뻐요.)
우냐?	Are you crying? ➡ No. (아니요.)
우라질!	① [원망] 〈비속어〉 Goddamn! = Fuck! = Hell! = Damn it! ② [불신 · 경멸 · 실망] Crap!
우리가 남인가요?	① Are we strangers to each other? ② Don't we know each other?
우리가 어떤 사이냐!	What are we?
우리끼리 비밀로 합시다.	Let's keep it between you and me. = Let's keep it a secret. = Let's keep it secret.
우리끼리 얘기합시다.	① Let's have a talk only between us. ② [은밀히] Let's have a talk alone.
우물 안 개구리.	A frog in a small pond.
우물에 가서 숭늉 찾는다.	[속담] To seek hot water under cold ice.

우물우물!	[음식물 먹는 소리] Mumble.

우물정자(#) 버튼을 누르세요.	Press the pound button. = Press pound.
	// Press the pound button after entering your phone number. (전화번호를 다 누르고~)
	// Leave your message and press the pound button, please. (메시지를 남기고~.)

우박이 내립니다.	It's hailing. // It's hailing outside. (밖에 마침~)
우산 가져왔습니까?	Did you bring your umbrella? ➡ ⓐ Yes! (예!) ⓑ No. (아니요.) ⓒ I forgot. (깜빡했어요.)
우산 좀 빌려주세요.	Can I borrow your umbrella? = Would you lend me your umbrella?
우습다!	That's funny!
우승했습니다.	You won. // He won. (그가~)
우연히 만났습니다.	It was coincidental to meet. = It was just by chance. // It was coincidental to meet him. = I ran into him. = It was just coincidence that I met him. = It was just by chance that I met. (그 사람을~)
우열을 가리기 힘듭니다.	① Can't say who wins and who loses. ② Can't compete with each other. = They're equally great. = Can't choose one between the two. (두 사람은~)

우울합니다.	I feel down. = I feel blue. = I feel depressed.
	// I feel down today. (오늘~)
	// I feel down on rainy days. (비오는 날은 기분이~)

우유를 마시겠습니다.	I'm going to drink milk.
우정을 영원히 잊지 않을 것입니다.	I won't forget the friendship ever. // I won't forget our friendship ever.

	= I will remember our friendship forever. (우리들의~)
우정을 위하여 건배!	Cheers to friendship! = Toast to friendship!
우체국이 있습니까?	Is there a post office? // Is there a post office near here? (부근에~) ➡ Yes. (있습니다.)
우체통이 어디에 있습니까?	Where is a post box? = Where is a mailbox? ➡ At the intersection. = At the crossroads. (사거리에요.)
우편번호를 써넣는 것 잊지 마세요.	Don't forget to write the zip code.

욱

욱하는 성질이 있습니다.	I have a hot temper. = I have a bad temper.

운

운 좋다!	You're lucky! = Lucky! // You're so lucky! (정말~)
운 좋은 줄 알아!	Consider yourself lucky! // Consider yourself lucky today! (오늘~)
운동 좋아합니까?	Do you like to exercise? = Do you like to work out? ➡ Of course, I do. (물론 좋아하지요.) // What exercise do you like? (무슨~)
운동을 잘합니까?	[구기운동] Are you good at sports? ➡ ⓐ Yes. (잘합니다.) ⓑ Just so so. (보통입니다. // 그저 그렇습니다.) ⓒ Not good. (잘 못합니다.)

	ⓓ Bad. (못 합니다.) ☞ 축구를 잘합니까? // 수영을 잘합니까?
운명이야!	① Fate! = Destiny! // This is a destiny! (이건~) ② [사망] Dead! = Died! = Passed away!
운명을 하늘에 맡기는 수밖에.	I left my fate to God.
운이 안 따르네.	I have no luck. = It's unlucky.
운이 억세게 좋았습니다.	I was so lucky. = I was incredibly lucky.
운이 없습니다.	So unlucky. // He has no luck. = He's so unlucky. (그는 정말~)
운전 잘합니까?	Can you drive well? // Can he drive well? (그는~) ➡ ⓐ Yes. (잘합니다.) ⓑ Not well. (잘 못합니다.) ⓒ No. (못 합니다.)
운전 조심하세요.	Drive safely. = Safe driving. = Drive carefully.
운전면허증 좀 제시해주세요.	Show me your driver's license, please. = Can I see your driver's license?
운전면허증과 신분증을 제시해주세요.	Show me your driver's license and ID, please. ➡ Here they are. = Here we go. (여기 있습니다.)

운전할 줄 압니까?	① [배워서] Did you learn how to drive?
	➡ ⓐ Yes. (예.) // Yes. (할줄 압니다.)
	ⓑ No. I'm still in training. (운전교습 중입니다.)
	ⓒ No. (아니요.)
	// No, I don't know how to drive.
	(할 줄 모릅니다.)
	② [능력] Can you drive?
	= Do you know how to drive?
	➡ ⓐ Yes. (예.) ⓑ No. (아니요.)

울

울고 싶습니다.	I wanna cry.
울고불고 난리야.	Crying like crazy. // She's crying like crazy. (그 여자~)
울지 마세요!	Don't cry!
울화통 터지네!	I'm losing my temper! = I'm blowing my top!

움

움직이기 싫어요.	[몸 등을] I don't wanna move.
움직이지 마세요.	① Don't move, please. = Stop moving, please. ② 〈경어〉 Would you please stop moving.

웃

웃기네!	① [가소로운 말에] That's hilarious!
	= That's ridiculous.
	// That's very hilarious! (정말~)
	② [농담] That's funny.
	// This is so funny. (이거 정말~)
	③ [시치미 떼는 말에] That's bullshit!

웃기지 마세요.	① [놀림에] Don't make fun of me. = Don't pull my leg. = Stop kidding around. // Don't make fun of me. That doesn't make sense! (~말도 안 돼!) ② [잘난 척에] Don't be ridiculous.
웃는 낯에 침 뱉으랴.	[속담] A soft answer turns away wrath.

웃어봐!	① Smile a bit! (좀~) ② [사진] Cheese!
웃으면 십 년은 젊어집니다.	〈직역〉 Smile, and you'll live 10 more years. // Smile once, and you'll live 10 more years. (한번~)
웃음 속에 칼을 품다.	〈직역〉 There's a sword hidden in the smile.

웅

웅!	[모기 · 파리 · 비행기의 소리] Buzz!

원

원 샷 좋지!	I like bottoms up!
원 샷!	Bottoms up! = Empty your glass! = Finish your drink!
원망스럽다.	I hate you. = I feel bad about you. // I really hate you. = I feel really bad about you. (네가 너무~)
원망을 마음에 담지 마세요.	Don't hold grudges. = Don't bear any malice.
원망하니?	Do you resent me? // Do you still hate me? (아직도 날~) ➡ No. (아니.)
원망하지 마세요.	Don't hate. = No malice.
원수가 따로 없네!	Like my enemy! // 〈비속어〉 The bastard is like my enemy! (그놈이 ~)
원수는 외나무다리에서 만난다더니.	It's like meeting bad luck one cannot escape.

ㅇ

원숭이도 나무에서 떨어질 때가 있다.	[속담] Even Homer sometimes nods. = A good marksman may sometimes miss.
원피스가 정말 어울립니다.	The dress looks great on you.
원하는 게 뭐냐?	① [의도 · 시비] What do you want? // What the hell do you want? (도대체~) ② [물건] What are you looking for? ➡ Nothing. (아무것도 없습니다.)

월

월경이 안 왔어요.	I've skipped a period. // I didn't have a period last month. = I had no period last month. = I didn't get my period last month.
월급날입니다.	It's my payday. // This is my first paycheck. Today is my payday. (이거 내 첫 월급이예요. 오늘~)

위

위가 아픕니다.	I have soreness in my stomach. = I have a stomachache.
위로해주세요.	Please comfort her. = Please console her. (그녀를~)
위로해줘서 고마워요.	Thank you for comforting me.
위반자는 벌금!	[경고문] Violators will be fined!
위아래도 몰라보네.	Can't you tell the difference between high and low?
위층에 삽니다.	I live upstairs.

위치가 어딥니까?	① Where is it? ② What's the location there? (거기~) ➡ Five miles northeast. (동북방향 5마일입니다.)
위치로!	① [군대 용어] To the position! ② To your place! (각자~)
위하여!	[건배 구호] Cheers!
위해서야!	All for you! // This is all for you! (이건 전부 널~)

위험해!	It's dangerous! = It's a danger!
	// It's very dangerous! (너무~)
	// This is very dangerous! (이 일은 너무~)
	// You're in danger! (당신 ~)

윗

윗물이 맑아야 아랫물이 맑다.	[속담] Parents are patterns. = The fish always stinks from the head downwards. = A servant is only as honest as his master.

윙

윙윙!	[바람소리] Hiss!
윙크했어.	I winked. // He winked at me. (저 사람이 나한테~)

유

유감입니다.	① I'm sorry. =That's bad. // I'm so sorry. = That's too bad. (정말 너무~) ② [들은 말] I'm sorry to hear that. ③ [놀라움] Oh no, what bad luck!

ㅇ

유난떨기는!	[까다로움] You're too particular! = You're too picky! = You're too choosy!
유리를 닦을게요.	I'll wipe the window. // I'll go and wipe the window. (제가 가서 ~)
유리에 베었어요.	I got a cut from the glass.

유명한 사람입니다.	A famous person.
	// He's a famous person. (그분은~)
	// The movie director is very famous.
	(영화의 감독은 아주~)

유명해질 거야.	You'll be famous. = You'll have fame.
유부남입니다.	A married man. // I'm a married man. = I'm married. (저는~)
유부녀입니다.	A married woman. // I'm a married woman. = I'm married. (저는~)
유유상종.	[속담] Each follows its own kind. = Birds of a feather flock together.
유치원에 다닙니다.	My daughter goes to kindergarten. (딸은~)
유치해!	Childish! = Immature! // So childish! (정말~)
유턴됩니까?	Can I make a U-turn? // Can I make a U-turn ahead? (앞에서~) ➡ Sure. (됩니다.)
유턴해주세요.	Make a U-turn, please. // Make a U-turn ahead, please. (앞에서~)
유통기한이 지났습니다.	It's expired. = It's past the expiration date.
유학 갑니다.	I'm going to study. // I'm going to America to study. (미국으로~)
유학생입니다.	I'm an international student. (저는~)
유행성감기 증세입니다.	It's a symptom of the flu.

	// This is a symptom of the flu. (이는~)
유행이 아니에요.	It's out of style. = It's old-fashioned.
유혹하는 겁니까?	Are you seducing me? = Are you tempting me? ➡ ⓐ No. (아니요.) ⓑ There's nothing like that. (그런 거 없습니다.)
유효기간이 지났습니다.	It's not valid anymore. = It's no longer valid.

으

어디로 // 무엇으로	① [방향] to = towards // Go to the front. (앞~ 가.)
	② [장소] to
	// Take me to Myeong-dong. (명동~ 가주세요.)
	// How can I get to Seoul Station.
	(서울역~ 가려면 어떻게 갑니까?)
	③ [항공] to // There is a flight to New York everyday. (매일 뉴욕~ 가는 항공편이 있습니다.)
	④ [용도] for
	// What's this for? (이건 무엇~ 사용될 겁니까?)
	⑤ [재료 또는 출처] from // Where is this from?
	(이건 무엇~ 만든겁니까?)

은

은행에 갑니다.	I'm going to the bank.
은행에서 일합니다.	I work at a bank. (나는~)
은혜를 원수로 갚다니!	You return evil for good!
은혼식을 축하합니다.	Congratulations on your silver wedding anniversary! // Mom and Dad, congratulations on your silver wedding anniversary! (엄마, 아빠~)

ㅇ

읕

~읕(무엇을)	Drop the gun! (총을 내려놔!)

음

음료를 드시겠습니까?	Would you like something to drink? // What would you like to drink? (무슨~) ➡ Apple juice, please. (사과주스요.)
음매!	① [소 울음소리] Moo! ② [양 울음소리] Baa!
음식 주문합시다.	Let's order some food.
음식배달입니다.	It's a food delivery.
음식솜씨가 훌륭합니다.	You cook very well. = You're a good cook.
음식을 가려서 먹으면 안 된다.	Don't pick at your food. = You shouldn't be picky about food.
음식이 쉰 것 같습니다.	The food seems to go bad.
음식이 입에 맞았으면 합니다.	Hope you like the food.
음악 좋아합니까?	Do you like music? // What kind of music do you like? (무슨~) ➡ ⓐ Yes. (좋아합니다.) ⓑ I like modern. (현대음악을 좋아해요.)
음치입니다.	I'm so poor at singing. = I'm a terrible singer. = I can't sing at all. = I'm tone-deaf. = I can't carry a tune in a bucket.
음탕한 계집!	[비속어] Whore! = Slut!

음흉합니다.	He's so sneaky. = He's so wicked. = He's so cunning. (그는 너무~)

응

응!	① [대답] Yes! ☞ 예! ② [응답] Yeah!
응원할 게! // 응원해줄게!	① [응원] I'll cheer! // I'll cheer for your team! (너희 팀을~) ② [지지] I'll back you up! = I'll support you!

의

의견에 동의합니까?	Do you agree? // Do you agree with me? = Are you with me? (저의~) ➡ Yes. (동의합니다.)
의견이 없습니다.	I have no idea.
의견차이가 큽니다.	The opinions are too different. // The opinions between us are too different. = We have too different opinions. (우리 사이~)
의기소침하다.	You're discouraged. = You're in low spirits.
의기양양하다.	You're in high spirits. = You're triumphant.
의리 없다!	You are ungrateful! = You're insincere! = You have no sense of duty and humanity. // You're so ungrateful! (너무~)
의사를 불러주세요.	Call the doctor, please. // Call the doctor quickly, please. (어서~)
의심스럽습니다.	I doubt it. = It's doubtful. // There's something fishy about this place. = There's something suspicious about this place. (여기가~)

의심의 여지가 없습니다.	① There's no doubt. = There's nothing to doubt. ② [혐의] There's nothing to be suspicious about.

이

이 녀석!	You, rascal! = You, dude!
이 안에 너 있다.	I have you in here. = You're in here.
이 인분 주세요.	Give me two servings, please. = Give me two helpings, please.
이가 부러졌습니다.	My tooth is broken. = I have a broken tooth.
이가 빠졌습니다.	My tooth fell out. = I got a tooth pulled out.
이가 아픕니다.	I have a pain in my tooth. = I have a toothache.
이거 어떻습니까?	How do you like this? = What about this? ➡ ⓐ Very good. (아주 좋아요.) ⓑ It's OK. (그런대로요.)
이거 주세요.	Let me have this. = I'll take this. = Give me this, please.
이것 좀 봐!	Look at this! = Have a look at this!
이것저것 좀 샀습니다.	I bought this and that. = I bought a few things. // I just bought this and that. (그냥~)
이게 누구야!	① [우연한 만남] Look who's here! ② [반감] Who the hell is here!
이게 뭐야?	① [일에 대한 불평] What's this! ② [모양 · 꼴] What the hell? = What the heck is this? ➡ This is not so bad. (이건 그런 대로 나은 편이야.) ③ [일의 결과에 대한 불평] What's going on?

	➡ I don't know, either. (나도 모르겠어요.)
이게 뭡니까?	[물건] What's this? ➡ It's a present for my friend. (친구한테 선물할 겁니다.)
이겼어!	I won! // I won! But it was so hard. (어렵게~)
이곳.	Here.
이기적으로 굴지 마세요.	Don't be selfish. = Stop being selfish.
이기적입니다.	Selfish. // He's so selfish. (그는 너무~)
이년아!	〈비속어〉 You bitch!
이놈의 자식!	〈비속어〉 You son of a bitch!
이등 하고 은메달을 땄습니다.	I got second place, and I got a silver medal. = I came in second, and I got a silver medal.
이등은 설자리가 없어!	There's no place for the second!
이따가 다시 얘기합시다.	Let's talk again later. = Let's continue to talk later. = Let's have a talk again later.
이따가 다시 오세요.	Please come again later.
이따가 다시 전화하겠습니다.	I'll call back later.
이따가 다시 전화하세요.	Please call back later.
이따가 봅시다.	① [만남] See you later. = See you again. = See you next time. ② [대화] Let's talk later.
이래도 되는 거야?	How could you do this? = How possibly could you do this? ➡ What did I do? (내가 어쨌다고!)

이래라저래라 하지마세요.	Don't tell me to do this and do that. = Don't boss me around.
이러고 있으면 어떻게 해?	① [동작이 뜸] Why are you so slow? ② [무대책에 대해서] What are you doing? // What are you doing? Come up with ideas! (~방법을 좀 생각해봐!)
이러고 있을 시간이 없습니다.	You don't have time to waste like this. = You have no time to lose. // You have no time to lose like this. (한가하게~)
이러면 안 되지!	You shouldn't do this! = You can't do this! // You shouldn't do this to me! (나한테~) ➡ Try to figure out why I am doing this to you. (왜 그런지 잘 생각해봐.)
이러면 안 됩니다.	☞ 이러지 마세요. // 이렇게 하면 안 됩니다.
이러지 마세요.	① Don't do this. = Stop doing this. ➡ Nobody can stop me. (누구도 나를 막을 수 없어.) ② [상투적인 수법에 대해] You shouldn't do this. // You shouldn't do this next time. (다음에 ~) ③ ☞ 그러지 마세요.
이러쿵저러쿵 말마세요.	① Don't talk about me behind my back. (뒤에서 저에 대해~) ② Don't say this and that.
이런 것으로 주세요.	Give me a thing like this.

이런 게 아닙니다.	① [확인] This is not right.
	= This is not the way.
	// Sir, this is not right. (선생님, ~)
	// This is not the way. (일이~)
	② This is not what you think. (당신이 생각하는~)

이런 경우가 어디 있습니까?	What kind of case is this? ➡ I don't get it either. (나도 이해가 안 돼!)
이런 느낌 처음입니다.	I haven't felt this way before.

이런 소리하지 마세요.	Don't say such a thing. = You shouldn't talk this way.
이런 일 없었습니다.	There's never been a case like this. // There's really never been a case like this. (정말~)
이런 적이 어디 한두 번이냐!	It's not the first time! = Didn't you do this before? = Haven't you done this before? = How many times have you done this?
이런!	① 〈비속어〉 Damn! = Shit! ② [불평] Gosh! ③ [놀람] Oh, dear! = Geez! ④ [실수] Yikes!
이런다고 뭐가 달라지죠?	What's the difference? = Does it make a difference? ➡ Be quiet. (조용히 해.)
이럴 수 없습니다.	① [상대방] You can't do this. // You can't do this. Never. (~절대 안 됩니다.) ② [어떤 일에 대해] This can't be happening.
이럴 수 있냐?	How could you? = How dare you? // How could you do this? (어쩜 나에게~)
이럴 줄 알았다!	① I knew it! ② [의심하고 있던 상태] I was already suspicious about it! = I have doubts about it already!
이럴 필요 없습니다.	① ☞ 그럴 필요 없습니다. ② This is not necessary. // This is really not necessary. (정말~)
이렇게 된 겁니다.	[상황설명] This is the way it goes. = This is how it goes.
이렇게 될 줄 알았습니다.	[예상] I knew it.
이렇게 말이야!	[상대가 원하는 동작을 취하면서] This is it! = Like this!
이렇게 말하지 마세요.	Don't talk like this. = Don't say things like this.

이렇게 맛있는 음식은 처음 먹어봅니다.	I've never had such delicious food. = I've never had food this delicious before in my life.
이렇게 빕니다.	[간청] I'm begging you.
이렇게 생각 안합니다.	① I don't think like this. = I don't think this way. ② I don't think like this, either. (저도~) ③ [의심] I don't think so.
이렇게 생각합니다.	This is what I think. // I think so, too. (저도~)
이렇게 오시게 해서 죄송합니다.	I am sorry to have made you come here. = I am sorry that you had to come all this way.
이렇게 찾아주셔서 감사합니다.	[음식점] Thank you for coming.
이렇게 하면 되겠습니까?	What about doing this? = What about doing it like this? = What about doing it this way? = How about doing like this? ➡ Good. (좋아요.)
이렇게 하면 됩니까?	How about doing like this? ☞ 이렇게 하면 되겠습니까? ➡ ⓐ OK. (됩니다.) ⓑ Good. (좋아요.)
이렇게 하면 안 됩니다.	① [지적] You can't do this. = You can't do it like this. = You can't do it this way. ② [판단] Don't do this. = Don't do it like this. = Don't do it this way. ③ [금지] You shouldn't do this. = You shouldn't do it like this. = You shouldn't do it this way. ④ [부당함] It's unfair to do this. = It's unfair to do it like this. = It's unfair to do it this way.

	⑤ [허가] You're not allowed to do this. = You're not allowed to do it like this. = You're not allowed to do it this way.
이렇게 할 수 없습니다.	I can't do this. = I can't do it like this. = I can't do it this way.

이렇게 합시다.	① [합의] Let's do it this way.
	= Let's do it like this.
	// OK. Let's do it this way. (좋아요. ~)
	② [결정] Let's decide on this.
	// OK. Let's decide on this. (좋아요. ~)

이렇다고 생각 안합니다.	I don't think so.
이력서 하나 쓰세요.	Write a resume, please. // First off write a resume, please. (우선~)
이론은 빠삭해도 실천은 약합니다.	I know all the theories but lack action. // She knows all the theories but lacks action. (그녀는~)
이르시군요!	[아침인사] It's so early!
이를 악물고 참아야합니다.	Clench your teeth and endure it. = Grin and bear it.
이를 어쩌나?	God! What happened!
이를 하나 빼야 합니다.	You need to get a tooth pulled. = You need to get one of your teeth pulled.
이름을 말씀해주세요.	Say your name, please.
이름이 뭐냐?	What's your name? ➡ My name is Seri. (이름이 세리라고 합니다.)
이름이 뭐랬지? // 이름이 뭐였더라?	[기억을 더듬으면서] Let me think about the name. = What was the name? // What was his name? (그 남자 ~) ➡ It's Yuri. (유리야.)

이름이 뭡니까?	What's your name? = How can I call you? ➡ Call me Jinsu. (저를 진수라고 부르시면 됩니다.)
이리 오세요.	Please come here.
이리 와!	Come here!
이리 와서 도와주세요.	Please come here to help.
이리 와서 앉아요.	Come here and sit, please.
이리 와서 좀 봐요.	Please come and look here.
이리 좀 와 봐요.	Come here, please.
이리저리 재다.	She's calculating this and that. (그녀는 ~)
이만 가보겠습니다.	I should leave now. = I must go now.
이만 하자!	[대화나 일을] Let's finish! // Let's finish it for today! (오늘~)
이메일(E-mail)로 보내주세요.	Please email it to me. = Send it to me via e-mail, please.
이메일(E-mail)있습니까?	① [계정] Do you have an e-mail account? ➡ Yes. (있습니다.) ② [주소] Do you have an e-mail address?
이메일(E-mail) 주소입니다.	It's my e-mail address. // This is my e-mail address. (이것은 나의~)
이발해주세요.	① I'd like to get my hair cut. ② 〈경어〉 Would you please cut my hair?
이번 연휴에 어디 갑니까?	Are you going somewhere this weekend? ➡ I'm going to Washington. (워싱턴요.)
이번 주 토요일은 친구 생일입니다.	This Saturday is my friend's birthday.

이번 주말에 시간 있습니까?	Do you have time this weekend?
	= Will you be free this weekend?
	➡ I have a date. (데이트가 있는데요.)
	
	관련표현
	this week (이번 주) // this Monday (이번 주 월요일)
	// this Tuesday (이번 주 화요일)
	// this Wednesday (이번 주 수요일)
	// this Thursday 이번 주 목요일)
	// this Friday (이번 주 금요일)
	// this Saturday (이번 주 토요일)
	// this Sunday (이번 주 일요일)

이번에는 끝장입니다!	[일이 잘못됨] I'm doomed! = I'm dead!
이번에는 또 뭐야?	What's next? ➡ A novel. (소설책입니다.)
이번에는 알아들었어요.	I understand this time. = I got it this time.
이번이 처음입니다.	This is my first time.
이별을 받아들일 수 없습니다.	I can't get over my breakup. // I can't get over the breakup with you. (너와의~)
이보 전진을 위한 일보 후퇴.	[속담] Better bend than break.
이봐요!	① [사람을 부름] Hey! ② You! ③ [남자] Sir! [여자] Ma'am!
이분은 누구십니까?	Who's this? = Who is this person? ➡ ⓐ This is our tour guide. (이분은 우리 가이드입니다.) ⓑ This person is a writer. (이분은 작가입니다.) ⓒ This person is an artist. (이분은 화가입니다.) ⓔ This is our president. (이분은 사장님입니다.) ⓕ This is my friend, Daniel. (이분은 저의 친구 다니엘입니다.) ⓖ This is my boss. (이분은 제 상사입니다.) ⓗ This is Mr. Gim. (이분은 김 선생입니다.)

이불 개세요.	Please fold your blanket.
이불 잘 덮고 자세요.	Make sure you cover youself with the blanket. = Be sure you cover yourself with the blanket.
이불 펴세요.	Unfold the blanket, please.

이불에 오줌을 싸냐?	You wet the bed?
	// You wet the bed again? (또 ~)
	// You wet the bed? How old are you? (나이가 몇 살인데, ~)

이사 가면 전화주세요.	Please give me a call when you move to your new place. = Please give me a call when you move.
이사하신 걸 축하합니다.	Congratulations on moving in.
이상!	[보고 완료] **That's all!** = **That's it!**
이상입니다!	① [말을 끝냄] I'm done! ② [보고] That's all! ☞ 이상! ③ [질문 없음] No more! ④ [상사가 회의나 소집을 해산] Dismissed!
이상하게 생각마세요.	Don't take it strangely.

이상하네!	① **It's weird!**
	② [헷갈림] It's confusing!
	// It's very confusing! (정말~)
	③ [판단] It's strange!
	④ [귀신에 홀린 듯] It's bizarre!
	// It's really bizarre! (정말~)

이상한 일이네!	It's a weird thing!
이상합니다.	① It's weird. // It's a little weird. (약간~) ② [상황] It's confusing. // It's a little confusing. (약간~)

	③ [평소와 다름] It's strange. // She's strange. (그녀가~)
이성을 잃었습니다.	He lost his temper. (그는~)
이야기.	A story.
이에 대해 정말 죄송스럽게 생각합니다.	I'm so sorry about this.
이열치열도 모르냐?	Don't you know like cures like? ➡ No! (몰라!)
이유가 뭡니까?	① [원인] What's the reason? // What on earth is the reason? (도대체~) ② [이유] Why? = How come?
이유를 잘 모르겠습니다.	I don't know why. // I also don't know why. (저도~)
이의 없습니다.	I have no objection.
이의 있습니다.	I have an objection. = I object.
이인실로 주세요.	Give me a room for two, please. = A two bedroom, please.
이점에 동의합니다.	I agree with this point.
이제 가봐야겠어요.	[시간이 돼서] I've gotta go now.
이제 곧 나옵니다.	[주문한 것] It'll be here soon. = It'll come out soon. // The food will be here soon. (요리가~)
이제 그만 끊어야겠습니다.	[전화] I should hang up now.
이제 그만해!	① [잔소리] Stop now! = Cut it out! = Knock it off! ② 〈비속어〉 Knock off the bullshit! = Fuck the bullshit!

ㅇ

이제 알겠습니다.	Now I got it. = Now I understand.
이제 지겨워!	I'm sick of it now! = I'm fed up with it now! = I can't take it anymore! = I'm disgusted with it!
이중인격자야!	He's two-faced! = He's double-faced! = He's the devil in disguise! (그는 ~)
이쪽에 앉으세요.	Please sit here.
이쪽으로 가세요.	Go this way, please.
이쪽으로 오세요.	① Come this way, please. ② This way, please. ⬅ Which way should I go? (어느 쪽으로 갑니까?)
이쪽으로 차타세요.	Please get in the car this way.
이쯤에서 끝내자!	Let's finish it now!
이차 가자!	[술자리] Let's go for a second drink! (우리~)
이참에 마음을 정리해.	You'd better clear your mind this time.
이틀 묵습니다.	I'd like to stay for two nights. = Two nights, please.
이판사판이야!	[사생결단] All or nothing! = Dead or alive!
이해가 안 됩니다.	① [분별] It doesn't make sense. ② [납득] I don't get it. = I can't understand. // I really can't understand you. (저도 진짜~)
이해심이 많네.	You're so understanding. = You're so considerate.
이해합니까?	① [분별] Do you get it? = Do you understand it? = Does it make sense to you? = Are you with me? ➡ ⓐ I understand. = I see. (이해합니다.)

	ⓑ I don't get it. (모르겠어요.) ② [납득] Can you understand? ➡ I understand him. (그 사람을 이해합니다.)
이해해주세요.	① [양해] Please understand. ② [납득] Please understand my point.
이해했습니까?	Did you get it? ➡ ⓐ I got it. (이해했습니다.) ⓑ I finally got it. (마침내 이해했습니다.)
이혼하자!	Let's divorce! = Let's get divorced! (우리~)

익

익숙해졌습니까?	Are you used to it? = Are you accustomed to it? = Are you familiar with it? // Are you used to the life here now? = Have you gotten used to the life here now? (이제 여기 생활에~) ➡ Somewhat. (그런대로요.)
익숙해졌습니다.	☞ 습관이 됐습니다.
익었어요?	① [육류 등] Is it done? ➡ Too well done. (너무 익었어요.) ② [면 · 라면 등] Is it cooked? ➡ Soon. (곧 됩니다.)

인

인과응보.	[속담] As one sows, so shall he reap. = Every herring must hang by its own gill. = Garbage in, garbage out. = An onion will not produce a rose.

인과응보야!	You reap what you sow! // You reap what you sow! (이건 다~)
인기 있는 요리가 뭡니까?	What's the most popular dish? = What' popular? // What's the most popular dish here? (이곳에서~) ➡ It's a roasted duck. (오리구이입니다.)
인명은 재천.	[속담] Only god knows the fate.
인사 나누세요.	Please greet. // Please greet. This is Ms. Gim. (~이분은 미스 김입니다.)
인사 나눕시다.	[처음 만나 사람과 교제] Let's greet. // Let's greet each other. (우리~)
인사 나눴어요.	We greeted each other. = We said hello to each other. // We exchanged simple greetings with each other. (간단히~)
인사드리세요.	Please say hi. = Say hello, please. // Go and say hello to Mom, please. (가서 어머님께~)
인사만 여쭙겠어요.	I just want to say hi. // I just want to say hi to him. (그에게~)
인사만하고 가세요.	Just say hi and leave.
인상은 어떻습니까?	What does he look like? = What's your first impression of him? (그 사람~) ➡ Very good. (매우 좋습니다.)
인생은 한 편의 연극이다.	Life is like a play.
인생이란 이런 거야.	① Life is just like that. ② [속담] Life has ups and downs.

인정 못해!	① [인정] I can't approve it! ② [불복] I can't get it! = I can't take it! = I can't accept it!
인정합니다.	I admit. // I admit that I love you. (당신을 좋아한다는 걸~)
인터넷광입니다.	Crazy about the Internet. // He's so crazy about the Internet. (그는 진짜~)
인터넷뱅킹으로 넣어드리겠습니다.	I will transfer the money through the Internet banking. // Tell me your account number. I'll transfer the money through the Internet banking. (당신의 계좌번호 말해보세요. ~)
인터넷으로 채팅을 할 수 있습니다.	I can chat online.

일

일 개월.	A month.
일 났어!	[사고] Something terrible happened!
일 년은 며칠입니까?	How many days are in a year? = How many days are there in a year? ➡ Three hundred sixty-five days. (365일입니다.)
일 년은 몇 개월입니까?	How many months are in a year? = How many months are there in a year? ➡ Twelve months. (12개월입니다.)
일 년은 몇 주입니까?	How many weeks are in a year? = How many weeks are there in a year? ➡ Fifty-two weeks. (52주입니다.)
일만 하고 놀지 않으면 바보 된다.	[속담] All work and no play makes Jack a dull boy.

일 분은 몇 초입니까?	How many seconds are in a minute? = How many seconds are there in a minute? ➡ Sixty seconds. (60초입니다.)
일 있어서 나가봐야 합니다.	I've gotta go out for work.
일 있으면 전화주세요.	Please call me if anything comes up. ➡ I will. (그러죠.)
일(1)인실을 원합니다.	I want a one bed room. // I want a one bed room with a bathroom. (욕실 딸린~)
일거양득. // 일석이조.	[속담] To kill two birds with one stone.
일기예보를 들었습니까?	Did you hear the weather forecast? ➡ They said it would be snowy. (일기예보에서 오늘 눈 온다고 했습니다.)
일남 일녀입니다.	I have a son and a daughter.
일단 드셔보세요.	Please just try the food.
일등 복권 당첨을 축하합니다.	Congratulations on winning the lottery.
일등하고 금메달을 땄습니다.	I got first place and got a medal.
일류대에 합격한 걸 축하드립니다.	You've been admitted into one of the best universities. Congratulations. // Your son has been admitted into one of the best universities. Congratulations. (아드님이~)
일리가 있습니다.	That makes sense. = That sounds good. = That sounds reasonable.
일마다 순조롭길 빕니다.	My best wishes for all of your business.

일반석으로 예약해주세요.	[비행기] I'd like an economy seat. // I'd like an economy seat from Seoul to Beijing. (서울에서 북경까지~)
일반석은 다 팔렸고 특실만 남았습니다.	[기차] All economy seats are sold out. We just have first class seats.
일반인 출입금지!	[경고문] No civilians!
일방적이야!	[독선] You're opinionated. // You're too opinionated. = You're too egocentric. (너무~)
일방통행로!	One way!
일 보세요.	Mind your own business.
일부러 그런 거지요?	You did it on purpose! = You did it intentionally! ➡ No. I didn't do it on purpose. (일부러 그런 게 아닙니다.)
일석이조.	☞ 일거양득
일손이 부족합니다.	I need more hands. = I'm in need of more help.
일시불로 하시겠습니까, 할부로 하시겠습니까?	Would you like to pay at once or in installments. ➡ Once. (일시불로 해주세요.)
일심동체.	☞ 한마음 한 뜻이 되어야 합니다.
일어나 식사하세요.	Please get up and eat.
일어나 학교 가야지!	① [재촉] Wake up now. Time for school! (어서~) ② [학교 갈 시간이 됨] Get up now. It's almost time for school.
일어나세요!	① [기상] Wake up! = Get up! = Up! // Get up now! (빨리~) ② [앉아있는 경우] Stand up!

	③ [누워있는 경우] Get up!
일요일 우리 집에서 점심이요.	How about lunch at my home?
일원의 가치도 없습니다.	That's not even worth one penny.
일으켜주세요.	[부축해서] Would you hold my arms and help me stand up? // Would you hold his arms and help him stand up? (그를~)
일은 바쁩니까?	[인사] Are you busy with work? ➡ ⓐ Yes. (바쁩니다.) ⓑ Not so much. (그저 그래요.) ⓒ Not at all. (별로 바쁘지 않습니다.)
일은 별로 힘들지 않아요.	The work isn't that hard. = The work is fine with me.
일은 잘됐습니다.	Everything went well.

일을 끝냈습니다.	I'm done with the work. = I finished the work.
	// I finished the work early. (우리는 미리~)
	// He's done with the work. (그~)

일을 방해하지 마세요.	Don't disturb my work. // Stop disturbing my work. (자꾸~)
일을 해도 해도 끝이 없네.	There's no end to work.
일을 확대시키지 마세요.	Don't make the situation bigger. = Don't make the situation worse than it already is.
일이 그 정도까진 아닙니다.	It's not that much.
일이 그렇게 간단한 게 아닙니다.	It's not that simple.

일이 그렇게 된 겁니다.	[설명] That's the way it goes.
일이 많습니다.	I have a lot of work.
일이 바쁩니까?	Are you busy with work? ➡ Yes. (바쁩니다.)
일이 방금 끝났습니다.	I've just finished the work. = I'm done now.
일이 생겼어요!	[사고] Something happened! = I had an accident!
일이 어떻게 이럴 수 있죠?	① How is it possible? ➡ Who knows? (누가 알겠어요!) ② How did it happen? ➡ This is not what I expected. (이건 제 본의가 아닙니다.)
일이나 잘해!	Concentrate on our work!
일정이 어떻게 됩니까?	How's your schedule? // How's your schedule today? (오늘~) ➡ I will go to the post office in the morning and school in the afternoon. (오전에 우체국에 가고, 오후는 학교에 갑니다.)
일주일 동안 너무 바빴습니다.	I have been so busy this week.
일주일은 며칠입니까?	How many days are in a week? = How many days are there in a week? ➡ Seven days. (7일입니다.)
일직입니다.	You're on duty. // I'm on duty today. (오늘은 제~)
일찍 갔다 일찍 오세요.	Leave early and come back early.
일찍 들어왔네.	[귀가] You've come home early. // You've come home early today. (오늘~)
일찍 쉬세요.	Take an early rest.

ㅇ

일찍 왔네요.	① [약속이나 출근시간] You're early.
	= You've come early.
	// You're so early. (정말~)
	// You're very early. (아주~)
	② [불만] How early! (너무~)
	③ [귀가] ☞ 일찍 들어왔네.

일찍 일어나는 새가 벌레를 잡아먹는다.	[속담] The early bird catches the worm.
일찍 일어났네.	You got up early. = You woke up early.
일찍 자고 일찍 일어나세요.	Go to bed early and get up early.
일편단심.	Whole-heartedly.
일하는 중입니다.	I'm working.
일하지 않는 자는 먹지 마라.	Don't eat if you don't work. = No work, no food.
일합니까?	Do you work? // What does your father do? (아버님은 무슨~) ➡ He's a doctor. (의사이십니다.)
일행이 있습니까?	① Do you have company? = Are you with anyone else? ② [기다리는 중일 경우] Are you waiting for anyone?

읽

읽어드릴게요.	Let me read for you. = I'd like to read for you.
읽어보세요.	① [낭독] Please read it. ② [독해] Why don't you read it? // Why don't you read it again? (다시 한 번~)

잃

잃고 싶지 않다.	I don't wanna lose. // I don't wanna lose you. (널~)
잃어버렸습니까?	Did you lose something? ➡ ⓐ Yes, I did. (잃어버렸어요.) ⓑ No, I didn't. (잃어버리지 않았어요.)
잃어버렸습니다.	I lost it. // I lost my bag. (제 가방을~)
잃어버리지 마세요.	[물건 등] Don't lose it. // Don't lose it, please. (제발~)
잃어버린 물건을 속히 찾아주세요.	Please hurry and find my lost stuff.

임

임기응변으로 했어요.	I improvised. = I did it impromptu. = I ad-libbed.
임신했습니다.	I'm pregnant. = I'm expecting a baby. // My wife is pregnant. (아내가~)
임자가 있습니다.	I'm taken.

입

~입니까?	Is this yours? (이건 당신 것~) ➡ ⓐ Yes. (예.) ⓑ No. (아닙니다.)
~입니다.	① It is Seoul. (서울~) ② My home is in Daejeon. (집은 대전~)
입 냄새가 납니다.	I have bad breath.

입 냄새가 심합니다.	I have terribly bad breath.
입 닥쳐!	① Shut up! ② 〈비속어〉 Shut the fuck up!
입 밖에 꺼내지 마세요.	Don't say it. = Don't even think about saying it. = Hold it in your mouth. // Please don't say it. (제발~)
입 벌려보세요.	Open your mouth.
입 벌리고 "아" 하세요.	① Open your mouth and say "Ah." ② 〈경어〉 Would you please open your mouth and say, "Ah?"
입 조심해!	① [경고] Watch your mouth! ➡ You watch your mouth! (너나 조심해!) ☞ 말조심해. ② [당부] Please be careful with your mouth!
입구가 어디에 있습니까?	Where's the entrance? ➡ On the left. (왼쪽이요.)
입국목적은 무엇입니까?	[공항에서] Why did you come here? ➡ For sightseeing. (여행입니다.)
입국신고서도 주세요.	[기내에서] Let me have an immigration form, too. = Can I have an immigration form, too?
입덧이 너무 심합니다.	I have terrible morning sickness. = My morning sickness is terrible.
입맛에 딱 맞습니다.	It tastes so good to me.
입맛에 맞는지 모르겠습니다.	I don't know if you like it. = I don't know whether you will like it or not.
입맛에 맞습니까?	Does the food taste good to you? = Do you like the food? // Do you like this food? (이 요리가~) ➡ It's OK. (그런대로요.)

입맛이 까다롭습니다.	I'm so picky about food.
입맛이 없습니다.	I lost my appetite. = I have no appetite.
입방아를 찧다.	They're gossipping about her. (그들은 그녀에 대해 ~)
입상했습니까?	Did you receive a prize? // Did he receive a prize, too? (그도~) ➡ No, he didn't. (이번엔 입상하지 못했습니다.)
입술이 다 텄습니다.	My lips are chapped. // Your lips are chapped. (당신~)
입술이 없으면 이가 시리다.	Your teeth would be cold without your lips.
입씨름하지 마세요.	Don't have an argument. = Don't argue. // Don't have an argument against her. (그 여자와~)
입어 봐도 됩니까?	Can I try this on? ➡ ⓐ Go ahead. (그러세요.) ⓑ No, you can't. (안 됩니다.)
입어보니 너무 작아요.	It's too small for me.
입어보니 약간 안 맞아요.	It didn't fit me.
입어보세요.	Try it on. // Try this on. (이걸 좀~)
입에 발린 소리!	That's superficial!
입에 침이 마르도록 칭찬하다.	He never stops speaking highly of her. = He can't stop praising her. (그는 그녀를 ~)
입에 침이나 발라라.	[거짓말] Stop lying. = Don't tell a lie.
입원했습니다.	He's hospitalized. = He's in the hospital. (그가~)
입은 거칠어도 마음은 비단결이다.	She has a harsh tongue but a beautiful heart. (그녀의 ~)

입을 막지마세요.	[손으로] Don't cover your mouth with your hand.
입을 못 다물어요.	① I can't close my mouth. ② [행복] I can't stop smiling. // He's so happy that he can't stop smiling. (그는 좋아서~) ➡ That's right. He's smiling from ear to ear. (맞아요. 입이 귀에 걸렸네요.)
입을 쭉 내밀어보세요.	Please stick your mouth out.
입을 틀어막아!	① [재갈] Muzzle him! (저놈의~) ② [말] Stop him! (저놈의~)
입이 가벼워.	You have a big mouth. = You're so talkative. // He has a big mouth. (그는~)
입이 무겁네요.	You're reticent. // He's very reticent. (정말~)
입이 무겁습니다.	I'm reticent. // He's reticent. (그는~)
입이 방정입니다.	You're careless with your tongue. = You're impulsive with your words. // I'm careless with my tongue. (제가~)

입이 싸서 탈이야!	Such a problem with the talkative mouth!
	// Such a problem with his talkative mouth. (그는~)
	// Such a terrible problem with her talkative mouth. (그녀는 정말이지~)

입이 얼얼합니다.	① [매운 맛] My mouth is burning. ② [아픔] It bites my mouth.
입이 열 개라도 할 말이 없다.	I wouldn't say a word even if I had ten mouths.
입장권은 어디서 삽니까?	Where can I buy tickets? ➡ At the ticket office. (매표소요.)
입장료는 얼마 입니까?	How much is an admission ticket? ➡ Five dollars. (5달러입니다.)

입장에서 생각해보세요.	Think as if you were in his shoes. (그의~)
입장을 바꿔놓고 생각해 보세요.	Let's think from each other's point of view.
입 조심해!	Watch your mouth! // 〈비속어〉 Watch your fucking mouth! (망할 ~)

있

있는 것들이 더해요.	① [속담] The more one has, the more one wants. ② The rich want more.
있는 것이 없는 것보다 낫습니다.	Having something is better than having nothing.
있는 대로 먹자!	Let's eat what we have!
있는 척하기는?	Do you pretend you're rich? = Are you acting as if you're rich?
있습니까?	① [소유] Do you have ~? // Do you have a computer? (컴퓨터~) ➡ ⓐ Yes, I do. (있습니다.) ⓑ No, I don't. (없습니다.) ② ☞ 계십니까?
있습니다.	① [소유] I have it. ② [출석] I'm here. = Here I am. ③ [빈자리문의나 노크에 대한 대답] It's taken.
있을 때 잘해!	Be nice when I'm with you!
있었어요. // 있었습니다.	① [과거소유] I had. // I had a boyfriend. (남자 친구가 ~) ② [과거존재] It existed. (그것이 ~) ③ [자리함] I've been here awhile. (여기에 잠시 ~)

잉

잉꼬부부라고 했는데.	I was told they're a happy husband and wife. // Everybody said they're a happy husband and wife. (다들~)

잊

잊어버려!	Snap out of it! = Take your mind off it!
잊어버렸습니까?	[망각] Did you forget it? = Was it out of your mind? = Did it slip your mind? ➡ ⓐ It slipped my mind. (깜빡했습니다.) ⓑ I forgot. (까먹었습니다.) // I completely forgot. (정말로 까먹었습니다.) ⓒ It slipped my mind. (잊어버렸습니다.)
잊을 뻔 했네요.	I almost forgot. (깜박~)
잊을 수 없습니다.	① I can't forget. // I can't forget her. (그녀를~) ② [고집] I wouldn't forget.
잊지 마세요.	① [망각] Don't forget. // Don't forget, please. (제발~) ② [기억] Please don't forget about your wallet and keys. (지갑과 열쇠 챙기는 거~)
잊지 않을 겁니다.	I won't forget. // I won't forget about today. (오늘을~)

자

자!	① [받아] Take it! = Here! = Here it is! ② [주의 환기] Hey! = Look! = Here! = Come on! // Come on! Let's drink a toast! (~건배합시다.)
자, 어서!	[동작을 유도] Come on!

자거라!	① Go to sleep! = Go to bed!
	// Go to bed now! (어서~)
	// Go to bed and sleep! (가서~)
	② [취침인사] Good night! = Have a good night!

자격미달이야!	You're not qualified! = You're not good enough! // He's not qualified! (그 사람은~)

자고 갈래요?	Would you like to sleep?
	// Would you like to sleep here? (여기서~)
	// Would you like to stay for a night here? (여기서 하룻밤~)
	➡ ⓐ Sure. (좋아요.)
	ⓑ No. I have something to do at home.
	= I've gotta go home and work.
	(아니요, 집에 가서 할 일 있어요.)

자고 싶어요.	I wanna sleep. // I wanna sleep more. (좀 더~)
자극 받았어요.	I was motivated. = I was inspired. = I got a kick in the butt.
자기 꾀에 자기가 넘어가다.	He fell into his own trap. = He's deceived by his own trick.
자기가 뿌린 씨는 자기가 거둔다.	[속담] One reaps what he sows. = One harvests what he has sown.
자기만 알고 남은 모른척합니다.	He knows only himself and no one else. (그는~)
자기분수를 알아야지.	Know yourself. = Don't forget who you are.

ㅈ

자기야!	① [남녀에게 다 씀] Honey! = Sweetheart! = Baby! = Darling! ② [여자에게만 씀] My queen! = My princess!
자라 보고 놀란 가슴 솥뚜껑 보고 놀란다.	[속담] Once bitten, twice shy. = A burnt child dreads the fire. = A scalded cat fears cold water.
자랑스럽다!	I'm proud! // I'm proud of you! (네가~)
자리 있습니까?	① [음식점] Do you have seats? // Do you have seats for tonight? (오늘 저녁~) ➡ ⓐ I will try to make some. (없어도 만들어 드려야지.) ⓑ Sorry, but there are no seats available. (죄송합니다. 없습니다.) ② [빈자리 확인] Is it taken? (여기~) ➡ ⓐ Yes, it's taken. (사람 있습니다.) ⓑ It's not taken. (빈자리입니다.)
자리 좀 바꿀 수 있을까요?	Can we switch the seats?
자리 좀 봐주세요.	Would you watch the seat? = Please hold the seat for me? = Do you mind saving the seat for me? // Would you watch this seat? (이~)
자리로 돌아가 주세요.	① Please return to your seat. (당신~) ② Please back to your own seat. (제~)
자리를 바꾸고 싶어요.	Can you change seats?
자리를 양보해주세요.	Please offer your seat. // Please offer your seat to her. (저 여자에게~)
자리를 예약하려고 합니다.	[음식점] I'd like to make a reservation. = I'd like to reserve some seats.
자리를 예약했습니까?	Did you reserve seats? = Did you make a reservation? // Did you reserve this seat? (이~)

ㅈ

	➡ No. (아니요.)
자리에 사람 있습니까?	Is it taken? = Is it occupied? = Somebody took it? // Is this taken? (이~) ➡ It's not taken. (사람 없습니다.)
자리에 앉아주세요.	① [회의 시작] Please sit. = Have a seat, please. ② [휴식 후에] Grab a seat, please. ③ [기내] Return to your seat.
자리에 앉아주시기 바랍니다.	Would you please sit down?
자리에 없습니다.	① [부재] He's not here. (그는 지금~) ② He came to work, but he's not at his desk. (그는 회사 안에 있지만, 지금~)
자만하지 마라.	Don't be too proud of yourself.
자매학교입니다.	It's our sister school.
자명종은 8시에 맞춰놨어요.	I set the alarm for 8.
자상하십니다.	① [보살핌] You're caring. // My grandfather is very caring. (할아버지는 무척~) ② You're kind. // My grandfather is very kind. (할아버지는 무척~)
자세히 한 번 보세요.	Please look carefully.
자식!	① You fellow! = Fella! ② [비속어] You son of a bitch!
자식을 낳아봐야 부모 은혜를 안다.	One can understand when he/she has a child.
자신 없습니다.	I have no confidence. // I have no confidence in my heart. (마음에~)

ㅈ

자신 있습니까?	① Can you do it? ➡ Yes. (있습니다.) ② Do you have confidence? = Are you confident? ➡ ⓐ Of course. (물론이죠.) ⓑ I'm confident. (자신 있습니다.) ⓒ Sure. (그럼요.)
자신을 가져!	① Have confidence! = Be confident in yourself. ② ☞ 포기하지 마세요.
자신의 능력을 믿어!	Believe in yourself!
자업자득이야!	① You've got yours! = It serves you right! = You deserve it! ② One reaps what he sows!
자자!	Let's sleep! // Let's sleep! Turn off the light! (~, 불 꺼!)
자전거 탈 줄 압니까?	Can you ride a bike? = Do you know how to ride a bike? ➡ ⓐ Of course. (타고 말고요.) ⓑ I haven't learned how to ride a bike. (아직 안 배웠어요.)
자주 놀러오세요.	Please visit me often. // Please visit me often from now on. (앞으로~)
자주 만납시다.	Let's meet more often. Let's meet more often from now on. (앞으로~) ➡ ⓐ Sure. (물론이지요.) ⓑ That's not difficult. (어렵지 않지요.)
자주 연락합시다.	Let's contact each other more often. // Let's contact each other more often from now on. (앞으로~)
자주 연락해!	Please call me more often!
자책하지 마세요.	Don't be hard on yourself. = Don't blame yourself. // Don't be too hard on yourself. (너무~)

ㅈ

자포자기 하지 마세요.	Don't be so discouraged. = Don't be so depressed. = Don't give up on yourself. = Don't be disappointed in yourself.
자화자찬.	You toot your own horn. = You blow your own trumpet. (너 ~한다)

작

작년에 졸업했습니다.	I graduated last year.
작별인사하고 싶지 않아요.	I don't wanna say goodbye. // I don't wanna say goodbye to you. (당신과~)
작습니다.	① [크기] It's small. // It's too small. (너무~) ② [키가] He's too short. (그는 너무~)
작심삼일.	① An unsteady plan. ② 〈직역〉 A decision cannot last for three days.
작업 거는 겁니까?	[연애] Are you hitting on me?
작업 들어가는거야.	[연애] I'm going to hit on her tonight. = I'm going to put the moves on her. (오늘 저녁 그녀에게~)
작업 중입니다.	① [여자를 상대로] I'm hitting on a woman. ← What's up? (뭐해요?) ② [일] I'm at work. = I'm doing my work.
작은 것 같습니다.	[옷 · 신발] It's small. // It's a little small. (좀~) // These shoes are a little small. (이 신발이 좀~)
작은 것은 없습니까?	① [기본적으로 작은 것] Don't you have small ones? // Don't you have a smaller one? (좀~) ② [더 작은 것] Don't you have it in a smaller size? (좀~)
작은 고추가 더 맵다.	[속담] The smaller, the shrewder.

ㅈ

작은 성의표시일 뿐입니다.	It's a little thing from my sincere heart.
작작 좀 해라!	**Enough!** = That's too much! // Enough! I'm really sick of it. (~지겨워 정말!)
작전타임!	Time for strategies!

잔

잔 비웁시다.	Let's finish the drink.
잔꾀 부리지 마!	[술수] Don't do tricks!
잔돈 없습니다.	I have no change. = I don't have change.
잔돈 좀 바꿔줄래요?	① Would you change some money? ➡ ⓐ Yes. (예!) ⓑ How much do you want to change? (얼마 바꿔드릴까요?) ② Can you change this 10 dollar bill to quarters? (10달러를 25센트짜리 ~) ➡ Yes. (예.)
잔돈 필요 없습니다.	[거스름돈] **Keep the change.** = I don't need change.
잔디를 함부로 밟지 마세요.	① Don't step on the grass. ② [경고문] Keep off the grass. = Stay off the grass. = Keep out of the grassy area.
잔디밭에 들어가면 안 됩니다.	You shouldn't go onto the grass.
잔뜩 먹었습니다.	I've had enough. = I'm full.
잔머리 굴리지 마!	Stop doing tricks!
잔소리 좀 그만해!	① Stop lecturing! = No more lecture! ② [귀찮음] **Stop nagging me!**

ㅈ

	③ [중단을 요구] Cut it out! = Knock it off! ④ [설교 같은 잔소리] Enough of your preaching! = No more preaching! = That's enough of your preaching.
잔인합니다.	You're cruel. = You're harsh. // You're too cruel. (너무~)

잘

잘 가!	① [작별인사] ☞ 안녕! ② [여행 인사] Good luck with your trip!
잘 갔다 오세요.	① Have a good trip. (여행~) ② [길조심] Take care. = Take care of yourself.
잘 갔다 왔니!	How was your day?
잘 기억해둬!	Keep it in mind! = Remember it!
잘 다녀가십시오.	☞ 안녕!
잘 들립니까?	Can you hear well? ➡ ⓐ Yes, I can. (잘 들립니다.) ⓑ No, I can't hear well. (잘 안 들립니다.)
잘 들어!	① [전하는 말] Please listen up! = Please listen carefully! ② [물건] Please hold it!
잘 먹겠습니다.	Thank you so much for the food.
잘 먹습니다.	① [많이 먹음] He eats much. = He has a good appetite. (그 사람은~) ② [기호] I like Chinese food. (중국 요리를~)
잘 먹었습니다.	I liked the food. = I enjoyed the food. // I enjoyed the food today. (오늘~)

ㅈ

잘 모르겠습니다.	① [사실을] I don't know it well.
	② [자세히] I don't know it in detail.
	③ [이치나 도리] I have no idea.
	④ [구체적으로] I'm kinda ignorant of it.
	// I'm also kinda ignorant of it. (저도~)
	// I'm kinda ignorant of it. Please understand. (~. 이해해 주세요.)
	⑤ [길을] I'm new here.
	= I'm unfamiliar with this area.
	⑥ [이해과정] I don't understand. = I don't get it.
	// I don't get it, either. (저도~)
	// I don't get it because it's too difficult. (너무 어려워서~)
	// I don't get it because he talks a lot. (그가 말이 너무 많아서~)
	⑦ [사람을 이해] I don't understand him. (그 사람을~)

잘 보관하십시오.	Please keep it. = Please take good care of it.
잘 보내세요!	① Have a good time! // Have a good weekend! (주말~) ② [파티 등 모임] Have fun! ③ Congratulations on your birthday! (생일~)
잘 봐!	[시범을 보임] Look carefully! // Look at me carefully! (날~)
잘 사세요!	[신혼부부에게] Live happily ever after!
잘 살아요.	[격려] Live a happy life.
잘 생각해봐!	① [기억] Try to remember! ② [고민] Think hard! ③ [경고성] Try hard!
잘 생각해봤니?	Have you thought about it? ➡ Yes, I have. (잘 생각해봤어.)
잘 생각했어!	① [결정] An excellent decision! ② [판단] Good judgment!

	③ [아이디어] That's a good idea!
잘 생겼습니까?	① [남자] Does he look nice? = Is he a good-looking man? = Is he handsome? (그 남자~) ➡ ⓐ Yes, he is. (잘 생겼어요.) ⓑ No, he's ugly. ☞ 못생겼습니다. ② [여자] Does she look nice? = Is she a good-looking woman? = Is she pretty? (그 여자 ~)
잘 속아요.	I'm too naive. = I'm easily deceived. = I'm gullible. (난~)
잘 쉬세요.	☞ 푹 쉬세요.
잘 시간입니다.	Time to sleep. = Time for bed.
잘 썼어요.	[글 쓴것 칭찬] Good writing! = You wrote it very well.
잘 안 들립니다.	I can't hear you well.
잘 안 보입니다.	I can't see well.
잘 알고 있습니다.	① [잘 이해함] I know him. (그를~) ② [자신 스스로를] I know myself. ③ [말하는 사람에 대해] I got you.
잘 알면서.	You knew it already.

잘 어울립니다.	It looks good on you.
	= It goes well with you.
	// It goes very well with you. (너무~)
	// The dress looks great on you. (이 옷을 입으니~)

잘 왔어요.	Good to see you. // Good to see you now. (마침~)
잘 자!	Good night!
잘 잤습니까?	Did you have a good night? = Did you sleep well?

ㅈ

	➡ ⓐ I feel good. (기분이 좋습니다.) ⓑ No. (별로요.)
잘 잤습니다.	I had a good night. = I slept well.
잘 주무세요!	① Have a good night! ② [취침] ☞ 안녕히 주무세요.
잘 주무셨어요?	① Did you have a good night? ② [취침] Did you sleep well? ➡ ⓐ Yes. (잘 잤어요.) ⓑ It was OK. (그런대로요.) ⓒ The bed was not comfortable. I couldn't sleep well. (잠자리가 맞지 않아, 잠을 못 잤어요.) ③ [취침] Did you have a good sleep? // Did you have a good sleep last night? (어제 밤~) ➡ Yes, I did. (잘 잤습니다.)
잘 지내고 있습니까?	How have you been? ➡ I have been fine. (잘 지내고 있습니다.) // I'm fine now. (지금~)
잘 지내고 있습니다.	I have been fine. = I'm doing well.
잘 지내셨습니까?	[아는 사이의 안부인사] ① How are you? ➡ Fine. (잘 지냈어.) ② How have you been? (그동안~) ➡ I'm OK. (그런대로요.) ③ What's up these days? = What have you been up to these days? (요즘~) ➡ ⓐ Not much. (잘 지냈습니다.) ⓑ I'm OK. (그런대로요.)
잘 지냅니까?	How are you? // How's he? (그 사람~) ➡ Fine. (잘 지냅니다.) // How's everybody? (모두~)
잘 지냈습니까?	[서로 아는 사이, 오랜만에 만나는 경우] How have you been? ➡ Fine. (잘 지냈어요.)

잘 지냈습니다.	I have been fine. // I have been fine. Thank you for asking. (~, 감사합니다.)
잘 한다!	① [일 · 행위 등을] Great! = Good job! ② [구기운동] You're a great basketball player! (농구~) // You're a good soccer player! (축구~) ☞ 노래 잘 한다!
잘난 척은!	① Stop putting on airs! ② [차림새] Look at how he dresses! = Look at what he's wearing! ③ [교만] She thinks she's something! (저 여자~) ④ [비난] What a dude!
잘난 척하냐?	Are you putting on airs? ➡ Who's putting on airs! (누가 자랑한데!)
잘난 척하지 마!	① [외모] Don't put on airs! ② [독선] Don't be egocentric! ③ [교만] Stop the arrogance!
잘났다!	[비난] ① [아는 체에 대해; 남녀 구분 없음] You're Mr. know-it-all! = You're a know-it-all! (너~) ② [똑똑한 척에 대해] How smart! (너~) ③ [교만] How excellent!
잘 됐다!	Good! = Fabulous! // It's good! (그거~) // It's really good. (정말~)
잘 돼 갑니까?	[장사 · 사업] How's your business going? ➡ ⓐ Going well. (잘 돼 갑니다.) ⓑ Not so good. (순조롭지 않아요.)
잘되고 있습니다.	[공부 · 일 · 사업] It's good.
잘되기만을 바라냐!	[실천은 않고] How could you wish for success without trying?

ㅈ

잘렸습니다.	I was fired. // I got fired from the job. (그 직장에서~)
잘못 걸었습니다.	[전화] You've got the wrong number.
잘못 먹었냐?	[이상한 행동에] Did you eat something bad? What's wrong with you? // What did you eat? What's the matter with you? (뭐~) ➡ I'm fine. (아주 정상이야.)
잘못 봐서 죄송합니다.	I'm sorry that I have mistaken you.
잘못 봤습니다.	I have mistaken you.
잘못 알았습니다.	You got it wrong. (당신이~)
잘못됐어!	① [오류] That's wrong! ② [그릇됨] That's false!
잘못될 리 없습니다.	That can't be wrong.
잘못을 비세요.	Beg for forgiveness. // Go quickly and beg him for his forgiveness. (어서 가서 그에게~)
잘못을 알고 있습니다.	I know your fault. // I know my fault. (제~)
잘못을 인정합니다.	I admit my mistake. // I admit to you my mistake. (당신에게~)

잘못이 아닙니다.	It's not my fault. = It's not my bad.
	// This is not your fault. (이건 당신~)
	// This is not my fault. (이건 제~)

잘못입니다.	① [과오] It's all my fault. (모두 제~) // This is my fault. (이건 제~) ② [실수] It's all my mistake. (모두 제~)
잘 못합니다.	① [일을] I'm not a good worker. ② [구기운동] I'm not good at sports. ③ [축구를] I'm not good at soccer.

	④ [영어 등을] I've learned English for 2 years. But I can't speak well. (2년이나 배웠는데 말을~)

잘못했습니다.	① [사과] I'm sorry. = I apologize.
	// I'm so sorry. (너무~)
	// I'm sorry. It's my bad. (죄송합니다, 제가~)
	➡ That's alright. (괜찮습니다.) ☞ 죄송합니다.
	② [실수] It's all my fault. = It's my bad.
	// I was bad. It's all my fault. (제가 나빴습니다, ~)
	③ [판단] I misjudged it. (제가~)
	➡ Please be careful next time. (다음번에는 조심하세요.)

잘하는 요리가 뭡니까?	What do you cook well? (여기~) // What do you cook best? (여기서 제일~) ➡ Bibimbap. (비빔밥입니다.)
잘한다!	[칭찬] Good! = Great! = Excellent! // Very good! (너무~) // So good! (정말~)
잘할 겁니다.	You'll do better. // I'm sure you'll do better. (틀림없이~)
잘합니까?	① [말을] Can you speak … well? // Can you speak Chinese well? (중국어~) ➡ ⓐ Yes, very well. (아주 잘합니다.) ⓑ So so. (별로입니다.) ⓒ Not so well. (못합니다) ② ☞ 운동을 잘합니까?
잘합니다.	I'm good. // I'm good at basketball. (농구를~) // I'm good at Chinese. (중국어를~)
잘해드리겠습니다.	[상점] We'll give you the best service. = We'll serve you well.
잘해봅시다.	[협력관계] Let's work hard together. (우리 함께~) ➡ Sure. Let's do it. (좋아요, 그렇게 합시다.)
잘해봐!	① [행운을 빔] Good luck! = I wish you good luck! = I wish you luck!

ㅈ

	② I hope you do well. ③ [교제] Good luck with the man! (그 남자하고~)
잘해줍니다.	She's nice to me. (그녀는 저한테~) // He's nice to me. (그는 저한테 ~)
잘해줘!	① [상대] Be nice to me! // Be nice to her! = Be kind to her! (그녀한테~) ② [보살핌] Take good care of her. (그녀에게~)
잘해줘서 고마워요.	Thank you so much for being nice / kind to me. = I appreciate you for being nice / kind to me.
잘했어!	① [행위에 대한 칭찬] Good! = Great! = Excellent! = It's nice of you! = It's kind of you! // How nice! (정말~) ② [구기운동] Good! = Great! = Good job! = Excellent! = Hooray! = Way to go! ③ [특출한 성적을 낸 상대를 칭찬함] Well done! = Bravo! = Good for you! = You did a good job! = You did well! = That takes the cake! = Excellent work! ④ [맞게 동작한 경우] Good! = Way to go! = That's the way to go! = Keep it up!

잠

잠 깨웠지?	[떠드는 소리에] Did I wake you up? ➡ No. I'm fine. (아니, 괜찮아.)
잠 잘 잤습니다.	☞ 잘 잤습니다.
잠깐 나갔다오겠습니다.	I'll be out for a while. = I'll be right back.
잠깐 누워 계세요.	Please lie down a while. // Please lie down over there a while. (우선 저기서~)

ㅈ

잠깐 봅시다.	[할 말이 있음] Can I talk to you a minute?
잠깐 쉽시다.	Let's take a rest for a while. = Let's rest for a short time. = Let's have a short break.
잠깐 실례합니다.	[잠시 자리를 뜸] Excuse me. = Pardon me.
잠깐만!	① [대기] Wait. Let me think! (~생각 좀 해보고.) ② [전화대기] Hold on! = Don't hang up! = Wait a second! ③ [가던 길을 멈춰 세움] Wait! = Stop! ④ [취하려던 동작을 제지함] Stop it! = Hang on!
잠깐만 기다리세요.	〈경어〉 Would you please wait a second? = Would you wait a minute? = Could you please wait a minute? = Could you wait a second?
잠꼬대를 자주합니다.	I often talk in my sleep.
잠옷으로 갈아입으세요.	Change into sleeping clothes. = Change into pajamas.
잠은 잘 주무십니까?	Do you sleep well? = Do you have a sound sleep? ➡ ⓐ Yes. (잘 잡니다.) ⓑ Not really. (별로입니다.) ⓒ No, I don't sleep well. (잠을 통 못 잡니다.)
잠을 깊이 잡니다.	I sleep like a log. = I am a deep sleeper. = I sleep deeply. = I sleep soundly.
잠을 못 잡니다.	I can't sleep well. = I have trouble sleeping. // I can't sleep well these days. (요즘 늘~)
잠을 통 못 잡니다.	I have trouble sleeping. = I'm totally sleepless.
잠을 한숨도 못잤습니다.	I couldn't sleep at all.

ㅈ

잡

잡아떼지 마!	Stop denying it! = Don't pretend you don't know it!
잡아라!	① [체포] Arrest! // Arrest that person! (저 사람 ~) ② 〈비속어〉 [손으로 몸을] Seize that bitch! (저년을~)

장

장가가고 싶습니다.	I wanna get married. = I wanna have a wife. = I want marriage.
장가갔습니다.	I'm married. = I got married. = I'm taken. = I have a wife. // The man is married. (그 사람은~)
장난이 아니야!	It's not a joke! = I'm not kidding!
장난치지 마!	① [농담] No kidding! // Stop kidding me! = Don't pull my leg! = Stop making a fool of me! (나한테~) ② [심한 장난] Stop it! ③ [소란] Don't make a fuss! = Don't fuss! = Stop the noise! = Stop the fuss! ④ [놀림] Don't pick on me!
장난친 거야.	① [농담] I was kidding. ② [놀림] I made fun of you. ③ [못된 장난] I made fun of you. // He made a fool of you. (그가~)
장담하지 말아요.	Don't boast. = Don't be certain like that. = You're too sure of yourself.
장보러 왔어요?	[인사] Are you here for shopping? ➡ Yes! (예!)
장사 잘됩니까?	① How's your business going? = How's your business?

ㅈ

	// How's your business these days? (요즘~) ➡ ⓐ Fine. (잘됩니다.) ⓑ It gets me to eat. (먹고 살만합니다.) ⓒ It's so slow. (불경기입니다.) ⓓ Fine. Thank you for asking. (덕분에 그럭저럭요.)
장수를 잡으려면 말부터 쏘아야 한다.	[속담] If you had not plowed with my heifer, you would not have solved my riddle. (성서 사사기14:18)

재

재미가 하나도 없습니다.	① I have no fun. = It's not fun at all. ② [놀이] It's not interesting. = It's not exciting!

재미없습니다.	① ☞ 재미가 하나도 없습니다.
	// This book is not interesting. (이 책은~)
	// This subject is no fun at all. (이 과목은 정말~)
	// This game is not exciting at all. (이 게임은 정말~)
	// This program is not interesting.
	= There's no fun in this program. (이 프로는 정말 ~)
	② [썰렁한 농담에] That's not funny.
	// That's not funny at all. (정말~)

재미있습니까?	Is it interesting? = Is it exciting? // Is this interesting? (이거~) ➡ ⓐ It's very interesting. (매우~) ⓑ It's really interesting. (정말~)
재미있습니다.	① [놀이] It's fun. // It's lots of fun. (정말~) ② [흥미] It's exciting. // It's really exciting. (정말~)
재미있을 것 같습니다.	① [책 · 영화] It looks interesting. // It looks very interesting. (아주~)

	② [보기에] It seems exciting. // It seems very exciting. (아주~) ③ [모양] It seems funny.
재수없네!	① [운수] Bad luck! = Not lucky! = So unfortunate! // How bad! (정말~) ② [행운] I have no luck! ③ [사람이] He has no luck! (그는 정말~)
재수 없는 놈은 뒤로 자빠져도 코가 깨진다더니!	[속담] The bread never falls but on its buttered side.
재수없어!	☞ 재수없네!
재수 옴 붙었네.	☞ 재수없네!
재수가 좋아요.	I'm lucky. = I have good luck.
재주는 곰이 넘고 돈은 되놈이 받는다.	[속담] One beats the bush and another catches the birds. = Two dogs strive for a bone, and a third runs away with it.
재촉하지 마세요.	Don't push me. = Don't rush me. = Don't hurry me up! // Don't push me like that. (그렇게~)

저

저 사람을 압니다.	① [면식] I know that person. = I'm aware of that person. = I'm acquainted with that person. ② [친밀도] I'm close with that person.
저것과 같은 것으로 주세요.	[주문, 요구] I'd like to have the same one as that one. = Same as that.
저것은 뭡니까?	What's that? ➡ That's an ad. (저건 광고입니다.)
저기 봐!	Look over there! = Look at that!

저기요!	① [사람을 부름] Excuse me! ② [사람을 불러 세움] ☞ 이봐요! ③ [실례] Excuse me! ④ [장소를 가리킴] Over there!
저녁 같이해요.	Have dinner with me. // Let's have dinner together. = How about having dinner together? (우리~)
저녁 시간은 다 좋습니다.	I'm free all evening. = Any time in the evening is fine with me.
저녁 잘 먹었습니까?	☞ 잘 먹었습니다.
저녁밥 다 했어요?	Have you finished preparing the dinner? ➡ So soon. = In a minute. (곧 됩니다.)
저녁에 기다리겠습니다.	I'll wait in the evening.
저는 서진희입니다.	[이름] I'm Jinhui Seo. = My name is Jinhui Seo.
저도 그렇게 생각합니다.	I think so, too.
저도 그렇습니다.	Me, too. = Same here.
저도 마찬가지입니다.	☞ 저도 그렇습니다.
저런!	① [놀람] Oh dear! = Oh my! = Good heavens! = Goodness! = Good gracious! ② [비난] Oh, boy! = What the hell!
저를 압니까?	Do you know me? ➡ Yes. (압니다.)
저리 가!	① [반대편으로] That way! ② [한쪽으로 비키라는 말] Go away! = Move! = Move out of my way! = Get out of my way! = Clear the way! = Out of my way! ③ 〈비속어〉 ☞ 꺼져! ④ [몸에서 떨어지라고] Get off of me!

ㅈ

저리 꺼져!	**Get the hell out of here!** ☞ 꺼져!
저리 비켜!	Go away! ☞ 저리 가!
저리로 좀 가줄래요?	Would you move over there? // You're too close to me. Would you move over there? (가까이 있지 말고~)
저리로 좀 가지.	① Why don't you move a bit? // You're too close to me. Why don't you move a bit? (가까이 있지 말고~) ② Move over there.
저밖에 몰라요.	I'm the only one with the answer. = I'm the only one who knows it. = Only me.

저분은 누구십니까?	Who's that? = Who's that person?
	➡ That is my teacher. (저분은 선생님입니다.)
	// That person is a doctor. (저분은 의사입니다.)
	// That's my father. (저분은 우리 아버지입니다.)

저의 명함입니다.	It's my business card. // This is my business card. (이건~)

적

적당할 때 그만둔다고 하는 거야.	This is called quitting at a proper time. (이런 걸~)
적당할 때 그만둬.	Drop it at a proper time. = Drop it when it's time. = Quit when it's time to quit.
적당합니까?	What time is convenient for you? (언제 가면~) ➡ Tomorrow is good. (내일이요.)
적당히 얼버무리지 마세요.	① [애매한 말] Don't speak ambiguously. = Don't shuffle. ② [대답회피] Give me a clear answer. = Don't evade the question. (질문에~)

ㅈ

	③ [실수무마] Don't smooth over your mistake. (실수를~) ④ [그럴듯한 포장] Don't sugarcoat it.
적반하장도 유분수지.	[속담] The thief turns on the master with a club. = Save a stranger from the sea, and he'll turn your enemy.
적으세요.	Write it down. = Copy it. = Take notes. // Write it down here. (여기에~)
적응이 됩니까?	Are you adjusting well here? = Are you getting in the swing of things here? = Are you fitting in well here? (여기 생활에~) ➡ ⓐ Now I feel comfortable with everything. (지금은 적응이 좀 됩니다.) ⓑ I haven't adjusted yet. (아직 적응이 안 됩니다.)
적임자예요.	He's qualified for this job. = He is a good choice for this work. = He is the right man for this work. = He is well-fitted for this job. (그가 이 일에~)

전

전 아닙니다.	① [Are you~?로 물은 경우] No, I'm not. ② [Do you~?로 물은 경우] No, I don't.
전 안됩니까?	Can't I? ➡ ⓐ You can. (됩니다.) ⓑ You will be able to. (될 거야.)
전공은 무엇입니까?	What is your major? = What are you studying? ➡ ⓐ My major is English Education. (전공은 영어교육입니다.) ⓑ I'm studying Business Administration. (전공은 경영학입니다.)
전기가 나갔어요.	The power went out.

전기가 들어왔어요!	The power is in! // The power is back! = The electricity is back. (다시~)
전달해주세요.	① Please convey my message to him. = Please get my point across to him. (내 뜻을 그에게~) ② [물건을 전달할 때] Please hand it to him. (그에게 그걸~)

전도가 유망해.	The future is bright before us.
	// You have a bright future before you.
	= The world is all before you. (자네는~)
	// He is a very promising man. (그는 ~)

전등을 끕시다.	Let's turn off the light. = Let's switch off the light.
전문가입니다.	He is an expert. = He is a specialist. = He is a professional. (그는~) // He is a pottery professional. = He is an expert in pottery. (그는 도자기~)
전문이지.	That is my specialty. = That is in my line. = That's my cup of tea. // Girl things are my specialty. (여자의 일이라면 내가~) ☞ 주특기지.
전반전이 끝났어요.	The first half is over.
전번처럼 해주세요.	Like you did last time. = Like you did previously.
전보다 좀 좋아졌어요.	① [실력] I improved a little compared to last time. = I changed for the better. ② [병세] I feel a little better than last time.
전보다 훨씬 좋아졌어요.	① [실력] I improved a lot. = I'm a lot better now. ② [병세] I feel a lot better now.
전부 너만 믿는다.	[부탁 · 당부] I absolutely trust you. = I have full confidence in you. = I have full trust in you.

ㅈ

전적으로 동의합니다.	I totally agree with you. = I'm absolutely going with you. = **I'm all with you.**
전적으로 지지합니다.	I'll all for that. = I absolutely support it. // I'm with you. = I'll stand by you. (당신을~)
전진!	① Proceed! = Go ahead! ② [운전 시에] Drive ahead!
전철역에 가려면 어떻게 갑니까?	How can I get to the subway station? = Can you show me the way to the subway station? ➡ ① Go straight. (앞으로 곧장 가세요.) ② There's one over there. (저기 저쪽에 하나 있습니다.)
전학가려고?	Why do you want to transfer? = Why do you want to change schools? (왜~) ➡ I don't like this school. = I don't want to be in this school. (전 지금의 학교가 싫어서요.)
전할 말이 있습니까?	Do you want to leave a message? = Do you have a message to leave? ➡ ⓐ No, nothing special. ⓑ What can I say to him? (무슨 할 말이 있겠어요?)
전할 물건이 있습니다.	I have something to give her. (그녀에게~)
전해드릴게요.	① [말을] I will make sure she gets the message. ② [물건을] I will make sure she gets it. (그녀에게~)
전해주세요.	① [말을] Please convey this message to him. = Please get this message across to him. (그에게~) // Please tell him so. = Please tell him like that. (그에게 그렇게~) ② [물건을] Please hand this to him. (그에게~)
전혀 가망이 없습니다.	Not a chance. = Hopeless. = Not in the least.

ㅈ

전혀 모르겠습니다.	I don't get it. = I don't understand at all. = I have no idea. = I have no clue. = I don't have the slightest idea. = I don't have the faintest idea. = It's all Greek to me. ☞ 하나도 모르겠어요.
전혀 안 들립니다.	I can't hear anything. = I hear nothing.
전화 끊겠습니다.	Let me hang up the phone. = Let me go.
전화 끊는다!	Let me hang up the phone! See you! (~, 안녕!)
전화 끊지 마세요.	Don't hang up. = Hold the line, please.
전화 끊지 말라고 했잖아.	I told you not to hang up on me.
전화 돌려드리겠습니다.	I will get you on to him. (그에게~)
전화드리겠습니다.	Let me call you back. = I'll call you again. = I will give you a call again. (다시~)
전화 바꿨습니다.	This is he/she speaking. // [자신의 이름을 말하며] Mike/Jane speaking.
전화 받기가 곤란합니다.	He cannot answer the phone now. = He is not available now. = I can't get you on to him. (그는 지금~)
전화 받아!	① [전화 바꿔주며] It's for you! ② [명령] Get the phone! = Answer the phone! = Pick up the phone!
전화 받지도 않고, 문자도 씹어.	He never calls back and ignores text messages. (그는~)
전화왔어!	A phone call for you! = You've got a call. = The phone's for you.
전화 잘못 건 것 같습니다.	Sorry, you've got the wrong number. (미안합니다, ~)
전화 좀 써도 될까요?	May I use your phone? = If you don't mind, I'll use your phone.

ㅈ

전화 주셔서 감사합니다.	Thank you for calling. = I appreciate that you gave me a call.

전화 주세요.	Give a ring. = Give me a call.
	// Call me later. = Give me a call later. (나중에~)
	// Don't forget to call me. (잊지 말고~)

전화 한 통도 없네.	There's no phone call at all.
전화 한 통만 쓰겠습니다.	Let me use your phone for just one call. = Can I use your phone for just one call?
전화가 끊겼습니다.	[사용정지] Your telephone line is disconnected.
전화가 끊어졌어요.	The call was disconnected. = The call was cut.
전화가 먹통입니다.	The phone is out of order. = The phone doesn't work.
전화가 불통입니다.	The line is dead.
전화가 안 됩니다.	I cannot get a hold of her. = I cannot get through to her on the phone. = I cannot reach her on the phone. (그녀에게~)
전화가 연결됐습니다.	You are on the line.
전화기가 꺼져있습니다.	[음성녹음] The number you called is off now. = The phone you called is turned off now.
전화를 돌려주세요.	[내선] Can you put me on to number 103[one, o, three]? = May I have extension one-o-three? = Extension 103[one-o-three], please. = Give me extension 103[one-o-three], please. (103번으로~)
전화를 받을 수 없어, 소리사서함으로 연결됩니다. 연결된 후에는 요금이 부과됩니다.	[음성녹음] The person you phoned cannot answer. You will be forwarded to an automatic voice mail service. After connected, you will be charged for recording your message.

ㅈ

전화번호는 몇 번입니까?	What is your phone number? ➡ My number is 2034-1233[two, o, three, four, one, two, three, three]. (전화번호는 2034-1233입니다.)
전화번호를 가르쳐줄 수 있습니까?	Can you give me your number? ➡ Sure. Here you are. (그러죠. 여기 있습니다.)
전화번호를 남겨주세요.	Leave your number, please. = Can you leave your number? = Can I take your number?
전화번호를 말씀해주세요.	Please ell me your number. = Give me your number, please. (당신의~)
전화벨이 울렸어요.	The phone rang.
전화비는 당신이 지불합니까? 상대방이 지불합니까?	Are you paying the charge, or is the receiver paying? ➡ ⓐ I'm paying. = The charge is on me. (제가 냅니다.) ⓑ Collect call, please. (수신자 부담입니다.)
전화비가 너무 많이 나왔어요.	The phone bill is too high. = I've got an unreasonably high phone bill.
전화위복이 될 수 있습니다.	Bad luck often brings good luck. = A misfortune turns into a blessing.

전화주세요.	Give me a call. = Call me.
	= Give me a holler. = Give me a shout.
	// Call me anytime.
	= Give me a ring anytime. (언제든지~)
	// Call me when you are back.
	= Give me a ring as soon as you're back.
	(돌아오시면~)

전화카드 한 장에 얼마입니까?	How much is a phone card? // How much is an international phone card? (국제~)
전화카드가 있습니까?	① [상점] Do you have phone cards?

	// Do you carry international phone cards? (국제~) ➡ We have many. What kind do you want? (여러 가지가 있는데, 어떤 것을 원하십니까?) ② [소유] Have you got a phone card with you?
전화하려던 참이었어.	I was about to call you. (막~)
전화하지 마세요.	Don't call me. // Stop calling me anymore. (더 이상~)
전화한 사람이 누구죠?	① [방금 전] Who was that on the phone? ② [지금] To whom am I speaking? = Who am I speaking to?
전화해주세요.	Call again after ten minutes. = Call me back in ten minutes. (10분 후에 다시~)
전화해도 될까요?	Can I call you? = Is it okay if I called you?

ㅈ

절

절 받으십시오.	Let me make a bow to you.
절대 그런 일 없습니다.	There's no such a thing. = I swear to God that there's no such a thing.
절대 안 됩니다!	You can't do that. Never! = No way! // Over my dead body! (내 눈에 흙이 들어가기 전까진 안 됩니다.)
절망적입니다.	① [상황] The situation is hopeless. = It's a disastrous situation. ② [심정] I'm devastated.
절에 간 색시.	[줏대 없는 사람] He lacks a backbone. = He doesn't have a backbone. = His opinions change like the weather changes. (그는~)

절약이 최대의 수입이다.	Thrift is revenue.
절약 좀 해야겠다.	You should economize. = You should tighten your belt. = You should cut corners.
절차가 그렇습니다.	That's the way it is. // That's the way you do it here. = That's how you do it here. (여기는~)
절차가 까다롭습니다.	There's a lot of red tape here. (여기는~)
절차상에 문제가 있습니다.	There are some procedural problems.
절호의 기회입니다.	This is a golden opportunity. = This is a great chance. = This is a heaven-sent opportunity. (이번이~) ☞ 하늘이 내려준 절호의 기회입니다.

젊

젊어 보입니다.	You look young.
	// You look younger than me. (나보다~)
	// You look younger than your age.
	= You look younger for your age. (나이보다)

젊어서 고생은 사서도 한다.	[속담] It does a young man good to suffer some privations in the world.
젊어지십니다.	You are getting younger and younger. (점점~)

점

점심 먹었습니까?	Did you have lunch? ➡ No, not yet. (아직요.)
점심 먹읍시다.	Let's have lunch. = Won't you have lunch with me?

	= What do you think of having lunch with me? (우리 같이~)
점심 식사하러 나갔습니다.	He's out for lunch. (그는~)
점심 제가 사겠습니다.	This lunch is on me. = Let me treat you to lunch. = I'll pay for lunch.
점심 좀 사줘요.	Please buy me lunch.
점심약속 있습니까?	Do you have a plan for lunch? ① ➡ ⓐ I have a plan. (선약 있는데요.) ⓑ No, I don't. (없습니다.) ② [데이트] ➡ Who's gonna want to go on a date with me? (누가 나하고 약속[데이트]하겠어요?)
점심에 약속이 있습니다.	I have a plan for lunch. = I have an appointment for lunch. ➡ With whom? (누군데?) ➡ Someone you don't know. (당신이 모르는 사람입니다.)
점을 본 적이 있습니다.	I've been to a fortuneteller before. // I happened to run into a fortuneteller before I came here. (여기 오기 전에, 우연히~)
점잔 빼기는.	You are putting on airs. = You are putting on frills.
점잖게 굴어!	[아이들에게] Behave yourself! = Act your age! = Be nice! (좀~)
점잖게 행동하세요.	① [신사답게] You are a gentleman. Behave yourself. (좀~) ② [배운 사람답게] You are an educated man. Behave yourself. (좀~) ③ [예의 있게] Show your manners. (좀~)
점잖게 좀 행동합시다.	Let's behave properly. = Let's behave ourselves. (모두들~)

ㅈ

점잖은 강아지 부뚜막에 먼저 올라간다.	[속담] A girl who seems well-behaved may disappoint you first.

접

접니다.	① [전화에서] This is Mike/Jane.(이름) // This is he/she Speaking. ② [노크 할 때] It's Mike/Jane.(본인 이름) = It's me.
접수는 며칠까지 입니까?	[등록] Until when do you accept applications? ➡ Till the twenty-fifth. (25일입니다.)
접수는 어디서 합니까?	[병원] Where is the receptionist? ➡ At the main entrance. (현관 입구에서요.)
접수는 어디에 가서 해야 합니까?	① [분실신고] Where can I report the lost article? ② [학교에서 전학] Where can I report the transfer? ➡ At the office of school affairs. (교무부요.) ③ [상표] Where can I register a trademark?
접시 닦을게!	① [설거지] Let me wash the dishes! ② I will wipe the dishes!
접시 하나만 주세요.	Can you get me a plate? // Can you get me a small plate? (작은~)

젓

젓가락을 사용할 줄 압니까?	Do you know how to use chopsticks? ➡ ⓐ I know how to use them. (사용할 줄 압니다.) ⓑ I don't know how to use them. (사용할 줄 모릅니다.)

ㅈ

정

정각입니다.	O'clock. // Twelve o'clock. (12시~)
정들려고 했는데.	I was about to be fond of you. = I was about to like you.
정들었습니다.	I've grown fond of you. = I've grown attached to you. = I've grown to like you. = You've grown on me. = I've gotten used to you. = I've gotten used to having you around. = Now I feel close to you.
정리 끝났습니다.	I have finished getting things organized. = I'm done with tidying things up.
정리 다 했습니까?	Did you finish organizing things? = Are you done with tidying things up? (물건은~) ➡ All done. (다 했어요.)
정리하겠습니다.	① [정리] Let me get them organized. (제가~) ② [청소] Let me put them away neatly. (제가~)
정말 그래!	[맞장구] You can say that again!
정말 좋겠다!	[감탄] Wow! That is good for you! = How lucky you are!

정말입니다.	You can take my word for it.
	= I'm speaking the truth.
	= You can bet your last dollar on it.
	// I'm serious. I'm not kidding. (농담이 아니고~)
	// That's not just an expression. I mean it.
	(빈 말이 아니고~)

정말일까요?	① [가능] Is it possible? ② [사실] Is it true?
정말입니까? // 정말이야?	① [대화 중에 믿기지 않는 경우] Really? = Are you sure? = Did I hear you right?

ㅈ

	= Are you serious? = You bet. (그게~) ➡ I'm (dead) serious. = I bet. (정말이야.) ② [사실여부 확인] Is it true? ➡ It's true. (정말입니다.) // This is true. (이건~)
정반대입니다.	It's just the opposite. = It's the other way round.
정상대로 문을 엽니다.	We are open as usual.

정상이 아닙니다.	He is not in a normal condition. (그는~)
	// He is not himself now. (그는 지금~)
	// He's out of his mind now. (그는 지금 정신이~)

정시 도착입니다.	I'm arriving on time.
정시에 가겠습니다.	I'll be there on time.
정시에 출발합니까?	[비행기] Is the flight number 902[nine-o-two] taking off on schedule? (902편은~) ➡ Yes, it is taking off on time. (정시에 이륙합니다.)
정식으로 저녁 초대를 했습니다.	He formally invited me to dinner. (그가~)
정신 똑바로 차려!	① Hold yourself together! = Keep your eyes peeled! = Get a grip! ② [정신없는 사람에게] Come to yourself! = Open your eyes! = Wake up!
정신 빠진 놈!	You are out of your mind! = You are crazy or something! = You have a screw missing!
정신 좀 봐!	How forgetful I am! (내~)
정신 좀 차려!	① [격려] Cheer up! ② [혼수상태] Hold yourself together! ③ [즐거움에 멍하니] Hey! Come back to earth! = Wake up! ④ [각성] Pay attention to what you are doing!

ㅈ

	⑤ [이성을 잃음] Come to your senses! ⑥ Get a grip!
정신만 차리면 괜찮아!	Look sharp! Then you will be okay.
정신없어.	① [소란스러움에] I don't know what's happening because of the noise. = The noise distracts me. ② [바빠서] I'm so busy that I feel like I'm on another planet. = I'm too busy, and I'm so out of it.
정신없었습니다.	① I was so absent-minded. = I was so out of it. ② [정신없이 바쁨] I was too busy with the work. (일 때문에~)
정신을 집중해!	Concentrate! = Pay attention! // Put your brain on it. (그것에~)
정신이 드니?	Are you feeling all right? = Are you okay? = Are you back with me now? = Have you come to yourself? ➡ ⓐ Yes, I'm all right. (응!) ⓑ I feel a lot better. (많이 좋아졌어요.)
정신이 들 겁니다.	He will come to his senses. (그는~) // He will regain consciousness soon. (곧~)
정신이 있는 거냐?	Are you out of your mind?
정신이 정상이 아닙니다.	I'm not myself. // I'm foggy today. = I'm not with it today. (오늘~)

정액권이 있습니다.	I've got a commuter ticket.
	// I've got a weekly pass. (일주일~)
	// I've got a monthly pass. (한 달~)

정을 붙여야 합니다.	We have to see each other often to form a friendship. = We have to grow attached to each other. = We should be getting closer to each other. (우리 서로가 자꾸~)

ㅈ

정직이 최선이야.	Honesty is the best policy.
정직하면 두려울 게 없다.	If you are honest, there's nothing you should be afraid of. = If you are honest, there's nothing to be afraid of.
정찰제입니다.	The price is fixed. = The price is set. = The prices are as marked. // Marked price. There's no overcharge. (~ 에누리 없습니다.)
정확합니다.	Exactly. = You are absolutely right. = You hit the bull's eye.
정황을 살펴라.	① [관찰] See what others do first. (먼저~) ② [상황을 두고 봄] See how the land lies first.

ㅈ

젖

젖 먹던 힘까지 다 쏟아!	Put in your best effort! = Put your heart and soul into it! = Give it your all!

제

제 갈 길 가도록 내버려 둬.	Let him make his own journey. = Let him make his own choice. = Let him make a decision on his own. (그가~)
제 꾀에 제가 넘어가다.	You are falling into the trap set by yourself. = You are polling the noose around your own neck. = You are digging your own grave.
제 논에 물 대기.	[아전인수] That is drawing water to one's own mill. = That's too self-centered a point of view.

제 눈에 안경이다.	① Beauty is in the eye of the beholder. (미의 기준은 보는 이에 따라 다르다.) ② Love sure makes people blind. (사랑하는 사람은 절로 예뻐 보인다.)
제 도끼에 발등 찍힌다.	It's like warming a snake in your bosom.
제 말이 바로 그 말이에요.	That's exactly what I want to say. = You took the words right out of my mouth. = You can say that again. = I totally agree with you. ☞ 동감입니다.
제 멋에 사는 겁니다.	He lives on his own fancy. = He lives on his own style. (그는~) // Everyone got his own thing. (모두들~)
제 무덤 파기야.	That's cutting your own throat. = That's digging your own grave.
제 밑 들어 남 보이기.	[약점을 드러냄] It's washing one's dirty linen in public. = It's airing your dirty laundry in public.
제 버릇 개 못 준다더니!	① It's a pattern of behavior! ② A fool can never throw away his bad habits! (버릇은 고치기 힘들다.) ③ [속담] A leopard cannot change his spots! (본성은 바뀌지 않는다.)
제 얼굴에 침 뱉기.	[속담] Chickens come home to roost. = Harm watch, harm catch! = It's like cutting off your nose to spite your face. = It's like spitting in the wind.
제 탓입니다.	That's my fault. = I have to blame myself for it. = Put the blame on me. = I'm responsible for it.
제 탓 하지 마세요.	Don't pin that on me. = Don't blame me for that.

ㅈ

제 풀에 흥이 나다.	You are full of your enthusiasm.
제가 낼게요.	Please be my guest. = Let me settle the bill. = Let me treat you. = It's on me.
제가 받을게요.	I'll get it. = Let me answer it. (전화~)
제가 알기로는 그래요.	As far as I know, that's true. = As far as I'm concerned, that is correct.
제가 해 드릴게요.	I'll do it for you. = Let me do it for you.
제기랄!	① 〈비속어〉 [자신의 실패를 후회] Damn it! ② [불행을 초래하는 사람에게 하는 욕] Go to hell!
제대로 되는 일이 없습니다.	Everything I do goes bad. = I'm screwed up.
제대로 오신 겁니다.	[상점 등에서] You are in the right spot. = You are in the right place. = You've found the right place. = This is what you're looking for.
제때에 돌아와 주세요.	Please come back on time. = Please be back on time.
제때에 드세요.	Eat it at a good time. // Have regular meals, please. = Be regular in your diet, please. (식사~)
제때에 왔구나!	You came at the right moment! = You came at a good time! = Your arrival is the perfect timing!
제멋대로야!	You are doing at your own pleasure! = You are running riot! = What a liberty!
제명에 못 살 것 같아.	I don't think I can die a natural death.
제발 나가주세요.	[명령] Please get out of here. = Please be gone.
제발 늦지 마세요.	[당부] Don't be late, please. = Be on time, please.

ㅈ

제발 신경 좀 꺼주세요.	Please don't mind me. = Please don't bother me. = Please stop poking your nose in my affair.
제발 이러지 마!	① [경고] You shouldn't do this. ② [간구] Please don't do that.
제발!	For God's sake! = For Pete's sake! = For the love of God!
제법인데!	You are doing pretty good! = That's pretty good!
제비뽑기하자.	Let's draw straws. = Let's draw for it. = Let's draw numbers.
제삿날이다.	Today is your last day. (오늘이 네~)
제시간에 가지 못할 것 같습니다.	I will never make it on time.
제안에 반대합니다.	① I'm against his suggestion. = I don't agree with his suggestion. (그의~) ② [회의에서] I don't second the motion. = I have an objection to the motion.
제안하고 싶습니다.	I'd like to suggest one thing. = I have a suggestion. = I'd like to make an offer. (한가지~)
제의가 있습니다.	I'd like to make a recommendation. = I'd like to recommend one thing. ➡ Recommendation again? How many more do you have? (또 건의야. 무슨 놈의 건의가 그렇게 많으냐?)
제일 잘하는 노래가 있습니까?	Do you have a song you can sing the best? ➡ I don't have anything. (없는데요.)
제일 좋아하는 영화입니다.	This is my favorite film. (이것은 내가~)
제자가 스승보다 낫다.	A pupil excels his master. ☞ 청출어람

ㅈ

제자로 받아주세요.	Please be my master. = I want to be your student. = I want to learn from you. (저를~)
제자를 보기에 스승만한 눈이 없다.	A master recognizes his pupils.
제자리에 갖다 놔요.	Put this back in its place. = Put this back where it was. = Put this in the original place. (이것을~)
제정신이 아니구나!	You are insane! = You are out of your mind! = You are out of your tree! = You've lost your mind!

젠

젠장!	[쓸데없는 말에] Damn it!

졌

졌다!	I give up! ☞ 손들었다!
졌습니다.	① [경기] I lost the game. ② [패배를 인정] I throw in the towel. = I give up. = You've got me.

조

조건이 맞아요.	The conditions are perfect for me. (나에게~)
조금도 말할 줄 모릅니다.	I cannot speak at all. // I cannot speak Japanese at all. (일본어는~)
조금만 더 참아!	① Endure a little more! = Hang in there a little more!

	② [고통] Bite the bullet a little longer!
조금만 마셔!	Take a sip! = Drink a little!
조금만 먹어!	Have a bite! = Have some!
조금만 참아!	[화] Have some more patience! = Keep your temper under control!
조급해 하지 마세요.	① Don't be so hasty. = Don't rush. (너무~) ② Don't fret about like that. (그렇게~)
조마조마해 죽겠어요.	I'm really nervous. = I feel uneasy. = I'm really anxious. = I definitely have butterflies in my stomach.
조만간에 성공할 겁니다.	We will succeed soon. = We'll make a success sooner or later. = We'll make a hit soon. // We'll make it soon. (조만간에 해낼 겁니다.)
조만간에 찾아뵙겠습니다.	I will come and see you sooner or later. = I will drop by soon.
조심성이 없었습니다.	I was not paying attention enough. // I was too careless. (너무~)
조심하겠습니다.	I will be careful. = I will be cautious. = I will keep my eyes open.
조심하세요!	① [눈에 보이는 위험] Watch out! = Look out! ② [눈에 보이지 않는 위험] Be careful!
조심하지 않았습니다.	I was not careful.= I was careless. = I was not paying attention. = I was not attentive. ☞ 조심성이 없었습니다.
조심해서 가세요.	① [여행] Have a safe journey. ② [귀가] Take care!
조용한 데 가서 얘기 좀 합시다.	Let's go to a quiet place and talk more. = Let's get a room and talk it over. (우리~)

ㅈ

조용합니다.	This place is very quiet. = It's very quiet here. (여기는 참~)
조용히(해)!	① [명령] Be quiet! = Hold your tongue! // Put a lid on it! = Shut up! ② Keep it down!
조용히 못하겠어!	① [명령] Stop that noise! ② Knock it off! ③ 〈속어〉 Shut up! ☞ 입 닥쳐!
조용히 처리합시다.	Let's take care of it quietly.
조용히 해주세요.	Be quiet, please. = Keep it down, please.
조족지혈입니다.	It's a drop in the bucket. ☞ 새 발의 피야.
조퇴했습니다.	① He went home early. (그는~) ② [학교] He left school early. // He skipped school. (무단으로~) ③ [직장] He left the office early. = He left work early. = He took the rest of the day off. = He had a short day.
조회 끝!	Morning meeting finished!

존

존경스럽습니다.	[탄복] I respect you.
존경합니다.	I respect him very much. = I look up to him very much. (그를 매우~)
존함은 많이 들었습니다.	[첫 대면 인사] I've heard a lot about you.
존함이 어떻게 되십니까?	What is your name? ☞ 성함이 어떻게 되십니까?

졸

졸려!	I'm sleepy. = I feel drowsy. = My eyelids are heavy.
졸려 죽겠어요.	I'm dead sleepy.
졸업 축하한다.	Congratulations on your graduation! // Congratulations! You're graduating with honors. (훌륭한 성적으로~)
졸업장은 따라!	You need a high school diploma at least! (고등학교~)
졸업합니다.	I'm graduating next year. (내년에~)
졸업했습니다.	I already graduated. (이미~) // He graduated from Columbia University. (그는 콜롬비아 대학을~)
졸음밖에 안 옵니다.	I feel nothing but sleepy. // His words make me sleepy. (그의 말은~)
졸지 마세요.	Do not doze off. = Don't knock a nod. ☞ 꾸벅꾸벅 졸지 마세요.

좀

좀	① [양] A little. = A dash. = A small quantity. ② [수] A few. = Some. = A small number. ③ [정도] Somewhat. = A little. = A bit. = To some degree.
좀 됐어요.	[시간] It's been a while. // It's been a few minutes. (몇 분~)
좀 쉬어야 합니다.	① [휴식] You need to take some rest. (좀~) ② [호흡] You need to breathe in some air. (숨을 좀~)

ㅈ

좀 일찍 가세요.	Leave a little early. = Be off a little early.
좀 있다가…	Later. = Some time later. = A little later.
좀생이!	① [인색한 사람에게] You are stingy! = You are so cheap! = You are a cheapskate! ☞ 치사하다! ② [속 좁은 사람에게] You are small-minded! = You are so narrow-minded.
좀스럽기는!	What a petty person you are!

종

종례는 매일 몇 시에 있습니까?	What time do we have our final meeting every day? ➡ At four o'clock. (4시 정각이요.)
종로에서 뺨맞고 한강 가서 눈 흘긴다.	[속담] A coward vents his anger on a third person. = Go home and kick the dog.
종류별로 하나씩 주세요.	I want one of every kind.
종아리 걷어라.	Turn up your pants to the knees. You are gonna be whipped on the calf. (~. 종아리를 맞을거야.)
종업원 좀 불러주세요.	① [상점] Can you call me a clerk here? ② [음식점] Can I have a waiter here? (남자~) // Can I have a waitress here? (여자~)
종이봉투에 넣어주세요.	Can you put it in a paper bag? // Put it in a brown paper bag, please. (갈색~)
종이와 펜을 가져올게요.	Let me get you a pen and paper.
종일 바빴어요.	I was tied up all day. // I was busy all day long today. (오늘~)
종잡을 수 없습니다.	I don't get what he says at all. = I can't make out what he says at all. (그 사람 말은~)

ㅈ

종점은 어디입니까?	Where is the final stop of this bus? (이 버스의~) = What is the last stop of this bus line? ➡ The final stop is the airport. (종점이 바로 공항입니다.)
종종 모입시다.	Let's get together often. (앞으로~)

좋

좋게 말할 때, 비켜!	① [명령] I'm telling you, make off! = I'm telling you, get off my way! = Step back! = Step aside! ② Get lost! = Get off me! = Get away from me!
좋게 보입니다.	It looks nice. = Looks good!
좋게 생각해.	[상황을 좋게 생각하길 바람] Take it positively. = Look on the bright side.
좋겠다!	Good for you! = You must be very happy!
좋기는 뭐가요!	[좋지 않음] That is nothing good!
좋기는 좋은데 너무 비쌉니다.	It is good but expensive.
좋다고 생각합니다.	I think it is good. // I think this book is the best one. (이 책이 제일~)
좋다 말았네!	I almost had it! = It would have been nice!
좋습니까?	When is good for you? = When is convenient for you? (언제가~) ➡ ⓐ The sooner, the better. (빠를수록 좋습니다.) ⓑ Anytime is good.(언제든 다 괜찮아요.)
좋습니다.	① [수락] That sounds good. = That's a good idea. = It's a deal.

ㅈ

	= I agree. // That's good with me. (저는~) ② I love rock music. (락음악이~) // I really love it. = I'm really into it. (그것이 정말~)
좋아는 마세요.	Don't be too happy with that. = Don't get too excited over that. (너무~)
좋아서 기절하는 줄 알았어요.	I was so happy that I almost fainted.
좋아서 난리입니다.	Everybody is so excited about that. = Everybody's so delighted about it. = Everybody's jumping with joy. (모두들~)
좋아서 이러는 줄 아세요?	I didn't choose to do this. = I'm not doing this voluntarily. = I'm not doing this because I want to! (누군~)
좋아서 하는 일인데, 뭘!	I chose to do this! (내가~)
좋아서요.	[마음이 내켜서하는 일] I'm willing to do this. = I love to do this. (내가~)
좋아 죽는다!	You are so crazy about it!
좋아질 겁니다.	① [상황] Things will get better. ② [건강] You will get better. = Your health will get better.
좋아하는 거면 다 좋아해.	I like whatever you like. (네가~)
좋아하는 것 같습니다.	He seems to have a crush on me. (그가 나를~)
좋아하는 사람 생겼구나?	You have someone special, don't you? ➡ ⓐ No, not yet. (아직 없습니다.) ⓑ Sure, I have. (당연히 있지.) ⓒ Who said that? (누가 그래?)
좋아한 적 있습니다.	I have had a crush on him before. (전에 그를~)
좋아합니다.	I like it. // I really love it. = I like it very much.

	= I'm really into it. (아주~) ☞ 좋습니다.
	// I like it, too. (저도~)
	// I like her very much. (정말 그녀를~)
	// I like you with all my heart. (진심으로 당신을~)
	// I like only you. (당신만을~)

좋았어!	[감탄] That was good! = You did a good job! = Excellent! = Great! // Awesome! (정말~)
좋으면 좋은 거고, 싫으면 싫은거지!	You either like it or you don't.
좋으면서!	You like it, don't you? = I know you like it! = I see you like it!
좋은 곳을 알고 있습니다.	I know a good place. // I know a nice place to hang out. (놀만한~)
좋은 기회 놓치지 마세요.	This is a good chance. Don't miss it. = This is a golden opportunity you should not pass up.
좋은 기회입니다.	This is a good opportunity. // This is a real good opportunity. (정말~)
좋은 꿈꾸세요.	Sweet dreams!
좋은 날씨네요!	The weather is great today! = Nice weather! (오늘~) ☞ 날씨가 좋다!
좋은 남자 만나서 결혼해.	Find a nice guy and marry him.
좋은 놈이라곤 한 놈도 없다.	There's no good man among your friends. (네 친구 중에~)
좋은 놈이야.	You are a really good man. (넌 참~)
좋은 말도 세 번 하면, 듣기 싫어한다.	Even good words, three times repeated, make you irritated.
좋은 분입니다.	He is a good man. = He is a nice person. (그는~)
좋은 사람 같지 않습니다.	He doesn't look like a good man. = I don't think he is a nice person. (그는~)

ㅈ

ㅈ

좋은 사람 만나서 잘 살자.	Let's find a good partner separately and live happily. (우리 각자~)
좋은 사람 있으면 소개시켜 줘.	Hook me up if there's a good person.
좋은 사람입니다.	He is a good man. (그는~) ☞ 좋은 분입니다.
좋은 생각이 있습니다.	I have a good idea. = I've got an idea. = An idea hit me.
좋은 생각이야!	That's a good idea. = That sounds good. (그거~) ☞ 좋습니다.
좋은 소식 기다리겠습니다.	I will be looking forward to hearing good news.
좋은 시간되십시오.	① Have a good time! ② [레스토랑] Enjoy your meal!
좋은 시절이 다 갔습니다.	His good days are all gone. (그의~)
좋은 아침입니다.	Good morning.
좋은 약은 입에 쓰다.	Good medicine tastes bitter.
좋은 의견입니다.	That is a good opinion.
좋은 일이 있습니까?	Did something good happen to you? = Do you have some good news? = Is there any good news? (무슨~) ➡ No, nothing. (아무것도 없습니다.)
좋은 쪽으로 생각하세요.	Think positively. = Look on the bright side. ☞ 좋게 생각해.
좋은 책입니다.	This is a very good book. (이건 매우~) // This book got it all. (내용이 알찬~)
좋은 하루 되세요.	Have a nice day! = Enjoy your day!
좋은 게 좋은 거지 뭐.	If it's nice, then it's nice.

좋을 게 뭐가 있어?	Is there anything good in you? = I can't find anything good in you. (너한테~)
좋을 대로 하세요.	Do as you like. = Suit yourself. = It's up to you. = Whatever you say. = It's your decision. = I don't care what you do. = By all means. ☞ 맘대로 해!
좋지!	[어떤 결정에 대한 대 만족] That's great! = That sounds good! = That's a good idea. = That sounds perfect! ⬅ Let's have pizza for dinner. (저녁으로 피자 먹자.) ☞ 좋은 생각이야. // 좋습니다.
좋지 않습니다.	① That's not good. = That is no good. (그건~) ② [효과] That doesn't work well.

좌

좌석은 오른쪽 창가에 있습니다.	Your seat is next to the window on the right.
좌석을 바꿀 수 있을까요?	Can I change my seats? ➡ ⓐ Sure. (그러세요.) ⓑ Sorry, you can't. (안됩니다.)
좌석을 예약하기 어렵습니다.	It's hard to reserve a seat because it's peak season these days. (지금은 성수기라~)
좌석이 있습니까?	Is there a seat available? // Do you have seats available to Seoul today? (오늘 서울 가는~) ➡ Yes, we do. (있습니다.)
좌절하지 마세요.	Don't be frustrated. = Don't break down, please.
좌측	On the left. // It's on your left. (~에 있습니다.)

좌회전!	Turn left! ☞ 왼쪽으로 도세요.

죄

죄 값을 받은 거야!	You deserve that! = That serves you right!
죄송합니다.	① [실수에 대한 사과] I'm sorry. It's my fault. ➡ That's okay. (괜찮아요.) ② [미안함] I'm so sorry. (정말~) ③ [정중한 사과] I apologize. = I owe you an apology. ④ [실례] Excuse me. ⑤ [말실수에 대한 사과] I'm sorry. It was a slip of the tongue. ☞ 미안합니다.
죄 짓고는 못산다.	Nothing hurts like the truth. = A guilty conscience needs no accuser. ☞ 도둑이 제 발 저리다.

주

주둥이나 깨끗이 닦고 말해!	Wipe your mouth and talk! = Clean your mouth and talk!
주량 것 드십시오.	Drink to your capacity. = Drink to your limit.
주량이 셉니다.	I am a heavy drinker. = I drink much. = I drink like a fish. (저는~)
주량이 약합니다.	I can't drink much. = I'm not a heavy drinker.
주량이 정말 세구나!	You are a heavy drinker! = You drink like a fish!
주말 잘 보내세요.	Have a nice weekend. = Enjoy your weekend.
주말에 시간이 있습니까?	Are you available on weekends? // Are you available this weekend?

	= Do you have time this weekend? (이번~) ➡ Yes, I do have time. (있습니다.)
주머니 사정이 안 좋습니다.	I'm short of money lately. = I'm low in my pocket lately. = I have been in the red lately. = I can hardly keep my head above water. = I'm having a hard time making ends meet. (요즘~)
주먹은 가깝고 법은 멀다.	It's easy to rely on physical strength rather than law.
주목해!	① Attention! = Listen up! = Give me your attention! // Keep an eye on him! (저 사람을~) ② ☞ 들어봐!
주무세요.	Good night! = Have a good night's sleep. ☞ 잘 주무세요!
주무셨어요?	Did you have a good night's sleep? = Did you sleep well? (잘~) ☞ 잘 주무셨어요?
주문 제작입니다.	① It's custom-made. ② [집 · 가구 · 소파 등] It's custom-built. ③ [재단] It's custom-tailored.
주문을 바꿔도 됩니까?	Can I change my order? ➡ Sure, you can. (그럼요.)
주문을 해도 됩니까?	Can I order now? = Can you take my order now?

주문하실래요?	[식당] Can I take your order?
	= Are you ready to order?
	= Are you all set?
	// What would you like to have? (뭘~)
	// What will you have today? (오늘은~)

주문하지 않았는데요.	[음식] We didn't order this. = This is not the food we ordered. (이것을~)

주문한 것 좀 빨리 갖다 주세요.	Please get us the food we ordered quickly. = Can we have our food in a minute? ➡ Sorry, we need some more time. (죄송합니다만, 시간이 조금 더 필요합니다.)
주문한 요리가 아닙니다.	This is not the food I ordered. (이것은 제가 ~) ☞ 주문하지 않았는데요.
주문한 요리가 아직 안 나왔는데요.	The food we ordered hasn't come out yet. = Our food is not served yet. (우리가~)
주문했습니다.	[물품 등] I ordered it already in the afternoon. (낮에 벌써~)
주부입니다.	My mother is a homemaker. = My mother is a housewife. (어머니는~)
주사 맞기 싫어요.	I don't want to get an injection. = I don't want a shot.
주사가 없습니다.	I am not a bad drinker. ☞ 술버릇이 없습니다.
주사위는 던져졌습니다.	The die is cast.

주세요!	① [주문] This one, please. (이걸~)
	② [요구] Give it to me! (그것을~)
	// Give me some money. (돈 좀~)
	// Give me a book. (책 한 권~)
	// Let me take a look at it!
	= Show it to me! (좀 보여 줘!)

주소로 가주세요.	[택시기사에게] Please take me to this address. (이~)
주소로 배달해주세요.	Please deliver it to this address. (이~)
주스 주세요.	Juice, please. = Please get me juice. // A glass of juice, please. = Please get me a glass of juice. (주스 한잔 주세요.)
주연이 누구인가요?	Who is starring in the film? = Who is the main actor/actress in the movie? (그 영화~)

ㅈ

주워오세요.	Pick it up and bring it to me. (그것을~)
주워들었어요.	I overheard it. // I picked up the story from others. (그 이야기를~)
주유소에서 기름 넣고 갑시다.	Let's drop by the gas station and fill up the tank.
주의시키겠습니다.	I will give him a word of caution. (그를 잘~)
주의하세요!	[조심] Be careful! = Be cautious! = Look out! = Watch out!
주의할게요.	[조심] I'll be careful. = I'll look out. = I'll watch out. = I'll be cautious.
주인 마음대로 하세요.	[접대] You are the host. Do it your own way. = It's up to the host.
주인을 찾고 있습니다.	[분실] I'm looking for the owner of this.
주저 말고 말해보세요.	① Don't hesitate to say anything. ② [대답] I want your prompt answer.
주전부리를 너무 많이 했어요.	[준비] I prepared too many snacks.
주제넘게 참견은!	What impudence to step in my business! = It's none of your business!
주제넘었지요.	I was too impudent. = I was too saucy. (너무~)
주제를 몰라요!	He doesn't know himself! = He doesn't know who he is! (그는 자신의~)
주제를 벗어났습니다.	We got off the subject. Let's get back on track. = Let's return to the subject. (~우리 본론으로 들어갑시다.)
주제파악 좀 하세요.	Know yourself! = Know who you are! = Who do you think you are?

ㅈ

주제파악을 못하는구나!	You don't know yourself! = You don't know who you are.
주차금지입니다.	This is a no-parking area. = This is not a parking area. = You cannot park your car in this area. (여기는~)
주차하지 마세요.	① [경고문] No parking. ② Don't park here. (여기에~)
주차해드리겠습니다.	Let me park your car.
주책부리지 마세요.	Don't behave senselessly. = Don't be shameless.
주특기지.	That's my cup of tea. = That's my specialty. ☞ 전문이지.

죽

죽 먹을래요.	Let me have some porridge. = I'd like some porridge.
죽 쒀서 개 줬네.	Everything gone to the dogs.
죽 쒀서 남 주다.	You do the good thing, but others take the credit for it.
죽 한 그릇 주세요.	I'd like a bowl of porridge. = Please get me a bowl of porridge.
죽고 싶냐!	Do you want to be dead-meat? // Does he want to be dead-meat? (저사람~)

죽고 싶습니다.	I wish I would die.
	// He is killing me. (그 사람 때문에 아주 ~)
	// The heat is killing me. (더워서~)

죽기 아님 살기야!	[사생결단] This is a life-and-death situation! = I'm risking my life here!

죽느니만 못합니다.	I am in such a pathetic situation. = My situation is so pathetic. = I cannot but live such a miserable life like this. (정말~) // I have no life these days. (요즘~) ➡ Don't despair. = Don't be frustrated. (절망하지 마세요.)
죽는 길밖에 안 남았어요.	There's no other way than to die. = No other thing is left to me than to die.
죽는 소리마세요.	Never say die!
죽도 밥도 아니다.	① It comes to nothing. // If you stop here, it comes to nothing. (만약 여기서 중단하면~) ② [엉망진창] Everything is messed up. = Nothing went right.
죽도록 마셔보자!	Let's go all the way tonight! = Let's get messed up tonight! = Let's hit the bottle tonight! (오늘밤~)
죽마고우	A buddy from my old stomping grounds. ① [남자] He is my old buddy. (그는 나의 오랜 친구입니다.) ② [여자] She is my old friend. (그녀는 나의 오랜 친구입니다.)
죽어났다!	We are all dead! (우리~)
죽어라 합니다.	[어려움에 처함] We're in real distress now. (지금~)
죽어야 돼!	[자신을 탓함] How stupid I am! = I'm worthless! = I'm good for nothing!
죽었다!	You are dead! (너는~)
죽었다 깨어나도 못합니다.	I can't do it - not in a million years.
죽었다고 봐야지요.	[망함] We're done. = We're finished. // We're done this time. (이번에는~) ☞ 망했어요.

ㅈ

죽었어요.	He's dead. = He passed away. = He kicked the bucket. = He bit it. (그 사람~)
죽여 버려!	[살인] Kill him. = Get rid of him. (그놈을~)
죽여준다!	That's awesome! = Wow, that's really killing me! (정말~)
죽은 정승이 산 강아지만 못하다.	[속담] A dog alive is better than a prime minister dead.
죽을 너무 되게 끓였어요.	The porridge is too thick.
죽을 때 싸 짊어지고 갈 거야?	Are you taking it to the grave? You'd better use it up. (~ 써버리는 게 좋아.)
죽이는데!	① That girl is awesome! = She is the bomb! = She is a killer! (저 여자~) ② [차림새] Look at you! You look awesome!
죽일 놈!	Damn you!

준

준비 잘하세요.	Prepare well.

준비가 덜됐습니다.	I'm not ready yet.
	// I'm not ready for the test. (시험~)
	// I'm not ready for the wedding. (결혼~)

준비됐습니까?	Are you ready? = Are you all set? ① Are you ready to go swimming? (수영할~) ➡ ⓐ Yes, I'm ready. (다 준비됐어요.) ⓑ Not yet. (아직 준비가 덜 됐어요.) ② [회의장 등] Everything is set? (모든 것이 다~) ➡ All set. (다 준비됐습니다.)
준비하세요.	Please get ready. // Whip it up, please. (빨리~)

준치는 썩어도 준치다.	[녹슬지 않은 실력] An old eagle is better than a young crow.

줄

줄 수 없습니다.	I cannot give it to you. = You can't take it from me. (당신에게~)
줄 게 아무 것도 없습니다.	I don't have anything to give you.
줄담배를 피웁니다.	He is a chain-smoker. = He's smoking nonstop. (그는~)
줄 뒤쪽으로 가세요.	Go to the back of the line.

줄 서세요.	Line up. = Stand in line, please.
	= Stand one behind another.
	// Line up here. (여기로~)
	// Line up over there. (저쪽으로~)

줄을 서야 합니다.	You have to get in line. = You have to wait in line.
줄줄이 사탕이야!	It's nonstop!

줏

줏대 없는 놈!	You are lacking a backbone!

중

중간에서 입장 곤란해요.	I'm in an awkward situation between the two. = I'm stuck between the two. (그 둘의~)
중간입니다.	① [실력 · 수준] I'm in the middle. (저는 ~)

ㅈ

	② [사물의 위치] It's halfway between. = It's in the middle.
중고등학교에 다닙니다.	He goes to secondary school. (그는~)
중도에 포기하지 마세요.	Don't give up in the middle.
중독되었습니다.	① [독성분에~] It's poisoned. (그것은~) ② [끊을 수 없게~] I'm addicted. = I'm an addict. = I have a monkey on my back. (저는~) // He is addicted to cigarettes. (그는 담배에~)
중량을 초과한 짐들은 꺼내서 들고 가겠습니다.	I will take out some items of the luggage that is over the weight limit and carry them with me.
중량초과 비용을 내야 합니다.	You have to pay for being over the baggage weight limit.
중량초과입니다.	It's over the weight limit.
중립을 지키겠습니다.	[싸움 · 시합] I will stand in the middle. = I'm going to sit on the fence. = I won't support any team. = I won't be on any side.
중매를 설까 해서 자네를 보자고 했네.	I want to introduce you to someone. = I want to set you up with someone. = I want to hook you up with someone.

중요하지 않습니다.	It's not important. = It doesn't count.
	= It's not a big deal. (그건~)
	// The matter is of little importance.
	(그 문제는 별로~)
	// He is a fifth wheel. (그 사람은~)

중요한 것은 여권입니다.	① The important thing is the passport. ② [일 진행의 관건] The passport is the key to this.
중요한 것은 외모가 아니고 내면입니다.	The important thing is not the looks but the inner beauty.

ㅈ

중요한 순간에 일이 터지는 거야.	An accident happened at the very important moment.
중요한 약속이 있어서 그만 가봐야겠습니다.	I have an important appointment, so I have to go. = I've got to go for a very important meeting.
중요한 약속이라도 있습니까?	① [모임] Have you got an important meeting? ② [데이트] Have you got a date?
중요합니다.	① It's very important. = It is crucial. (그건 정말~) ② [긴급] It's a very urgent matter. (그 문제는~)
중이 제 머리 못 깎는다.	You cannot scratch your own back.
중학교 동창입니다.	He and I went to the same middle school. (그는~)

중학교에 다닙니다.	He goes to middle school. (그는~) // My brother attends middle school. (남동생은~)
	관련표현
	the first grade of middle school (중학교 1학년) // the second grade of middle school (중학교 2학년) // the third grade of middle school (중학교 3학년)

쥐

쥐 죽은 듯 고요합니다.	It's still as the grave. = It's quiet as a mouse.
쥐가 났어요.	I got a cramp in my leg. (다리에~)
쥐구멍에도 볕들 날이 있다.	[속담] Every dog has his day.
쥐구멍이라도 들어가고 싶은 심정입니다.	I feel like sinking into the ground. = I wish the floor would open and engulf me.
쥐꼬리만큼 법니다.	I earn just chicken feed.

ㅈ

쥐도 새도 모르게.	In secret. = Behind the scenes.
쥐뿔도 모르다.	I don't know anything about it. = I know nothing about it. = I don't know beans about it. (그것에 대해~)
쥐새끼 같은 놈들!	Paltry fellows!

즉

즉각 돌아오겠습니다.	I'll be back right away.

즐

즐거운 명절 되세요.	Happy holidays!
즐거운 시간됐습니까?	Did you have a good time? = Did you enjoy a lot? = Did you have fun? ➡ Yes, I enjoyed myself a lot. = Yes, I enjoyed it a lot. (아주 즐거웠어요.)
즐거운 시간되세요.	① [파티 등] Have fun at the party. ② [극장] Enjoy the movie.
즐거운 여행되세요.	Have a pleasant trip! = I hope you have a good trip! = I wish you a good trip!
즐거운 하루되세요.	Have a nice day! = Enjoy your day!
즐거워요.	① [기분이 좋음] I'm so happy. ② [즐기고 있음] I'm having fun. = It's a lot of fun.
즐거웠던 적이 없습니다.	I've never been happy like this before. = I've never been this happy before. (이처럼~)
즐거웠어요.	It was a lot of fun. = I had so much fun.

	= I enjoyed myself a lot. (정말~)
	// I really enjoyed talking to you. (당신과의 얘기가~)
	// I had a great time, too. (저도~)
	// I had a ball last night. (어제 저녁~)

즐겁게 노세요.	Have fun. = Have a good time. ☞ 즐거운 시간되세요.
즐겁게 놀았습니까?	Did you have fun? ➡ Yes, I did. (즐거웠어요.)
즐겁게 지냈습니까?	Did you have a good time today? (오늘~) ➡ Yes, I did. (즐겁게 지냈어요.)

증

증명사진을 8장 찍어주세요.	I need eight portrait shots. // I need eight bust shots. (상반신~)
증명할 수 있나요?	Can you prove it? = Can you verify it? // Can you verify that you didn't do it? (당신이 하지 않았다는 것을~) ➡ Sure. I can give you enough evidence. (네, 증거가 충분히 있습니다.)
증상이 심각합니까?	Is he in serious condition? (그의~) ➡ Not too serious. (큰 문제는 없습니다.)

지

지각이야.	We're late. = We're running behind. = We're running late. = We're behind time. (우리~) // We must be late today. (오늘 틀림없이~)
지각하겠어요.	We're going to be late. (우리~)
지각하면 야단맞을거야.	If we're late, we'll be scolded.

ㅈ

ㅈ

지각하지 마라.	Don't be late.
지각하지 않을게요.	I won't be late again. = I promise I will not be late again. (앞으로 다시~)
지각했어요.	I was late. // I was just five minutes late. (다만 5분~)
지갑 챙기는 거 잊지 마세요.	Don't forget to bring your wallet.
지갑과 여권을 도둑맞았어요.	I had my wallet and passport stolen.
지갑과 열쇠를 빠뜨리지 마세요.	Don't forget your wallet/purse and key. ※ wallet : 남녀 공용지갑, purse : 여성용지갑
지갑을 깜빡했어요.	I forgot to bring my wallet/purse.
지갑을 도둑맞았어요.	My wallet was stolen. = I got my wallet stolen.
지갑을 잃어버렸어요.	I lost my wallet/purse.
지갑이 없어졌어요.	My wallet/purse is gone. = My wallet/purse disappeared.

지겨워!	① [지겨움] I'm sick and tired of it!
	= It really sucks! (정말~)
	// I'm sick and tired of this work!
	(이 일은 정말~)
	// I have had enough! (이젠~)
	② [귀찮음] It's really annoying! (정말~)
	// It's not annoying at all! (하나도 안~)
	// This work is a real nuisance! (이 일은 정말~)
	③ [혐오] It makes me sick!
	④ [지루함] What a drag! = How boring!
	= How dull!
	⑤ [스트레스 받음] It gets on my nerves! (정말~)
	// I can't stand it anymore! ☞ 이제 지겨워!

지금 가야 합니다.	I must be going now. = I have to go now. = I gotta go.
지금 갈게!	I'll be right over. // I'll be right over to you. = I'll come to you right away. (너에게~)
지금 막 왔어!	I have just arrived. = I'm just back.
지금 몇 시입니까?	What time is it now? = Do you have the time? ☞ 몇 시입니까?
지금 이대로가 좋아.	I like it as it is.
지긋지긋해!	I'm sick and tired of it! = I'm fed up with it! = I've had enough of it! ☞ 질린다. // 지겨워.
지기 싫어 그러는 거야.	I don't want to be a loser. = I don't want to lose.
지껄여봐!	Speak one more word! (한 번 더~)
지나가겠습니다.	Let me pass by. (옆으로~) // Let me pass through. (가운데로 좀~) // Let me pass through between you. (당신들 사이로 좀~)
지나가는 길에 들렀습니다.	I happened to be passing by so I dropped in.
지나가는 길입니다.	I'm just passing by. (그냥~)
지나갑니까?	Does this bus pass through the square? (이 버스는 그 광장을~)
지나는 길이었습니다.	I'm just passing by. ☞ 지나가는 길입니다.
지난 일에 연연하지 마라.	Don't live in the past. = Don't cling to past days. = Don't cling to bygones.
지난 일은 잊어버리세요.	Let go of the past things. = Let bygones be bygones.
지난 일이야!	It's all gone. = It's water under the bridge. (다~)

ㅈ

지난달에 왔습니다.	I came here last month. = I arrived here last month. (여기에~)
지난번 수업을 빠졌어요.	I missed the last class. = I was absent from the last class.
지난번 여행 같이 갔었죠?	We went on the last trip together, didn't we? (우리~) ➡ No, you seem to be confusing me with someone else. = No, you must have me confused with someone else. (아니요, 잘못 알고 있는 것 같습니다.)

지난주에 어디 갔습니까?	Where did you go last week?
	➡ I went to Busan on business.
	(부산에 일보러 갔습니다.)
	
	관련표현
	last week (지난주) // last Monday (지난주 월요일)
	// last Tuesday (지난주 화요일)
	// last Wednesday (지난주 수요일)
	// last Thursday (지난주 목요일)
	// last Friday (지난주 금요일)
	// last Saturday (지난주 토요일)
	// last Sunday (지난주 일요일)

지낼 만합니까?	Are you getting along well? = Are you doing good? // Are you getting along well here? (여기서~) ➡ Yes, I'm doing good. (지낼 만 합니다.)
지냈습니까?	How was your day? (오늘 어떻게~) ➡ ⓐ It was fun. (즐거웠어요.) ⓑ Just so-so. (그런대로요.) ⓒ Not so good. (별로입니다.)
지당한 말씀입니다.	Absolutely right. = Well said.
지도 한 장 주시겠습니까?	Can I have a map of this city? (이 도시~) // May I have a map of this town? (이 마을~)

지도교수님이십니다.	This is my advisor. (이분이 저의~)
지도에 표시 좀 해 주시겠습니까?	Will you mark it on my map? = Can you mark where it is on my map?
지도 편달 바랍니다.	I will appreciate your help and encouragement. (앞으로~)
지독하게 굴지 마라.	Don't be so senseless. = Don't be so vicious. = Don't be so mean!
지독하네요.	It's really awful. = It's really terrible. (정말~)
지독한 여편네!	Deadly girl!
지독합니다.	① [행위] It's so dreadful. (정말~) ② [날씨] The weather is awful today. (오늘~) ③ [냄새] The smell repels me.
지랄들 그만해!	Stop the madness!
지렁이도 밟으면 꿈틀한다.	① Even a worm will turn. = Tread a worn and it will turn. ② Even a fly has its anger.
지루합니다.	① [나의 상태] I'm bored. // I'm so bored. (정말~) ② [어떤 대상] This subject is so boring. (이 과목은 정말~) // This lecture is so boring. = Time passes so slowly in this lecture. = The lecture is a total drag. (이 강의는 정말~)
지방에 출장 중입니다.	He is out of town on his business trip. (그는 지금~)
지성이면 감천.	Sincerity moves heaven. = Faith can move mountains.
지식은 힘이다.	Knowledge is power. ☞ 아는 것이 힘이다.
지어낸 이야기입니다.	I made it up. (그건 내가~)

ㅈ

지역번호를 누르세요.	Press the area code.
지연되었습니다.	It was delayed. // It was delayed about an hour. (한 시간쯤~)

지저분하네요!	It's so messy/dirty!
	// This room is messy. (이 방은~)
	// This room looks like a tornado hit it!
	(이 방은 정말~)

지적받았습니다.	My mistake was pointed out. (실수에 대해~)
지적인 사람입니다.	He is a very intelligent person. (그는~)

지지합니다.	① [정당이나 정치인을] I support ~
	// I support the political party. (그 정당을)
	// I support him. (그를~)
	② [누군가의 편을 들 때] I'm going to bat for him.
	(그를~)

지체했습니까?	Why were you late? (어째서 시간을~) ➡ I got stuck in traffic. (차가 한참 막혔어요.)
지켜봅시다.	Let's see what else happens. (더~)
지켜봐 주세요.	① [부탁] Please be my backer. (뒤에서~) ② [감시] Keep an eye on this. (이것을 계속~)
지켜줄게.	Let me protect you. = Let me take care of you. (널~)
지퍼가 열렸어!	Your fly is open!
지피지기면 백전백승.	If you know your enemy and yourself, you can win every battle.
지하도로 내려가면 됩니다.	You can take the underpass.
지하철 3호선을 탑니다.	I take the subway line three.
지하철역은 어디에 있습니까?	Where is the nearest subway station? (제일 가까운~)

	➡ Go straight along this street. (이 도로를 따라 앞쪽으로 가시면 됩니다.)
지하철은 얼마 간격으로 운행합니까?	How often does the subway come and go? ➡ A subway comes and goes every two or three minutes. (대략 2~3분에 한 대요.)
지하철을 잘못 탔어요.	I took the wrong train.

직

직선적이지요.	① [말] He talks too directly. (그는 너무~) ② [성격(긍정적)] He is straightforward. (그는~)

직업은 무엇입니까?	What do you do?
	= What do you do for a living?
	= What's your job?
	= What's your occupation?
	➡ I am a public official. (공무원입니다.)
	// I am a teacher. (교사입니다.)
	// I sell cars. (차 팔아요.)

직업학교에 다니고 있습니다.	[고등학교] I go to a vocational high school.

직장 구한 것 축하합니다.	Congratulations on getting the job you wanted. (원하는~)
	// Congratulations on getting a good job. (좋은~)
	// Congratulations on getting a job so soon like this. (이렇게 빨리~)

직장은 어디 다닙니까?	Where do you work? ➡ I work at a trading company. (무역회사에 다닙니다.)
직장을 찾고 있는 중입니다.	I'm looking for a job. = I'm on the hunt for a job.

ㅈ

직접 가야 합니까?	Do you have to go yourself? (당신이~) ➡ Yes, I have to go myself. (예, 내가 직접 가야합니다.)
직접 말씀드리는 게 좋을 것 같아서요.	I thought I should talk to you in person.
직접 물어봐요.	Ask him in person. (그에게~)
직접 할게요.	[동작을] Let me do it myself. = I'll do it on my own. (제가~)
직진하다가 첫 번째 길목에서 왼쪽으로 돌면 바로 나옵니다.	Go straight and turn left at the next corner, and then you can see it.
직진하세요.	Go straight.
직진해서 우회전한 다음에 다시 직진하세요.	Go straight and turn right. And then go straight again.

진

진동으로 해놔야지.	Put your cell phone on vibrate. (핸드폰을~)
진땀이 납니다.	Even thinking about that time makes me sweat. (그때만 생각하면 지금도~)
진실을 밝혀야 합니다.	[사건의 진상] We have to reveal the real facts of the case. = We have to verify what is true in the case.
진심으로 사과를 드립니다.	I apologize for that with all my heart. = I apologize for that. I really mean it.
진심으로 용서를 빕니다.	I beg you to forgive me. = Please forgive me. I really mean it.
진심으로 축복합니다.	I wish you a blessing with my whole heart.

진심입니까?	Is it from your heart? // Are you serious? = Do you really mean it? (농담이 아니고~)
진심입니다.	I am serious. = I really mean it. = I'm not kidding. (내가 한 말은~)
진인사대천명.	Do your best and God will do the rest.
진작 깨웠어야지.	You should have woken me up earlier. = Why didn't you wake me up earlier?
진정(들) 하세요.	① [화내지 말고] Calm down. = Take it easy. = Pull yourself together. = Chill out. = Cool it. = Let your hair down. ② [너무 좋아하지 말고] Don't be too excited.
진지는 잡수셨습니까?	Have you had your meal? ➡ Yes, I have. (먹었다.)
진지할 수 없어?	Can't you be serious? // Can't you take what I'm saying seriously? I'm opening my heart to you. (너 좀~ 남은 속마음을 털어놓고 있는데.)
진짜 별로야.	[수준] It's not good at all.
진짜로 받아들이지 마세요.	[농담으로 한 말] Don't take it seriously. = I'm just kidding. = I don't really mean it.
진짜야!	① [물건 등이] This is real! = This is genuine! (이건~) ② [말이] This is true! = I'm speaking the truth! = I'm serious!= Take my word for it! = Trust me! (이건~)
진짜야?	① [사실 여부] Is it true? ② [진심 여부] Are you serious? = You're not kidding? = Do you really mean that?
진찰받으러 갑시다.	Let's go to see a doctor.
진퇴양난입니다.	I am stuck in a dilemma. = I'm facing pressure from two tides.

ㅈ

	= I am caught between a rock and a hard place. = I'm between the devil and deep sea. = I'm trapped in a catch twenty-two situation. (지금 저는~)
진행 중입니다.	It is in progress. = It is under way. = It is going on. = It is still in the works.

질

질 게 뻔해.	It's so obvious that we will lose this time. (이번엔~)
질 뻔했어요.	We almost lost it. = We came near losing it.
질렸어요.	I'm fed up with his jokes. = I'm tired of his jokes. (그 사람 농담은 이제~)
질린다!	① [불평 · 원망] I can't stand it anymore! = I can't take it anymore! (이젠~) ② [싫증] I'm sick and tired of it! = I've had enough of it! = I'm fed up with it! ☞ 지긋지긋해!
질문 있습니까?	Do you have any questions? ➡ No, I don't. (없습니다.)
질문 있습니다.	I have a question.
질문이 참 많네요.	You have so many questions. ➡ Sorry about that. (미안합니다.)
질색입니다.	I'm allergic to it. = I hate it. = I don't like it at all. (그건~)
질투난다.	I'm jealous. // I'm jealous of you. (너에게~)
질투심이 많아.	You are so jealous. = You are green-eyed. (넌 정말이지~)

질투하고 있는 겁니까?	Are you jealous of me? = Are you envious of me? = Are you green with envy? (나를~) ➡ No, I'm not. (그런 거 없습니다.)

짐

짐 가지고 나올게.	① I will bring my luggage out. ② [공항] Let me check my baggage out.
짐 꾸려요.	I'm packing my bag. = I'm packing up.
짐 좀 내려 주시겠습니까?	① Can you put down your baggage? ② [도움 요청] Can you help me? I'd like to take my baggage down.
짐 좀 옮겨주세요.	Please move this luggage. = Please take this luggage away. (이~)
짐 가방을 찾지 못했어요.	I couldn't find my suitcase. = I couldn't get my luggage back.
짐 가방이 없어졌어요.	My suitcase is gone. = My suitcase disappeared. = I can't find my suitcase.
짐 보관소는 어디에 있습니까?	Where is the checkroom? ➡ It's on the left of the hall. (홀 좌측에 있습니다.)
짐승!	Beast!
짐승도 은혜를 안다.	Even a beast returns the favor he received.
짐승도 제 새끼는 사랑한다.	The owl thinks her own young fairest.
짐승만도 못한 놈!	You are worse than a brute! = You are worse than a beast!
짐은 어디에 넣을까요?	Where can I put my bags?

ㅈ

	➡ Put it in the trunk. = Put it in the boot. (트렁크에 넣으세요.)
짐은 좌석 아래 두시면 됩니다.	You can put your belongings under your seat.
짐을 덜어드리고 싶습니다.	① 〈직역〉 I'd like to lighten your load. ② [부담감] I'd like to take your burden off your mind. = I'd like to take your load off your mind.
짐을 열어보세요.	[검사] Please open your suitcase.
짐을 옮겨야 합니다.	① [장소 이동] I have to move the baggage. ② [일 등] I have to carry my luggage.
짐을 저한테 주시죠.	Give your baggage to me. = Let me keep your baggage.
짐을 찾으면 바로 연락해주세요.	When you find your baggage, contact me right away, please.
짐을 호텔로 보내주세요.	When you find my baggage, send it to the hotel right away, please. (찾으면 즉시 제~)
짐이 나오지 않았습니다.	[공항] My luggage hasn't come out yet.
짐이 많아서 걱정입니다.	I'm worried that my baggage is too large.
짐이 보이지 않습니다.	I can't see my luggage.
짐이 중량초과입니까?	[공항] Is my luggage over the weight limit? (부치는~) ➡ Yes, it's five kilograms over the weight limit. (5킬로그램 초과입니다.)
짐작은 했어요.	This was my guess. = I expected it. = It was within my expectations. (이 점을 미리 ~)
짐작이 맞았어.	I guessed it right. (내~)

ㅈ

집

집들이 할 겁니다.	We're going to have a housewarming party.
집세를 못 내겠으면, 방 빼!	If you can't pay the rent, get/move out!
집안 망신 좀 시키지 마라.	Don't disgrace your family. = Don't make yourself a disgrace to your family.
집안에 할 일이 산더미처럼 쌓였어요.	I have a mountain of work to do at home. = I've got a mountain of chores to do. = I've got a mountain of housework to do.
집안이 차이가 나다.	They are from totally different families. = Their family backgrounds are so different.
집안이 화목해야 만사가 잘 된다.	When your home is happy, all goes well. ☞ 가화만사성.
집안이 환하고 깨끗하네요.	It's bright and clean in your house.
집안일은 정말 힘들어요.	Chores are hard to do. = Housework is so hard to do. = It's really demanding to do all the chores. = It's really demanding to do all the housework.
집어주세요.	[물건] Can you pick it up for me? = Can you pass it to me? (그것 좀~)
집어치워!	① [하던 말] Cut it out! ② [허튼소리] 〈속어〉 Stop the bullshit! = Cut the crap!
집에 가봐야 합니다.	I have to go home.
집에 가서 애나 봐라!	Mind your own business!

ㅈ

집에 가서 죽을 줄 알아!	You are dead when we get home!
집에 가셔서 푹 쉬세요.	Go home and take a rest.
집에 갑시다.	Let's go home.
집에 계시냐?	Is your dad at home? (아빠~) ➡ ⓐ Yes, he is. (집에 계십니다.) ⓑ No, he is out. (집에 안 계십니다.)
집에 놀러오세요.	Come over to our place next time. = I want to see you at our place again. (다음에 우리~)

집에 데려다줄게.	Let me take you home.
	// Let me give you a ride home. (자동차로~)
	// Let me walk you home. (걸어서)

집에 도둑 들었어요.	My house was robbed. = My house was broken into. = I've got a burglary in my house.
집에 돌아가는 게 좋겠어요.	I'd better go back home.
집에 돌아가도 좋습니다.	You can go back home now. (이제 그만~)
집에 들러주세요.	Come and visit my place anytime. (언제든지~)
집에 아무도 없습니다.	There's no one at home.
집에 안 계십니다.	① He is not at home. (그는~) ② [전화상에서] He is not in. = He is not available now. = He is out now.
집에 연락했습니까?	Did you call your home? ➡ Yes, I did. (했어요.)
집에 있는 것처럼 편하게 지내세요.	Make yourself at home. // Make yourself at home here. (여기서는~)
집에 있지도 않고, 날마다 밖으로만 싸돌아다닌다.	He never stays at home and wanders around. (그는~)

ㅈ

집에 전화하고 싶어요.	I'd like to call home.
집에 전화해야 합니다.	I have to call home.
집에 좀 일찍 가려고요.	I'd like to go home early.
집에 처박혀 있지 말고요, 밖에 좀 돌아다녀.	Don't lock yourself up in your room, and go out.
집에 한번 놀러오세요.	Come over to my place some day. = Drop by my place some day.
집에만 있으면 병납니다.	Staying at home every day makes you sick. (만날~)
집에만 처박혀있습니다.	I penned myself up in my room. = I locked myself up in my room.
집에서 가까운 게 최고야.	[직장 출근] The best thing is that it's near my house.
집에서 놀지요?	He has no job, right? = He doesn't have a job, does he? (저 사람~) ➡ He works at home doing chores. (살림해요.)
집에서 놉니다.	He is staying at home out of work. (그냥~)
집에서 만든 겁니다.	This was made at home. = This is home-made. (이건~)
집에서 몇 째입니까?	How many brothers or sisters do you have? = Are you the youngest or the oldest? = Where do you come in your family? = Where do you fall in your family? ➡ ⓐ I'm the eldest. (첫째입니다.) ⓑ I'm the second oldest. (둘째입니다.) ⓒ I'm in the middle. (가운데입니다.) ⓓ I'm the youngest. (막내입니다.) ⓔ I'm the only child. (독자입니다.) ☞ 몇째세요?

ㅈ

ㅈ

집에서 엄마 말 들어.	Stay with Mom at home today. = Stay with your mom at home today.
집은 어디입니까?	Where do you live? ➡ I live in Myeong-dong. (명동입니다.)
집은 어떻습니까?	What does this place look like? = What do you think of this house? (이~) ➡ It looks great. (훌륭합니다.)
집은 학교에서 멉니까?	Is your place far from your school? ➡ ⓐ No, it's not so far. (별로 멀지 않습니다.) ⓑ It's very close. = It's a stone's throw. (매우 가깝습니다.)
집을 나갔어요.	[가출] He left home. = He ran away from home. (그가~)
집이 아담합니다.	[칭찬] Your place is pretty and cozy.
집이 멋지네요.	[칭찬] You've got a lovely house. = Your house is very beautiful.
집이 최고야.	Home is the best above all things. (이러니저러니 해도 우리~)
집적거리지 않는 게 좋을 거다.	You'd better not try to hit on her. (그녀한테~)
집전화를 쓰세요.	Use the home phone.
집전화입니다.	This is the phone number of my place. (이게~)
집주소입니다.	This is my address. (이건~)
집중력이 떨어집니다.	You get less attentive if you study more than two hours. (공부는 2시간 이상하면~)
집중해!	① Attention! = Focus! = Concentrate! // Attention, everybody! (모두들~) ② [말을 집중해 듣기 원하는 경우] Listen up!

집중해서 일을 할 수 없습니다.	I cannot concentrate on the work. = I can't focus on what I'm doing.
집처럼 생각해요.	Make yourself at home. (자기~)
집합 5분 전!	Five minutes to gathering!

징

징그러워!	① [혐오] It's gross! ② [구역질] It's disgusting! ③ [소름] It's creepy! = It gives me the creeps!
징징대지 마!	Stop whining like a baby! (애처럼~)

짚

짚신도 제 짝이 있어요.	Every Jack has his Jill.
짚고 넘어가야 할 것이 있어.	We must resolve this matter. = This issue must be clarified.

짜

짜고 치는 고스톱이 아닌가요?	Is this a fixed game? (이것~)
짜고 치는 고스톱이네.	They are all fixed games. (다~)
짜증 좀 내지마.	[집사람의 바가지] Stop nagging me. = Stop annoying me. = No more tantrums, please!
짜증나!	① 〈비속어〉 I'm pissed off! ② I'm really annoyed!

짜증나게 하네.	It's really annoying. = It's really getting me into tantrums. (정말 사람~)
짜증나게 했어?	〈비속어〉 Who pissed you off? = Who made you pissed off? (누가 너를~)

짜증난다!	It's irritating. = It's really annoying.
	// The traffic here is really irritating. (이곳의 교통은~)
	// This work is really irritating. (이 일은 정말~)

짝

짝사랑하고 있습니다.	I have a crush on him. (그를~)
짝사랑했습니다.	I had a crush on her. (그녀를~)
짝퉁이지?	This is a fake, isn't it? = This is a counterfeit, isn't it? (이거~) ➡ You must be kidding. It may not be a fake. (그럴 리가요, 가짜는 아닐 겁니다.)

짠

짠!	① [건배] Cheers! ② [갑자기 모습을 드러내며] Look at me! = Look here! ☞ 봐!
짠 것을 좋아합니다.	[음식] I like salty food.
짠돌입니다.	① My boss is stingy. = My boss is a miser. (우리 사장님은 정말~) ② [상대방 호칭으로 부를 때] Hey, you cheapskate!

ㅈ

짧

짧게 깍지 마세요.	[두발] Don't make it too short. (너무~)
짧게 좀 잘라주세요.	[두발] I want to have my hair cut short.
짧게 할까요?	How short would you like it? (얼마나~) ➡ [손동작과 함께] This short, please. (이만큼요.)
짧아졌어요.	It's a lot shorter now. (이젠 많이~)

짭

짭니다.	It's salty. // It's too salty. (너무~) // It's really salty. (정말~)

짱

짱이다!	① [모양 · 생김새 · 차림새에 대한 칭찬] You look great! ② [한 일에 대한 칭찬] You did an excellent job!

째

째려보면 어쩔 건데?	For what are you staring at me like that? = Why are you staring at me like that? (그렇게~)

쨍

쨍그랑!	[물건 깨지는 소리] Clink-clank!

ㅈ

쩨

쩨쩨합니다.	He is stingy. = He is so cheap. = He is a cheapskate. = He is a miser. (그는~) ☞ 짠돌입니다.

쪼

쪼그려 앉아!	Squat down!

쪽

쪽박신세.	I'm totally broke.
쪽지를 남깁니다.	I leave this note after long thought. (한참 고민하다가 이~)
쪽팔려!	[창피함] What an embarrassment! = How embarrassing!
쪽팔리게!	You are embarrassing me! = You are an embarrassment!
쪽팔리게 왜 그래!	[창피함] Why are you doing this? You are embarrassing me!
쪽팔리게 하지 마라.	Don't embarrass me. (날~)
쪽팔린 건 아냐?	[부끄러움] Do you know it is an embarrassment? = Do you know you are embarrassing yourself?
쪽팔린 것도 모르냐!	[부끄러움] Don't you know it's an embarrassment? = Don't you know you are embarrassing yourself?

ㅈ

쫄

쫄딱 망했어요.	I'm completely ruined.
	// He lost his shirt. (그는 쫄딱~)
	// I failed in my business.
	= I went bankrupt. (사업이~) ☞ 망했어요.

쫄지 마!	Don't be afraid! = Don't panic! = Don't be a coward!
쫄지 말고, 떨지 말아요.	Don't be so afraid and nervous.

쫓

쫓겨났어요.	We were kicked out. (저희들은~) // My grandma kicked us out. (할머니한테~)
쫓아내지 마세요.	Don't kick me out. (저를~)

쫙

쫙 빼입었네.	You are dressed up.

쭉

쭉 가세요.	Go straight two blocks. (두 번째 블럭까지~)
쭉 드세요.	Drink this to the bottom. (이거~)

찌

찌개 다 식어요.	The stew is getting cold.

ㅈ

찌개 좀 들어보세요.	Try some of this stew. (이~)
찌뿌드드합니다.	I feel under the weather. = I feel out of sorts. (몸이~)

찍

찍습니다!	[사진] Let me go!
찍어서 드세요.	[소스 등에] Use this dip. = Dip it into this sauce. (여기에~)
찍어요.	[사진] Let's take a picture together. (같이~)
찍어주세요.	Can you take a picture with this camera? (이 카메라로도 좀~)
찍어둔 사람이 있나요?	Do you have someone in your mind?
찍었다!	[연애] I checked him out! = I got a thing for him. = He is on my list. (그 사람 내가~)
찍혔어!	① You are branded as a bad student by Mr. Wang! = You're on Mr. Wang's black list! (넌 왕 선생님한테 나쁜 학생으로~) ② [지적받음] I got pointed out! (나~)

ㅈ

찐

찐하게 한번 놀아봅시다!	Let's have a ball!

찔

찔리니?	Are you feeling guilty?

	= Do you have something to be ashamed of? (너~) ➡ No, I'm not feeling guilty of anything. = No, I don't have anything to be ashamed of. (아니, 난 찔릴 거 없어.)

찜

찜질방에 놀러올 돈은 있어!	You've got enough money to be here in the sauna!
찜찜했어요.	I felt something a little unpleasant. // I felt something uncomfortable about it. (그것에 대해~)
찜했다!	I checked him out! = He is on my list! (그를~) ☞ 찍었다!

찝

찝쩍거리지 마라.	Don't flirt with girls. // Don't try to come on to girls. (여자에게~)
찝찝합니다.	① [날씨] Today's weather is humid and damp. (오늘 날씨가~) ② [문젯거리] It's still bothering me. = It's still on my mind. = I'm still troubled by it.

찡

찡그리지 마세요.	Don't frown. // Don't distort your pretty face. (예쁜 얼굴~)

ㅈ

찢

찢어졌습니다.	① It was torn. ② [구멍이 남] Here is a hole. (여기~) // My skirt has a hole in it. (내 치마에~) ③ [찰과상] I got a scratch here. (여기~)
찢어지는 듯합니다.	My heart has broken. (마음이~)
찢어집시다.	① [각자 갈 길로] Let's each go our own ways. ② [남녀] Let's break up.

ㅈ

차

차 가지고 왔어요.	I brought my car. = I drove here.
차 같은 것 좀 마십시다.	Why don't we have something to drink, like tea?
차 돌려요!	Turn your car around! // Make a U-turn! (여기서~) ☞ 유턴해주세요.
차 문이 안으로 잠겼어요.	I am locked out of my car. // ~ I can't get in. (~ 안으로 들어갈 수 없어요.)
차 세워! // 차 세우세요.	① [명령] Stop your car! = Pull up your car! ② [갓길에] Pull over! // Pull over there! (저쪽에~)
차 조심하세요!	① [경고] Watch out for cars! = Look out for cars! ② [당부] You should be careful with cars.
차 좀 빼주실래요?	Will you move your car? ➡ Give me just a second. (잠시만요.)
차 좀 타올게요.	Let me make some tea for you.
차 좀 태워줄래요?	Can you give me a ride? // Can you give me a ride on your way? (가는 길에~) ➡ ⓐ Sure. Get in. (타세요.) ⓑ Okay. Then, let's meet in the lobby in five minutes. (좋아요. 그럼 5분후에 로비에서 봅시다.)
차 한 잔 합시다.	What about a cup of tea with me? // Why don't you go to a cafe or something and have some tea? (카페나 어디 가서~)
차가 막히는 모양입니다.	There might be a traffic jam. // It looks like a traffic jam ahead. (저 앞쪽에~)
차가 막힙니다.	The traffic is very slow.

ㅊ

	= We cannot move forward because of the traffic jam.
차라리 날 죽여라!	I would rather die than do such a thing! = It would be better to die than to do such a thing! (그런 일을 하느니~)
차렷!	Attention!
차례를 기다리세요.	Wait for your turn. // It's not your turn yet, so wait. (아직 차례가 아니니~)
차례야!	It's your turn! = Your turn has come around! (네~)
차로 바래다줄게요.	Let me give you a ride. = Let me take you to your destination in my car. // Let me give you a ride home. = Let me take you home in my car. (집까지~)
차를 갈아탑니까?	Do you transfer? // Where do you transfer? (어디서~) ➡ At the last stop. (종점에서요.)
차를 거꾸로 탔습니다.	[버스] I took the bus going in the opposite direction. // I took the wrong bus. (잘못~) // We took the wrong bus. (우리가~)
차를 렌트하려고 합니다.	I'd like to rent a car.
차를 바로 빼드리겠습니다.	I will move my car right away.
차를 빼주세요.	Please move your car right away. = Please take away your car right away. (빨리 좀~) ➡ Okay. (예.)
차를 저기에 세워도 될까요?	① [임시정차] Can I pull over my car over there? ② [주차] Can I park over there? ➡ Sure. Go ahead. (그러세요.)

ㅊ

차를 타오겠습니다.	Let me make some tea for you. ➡ Don't bother to. (신경 쓰지 마세요.) ☞ 차 좀 타올게요.
차를 한 번 갈아탑니다.	① [버스] I change/switch to another bus once. ② I transfer to another line once. (다른 노선으로~)
차린 건 없지만 많이 드십시오.	We prepared with all our heart. Help yourself.
차림새가 죽인다.	You look awesome today. = You look great today. (오늘~)
차멀미를 합니다.	I am prone to carsickness. = I easily get motion sickness.
차버렸어요.	I dumped him. (내가 그를~)
차별대우하지 마세요.	① Stop playing favorites. = Stop favoring certain people. // Treat us equally. (우리를~) ② [편견] Don't be biased.
차봐!	① [시계 · 안경] Try it on! = Put it on! ② [차 조심] Watch out! There's a car. = Look out! There's a car coming.
차분히 얘기해봐.	[진정하고] Calm down and tell me the story. = Relax first and tell me what you want to say.
차분히 잘 생각해보세요.	Think carefully. = Think it over carefully.
차비는 얼마입니까?	How much is the fare? // What is the fare from Seoul to Busan? (서울에서 부산까지~) ➡ The fare is twenty thousand won. (2만원입니다.)
차에서 내리세요.	Get out of the car, please. = Get out, please.
차 타세요.	Get in the car, please. = Get in, please.

ㅊ

차표를 보여주세요.	I'd like to see your ticket. = Can you show me your ticket?
차표를 어디서 삽니까?	[기차표] Where can I buy the train ticket? ➡ At the ticket booth. = You get it at the ticket office. (매표소요.)

착

착각은 자유야.	You are free to believe whatever you want to believe. = Just think what you want.

착각하지 마세요.	① [착각] Don't be confused.
	② [오해] Don't get it wrong, please. (제발~)
	③ Don't be confused with something else. (다른 것과~)
	// Don't be confused with someone else. (다른 사람과~)
	// Don't mix me up with somebody else. (다른 사람과 저를~)

착각했습니다.	① [착각] You made a mistake. (당신이~)
	// You were confused with something else. (다른 것과~)
	// You mixed it up with something else. (그것을 다른 것과~)
	// You were confused with somebody else. (다른 사람과~)
	② [오해] You misunderstood.
	= You got it wrong.

착하게 굴어!	① Be nice! // Be nice to others! (다른 사람들에게~) ② [예의바르게] Behave yourself!
착하게 살지 그랬니?	Why haven't you been nicer?
착하지!	① [남자 아이에게] Good boy! = Oh, that's a good boy!

ㅊ

	② [여자 아이에게] Good girl! = Oh, that's a good girl!
착한 여자입니다.	She is a good girl. = She is a lovely girl. (그녀는~)

찬

찬물도 위아래가 있다.	① 〈직역〉 Older before younger. = Always respect your elders. ② [모든 일에는 순서가 있다.] There's a proper order for everything.
찬밥 더운밥 가릴 때냐!	① [어려운 처지에] Beggars cannot be choosers! ② [감사해야 할 때에 그렇지 않은 경우] You are not to look a gift horse in the mouth.
찬성입니까? 반대입니까?	Do you agree with her, or not? = Are you for her opinion? Or against it? (그녀의 의견에~) ➡ ⓐ I'm with her. = I agree. = I'm for it. (찬성합니다.) ⓑ I don't agree. = I'm against it. (반대합니다.) ⓒ I give my hearty support to her. (쌍수를 들어 찬성입니다.)

참

참가하고 싶어요.	I'd like to join it, too. = I'd like to participate in it, too. = I'd like to take part in it, too. (저도 그 일에~) // I want to join you. (당신 하는 일에~)
참견하지 마세요.	Mind your own business. = It is none of your business. = It's no concern of yours. = Stay out of this.

ㅊ

	= You have nothing to do with this. = Butt out! (내 일에~) // You don't have a say in my affairs anymore. (앞으로 내 일에~)
참는 자에게 복이 있다.	Patience is a virtue. = Be patient toward all men.
참새가 방앗간을 그냥 지나치랴.	No man goes carelessly by a place where profit lies.
참석해주셔서 감사합니다.	Thank you for coming.
참으세요.	① [인내] Hang in there. = Stick with it. = Don't give up. (포기하지 말고~) ☞ 포기하지 마세요. ② [욕망] Be patient. // Have more patience. (좀 더~) ③ [성질] Keep your temper. = Cool it down. = Keep your shirt on. = Take it easy. = Hold your horses.
참지 못하겠어!	I can't take it anymore! = I can't bear it anymore! = I can't stand it anymore! = This is the last straw! = This is too much for me! ☞ 못 참겠어!

창

창가 쪽에 앉고 싶습니다.	[비행기 · 기차] I'd like a window seat. = Can I get a window seat?
창문 좀 닫아줄래요?	Will you please close the window? ➡ Sure. (그러죠.)
창문 좀 열어도 되겠습니까?	① Can/May I open the window? ➡ Sure. (그러세요.)

	② Do you mind if I open the window? ➡ No, I don't mind at all. = Not at all. (그러세요.)
창피해!	① [굴욕] It's a real humiliation! ② [부끄러움] It's a shame! = What a shame! ③ [입장이 곤란함] I'm embarrassed. = It's embarrassing. ④ [말하기가 곤란함] It's really hard to put into words.

찾

찾아보겠습니다.	① I will look for it.
	= Let me search for it. (그것을~)
	② [단어의 뜻] I'll look it up.
	= Let me look it up. (그것을~)
	// I'll look it up in the dictionary. (사전에서~)
	③ [장소] I'll locate where it is. (그곳을~)
	// Let me look up the place on the map. (지도에서~)
	④ [방법 · 해답] I'll figure it out.
	= I'll try to find a way.
	= I will come up with a solution. (해결책을~)

찾아오지 마세요.	Don't come and see me again. = Do not visit me again. (앞으로 다시는 날~)
찾아주신 것을 환영합니다.	[장소] Thank you for coming. = Thank you for visiting.
찾았습니다.	① [발견] I already found it. (벌써 그것을~) ② I was looking for it. = I was hunting for it. (그것을 찾고 있었습니다) ③ [사람] I was looking for you. (당신을~) ④ [은행] I withdrew some money from the bank. = I drew out some money from the bank. (돈을~) // I took out some money from the ATM. (현금지급기에서 돈을~)

찾으면 연락드리겠습니다.	We will let you know if we find it. (우리가 그것을~)
찾을 수 없습니다.	I can't find it.
찾지 못했습니다.	We haven't found it yet. (아직~)

채

채널 고정해 주세요.	Please stay tuned. // Stay tuned for more stories. = Stay tuned. More stories are coming up. (더 많은 이야기가 있으니~)
채널을 바꿔도 됩니까?	Can I change the channel? // Can I change the channel to ten? = Can I turn on channel ten? (10번으로~) ➡ Sure. Go ahead. (네, 바꾸세요.)
채였어요.	[헤어짐] I got dumped. Are you okay with it? (~만족하세요?)

책

책 한 권 주세요.	[서점] I'd like this book. = Can I have this book? = Can you get me this book? (이~)
책을 읽어!	Read a book! = Crack open a book! = Hit a book!
책망하지 마세요.	Don't blame yourself. = Don't reproach yourself. = Don't be severe with yourself. (자신을~)
책상이 지저분합니다.	Your desk is messy. = Your desk is a real mess.

ㅊ

책임질게요.	I'm responsible for it. = I'm liable for it. = Let me take the responsibility. = The buck stops with me. (제가~) // I'll fully responsible. = I'll take full responsibility. (모두~)
책임을 지세요.	You have to be responsible for what you did. = You have to take the responsibility because you did it. = You made your bed, now you'll have to lie in it. = Accept your responsibility. = You should answer for the consequences of what you did. (당신이 한 일에~)
책임을 전가하지 마세요.	Don't pass the buck to others. = Don't shift the responsibility to others. (다른 사람에게~)
책임을 회피하지 마세요.	Don't avoid your responsibility. = Don't shrink from the responsibility.
책임자가 누구입니까?	Who's calling the shots here? = Who's in charge here? (여기~)

ㅊ

처

처녀가 아이를 낳아도 할 말이 있다.	Even a criminal can have an excuse for what he did.

처리하겠습니다.	① [일처리] I'll take care of it. (제가~)
	// Let me handle it for you. (당신 대신~)
	② [맡아서] Let me take care of my own business.
	= Leave the matter to my discretion. (제 일은 제가~)
	③ [해결] I'll solve this matter. (제가 이 문제를 ~)
	// I'll solve this matter first. (우선~)

처리하기 곤란하군요.	[일처리] It's a tough call. = It's hard to take care of it.

	= It's difficult to decide what to do with it. = I don't know what to do with it. = I'm at a loss as to what to do with it.
처리해드리겠습니다.	Let me take care of it right away. = Let me handle it right away. (바로~)
처신 똑바로 해!	① [바른 행동] Behave yourself! = Behave properly! ② [나쁜 일에 휘말리지 않도록] Keep your nose clean! = Stay away from rough things!
처음 듣습니다.	I have never heard of this. = This is news to me. = This is a revelation to me. ☞ 금시초문입니다.
처음 만났습니다.	We met for the first time. = We've never met before. (우린~)
처음 본 순간 사랑하게 되었어요.	I fell in love with you at first sight. = I fell in love with you as soon as I saw you. (당신을~)
처음 뵙겠습니다.	Nice to meet you. = I'm very glad to meet you. = I'm happy to meet you.
처음부터 끝까지 발언하지 않았습니다.	I didn't say anything from beginning to end.
처음부터 다시 시작합시다.	Let's start it over again. = Let's do it all over again. = Let's start it afresh. = Let's just take it from the top again. (우리~)
처음부터 초를 쳐요.	Don't speak bad things before we get to start. = Don't spoil the mood before we start.
처치해!	Get rid of him! = Remove him! (그놈~)

척

척보고 알았어요.	I got it at first glance. = I knew the moment I saw it.

척하지 마!	Don't pretend! // Don't pretend not to hear!
	= Don't play deaf! (못 들은 척~)
	// Don't play a gentleman! (신사인 척~)
	// Don't pretend to know everything!
	= Don't let on that you know everything!
	(아는 척~)

척척박사구나!	You are good at everything you do! = You excel in everything! = You're multi-talented! = You are a well-rounded person! = You are well-rounded!

천

천기를 누설하면 안 됩니다.	① 〈직역〉 The secret of nature should not be revealed. ② The profound secret must not be divulged. = It's a precious secret not to be divulged.
천길 물속은 알아도 계집의 마음속은 모른다.	You can know about what it's like in the deep ocean, but you cannot understand what's like deep inside a girl's mind.
천 리 길도 한 걸음부터.	A journey of a thousand miles begins with a single step. ☞ 만 리 길도 한걸음부터.
천만에요!	① [감사에 대해] It's my pleasure! = The pleasure is mine! = Anytime! = Not at all! ← Thank you. = I appreciate it. (감사합니다.) ② [칭찬에 대해] Don't mention it! ③ [사과에 대해] That is no problem! = That's all right. = That's okay.

ㅊ

	← I'm sorry. (미안합니다.) ④ [사실과 부합하지 않음] That's not true. ← You overslept, didn't you? (늦잠 잤지?)
천박해!	① [교양] He is too shallow. = He is very lousy. (그 사람 너무~) ② [말투] He uses vulgar language. (그는 말이 ~)
천벌을 받은 거야!	You deserve it! = It serves you right! (결국~)
천벌을 받을 거야!	God will punish you for it! = You will be punished by heaven for it! (넌~)
천생연분이다.	**We're made for each other.** = We're a match made in heaven. (우린~) ☞ 하늘이 맺어준 인연입니다.
천성이야.	① [고칠 수 없는 습관] That's his second nature. = That is his old habit he cannot break. (그건 그의~) ② [속담] A leopard cannot change his spots. = You cannot make a crab walk straight.

천재야.	He is a genius. = He is a natural. (그는~)
	// He is a natural soccer player. (그는 축구 ~)
	// He is a natural singer.
	= He was born to sing. (그는 노래~)

천적이야.	He is a natural enemy to me. (그는 나의~)
천천히 드세요.	Take your time with your meal. // Enjoy the rest of your meal leisurely. (마저~)

천천히 말씀해 주세요.	Can you speak more slowly?
	// Can you slow it down a little bit? I can't follow you. (말씀이 너무 빠르시네요. ~)
	// Can you say that again slowly? (다시~)

천천히 합시다.	**Let's take our time.** // Let's not make haste. = Let's not rush. (서두르지 말고~)

ㅊ

철

철 좀 들어라!	Grow up! = Be a man! = **Act your age!**
철썩 같이 믿었어요.	I really pinned my faith on his sleeve. = I didn't have any doubt in him. = I had full confidence in him. (그를~)
철이 없습니다.	He is so immature. = He needs to grow up more. (그는~)

첫

첫 눈에 반했습니다.	I fell in love with you at first sight. = I fell in love with you the minute I laid eyes on you. = You struck me the moment I saw you. = I think I have taken a shine to you. (당신에게~)
첫 단추를 잘못 낀 거야.	You're starting off on the wrong foot. = **You are starting out wrong.** = You are making a mistake from the very beginning. (너는~)
첫눈이 내린다고 했는데.	We're supposed to have our first snow today. = I was told that there might be the first snow of the season today. (오늘~)
첫사랑도 못해봤습니다.	I've never been in love.
첫술에 배부르랴.	You must not expect too much on your first attempt. = **Rome wasn't built in a day.**
첫인상이 어땠나요?	What was your first impression of me? (나의~) // What was your first impression of her? (그녀의~)

ㅊ

청

청각에 문제가 있어요.	I can't hear well. = I have a problem with hearing. ☞ 듣는 데 문제가 있어요.
청산유수로군.	**He is a good talker.** = He is very eloquent. (그는~)
청소나 해!	Just clean it up! = Please get to clean it up! (어서~)
청소해주세요.	Please clean up my room. (방을~) // Please vacuum my room. = Please have my room vacuumed. (청소기로~)
청출어람.	Blue comes from indigo. = A pupil excels his master.
청혼했나요?	Did you propose to her? = Did you ask her to marry you? (그녀에게~) ➡ Yes, I did. But she declined it. (네. 하지만 거절당했어요.)

ㅊ

체

체구는 작아도 담이 크다.	She is so short and small but gutsy. = She's got a small frame but lots of guts. (그녀는~)
체면 깎이는 일은 하지 마세요.	Don't do any disgrace to yourself. = Don't disgrace yourself. = Do not make yourself lose face.
체면도 없군요.	You don't have any face. = You don't have any sense of honor. (정말~)
체면을 잃었습니다.	**He lost face.** = He failed to save face. = He failed to preserve his good standing. (그는~)

체면상 한 번 봐드리겠습니다.	I'll let you go for your honor's sake. = I'll ignore it to help you save face.
체온 좀 재봅시다.	Let me take your temperature.
체크아웃하려고 합니다.	[호텔] I'd like to check out. // I'm going to check out tomorrow morning. (내일 오전에~)
체크인해 주세요.	[호텔] I'd like to check-in. = Check me in, please.
체포되었습니다.	He got arrested. = He got collared. (그는~) // He got arrested by police. = Police caught him. (경찰에 의해 그는~)
체하려고 합니다.	I'm afraid something's lying heavy in my stomach. = I think something's disagreeing with my stomach.
체하지 않을까 걱정입니다.	I'm afraid something's disagreeing with my stomach because of the cold weather. (날씨가 싸늘해서~)

쳐

쳐다봐요.	The person is looking at me. = The person is staring at me. (저 사람이 날~)

초

초대장은 보냈습니까?	Did you send an invitation? ➡ ⓐ I already did. (벌써 보냈어요.) ⓑ Not yet. (아직이요.)
초대장이 있습니다.	I have an invitation. = I've got a letter of invitation.

ㅊ

초대해주셔서 감사합니다.	Thank you for inviting me. = Thank you for having me here.

초등학교에 다닙니다.	He goes to primary school.
	= He attends elementary school. (그는~)
	관련표현
	the first year of elementary school (초등학교 1학년)
	// the second year of elementary school (초등학교 2학년)
	// the third year of elementary school (초등학교 3학년)
	// the fourth year of elementary school (초등학교 4학년)
	// the fifth year of elementary school (초등학교 5학년)
	// the sixth year of elementary school (초등학교 6학년)

초보운전!	[표어] Learner! = Student! (운전연습 중)
초보입니다.	① I've just started to learn it. = I'm a beginner. // I'm just a novice. (저는 그냥~) ② [미숙한 사람] She is a babe in the field. (그녀는 그 분야에~)
초보치고는 잘 하는군요.	For a beginner, you're pretty good.
초상집에 갔었어요.	I was at a wake. = I attended a wake.
초저녁이야.	The night is still young. (아직~)

초조해하지 마세요.	Don't be nervous. = Don't be anxious.
	// You don't have to fret like that. (그렇게~)
	// Don't fret about it. (그것에 대해~)

초치지 마.	Don't ruin it. = Don't spoil it. = Don't mess it up. = Don't botch it up.
초행길입니다.	I am new here myself. = I've never been here, either. = I'm not familiar with this area, either. (저도~)

ㅊ

촌

촌스러워요.	[패션] The clothes are out of style. = The clothes are unfashionable. (그 옷~) // It's too corny. = It's too tacky. (너무~)

총

총각입니까?	Is he single yet? = He isn't married yet? (그는 아직도~)

최

최고다!	① It is the best! = It is second to nothing! // It is the best ever! (지금껏~) ② You are the best! = You are second to none! (네가~)
최선을 다 하겠습니다.	I will do my best. = I will try my best. = I will do all I can do. = I will do everything in my power.
최선을 다해 돕겠습니다.	I'll try my best to help you. = I will do all I can to help you. = I will do everything in my power to help you.
최선을 다해라!	Do your best! = Try your best! = Give your best shot!
최소한 10시간은 걸립니다.	It takes at least ten hours.
최신 영화입니다.	This is the latest movie. = This is the newest film. = This is a new release. (이것은~)

ㅊ

최악의 상황이야.	This is the worst thing that could happen. = We're in the worst situation. = There could be nothing worse than this. = We hit rock bottom. (이것은~)

추

추남!	Ugly boy!
추수감사절 잘 지내세요.	Happy Thanksgiving!
추억은 아름답습니다.	The memory of my old days is beautiful. (저에게~)
추우니까, 감기 조심하세요.	It's cold outside, so be careful not to catch a cold. // It's cold these days, so be careful not to come down with a cold. (요즘~)

추워요!	① [날씨] It's cold. // It's chilly.
	= It's a bit cold. (약간~) // It's too cold.
	= It's freezing cold. (너무~)
	// It's really cold today.
	= It's freezing cold today. (오늘은 정말~)
	➡ It really is. (그러게요.)
	// We've got another freeze today. (오늘도~)
	② [몸 상태] I'm cold. ☞ 춥습니다.

추워졌어요.	It's colder today. (오늘 날씨가~) // It's colder lately. (요즘 날씨가~)
추워죽겠어요!	① [추위] I'm dead cold! = I'm dying of the cold! ② [몸이 얼 정도로] I'm freezing! = I'm freezing to death!
추월금지	[도로 표지판] No passing!
추위를 타요.	The cold really gets to me. (전~)

추천 좀 해주세요.	Can you recommend one? (하나~)
	// Can you recommend me?
	= Can you put in a good word for me? (저를 ~)
	// Can you recommend me for the position?
	(저를 그 직책에~)

추태를 부립니다.	He makes a scene when drunk. = He behaves badly when he's drunk. (그는 술 먹고~)

축

축구경기를 자주 봅니다.	I watch soccer games often.
축구를 잘합니까?	Is he a good soccer player? (그는~) ➡ ⓐ Yes, he is. (잘합니다.) ⓑ So so. (보통입니다.) ⓒ He is not good. (잘 못합니다.) ⓓ He can't play. (못합니다.)
축복이 있기를!	God bless you! (신의~)
축제는 언제 시작합니까?	When is the festival going to start? ➡ It's going to start on October ninth. (10월 9일이요.)
축하합니다.	Congratulations! ➡ I'm so happy that I can't talk. = Happiness made me speechless. (기뻐서 말도 잘 나오지 않아요.)

출

출가외인.	A married daughter is no better than a stranger.
출국신고서를 써주세요.	Please fill out the departure card.

ㅊ

출근합니까?	Are you going to work? // What time do you start your work? = What time do you report for work? = What time are you supposed to be in? (몇 시에~) ➡ Seven-thirty in the morning. (오전 7시 반에요.)
출발합니까?	When are we going to leave? = When are we leaving? = When is our departure time? (우리 언제~) ➡ At six o'clock tomorrow morning. = We're leaving at six o'clock tomorrow morning. (내일 아침 6시요.)
출산 예정일이 언제입니까?	When is your baby due? = When are you expecting? // When is she expecting? (그녀는~)
출산했습니다.	She gave birth to a baby.
출생지는 어디입니까?	Where were you born? ➡ I was born in Seoul. (서울 태생입니다.)
출세하시길 바랍니다.	I wish you success in your life. = I wish you could make your way in the world. // I wish you would make a rapid rise in the world. (빨리~)
출세했네요.	You've made your way in the world. = You've achieved a rise. = You made a big success. = You've come up in the world. = You've pushed your way.
출입국신고서를 쓰셨습니까?	Did you fill out your landing card? = Did you fill out your disembarkation card? ➡ Yes, I did already. (이미 썼어요.)
출입금지!	[경고문] No entry! = No trespassing! // Off limits to minors! = No minors! (미성년자~)
출장 갑니다.	I'm going on the road. = I'm going on a business trip.

ㅊ

출장 갔다 왔습니다.	I'm back from my business trip. // I've just arrived from my business travel. (방금~)

춤

춤을 못 춥니다.	I'm not a good dancer. = I can't dance well. = I'm not good at dancing. = I've got two left feet. = I'm an abysmal dancer.
춤을 잘 추네요!	You dance well! = You're a great dancer! = You can really bust a move! = Wow! Can you move!
춤추실 줄 압니까?	Can you dance? ➡ ⓐ Just a little. (조금 합니다.) ⓑ I'm not a good dancer. (잘 못합니다.)
춤추자!	① Let's dance! ② [클럽에서] Let's take the floor!

ㅊ

춥

춥습니다.	It's cold.
	// It's freezing cold today. (오늘은 날씨가 아주~)
	// It's nippy.
	= It's biting cold.(살을 에듯이 ~)
	// It chills me to the bone.
	= It's piercing cold. (뼈 속까지~) ☞ 추워요!

춥지 않습니다.	It's not cold today. (오늘은~) // It's not so cold. = It's not that cold. (그렇게~)

충

충격이 컸던 것 같습니다.	He seems to have been really shocked.

	= I think he was deeply shocked. = I think he got a real shock. (그는~)
충고 감사합니다.	Thank you for your advice. = I appreciate your advice. (당신의~) // I appreciate the advice you gave me. (나에게 해준~)

충분합니다.	That's enough. (그 정도면~)
	// Five dollars is enough. (5달러면~)
	// Enough already. (벌써~)

취

취급 주의!	[경고문] Fragile - Handle with care!
취미가 뭡니까?	What is your hobby? = What do you do in your free time? ➡ ① ⓐ My biggest hobby is collecting stamps. (우표수집이 가장 큰 취미입니다.) ⓑ I don't have any hobbies. (아무 취미도 없습니다.) ⓒ My hobby is reading. (취미가 독서입니다.) ② I'm interested in chess. (장기에 취미가 있습니다.) ③ I enjoy watching movies. (영화감상입니다.)
취사 가능합니까?	[숙소] Can I cook for myself? ➡ ⓐ Sure, you can. (예, 가능합니다.) ⓑ No. There's no place you can cook in. = No. There's no kitchen. (아니오, 취사장소가 없습니다.)
취소하겠습니다.	① I want to take it back. (그 말을~) ② [계약 등] I want to cancel it. ③ [계획 등] I'll call it off.
취중진담.	Truth is at the bottom of the decanter.

ㅊ

	= One often tells the truth when drunk. = There is truth in wine. = What soberness conceals drunkenness reveals.
취직 좀 시켜주세요.	① Please give me a job. = Please hire me. // Please put me in any position here. (이 곳에 아무 직책이나~) ② [알선] Please help me get a job. = Please help me find a job.
취직됐습니다.	① I got a job. = I got employed. = I'm in collar now. // I got a job here. (여기에~) ② [채용시험] You are hired. = You got a job here. = You are employed here. = We'll put you in a position. (당신은~)
취하지 않도록 조금만 드세요.	Drink less not to get drunk.
취한 것 같습니다.	① I think I'm drunk. (제가~) // I'm a little tipsy. = I'm having a buzz. (약간~) ② I feel funny now. (기분이~)
취할 때까지 마셔봅시다.	Let's get blitzed today. (오늘 우리~)
취했습니다.	He's very drunk. = He got dead drunk. = He's high as a kite. (그는 매우~)

치

치과 약속이 있어요.	I have to go to the dentist. = I have a dentist appointment.
치료보다는 몸조리가 중요합니다.	Taking good care of your health is more important than getting medical treatment.

ㅊ

치사하다!	① [불평] What a shame! ② [인색] You are so cheap! = You are a cheapskate! = What a cheapskate! = You are so stingy! = That's a cheap shot! ③ [비열함] You are so mean! = You are so shameless!
치약은 어디에 있습니까?	Where is the toothpaste? ➡ It's in the bathroom. (화장실이요.)
치우세요.	① [정리] Tidy it up. (그것을~) ② [청소] Clean it up. (깨끗이~) ③ [제거] Remove it. = Get rid of it. ④ Hands off. = Get your hands off. (손을~) ⑤ [가져감] Take it away. ⑥ [따로 보관] Put it away.
치우지 말고 그냥 놔두세요.	[물건 등] Don't take it away. Leave it there. (거기에~)
치즈버거 하나 주세요.	A cheeseburger, please. = Can I have a cheeseburger?
치즈하고 웃으세요.	Smile! Say cheese!
치킨을 포장해주세요.	I'd like a fried chicken to go.

친

친구 따라 강남 간다.	[아무 생각 없이 따라 하는 행동] Willing mind makes a light foot.
친구 좋다는 게 뭐냐?	What are friends for? = You know what friends are for. = That's what friends are for.

친구가 있습니다.	I have a friend. // I have an American friend. =I have a friend from the United States. (미국~)
친구는 사귀어 봐야 안다.	You can't get to know a person until you make a friend of him.
친구는 옛 친구가 좋고 옷은 새 옷이 좋다.	A new dress is better than an old one, but it's the opposite when it comes to friends.

친구를 만났어요.	I met my friend.
	// I met my friend there. (거기서~)
	// I met a friend of mine on my way here. (여기 오는 길에~)

친구를 보면 그 사람을 알 수가 있어.	A man is known by his friends. = A man is known by the company he keeps.
친구를 소개해 드리겠습니다.	Let me introduce you to my friend. = Let me introduce my friend to you. = Please meet my friend. (제~)
친구야, 고맙다!	① Thanks, my friend! ② [남자들 사이에서] Thanks, buddy!
친구와 돈거래하면 친구를 잃는다.	Lend your money and lose your friend.
친구일 뿐입니다.	I'm just your friend. Nothing more than that. (전 다만 당신의~)
친구잖아.	I'm your friend. // We're all friends. (우린 다 같은~)
친구합시다.	Let's be friends. // Let's stay friends. (우리 그냥~)
친절에 감사를 드립니다.	① Thank you for your kindness. = How kind of you to do that. (당신의~) ② [환대에 대한 감사] Thank you for your hospitality.
친절한 것 같습니다.	People here seem to be friendly.

	= All the people here look very kind. (사람들이 다~)
친하게 지내서 나쁠 것 없어.	There's no harm in getting along well with your schoolmates. (학교 애들하고~)
친합니까?	Are you close to him? (그 사람과~) ➡ No, we're not close. (친하지 않아요.)
친합니다.	They are close. = They are close friends with each other. = They are in a very intimate relationships. (그들은~)
친해졌습니다.	We got really close. (우리는~) // We really hit it off. (우리는 금방~)

칠

칠 주의	[표지판] Wet paint! = Fresh paint!
칠면조 같다.	① [생김새] It looks like a turkey. ② [짐작] It appears to be a turkey. = I guess it is a turkey.
칠전팔기	If at first you don't succeed, try, try again.

침

침 뱉지 마세요.	① Don't spit here. (여기에~) ② [표지판] No spitting!
침구를 빌릴 수 있나요?	Can I borrow some bedding?
침대가 둘인 2인실로 주세요.	I'd like a twin room. = I want a room with twin beds.

ㅊ

침대도 있고 온돌방도 있습니다.	We have rooms with a bed and also rooms with an under-floor heating system.
침대차가 있나요?	[기차] Is there a sleeper on this train?
침소봉대	[지나친 과장] It's making a mountain out of a molehill.
침착하세요.	Chill out. = Calm down. (좀~)

칭

칭찬하는 거야? 비꼬는 거야?	Are you praising me or just being sarcastic now? = Is it a compliment or sarcasm? (지금~) ➡ I just got interested in you. (난 다만 너에 대해 호기심이 생겼을 뿐이야.)
칭찬해주셔서 감사합니다.	Thank you for your compliment. = I appreciate that you praised me.

카

카드 됩니까?	Can I pay by credit card? ➡ We accept cash only. (우린 현금만 받습니다.)
카드도 결재됩니다.	[신용카드] You can pay by credit.

칼

칼로 물 베기.	It's like cutting water with a knife. // The quarrels of a married couple are like cutting water with a knife. = Domestic quarrels are soon forgotten. = The quarreling of a married couple is like cutting water with a knife. (부부싸움은~)
칼로 흥한 자 칼로 망한다.	They that live by the sword shall perish by the sword!
칼이 잘 들어요.	The knife cuts well. ➡ Be careful with it. = Be careful handling it. = Handle it with care.(다룰 때 조심하세요.)

캠

캠퍼스 커플입니다.	They are college sweethearts. (그들은~)
캠퍼스 커플로 만났어.	They met in college. (그들은 대학 때~)

커

커닝 수법도 변한 게 없으니, 정말 실망이구만.	It's disappointing that cheating techniques haven't improved at all.

커서 훌륭한 사람이 되어라.	Forget the past days and become a good man. (지난 과거는 잊어버리고, ~)
커튼을 쳐주세요.	Draw the curtain, please. = Put the curtain down, please.
커피 마시고 싶습니다.	I'd like a cup of coffee.
커피 마시면 잠이 안 옵니다.	Coffee makes me stay up all night. = If I drink coffee, I can't sleep at all.
커피 좀 타오세요.	Please make us some coffee. (우리에게~)
커피 한 잔 주세요.	Can you get me a cup of coffee?
커피를 마시겠습니까?	Would you like some coffee? = Do you want to grab some coffee? // What kind of coffee would you like? (어떤~) ➡ Any kind. (아무거나요.)

컴

컴퓨터 그만 해라.	Stop playing on the computer.
컴퓨터가 다운되었습니다.	My computer went down. = My computer crashed. = My computer broke down.
컴퓨터가 바이러스를 먹었어요.	I think my computer has a virus.
컴퓨터가 이상합니다.	There's something wrong with my computer. = There seems to be a problem with my computer.
컴퓨터를 잘합니까?	Are you good with computers? ➡ ⓐ Yes, I am. (잘합니다.) ⓑ Not so good and not so bad. (보통입니다.) ⓒ I'm not so good. (별로입니다.) ⓓ I'm not good. (못합니다.)

컴퓨터를 할 줄 압니까?	Do you know how to use computers? ➡ ⓐ Yes, I do. (할 줄 압니다.) ⓑ No, I don't. (모릅니다.)

컵

컵라면 하나 먹었습니다.	I've just had cup noodles. = I've just had cup *ramyeon*. (방금~)

케

케이크 먹으면 살찝니다.	Cake makes you fat. = If you eat cake, you will get fat.
케첩과 겨자를 넣어주세요.	Add some ketchup and mustard, please.

ㅋ

코

코 파지 마세요.	Don't pick your nose.
코 푼 것 뿐입니다.	I just blew my nose.
코가 납작해졌다.	He got frustrated with shame. (그는 ~)
코감기에 걸렸습니다.	I've got the sniffles. = I have a runny nose.
코골면 안 됩니다.	You shouldn't snore at night. (밤에~)
코끝이 찡했어요.	It made my nose twitch. (그것 때문에~) // The film was so sad and made my nose water. (그 영화가~)
코를 곱니다.	I snore. // I snore every time I sleep. = I snore every time I'm asleep. (잠 잘 때 늘~)

코피가 납니다.	My nose is bleeding. // My nose bleeds often. (자꾸~)

콕

콕 찍어서 말해요.	Talk straightforwardly. // Don't beat around the bush and talk straightforwardly. (사람 헷갈리게 하지 말고, ~)

콘

콘돔 사용해봤습니까?	Have you ever used a condom? ➡ No, I haven't. (사용해본 적 없습니다.)

콧

콧물이 납니다.	I've got a runny nose.
콧대가 세다.	She is too snobby. = She is too proud of herself. = She is too arrogant. (그녀는 너무~)
콧대가 꺾였다.	He got cut down to size. = He's back in his place. = He was put in his place. (그는~)

콩

콩 심은 데 콩 나고 팥 심은 데 팥 난다.	As one sows, so shall he reap. = Every herring must hang by its own gill.
콩깍지가 씌었어요.	Love is blind. = You cannot love and be wise.

콩밭에 가있었어요.	I was thinking something else. = I was somewhere else. = I was daydreaming. = My head was up in the clouds. (마음이~)

콸

콸콸!	[물소리] Woosh woosh!

쾅

쾅!	① [뇌성 소리] Boom! ② [부딪치는 소리] Bang!

쿨

쿨쿨!	[코고는 소리] z-z-z

쿵

쿵!	[물건이 떨어지는 소리] Bang!
쿵쿵!	① [가슴이 뛰는 소리] Thump, thump! ② [부딪치는 소리] Boom, boom!

크

크게 말씀해주세요.	Can you speak more loudly? = Will you speak up a little bit? (좀 더~)
크리스마스 잘 보내세요.	Merry Christmas!

ㅋ

크림을 많이 넣어주세요.	[빵 크림] Put on a lot of cream.

큰

큰 것 같습니다.	① [옷이] It looks large on you. (당신에게) ② It looks like it is a little bit large. (약간~)
큰 것은 없습니까?	Do you have a bigger one? (더~) // Do you have a larger size? = Do you have it/this in a larger size? (사이즈가 더~) ➡ Yes, we do. (있습니다.)
큰 코 다쳐요.	You'll end up embarrassing yourself. // That will make you end up looking foolish. (그러다가~)
큰소리로 떠들지 마세요.	Don't talk loudly. = Don't make noise. = Don't make a sound.
큰일 날 뻔 했어요.	That was a close call.
큰일 났어요!	We are really in trouble! = We've got a problem! (우리 ~) // Your goose is cooked! (당신은 이제~)

키

키가 얼마나 됩니까?	How tall are you? = What is your height? ➡ I'm about one hundred and eighty centimeters. (1m 80cm 정도입니다.)
키스는 어떤 느낌인지 모르겠어.	I don't know what a kiss feels like.
키스하자!	Let's kiss! (우리~)

키스해줘!	Give me a kiss!

킬

킬로그램까지는 무료입니다.	It's free up to twenty kilograms. (20~)
킬로미터 마다 1달러씩 추가됩니다.	One dollar per one kilometer will be added.

킹

킹카입니다.	He's super hot. (그는~)

ㅋ

타

타고난 체질이에요.	I was born for this. = I was born to do this.
타산지석.	It is a good lesson for you. = Let another's shipwreck be your seamark. = It is good to learn at another men's cost.
타이가 잘 어울리시는군요.	That tie goes well with your suit. (그 옷과~)
타이르겠습니다.	① I will advise him. = I will give him a good talk. (그를~) ☞ 주의시키겠습니다. ② I will advise him not to do it again. (다시 못하게 그를~)

탁

탁구를 상당히 잘 하네.	You play table tennis well. = You are so good at table tennis.

탈

탈의실은 어디에 있습니까?	① [옷가게] Where's the fitting room? ② [공연장 · 체육관] Where's the dressing room? ③ [헬스장] Where's the locker room?

탑

탑승 수속은 언제부터 합니까?	[비행기] What is the check-in time for my flight? ➡ ⓐ You can check in right now. (지금 할 수 있습니다.) ⓑ Check-in is starting in five minutes. (5분 후에 시작합니다.)

ㅌ

탑승구는 몇번 입니까?	What is the number of the boarding gate? ➡ Gate number twenty-eight. (28번 탑승구입니다.)
탑승권 좀 보여주세요.	Can I see your boarding pass?
탑승은 언제부터 합니까?	What time does boarding start? = What time will you start boarding? ➡ Boarding starts at 3 p.m. (오후 3시에 탑승을 시작합니다.)

탓

탓하지 마세요.	Don't blame me. = Don't put the blame on me. (저를~) // Don't blame yourself. = Don't put the blame on yourself. (자신을~)

태

태어날 때부터 잘하는 사람은 없어요.	No one is good from the beginning. = Nobody starts off being good at something. = Everybody starts off a beginner.
태어났습니까?	Which year were you born in? (몇 년도에~) // When were you born? (언제~) ➡ ⓐ I was born in 1982(nineteen eighty two). (82년생입니다.) ⓑ I was born in 2001. (2001년생입니다.) ➡ I was born in Seoul. (서울에서요.)
태우지 마세요.	[음식 등] Do not burn it.
태클을 겁니까?	① [말로] Why do you keep arguing? (어째서 우리한테 자꾸~) ➡ Who are you talking about? (누가 누굴 걸었다고 그래?)

ㅌ

	② [행동으로] Why are you disturbing us? = Why are you interrupting us?
태클이나 걸지 마세요.	① [말로] Stop arguing. ② [행동으로] Stop disturbing me. = Stop interrupting me.

택

택배회사에서 당신에게 배달 온 물건입니다.	This is delivered to you by home delivery service. (이건~)
택시를 불러주세요.	Please call me a taxi.
택시 승강장이 어디입니까?	Where is the taxi stand? = Is there a taxi stand near here?
택시 타고 가세요.	[귀가] Please take a taxi home.

터

터놓고 얘기해 봅시다.	Let's have a heart-to-heart talk.
터무니없는 소리!	① That's nonsense! = What a ridiculous thing to say! = That's not very realistic! ② 〈비속어〉 That's bullshit!

턱

턱 좀 닦아요.	Wipe your chin.
턱도 없는 소리!	That's ridiculous! = What a ridiculous thing to say!

턱도 없어요.	① [실력] We don't have nearly enough talent. (우리는~) ② [금액] We don't have nearly enough money.
턱없이 비싸요.	① It's unreasonably expensive. = The price is unreasonably high. ② [바가지 쓰고 있다는 생각이 들 경우] It's a rip-off.

털

털도 돋지 않은 것이 날기부터 하려 한다.	He dares try to fly even though he's just a fledgling. (그는~)
털어놓고 말해보세요.	Get it off your chest. = Tell me frankly. // Come clean with me. (나에게~)
털어서 먼지 안 나는 사람 없어요.	Everyone has his faults. = Everyone has their shortcomings. = Everyone has his skeleton in his closet. = No one is perfect. = No one is without faults.
털끝만큼도.	Not in the least. (~ 그렇지 않아.)
털끝만큼도 의심하지 않아.	I don't doubt it at all. = I don't doubt it a bit.
털끝만큼의 양심도 없어.	He doesn't have an atom/ounce of conscience. (그는~)

텃

텃세가 심합니다.	They don't welcome newcomers here. = They don't take to newcomers here. (여기는~)

텅

텅 빈 것 같습니다.	It looks empty. // I feel empty in my heart. (마음이~)

테

테니스를 잘 칩니까?	Are you good at tennis? ➡ ⓐ Yes, I am. (잘합니다.) ⓑ I'm not that good. (별로입니다.) ⓒ I can't play tennis at all. (전혀 못합니다.)
테이블 좀 치워주세요.	Clear the table, please.
테이블을 예약하고 싶습니다.	I want to make a reservation for a table for eight people. (여덟 석~)

텔

텔레비전 끄세요.	Turn off the TV.
텔레비전 보고 있습니다.	I am watching TV.
텔레비전 켜세요.	Turn on the TV.
텔레비전에서 봤어요.	I've seen it on TV. (그것을~) // I've seen you on TV. (당신을~)

토

토 달지 마.	Don't pick at every word I say. = Don't criticize every word I say. (내 말에~)
토끼 둘을 잡으려다가 하나도 못 잡는다.	If you run after two hares, you will catch neither.

ㅌ

토끼를 다 잡으면 사냥개를 삶는다.	[토사구팽] When needed, it was appreciated. But when it becomes unneeded, it's abandoned. (필요할 땐 감사히 여기다가 필요 없어지면 버린다.)
토하려고 합니다.	I feel like throwing up. = I feel like vomiting. = I think I'm going to spew. // I often feel like throwing up. (자꾸~)
토할 것 같습니다.	[몸이 불편함] I feel nauseous. = I feel sick.

통

통과할 수 없습니다.	① You cannot go through here. (이 곳을~) ② [간판] No trespassing. = Dead end.
통역을 한 사람 부탁합니다.	I need someone who can translate for me. // I need an English interpreter. (영어~)
통역해주세요.	Translate this into English for that person. (이 말을 저 사람에게 영어로 ~)
통장을 만들려고 합니다.	I'd like to open an account.
통장을 분실했습니다.	I lost my bank book.
통증이 없어졌습니다.	The pain is gone.
통쾌합니다.	I'm greatly satisfied. (정말~) // It gives me a lot of pleasure. (그것 때문에~)
통하지 않아요.	① [제안 · 방법] It's not accepted. // This is not acceptable to me. (나한테는 이런 거~) // That method is not accepted anymore. (그 방법은 더 이상~) ② [변명 · 구실] You can't get by with that excuse anymore. (그런 변명은 더 이상~) ③ [관계] We don't have a connection. (우리는 잘~)

ㅌ

통했어요.	We clicked right away. = We hit it off immediately. (우리는 만나자 마자~) // We just clicked. (우리는 그냥~)
통행금지	① It's closed. (막혔습니다.) ② [간판] Closed for pedestrians. (보행자~) // Closed to all vehicles. (차량~)
통화가 안 되는군요.	① I can't get through to him. (그와~) ② [전화를 안 받는 경우] Nobody is answering.
통화중입니다.	① [신호음이 들리는 경우] The line is busy. ② [대화중에] He is on the phone. (그는~) ③ [전화상에서] He is on the other line. (그는~)

퇴

퇴근 후에 한잔 하는 거 어때요?	① Why don't we grab a drink after work? = Why don't we stop for a drink on the way home? ② [맥주] Why don't we grab a beer after work? ➡ Sounds good. (좋아요.)
퇴근하셨습니다.	He went home. = He's out. = He left for the day. = He is gone for the day. = He has punched out. (그는~)
퇴원할 수 있습니다.	I can leave the hospital. // I can leave the hospital in one or two days. (한 이틀 있으면~)
퇴원했습니까?	Are you out of the hospital now? (이제~)
퇴직합니다.	I retire from office next year. = I leave office next year. (내년에~)

투

투정부리지 마세요.	Stop whining.
투표로 결정합시다.	Let's decide by vote.
투표로 표결합시다.	Let's put it to the vote.

툭

툭하면 화냅니다.	He easily gets angry. = He is quick to get mad. (그는~)
툭하면 웁니다.	He just cries too often. (그는~)

튀

튀자!	Let's run! = Let's run away!
튀지 마라.	Don't stick out.
튀지 않아요?	① [색깔이나 모양] Doesn't it stand out? = Isn't it too funky? ☞ 눈에 튀지 않아요? ② [이상한 사람] Isn't he odd? = Don't you think he is an oddball? (그 사람~) ➡ Yeah, he is a real oddball. (예, 그는 정말 튀는 사람이에요.) ③ [눈에 띄는 사람] Doesn't he come on too strong? ➡ I think he is hot. (제 생각엔 멋지기만 한걸요.)

튕

튕기지 마라.	① Stop turning me down anymore. (더는~)

	② [연애] Stop playing hard-to-get. = Stop acting coy. = Stop playing games. = Stop playing hot and cold.

트

트렁크 좀 열어보세요.	[짐 가방] Open your suitcase.
트림하지 마세요.	Do not burp.
트집만 잡아요.	He keeps picking on me. = He tries to find faults with everything I do. (그는 내가 하는 일에 이러쿵저러쿵~)
트집 잡다.	① [말] find fault with~ ② [물건] pick a hole in~
트집 잡지 마세요.	Stop picking on me. = Stop finding fault with me.

특

특별대우를 해줄 수 없습니다.	We cannot provide special treatment only to you. = We cannot give red-carpet treatment only to you. (당신에게만~)
특별히 맞춘 겁니다.	[가구 등이 딱 맞도록] I had it specially made to order.

튼

튼튼합니다.	① [제품 등] This is sturdy. = This is durable. (이것은~) // These shoes are durable. (이 신발은~)

② [신체] He is so strong.
= He has a strong body. (그는 참~)
// He is a well-built man. (그는 체격이 ~)
③ [기초] It has a solid foundation. (그것은~)

틀

틀렸습니다.	① [행위나 일 등이] It went wrong. (그건~) // It went completely wrong. (완전히~) ② [가망이 없음] I'm hopeless. = The odds are against me. = There's no chance. ③ [생각] You're dead wrong. (당신 생각은 완전히~)
틀림없습니까?	① [확신을 묻는 경우] Are you sure? ➡ Yes, I'm sure. (틀림없습니다.) ② [계산이나 문법] Is it correct? ➡ Yes, it is. (틀림없습니다.)
틀림없습니다.	① [사실 확인] It's true. // It's nearly true. (거의~) ② [추측] It must be correct. ③ [의심의 여지가 없음] I have no doubt about it.

티

티켓 두 장 예약해 주세요.	I'd like to reserve two tickets.
티켓을 못 구해서 정말 아쉽네요.	I'm sorry that I couldn't get the tickets.
티 나니?	Does it show? ➡ Yeah, it shows. = Yeah, you can't hide it. (그래, 티나.)

팀

팀의 실력은 말이 아닙니다.	Our team plays terribly. (우리~)
팀을 나누자.	Let's make teams.

팁

팁 주지 마세요.	Do not tip me again. (다시는 저한테~)

ㅎ

파

파렴치하다!	He is a shameless guy. (그는~)
파마해주세요.	I want to have my hair permed.
파산했어요.	He went bankrupt. = He cannot make ends meet. = He went belly up. (그는~)
파세요!	Sell it! // Sell it at a cheap price. = Sell it at a loss. (싸게~)
파손 주의라고 표시해주세요.	Please put a sign that it is fragile.
파이팅!	① Let's go! = Way to go! ② [손을 드는 동작과 함께] Give me five! = Slap me five!
파트너는 어떻습니까?	[미팅] What is your blind date like? ➡ ⓐ I got stood up. (바람맞았어요.) ⓑ We are dating. (진행 중입니다.)
파트타임 일을 합니다.	I've got a part-time job. = I've got a side job. ➡ [밤에 부업하는 경우] I moonlight as a ~ // I moonlight as a bartender. (저는 밤에 바텐더로 부업합니다.)
파티하기로 했어요.	We'll have a party. // We are supposed to have a party at my place this weekend. (이번 주말에 저의 집에서~)

팍

팍팍 좀 먹어요.	Eat as much as you can.

ㅍ

판

판에 박은 듯하다.	He is a living likeness of his father. = He is the spitting image of his father. (그는 그의 아버지를~) // We go on in the same old rut. (판에 박은 듯 똑같은 일을 반복한다)
판매합니다.	① It's for sale. // ② [간판] For sale.

팔

팔렸습니다.	They are all sold out. (다~) // It sold like hot cakes. (날개 돋친 듯이~)
팔을 벌리세요.	Outstretch your arms.
팔이 무척 아픕니다.	My arms hurt badly.
팔자 좋다!	① [친구 사이] You are a lucky man! (남자일 경우) // You are a lucky girl! (여자일 경우) ② [비난이나 한가로움을 나타냄] How come you idle away all the time!
팔자걸음 좀 고치세요.	Break your habit of an out-toed gait.
팔자소관이지.	It is the luck of the draw.

팜

팜플렛 좀 얻을까요?	May I have a brochure? = Can I get a brochure?
팝니까?	① Is this for sale? (이거~) ➡ No, it's not for sale. (안 팝니다.) ② How much is this? (얼마에~) ➡ It's one hundred twenty dollars. (120달러요.)

ㅍ

③ How much is this for one kilogram?
(이거 킬로그램당 어떻게~)

➡ It's ten dollars a kilogram.
(일 킬로에 10달러입니다.)

④ How much is this each? (이거 개당 어떻게 ~)

➡ It's two dollars each. (한 개에 2달러요.)

⑤ Where can I buy this? (이거 어디서~)

➡ ⓐ Over there. (저쪽이요.)
ⓑ You can buy it anywhere. (어디든 다 있습니다.)

패

패 다시 돌려요.	[포커게임] Deal again.
패배를 인정합니다.	I admit my defeat. = I admit I lost the game. ⬅ Are you admitting your defeat? = Are you admitting you lost the game? (패배를 인정하는 거야?)
패션에 대한 센스가 있네요.	You have an eye for fashion.
패스트푸드점에 가서 햄버거 먹자.	Let's grab some burgers at a fast food joint.

팩

팩스 받았습니까?	Did you get the fax? = Did you receive the fax? ➡ Yes, I got it. (받았어요.)
팩스로 보내주세요.	Can you send it by fax? // Can you send this to him by fax? (이것을 그에게~)

펑

펑!	[포성] Pop!
펑펑!	[폭죽] Pop, pop!

펜

펜 좀 빌려주세요.	Can you lend me a pen? = Can I borrow a pen? = Can I use your pen?

펴

펴세요.	Open it. // Open the book. (책을~)
	// Spread the blanket. (이불을~)
	// Spread the bed sheet. (침대시트를~)

편

편도로 하나 주세요.	I'd like a one-way ticket. = I'd like a single ticket.
편도입니까, 왕복입니까?	One way or round trip? = Single or return? ➡ I'd like a round trip ticket. = I'd like a return ticket. (왕복표로 주세요.)
편리하네요.	[사용이] This is convenient for use. = This is easy to use. = This is really handy. (이거~)
편리한 시간은 언제입니까?	When are you available? ➡ I'm available anytime. (언제든지 다 됩니다.)

편식하나 봅니다.	You eat only what you like. // The child eats only what he/she likes. (저 아이~)
편안히 다녀오십시오.	① Have a safe trip. ② [비행기 여행] Have a safe flight. ③ [선박 여행] Have a safe cruise.
편안히 하세요.	① Relax. = Take it easy. ② [마음을] Make yourself at home. = Make yourself comfortable. ③ [긴장하지 말고] Don't be nervous and rest yourself.
편지 잘 받았습니다.	I've got your letter. // I've got the letter you sent me on September 10th. (9월 10일에 보낸~)
편지 좀 전해주시겠습니까?	Can you deliver the letter to him? (그에게~) // Can you deliver this letter to him? (이~ 그에게~)
편지를 부치려고 합니다.	I'd like to send this letter. = I'd like to mail this letter. = I'd like to post this letter.
편지주세요.	Give me the letter, please. (저에게~)
편하게 드세요.	Make yourself at home and help yourself.
편하게 앉으세요.	① Sit down and relax. = Sit down and rest yourself. ② [임산부 · 장애자에게] Get the weight off your feet.
편하게 입어도 돼.	You can dress down.
편히 가십시오.	[고인에 대한 인사] Rest his soul.
편히 쉬세요.	① Take a rest. ② [취침 전 인사] Have a good night's sleep.

편히 주무세요.	Good night. ☞ 안녕히 주무세요.
편히 하세요.	[대면하는 자리] Make yourself at home.

평

평범한 것 같습니다.	It looks plain. = It looks common. = It doesn't look/seem special.
평범한 사람입니다.	I'm an ordinary person.
평상시 그대롭니다.	It's not unusual. = It's a usual thing.
평생 당신을 잊지 않을 겁니다.	I won't ever forget you. = I'll remember you forever.
평생 당신의 은혜를 못 잊을 겁니다.	I will be eternally grateful to you. = I will not forget the mercy you showed me.
평생 너와 함께 하고 싶어.	I want to be with you for the rest of my life.
평생 사랑하며 행복하게 사시기를 바랍니다.	[신혼부부] I wish you happiness in your wedded life.
평소 재주도 멍석 펴놓으면 안 한다.	He shows his talent in private but never on a stage provided. (그는~)
평안감사도 저 싫으면 그만이다.	[속담] A man may lead his horse to water, but cannot make him drink.

폐

폐를 끼쳐드려 정말 죄송합니다.	I'm sorry for causing you so much trouble. = I'm sorry for the inconvenience. ➡ That's no problem. (천만에요.)

ㅍ

폐를 끼쳤습니다.	I have caused you trouble. ➡ Not a problem at all. (천만의 말씀입니다.)
폐를 많이 끼쳤습니다.	I have caused you a great deal of trouble. = I have caused you much trouble so far. (지금껏~) ➡ No problem. (뭘요.)
폐인이 다 됐어.	He is a basket case now. = He got devastated. = He got screwed up. (그는~)

포

포기만 하지 않으면 뭐든 해낼 수 있다고 생각합니다.	I think I can achieve anything if I don't give up.
포기하지 말고 내게 맡겨.	Don't give up. Just leave it up to me.
포기하지 마세요.	Don't give up. = Don't give up hope. = Stay with it. = Stick to/with it. = Hang in there. // Don't give up, please. (제발~)
포기해!	Give it up! = Pass it up! = Throw the towel in! = Let it go!
포기했어요.	I gave it up.= I passed it up. = I let it go. = I called it quits. // I gave it up completely. (완전히~)
포스터를 봤습니다.	I saw the poster. // I saw the poster on the wall in my school. (학교에 붙어있는~)
포옹해 주세요.	Give me a hug.
포인트 카드입니다.	This is a mileage card that you can use to save up points. (이것은~)

ㅍ

포장할까요?	[선물가게] Would you like me to wrap it up? ➡ Please wrap them up separately. (따로따로 싸주세요.)
포장해 드릴까요?	[음식점] Would you like a doggie bag? ➡ Sure. (그러세요.)
포장해 주세요.	① [선물] Can you wrap it, please? = Can you gift-wrap it? ② [음식] Please make that to go. = I'd like it take-away. ③ [남은 음식] Can I have a doggie bag?
포즈 잡아!	Strike a pose!
포커합시다.	Let's play poker.

폼

폼 잡지 마!	Don't put on airs! = Get real! = Get down to earth! = Get a job! = Get a life!

표

표 두 장 구했습니다.	I've got two tickets for a soccer game. (축구경기~)
표 두 장 주세요.	Two tickets for October 3rd. (10월 3일~)
표가 있습니까?	① Do you have tickets available? ② [표가 다 팔린 경우] When can I buy tickets for? (언제~) ➡ Tomorrow. (내일이요.) ③ [지정된 시간] When can I buy tickets for? (언제~)

	➡ You can get tickets for 10 days later. (10일 이후 것 있습니다.)
표정 짓지 마.	Don't give me that look. (그런~) ➡ What's wrong with my look? (내 표정이 어쨌다고?)
표정만 봐도 알아.	It's written all over your face. = I can read every expression on your face. = Your facial expression shows everything. (네~)

푸

푸대접한 적 없습니다.	I have never treated you badly. (당신을 지금까지~)
푸석푸석해졌어.	[음식 등] It became crumbly.

푹

푹 쉬세요.	Rest up. // Rest up on weekends. (주말엔~)
푹 쉬어야 합니다.	You have to allow yourself a long rest.
푹 잤습니다.	I slept like a dog.
푹푹 찐다.	[날씨] Another sizzler today. = Another sizzling day today. (오늘도~)

푼

푼수도 유분수지!	How come you are so thoughtless!

풀

풀어주세요.	① Unlock it, please. (자물쇠를~) ② [자유롭게~] Please let it go. // Please let him go. (그를~)

품

품위를 지키세요.	Keep your dignity.
품질은 보증합니다.	We guarantee the quality. (우리가~)

풋

풋내기네.	You are a novice. = You are a babe in arms. // He is wet behind the ears. = He has milk on his chin. (그는~) ☞ 머리에 피도 안 마른 것이!
풋내기가 아니다.	He was not born yesterday. (그는~)
풋사랑이었어요.	It was puppy love.

풍

풍경이 너무 아름답습니다.	The scenery is so beautiful.
풍덩!	[물건이 물에 빠지는 소리] Plop!

프

프러포즈 했어요.	He proposed to me.

ㅍ

	= He asked me to marry him. (그가 나한테~)
프림 두 스푼 주세요.	① Two spoons of cream, please. ② [커피] Can I have two spoons of cream in my coffee?
프림과 설탕을 넣을까요?	[커피] Will you have some cream and sugar in your coffee? ➡ Thank you, but that's okay. (감사합니다. 괜찮아요.)
프림은 넣지 말고, 설탕만 넣어주세요.	No cream, and just sugar, please. // [커피] No cream, and just sugar in my coffee, please.

피

피가 자꾸 납니다.	It bleeds often. // The wound bleeds often. (그 상처에서~)
피검사도 해야 합니까?	Do I have to get a blood test? ➡ You need a blood test. (피검사가 필요합니다.)

피곤합니다.	① I'm tired. // I'm so tired. (정말~)
	// I'm too tired. (너무~)
	// I'm still tired. (아직도~)
	// I'm a little tired. (약간~)
	② [피곤해서 녹초가 되었을 때] I'm exhausted.
	= I'm knocked out.
	③ [일 때문에 피곤할 때] I'm tired from all the hard work.
	= I'm tired because of all the hard work.

피곤해보입니다.	You look tired. = You look exhausted. // You look so tired. (많이~)
피곤해 죽겠어요.	I'm dead tired. = I'm drained.
피골이 상접하다.	You are reduced to a skeleton. = You are all skin and bones.

ㅍ

피는 물보다 진합니다.	Blood is thicker than water.
피부가 땡깁니다.	[건조함] My face feels tight. = My face feels dry.
피서 가고 싶습니다.	I want to go on holiday for the summer.
피시(PC)방 가서 인터넷을 합니다.	I go to Internet cafes to surf the Internet. // He often goes to Internet cafes to surf the Internet. (그는 자주~)
피아노를 잘 칩니까?	Do you play the piano well? ➡ ⓐ Yes, I play the piano well. (잘 칩니다.) ⓑ No, I don't play the piano well. (잘 못 칩니다.) ⓒ No, I can't play the piano. (못 칩니다.)
피자를 제일 잘 먹습니다.	Pizza is my favorite food.
피장파장입니다.	Now we're even. = That makes us even. = Let's call it even now. (이제~)
피차일반입니다.	① We are the same. = No difference between you and me. ② [같은 처지임을 강조할 때] We are in the same boat.
피하지 마세요.	① Don't avoid it. ② [문제 회피] Don't turn a blind eye to the problem. = Don't shut your eyes to the problem. (그 문제를~)
피하지 않을 겁니다.	① I will not avoid it. = I will face it. ② [도망] I will not escape from it.
피해!	① Dodge the car! = Step away from the car! (차를~) ② [몸을 숨김] Hide yourself!

필

필기도구 있습니까?	Do you have a pen or something? = Have you got something to write with? ➡ Here you are. (예, 여기 있습니다.)
필(feel)이 아직 안 옵니다.	I cannot feel something in her yet. = I'm not attracted to her yet. (그녀에게서~)
필름 있습니까?	Do you have camera film here? = Do you have film for cameras here? (카메라용~)
필름 팝니까?	Do you carry film for cameras here? ➡ Yes, we do. (팝니다.)
필름 한 통만 주세요.	A roll of film, please.
필름을 현상해주세요.	I want this film developed.
필름이 끊겼어요.	[음주] I blacked out. = I was dead drunk and cannot remember anything.
필요는 발명의 어머니.	Necessity is the mother of invention.
필요 없어요.	① [행위를 강요하지 않음] It is not necessary to do that. (꼭 할~) ② [거절] Sorry, I don't need that.
필요한 것 있으면 뭐든지 말씀하세요.	Tell me whatever you need. ➡ I will. (알겠어요.)
필요할 때 친구가 진짜 친구지.	[속담] A friend in need is a friend indeed.
필요합니까?	① Do you need this? (이것이~) ② [금전이나 물품] How much do you need? (얼마나~) ➡ About two hundred dollars. (2백달러 정도요.)

필요합니다.	① I need it. (그것이~) ② [업무상] We need you here. = We need you in this work. (당신이~) ③ I need this book badly. (이 책이 너무~)
필요해!	[연애] I need you so much. (난 네가 정말~)

핑

핑계 대지 마세요.	① Don't make an excuse. = No excuse, please. = Don't give me any excuses. ② 〈비속어〉 Don't give me any bullshit.
핑계 없는 무덤 없다.	A pretext is never wanting. = Everyone has their excuses. = Everyone always comes up with their excuses.
핑계라면 그럴싸하게 대라.	① That's not a good excuse. ② [항상 똑같은 핑계를 대는 사람에게] That's the same old excuse!

ㅍ

하

하겠습니다.	① I will do it. = Let me do it. (제가~) ② [일처리] I will take care of it. = Let me take care of it. (제가~)
하고 싶은 대로 해!	Do as you want! = Do whatever you want!
하기 싫어도 어쩔 수 없어.	You can't help it. = It's time to face the music.
하긴!	① [가벼운 동의] That's right! = You're right! ② [추측] It must be so!
하나 더 주세요.	Give me one more.
하나도 모르겠습니다.	I don't get it at all. = I don't understand at all. = I don't have the faintest idea.
하나 드릴까요?	Would you like one? ➡ Give me one, please. (하나 주세요.)
하나 먹어보세요.	Why don't you try one?
하나, 둘, 셋, 됐어요.	[사진 촬영] One, two, three. Well done.
하나, 둘, 셋, 세봐요.	Count one, two, three.
하나도 모르겠어요.	[상대방 말을] I don't understand at all what you are talking about.
하나도 변한 게 없어요.	You haven't changed a bit.
하나를 보면 열을 안다.	① A word to the wise is enough. ② [이해가 빠름] He is quick on understanding. (그는~)
하나만 알고 둘은 모른다.	You know a little, but not completely.
하나면 됩니다.	One is enough.

하나씩 포장해 주세요.	Wrap them separately.
하나에 얼마입니까?	How much is it each? ➡ It's two dollars. (2 달러입니다.)
하나에 2달러입니다.	It's two dollars each.
하느님!	God!
하느님 감사합니다.	Thank you, God.
하느님, 맙소사!	Oh, no! = Oh, my god! = Oh, dear!
하는 거 봐서.	It's up to you. = It depends on what you do. = I will see what you do. = Let me take some time and watch what you're doing.
하는 일 없이 바빠!	I'm busy with nothing special!
하는 일마다 되는 일이 없습니다.	Everything I do these days turns out bad. (요즘~)
하는 짓거리 좀 봐라.	Look at you! = What a sight! ☞ 꼬락서니 하고는!
하늘 높은 줄 모르는구나!	You think you are high in the sky!
하늘 안 무너지니까, 앉아서 천천히 말해.	There's no need to hurry, so sit down and take your time.
하늘과 땅 차이.	It's a world of difference. = They are as opposite as two poles. = They are polar opposites. = They are different as day and night.
하늘도 무심하시지.	God is indifferent!
하늘보다 높고 바다보다 깊다.	High up in the sky, deep under the sea.
하늘에 맡기는 수밖에.	My fate is in God's hands. ☞ 운명을 하늘에 맡기는 수밖에.

ㅎ

하늘에 맹세해!	I swear to God! // Honest to God, ~ = By God, ~ (하늘에 맹세컨데. ~)
하늘은 스스로 돕는 자를 돕는다.	[속담] Heaven helps those who help themselves.
하늘을 봐야 별을 따지.	There haven't been many opportunities. (기회가 많지 않았어.)
하늘을 찌를 듯.	Morale is high up in the sky. (사기가~)
하늘의 별 따기.	[불가능한 일] It's almost impossible. = It's like asking for the moon. = There's not much chance of that happening.
하늘이 무너져도 솟아날 구멍이 있다.	[속담] There is a way out of every situation, however bad. = If the sky falls, we shall catch larks. = Every cloud has its silver lining.
하늘이 준 절호의 기회입니다.	It's a heaven-sent opportunity. = It's a golden opportunity I cannot pass up.
하늘이 맺어준 인연입니다.	They are a match made in heaven. (그들은~) ☞ 천생연분이다.
하던 짓도 멍석 펴놓으면 안 한다.	He shows his talent in private but never on a stage provided. (그는~) ☞ 평소 재주도 멍석 펴놓으면 안한다.
하든지 말든지 맘대로 해.	Take it or leave it.
하라는 대로 해.	Do as I told you. ☞ 시키는 대로 해!
하루 벌어 삽니다.	I'm living paycheck-to-paycheck.
하루 이틀이 아니었어.	[잘못한 것이] It's not something that's happened just once or twice.
하루 종일 시간만 허비했어요.	I've wasted the whole day.

하루가 멀다하고.	A day cannot pass without it.
하루가 여삼추라.	A day is like three years. // A minute is like three years. = I feel a moment as if it were three years. (일각이 여삼추)
하루는 몇 시간입니까?	How many hours do we have in a day? ➡ We have twenty four hours in a day. (24시간입니다)
하루도 편할 날이 없다.	I haven't passed a day without worrying about you. (너 때문에~)
하루아침에 유명해졌습니다.	He woke up to find himself famous. = He became famous overnight. (그는~)
하루에 몇 시간 공부합니까?	How many hours do you study a day? ➡ I study six hours a day. (하루에 6시간 공부합니다.)
하룻강아지 범 무서운 줄 모른다더니.	① An ignorant person doesn't stand in awe of the great. ② Fools rush in where angels fear to tread.
하룻밤을 자도 만리장성을 쌓는다.	The Great Wall can be built in a night.
하마터면 기차를 놓칠 뻔 했어요.	I almost missed the train.
하마터면 큰일 날 뻔 했어요.	It was close. = It was a narrow escape. = It was a close call.
하면 하고 말면 말고.	If you want, put your feet in. If not, keep them out.
하숙하고 있습니다.	I'm staying in a boarding house. // I board at Mr. Clark's house. (Clark씨네 집에서 하숙하고 있습니다.)
하이(Hi)!	[인사] Hi. ☞ 안녕!

하

하자는 대로 할게.	I'll do as you want.
하지 말라는 건 기어코 하는구나.	Nothing can hinder you from doing what you are told not to do.
하품이 나옵니다.	I can't stop yawning. (계속 멈추지 않고~)
하품은 전염성이 있어.	Yawning is contagious.
하하!	[웃음소리] Ha-ha!
하혈합니다.	[증상 설명] I'm having vaginal blood discharge.

학

학교갑니다.	[등교] I'm going to school.
학교 다녀왔습니다.	I came back from school.
학교를 나오지 않았습니다.	He didn't come to school. = He was absent from school. (그는~)
학교 선생님입니다.	I am a school teacher. // My wife is a school teacher. (아내는~)
학교 정문에서 만나요.	Shall we meet at the main gate of school?

학교에 다닙니까?	Do you go to school?
	= Do you attend school?
	// What kind of school do you go to? (어떤~)
	➡ I go to college. (대학교에 다니고 있습니다.)
	// Which school do you go to? (어느~)
	➡ I go to Columbia University. (컬럼비아대학입니다.)

학벌이 없습니다.	He doesn't have an educational background. (그 사람~)
학생 여러분, 안녕하세요?	Hello, everybody?

학생은 할인됩니까?	Can students get a discount on this? ➡ You can get a fifty percent discount. (50% 됩니다.)
학생입니까?	Are you a student? ➡ ⓐ Yes, I'm a high school student. (예, 고등학생입니다.) ⓑ Yes, I'm a freshman in college. (예, 대학교 1학년 학생입니다.)

한

한 가지 물어보겠습니다.	Let me ask you one thing.
한 가지가 빠진 것 같습니다.	One thing is missing, I guess.
한 가지만 물어보겠습니다.	Let me ask you just one thing.

한 가지 더 있습니다.	There's one more thing.
	// There's one more thing to tell you. (할 말이~)
	// There's one more thing you have to take care of before we go.
	(우리가 가기 전에 처리해야 할 일이~)

한 개	One. ☞ ~개
한 게임 할래요?	[구기운동] Would you like a game with me? (저랑~) ➡ That sounds great. (좋지요)
한 곡 불러보세요.	Sing a song, please.
한 구간을 걸어야 됩니다.	You should walk one block.
한 권	① A book. ② [여러 권 시리즈 물 중 한권] A volume. ☞ ~권

ㅎ

한 권밖에 없습니다.	I have just one, too. (저도~)
한 귀로 듣고 한 귀로 흘려버리세요.	In one ear and out the other. = Let it pass without much thought. = Just ignore it. = Don't pay any attention to it.
한 끼에 얼마입니까?	How much is it a dish? ➡ It's 10 dollars. (10달러입니다.)
한 달에 얼마나 법니까?	How much do you earn a month? ➡ I earn fifteen hundred dollars. (1500달러요.)
한 달은 며칠입니까?	How many days are there in a month? ➡ Thirty or thirty-one days. (30일 혹은 31일입니다.)
한 달은 몇 주입니까?	How many weeks are there in a month? ➡ About four weeks. (약 4주입니다.)
한말 취소해!	Take it back! = Take back your words!
한 말은 끝까지 책임집니다.	A man's word is as good as a bond. = I'm responsible for what I said.
한 명	One person.
한 바퀴 돌고 오겠습니다.	① [조깅] I'm going to run all around the park and come back. (공원을~) ② [산책] I'm going to take a walk through the park and come back. (공원을~)
한 발 늦었어요.	You missed the boat.
한 번 더 말씀해주세요.	Can you say that again? = Say it again, please.
한 번 더 시도해보세요.	Try one more time, please.
한 번 더!	One more time!

ㅎ

한 번 웃으면 십 년 젊어집니다.	One laugh makes you ten years younger.
한 번도 못 봤습니다.	I've never seen it before.
한 번도 안 해봤습니다.	① I've never done that. ② [구기운동] I've never played before.
한 번도 이곳에 와보지 않았어요.	I've never been here. // I've never been here before. (전에~)
한 벌에 얼마입니까?	How much is this a set? ➡ One set is one hundred dollars. (한 벌에 100달러입니다.)
한 병 더 주세요.	One more bottle, please. // One more bottle of beer, please. (맥주~)
한 분	One person. ☞ 한 명
한 사람 가는 길로 가지 말고 열 사람 가는 길로 가라.	[속담] Choose the way ten other people take, not the one just a person takes.
한 사람 당 1달러입니다.	It's one dollar per person.
한 사이즈가 작은 걸로 주세요.	I need one size smaller than this.
한 사이즈가 큰 거 있습니까?	Do you have a larger size? (이 옷~) ➡ We have only this size. (이 사이즈밖에 없습니다.)
한 솥 밥을 먹다.	We live under the same roof like a family.
한 수 위야.	I am a cut above you. (내가 너보다~)
한 수 배우고 싶습니다.	[시합] I'd like to learn from you.
한 시간 안에 마칠 수 있습니까?	Can you finish it in one hour? ➡ We can't because we're short of time. = We don't have enough time to finish it. (시간이 너무 모자라서 도저히 다 할 수 없습니다.)

ㅎ

한 시간은 몇 분입니까?	How many minutes are there in an hour? ➡ There are sixty minutes. (60분입니다.)
한 쌍이 되신 것을 축하드립니다.	[결혼] Congratulations on your marriage.
한 알 먹어보겠습니다.	[알약] Let me take a pill.
한 우물을 파다.	① Don't chase after another. Stick to just one. ② [속담] Jack of all trades, master of none. (여러 일을 하다가는 한 가지도 제대로 못한다.)
한 일을 후회합니다.	I regret what I did. = I'm kicking myself on what I did. (내가~)
한 잔 더 주세요.	Can I have one more glass? = Pour me one more, will you?
한 잔 더 할까요?	[술자리 이동] Let's go for another round. = Let's go bar-hopping. = How about another drink somewhere else?
한 잔 드십시다.	① Let's have a drink. ② [건배] Cheers! // Let's toast! (우리~)
한 잔 들겠습니다.	Let me have a glass.
한 잔 살게.	I'll buy you a drink.
한 장에 얼마입니까?	How much is this per piece? ➡ It's two dollars. (2달러입니다.)
한 접시 주세요.	One plate, please.
한 줄로 서세요.	Stand in a line. = Stand in a queue.
한 짓이지!	You did this, didn't you? (네가~) ➡ No, I didn't. (아닌데요.)
한 치 앞을 못보다.	You see no further than your nose.

한 판 더 합시다.	① Let's have one more round. ② [구기운동, 바둑, 장기 등] Let's play one more game.
한 푼도 못 받아요.	You cannot get a penny for it.
한 푼도 안 깎아 줬어요.	They wouldn't go a penny under the asking price.
한 푼도 없습니다.	I have no money. = I'm broke. = I'm penniless.
한집에 살고 있습니다.	We're living together. (우리는~)
한가하게 이러고 있을 시간이 없습니다.	We don't have time to idle away.
한가하면 전화 좀 주세요.	Give me a call when you are free.
한가하지 않습니다.	I'm not free. (전~) // Nobody is free. (다들~)
한가한 시간이 있습니까?	Do you have some free time? ➡ No, I have a tight schedule. (아니요, 아주 빡빡합니다.)
한가합니까?	Are you free tonight? (오늘 저녁~) ➡ ⓐ Yes, I'm free tonight. (오늘 저녁 한가합니다.) ⓑ I'm free now. (지금 한가합니다.) ⓒ Sorry, I don't have time. (미안합니다, 시간이 없습니다.)
한국 음식은 뭐가 유명합니까?	Which Korean food is famous? ➡ *Bulgogi* is famous. (불고기입니다.)
한국 사람입니까?	Are you Korean? ➡ ⓐ Yes, I am Korean. (예, 저는 한국사람 입니다.) ⓑ No, I'm Chinese. (아니요, 저는 중국인입니다.)
한국 사람 다 되었네요.	You've become Koreanized. = You've turned into a regular Korean. = You could pass as a Korean.

한국어로 어떻게 합니까?	What do you call it in Korean? ➡ I don't know. (모르겠어요.)
한국어를 잘 못합니다.	I can't speak Korean well.
한국어를 할 줄 압니까?	Can you speak Korean? ➡ Yes, a little bit. (조금 할 줄 압니다.)
한국에서 온 김대명입니다.	I'm Daemyung Gim from Korea.
한눈에 너를 알아봤어.	I recognized you at first sight. = I recognized you as soon as I saw you.
한눈에 알아봤습니다.	I recognized it at first sight.
한눈팔까봐 불안해?	Are you afraid that he is cheating on you? (그가~)
한눈팔지 마.	① [집중] Keep your eyes on the ball. ② Don't even think about cheating on me! = Keep your eyes off other women! (다른 여자들에게~)
한다면 합니다.	I do whatever I say I'm going to do. (전~)
한동안 소식이 없더니.	[오랜만에 만난 경우] I haven't heard anything from you for so long. = I haven't seen you for so long. // How have you been? (그동안 어떻게 지냈니?)
한동안 안 보이더라.	I haven't seen you lately.
한마디도 안 들립니다.	I can't hear anything.
한마디로 급소를 찔렀습니다.	You made the point.
한마디로 다 말씀드릴 수 없습니다.	I can't express it in a sentence.

ㅎ

한마음 한 뜻이 되어야 합니다.	We have to be one all together. (우린~)
한물갔습니다.	① [사람의 전성기] He has taken a backseat. = He has passed his peak days. = He is past his peak days. (그는~) ② [유행] It is not in anymore. = It is out of date. = It's out of fashion. // That song is a has-been. (그 노래는~)
한발 늦었습니다.	You missed it just by a second.
한번 가보세요.	You have to go there.
한번 다녀왔습니다.	I have been to France once. (프랑스에~)
한번 보세요!	Come and take a look! (와서~)
한번 봅시다.	Let me take a look.
한번 엎지른 물은 다시 담지 못한다.	It's no use crying over spilt milk. (후회해보았자 소용없다) ☞ 엎질러진 물이야.
한번 해봐요.	Try it. = Give it a try. = Give it a shot. // Try again. = Give it one more try. = Give it one more shot. (다시~)
한번만 눈감아주세요.	[용서] Forgive me just one time!
한번만 믿어주세요.	Believe me just one time.
한번만 봐주세요.	Give me a break. Just once, this time. (이번~)
한술에 배가 부르랴.	You must not expect too much at your first attempt. ☞ 첫술에 배부르랴.
한술 더 떠.	He is worse. (그가~)
한숨 돌렸어요.	He was relieved after he got his report card. (자기 성적을 알고 나서야 그는~)

ㅎ

한숨 돌리자.	Let's take some breaths and start it again. (~그리고 다시 시작하자)
한숨도 못 잤어요.	I didn't get any sleep. = I didn't get a wink of sleep.
한시가 바쁘다.	I'm really busy. I have no time to idle away.
한심한 녀석!	You are pathetic!
한입 갖고 두말하네.	You are contradicting your own words. = You are going back on your words.
한입 건너 두 입.	[소문] A rumor spreads from one person to the next.
한입 먹어봐!	Have a bite!
한입으로 두말 안 한다.	I'm not going to contradict what I said.
한잔 더 합시다.	Let's go for another drink. = Let's go for another round.
한잔하러 갑시다.	Let's go for a drink. (우리 함께~) // Let's go for a round of beers. = Let's go and grab a beer. (맥주~)
한쪽으로 빠져 있어!	Take one step aside! ☞ 빠져있어!
한참 기다렸어요.	I have waited for you for a long time.
한참 됐습니다.	① It's been a long time. (일이 진행 된지~) ② [이미 일어난 일의 경우] It happened a long time ago. (일이 있은 지~)
한참 말렸어요.	I have persuaded her not to do it for a long time. (그녀를~)
한턱내겠습니다.	Let me treat you today. (오늘 제가~)

ㅎ

할

할 만합니까?	① Is your business going well? (사업~) ➡ ⓐ Just so-so. (그럭저럭.) ⓑ It isn't going as well as I wished. (뜻대로 잘 안되네요.) ② [일 등이] Things are going well. ➡ Everything is good. (모든 게 다 좋습니다.)
할 말 다 했습니다.	I have told you all I want to say.
할 말 더 뭐 있겠어요?	I have nothing more to say.
할 말 많다.	I have a lot of things to tell you. (너한테~)
할 말 없습니다.	① I have nothing to say. (뭐~) ② I have nothing to tell you. (너한테 뭐~)
할 말 없으면 조용히 돌아가세요.	If you don't have anything to say, just go back.
할 말이 있고 안 할 말이 있지.	Some things shouldn't be said. = Some things are better left unsaid. = It's better not to speak of such things.
할 말 있습니까?	Do you have something to tell me? (저한테~) ➡ No, I don't have anything to tell you. (없습니다.)
할 말 있습니다.	I have something to say. // I have something to tell you. = Let me tell you something. (당신에게~)
할 말 있어서 나오라고 했어.	I have something to tell you. That's why I asked you out. (너한테~)
할 말 있으면 말로 하세요.	[대화로 문제 해결] What are you doing? Use words, not violence. (뭐하는 거예요?~)
할 말 있으면 직접 하세요.	If you want to tell me something, just see me in person.

ㅎ

할 말은 하겠습니다.	I will say what I have to say. = I won't hesitate to say what I have to say.
할 말을 잃었습니다.	I am tongue-tied. = I am speechless.
할 수 없습니다.	① [일] I can't do this. (이 일은 도저히~) ② [처리] I can't handle it. ③ [방법] I can't take this way. (이렇게는~)
할 수 없이 샀습니다.	I couldn't help buying it. = I couldn't avoid buying it.
할 수 없이 이렇게 했습니다.	I couldn't help it. ➡ That's okay. You did your best. (괜찮아요, 최선을 다하신 걸요.)
할 수 있어!	[능력] You can do it! (넌~) = You are able to do it! // The sky is the limit for you. (넌 뭐든지~)
할 일 없습니까?	① Do you have nothing to do? ➡ ⓐ No, I'm very busy. (아니요. 무척 바빠요.) ⓑ Not now. (지금은 없습니다.) ② [한가함] Can't you see this? (보면 몰라요.[일이 많음])
할 일 없습니다.	I have nothing to do here. (여기서는~) // I have nothing to do now. (지금~)
할 일을 한 것뿐입니다.	[당연] That is what I have to do.
할 일이 그렇게 없어!	[불만 · 쓸데없이 간섭하는 경우] Mind your own business!
할 일이 꽤나 없는 모양이네.	Looks like you have nothing to do.
할 일이 많습니다.	I have a lot of things to do. = I have tons of things to do.
할 일이 좀 남았습니다.	I have something left to do.

ㅎ

할 일이나 해!	① [간섭에 대해] Mind your own business! ☞ 할 일이 그렇게 없어! ② Do what you are supposed to do!
할 줄 모릅니다.	I don't know how to do it. // I can't speak English. (영어를~)
할 줄 압니다.	I know how to do it. // I know how to do it a little. (조금~)
할거야? 말거야?	Are you going to do it or not? = Are you in or out? = Are you going to get to it or not? ➡ I'm not going to do it! (싫어!) // I will. (할게.)
할 거면 제대로 하고 아니면 하지 마!	Shape up or ship out! = Fish or cut bait!
할게요!	[적극적인 동작] Let me take care of it. (제가~) ➡ You step aside! (저쪽으로 가있어!)
할머니에게 자리를 양보해 주세요!	Why don't you give your seat to the elderly woman?
할머니입니다.	This is my grandmother. (이분이 제~)
할부는 30일에 끝납니다.	The installments are over on the 30th.
할부됩니까?	Can I pay by installments? = Can I pay for this in installments? ➡ Sure, you can. (그럼요.)
할부로 샀습니다.	I bought it on the installment plan.
할아버지에게 자리를 양보해주세요!	Why don't you give your seat to the gentleman?
할아버지입니다.	This is my grandfather. (이분이 제~)
할인권을 살 생각입니다.	I'd like to buy a discount ticket/coupon.

함

함부로 까불지 마세요.	① [덤비는 행위] Don't act recklessly. ② [위험한 동작을 시연] Don't act thoughtlessly.
함부로 돈 쓰지 마세요.	Don't spend money recklessly.
함부로 만지지 마세요.	Don't touch it carelessly. = Take care of it with extra care. // [주의] Handle it carefully. It's fragile. (~깨집니다.)
함부로 말하지 마세요.	Don't talk about that easily. = You're not supposed to talk like that. = Watch your mouth!
함부로 지껄이지 마세요.	Do not talk too freely. = Stop shooting off your mouth.
함부로 믿지 마세요.	Don't believe it too easily.

합

합격한 걸 축하합니다.	Congratulations on your acceptance/admission to Seoul National University. (서울대학에~)
합계가 얼마입니까?	How much is it in total? ➡ 20 dollars altogether. (모두 다 20달러입니다.)
합석해도 될까요?	① Can I join you here? (여기~) ➡ Sure. (그러세요.) ② [버스나 기차에서] Can I sit here next to you? ➡ Sure. (그럼요.)

핫

핫도그 두 개 주세요.	Two hotdogs, please.

ㅎ

항

항공사로 하겠습니까?	Which airline would you like? (어느~) ➡ ⓐ Korean Airlines, please. (대한항공이요.) ⓑ Asiana Airlines, please. (아시아나항공이요.)
항공편 시간을 좀 알고 싶은데요.	I'd like to know the flight schedule.
항공편을 말씀해 주세요.	Can you give me the flight number? // Can you give me your name and the flight number? (성함과~)
항복해?	Will you give in? = Will you surrender? ➡ ⓐ No, I won't. (항복 못해.) ⓑ I will. You won. (항복이야.)
항상 이런 식이야!	You are always like that. = That's what you are.

해

해가 서쪽에서 뜨겠네.	[놀라운 일] Wonders never cease. = Hell is going to freeze over.
해결하겠습니다.	Let me work it out. // Let me take care of him. (그는 내가 알아서~)
해고됐습니다.	You are fired. (당신은~) // I got/was fired. = I got sacked. = I got the pink slip. (저는~)
해낼 수 있습니다.	I can make it.
해냈어!	① [성취] I made it! ② [경기의 승리] I won! // We won! (우리가~)
해도 해도 너무 합니다.	You are being too harsh on me. (정말이지~)

ㅎ

해명할 필요 없습니다.	You don't have to make an excuse. = You don't have to make excuses.
해보겠습니다.	Let me try it.
해보세요.	Give it a shot. // Give it one more shot. (다시 한 번~)
해본 적이 없습니다.	I've never done that.
해볼게!	I'll try my best. = I'll give it a shot. = I'll give it a go. = I'll do what I can.
해볼 만해.	It's worth a try. = It's worth a shot.
해봐요!	① [동작 유도] Do it like this! (이처럼~) ② [시도] Give it a shot! = Give it a try!

핸

핸드폰이 꺼져 있습니다.	His cell phone is off. (그는~)
핸드폰사용이 금지되어 있습니다.	You can't use a cell phone on board. (기내에서는~)
핸드폰에 배터리가 나갔습니다.	My cell phone is dead. = The battery is dead.
핸드폰 배터리가 다 되어 갑니다.	My cell phone is dying.
핸드폰으로 연락주세요.	Contact me on my mobile. = Call me on my cell. (제~)
핸드폰은 몇 번입니까?	What is your cell phone number?
핸드폰을 꺼놨어요?	Have you had your cell phone off? = Did you turn your cell off? ➡ That's because the battery is dead. (배터리가 나가서요.)

핸드폰을 하나 사려고 합니다.	I want to buy a new cell phone.

햄

햄버거 하나와 콜라 한 잔이요.	A hamburger and a coke, please.

했

했습니다.	① I have done it. ② [완료] I have finished it. (제가~) ③ [확인] I did it. (제가~)

행

행동으로 좀 옮겨봐.	Why don't you match your words with your actions? = Why don't you put your words into action?
행방이 묘연합니다.	His whereabouts are not known. (그의~)

행복하세요.	[신혼부부에게] I hope you will be happy together.
	// I hope you will be happy together forever. (영원히~)
	// I hope you will be happy together for your whole ife. (평생~)

행복하시길 바랍니다.	I hope you will have a happy family. (가정이~)
행복한 신혼되세요.	I hope you will be happy in your married life. = I wish you happiness in your married life.
행복했습니다.	I was happy. // I was so happy in those days. (그때가 정말~)

행운을 빕니다.	① I wish you good luck. = I wish you the best of luck. = I will keep my fingers crossed! = Good luck to you! ② [공연 등에서] Break a leg! ☞ 성공하시길 빕니다.
행운을 빌어주세요.	Wish me luck, please. = Cross your fingers for me.
행운입니다.	It's good luck. = I was in luck. = I was lucky. = I was fortunate.

향

향수 하나 주세요.	① [여성용] Perfume, please. ② [남성용] Cologne, please.

허

허락합니다.	You are allowed to do it. = You've got permission. = You've got the green light.
허락해주세요.	① [결재] I need your approval for this. (이 일을~) ② [결혼] Please allow me to marry him. (그와의 결혼을 ~) ③ [승낙] Please say yes to this. (이 일을~)
허리 펴세요!	Get your back straight. = Stretch your back.
허리가 아픕니다.	My back is aching.
허리띠를 졸라매야 해.	[절약] We should tighten our belts. = We should economize. = We should cut corners. ☞ 절약 좀 해야겠다.
허리를 다쳤어요.	I hurt my back. = I threw out my back.

허세 부리긴!	You are running a bluff! = You are playing the peacock! = You are showing off!
허튼소리!	That's nonsense!
허튼소리 하지 말랬지!	① Don't talk nonsense! ② 〈비속〉 Cut the crap! ➡ I'm not joking. = I'm serious. (허튼소리 아니야!)
허튼소리하지 마세요.	Will you please stop talking silly things?
허튼수작 부리지 마세요.	Don't make yourself ridiculous. = Stop playing tricks.
허풍떠네!	You are talking big! = You are exaggerating! = All blow and no go! = You're full of hot air! = There are talkers and there are doers!
허풍 떨지 마세요.	Stop talking tall. = Stop talking through your hat.
허풍쟁이!	① What a braggart! ② 〈비속어〉 Full of shit!

ㅎ

헌

헌신짝 버리듯.	Just like throwing away an old hat. // He dumped her just as he would throw away an old hat. (그가 그녀를~)
헌팅 하러 갈까?	① [여자의 말] Can we go out and pick up some guys? ② [남자의 말] Why don't we go out to pick up some girls/chicks?

헐

헐값에 팝니다.	We are selling this for the scrap value. = We are selling this for the mud. (이것을~)
헐값에 샀어.	I bought this cheap as dirt. (이것을~)
헐값입니다.	This is dirt cheap. (이것은~)
헐뜯지 마세요.	Stop back-biting.

험

험담을 하지 마세요.	Don't speak bad of others. (다른 사람의~) = Don't speak ill of others. // Don't talk about him behind his back. (그를~)

헛

헛걸음하게 해서 정말 죄송하게 됐습니다.	I'm so sorry that you made a fruitless trip.
헛고생만 했습니다.	Everything I did was in vain. = I was on a wild goose chase.
헛물만 켜는 거야.	You're making vain efforts.
헛배 부르다.	I have gas in my stomach.
헛소리!	That's nonsense! = That's ridiculous!
헛소리하지 마세요.	① Don't talk nonsense. = Don't say silly things. ② 〈비속어〉 Cut the crap!

ㅎ

헤

헤어졌습니까?	[놀람] Did you two break up? (두 사람~) ➡ Yes, we broke up. (우리 헤어졌어요.)
헤어지고 싶어요.	I want to break up with you. = I want to end things with you. (당신과~)
헤어집시다.	① Let's break up. = Let's split up. (우리~) ② [작별인사] Let's say good-bye here. (여기서 그만 우리~)
헤엄을 잘 칩니다.	I am a good swimmer. = I swim well. ☞ 수영을 잘합니다.

헬

헬스장 다니나요?	Do you go to a fitness club? = Do you go to a gym? = Do you exercise at a fitness club?

혀

혀를 내밀어보세요.	Stick out your tongue.

현

현금 결제입니까, 카드 결제입니까?	Cash or credit? = Cash or charge? ➡ I'll pay by credit card. (카드로요.) = Credit card.

현금만 받습니다.	[거래] We accept cash only. (우리는~)
	// We accept cash only this time. (이번에 우리는~)
	// Sorry, we accept cash only. (미안합니다, 저희는~)

현금카드를 잃어버렸습니다.	I lost my debit card.
현명한 사람입니다.	He is a wise man. = He has a good head on his shoulders. (그는~)

혈

혈색이 좋지 않군요.	You look pale. = You don't look so good.
혈압이 낮습니다.	Your blood pressure is low.
혈압이 높습니다.	Your blood pressure is high.
혈액형이 O형입니까?	Are you blood type O? ➡ No, I'm type B. (B형이요.)

혐

혐오스러워요.	This man is disgusting. = This guy looks creepy. (이 남자는 정말~)

협

협조해주셔서 감사합니다.	Thank you for your cooperation.
협조해주세요.	I need your cooperation.
협박하는 겁니까?	Are you threatening me now? (지금~)

형

형광등이야.	[이해가 느림] He is slow-witted. (그는~)

ㅎ

형제자매는 몇입니까?	How many brothers or sisters do you have? ➡ I have two older brothers and two younger sisters. (형 둘, 여동생 둘입니다.)
형편없는 영화입니다.	It's a terrible movie. = The movie is awful. = The movie stinks.
형편없어!	It's terrible! = It sucks! // It's so terrible! (너무~) // This game is awful! (이 시합은 정말~)

호

호강 시켜 드릴게요.	[어머니에게] I will make you happy.
호들갑 떨지 마세요.	Don't make a big deal about it. = Do not make a fuss.
호랑이 굴에 들어가야 호랑이를 잡는다.	Nothing venture, nothing win.
호랑이 없는 산에 토끼가 대장 노릇 한다더니.	When the cat is away, the mice will play. = Among the blind, the one-eyed is king.
호랑이는 죽어서 가죽을 남기고 사람은 죽어서 이름을 남긴다.	Tigers leave only their skins when they die, but through his achievements a man's name lives on.
호랑이도 제 말하면 온다더니.	Speak of the devil.
호랑이를 잡으려면 호랑이 굴로 들어가야 한다.	Nothing venture, nothing win. ☞ 호랑이 굴에 들어가야 호랑이를 잡는다.
호랑이에게 물려가도 정신만 차리면 산다.	Drive gently over the stones.
호미로 막을 것을 가래로 막다.	A stitch in time saves nine.

ㅎ

호박씨 깐다.	He does something behind others' back. (그는 뒤로~)
호실을 말씀해주세요.	What is your room number? (방~) // What is your name and room number? (성함과~)
호의를 몰라주다니!	[비난] How come you ignore my goodwill!
호의에 감사드립니다.	Thank you for your favor. (당신의~) = Thank you for your kindness.
호칭은 어떻게?	What can I call you? = How can I address you? ➡ You can call me by name. (이름 부르면 됩니다.)
호텔은 어떻게 갑니까?	How can I get to the hotel? ➡ Go ahead just a little. (앞쪽으로 얼마 안가면 도착합니다.)

호텔 하나 추천해 주시겠습니까?	Can you recommend a hotel?
	// Can you recommend a cheap hotel? (값싼~)
	// Would you recommend a good hotel for me? (적당한~)

혹

혹 떼려다가 혹 붙이는 거 아냐.	You go for wool, but you can come home shorn. = The biter can be bitten.
혹시나 해서 당신에게 말한 겁니다.	I told you on the off chance.

혼

혼 좀 내줘!	① [훈계] Give him/her a warning! (개~) = Teach him/her a lesson!

	② [버릇을 고침] Give him/her what-for. = He/She has to pay for it! (개~)
혼나고 싶어?	You want to have a hard time?
혼자 가는 거야?	Am I going alone? (나~) ➡ ⓐ Yes, you are. (그래.) ⓑ No. You've got company. (아니, 둘이.)
혼자 끙끙 앓지 마세요.	Don't keep it bottled up.
혼자 내버려두지 마세요.	Don't leave me alone. (날~)
혼자 배웠습니다.	I learned it by myself.
혼자 삽니까?	① Do you live alone? ② [결혼여부] Are you single? ➡ Yes, I'm single. (혼자 삽니다.) ☞ 독신입니까?
혼자 있게 내버려둬요.	Leave me alone.
혼자 있게 해서 미안합니다.	Sorry for leaving you alone.
혼자 있고 싶습니다.	I'd like to be alone. // I'd like to be alone for a moment. (잠시 저~)
혼자 있으면 너무 답답합니다.	I feel uneasy when I'm alone.
혼자 지낼 만합니까?	Is is all right to live alone? ➡ Not too bad. (그런대로요.)
혼자입니까?	① Are you on your own? ➡ ⓐ Yes, I am. (예.) ⓑ I am on my own. (혼자입니다.) ⓒ No, there's one more. = No, I've got company. (아니요, 한 사람 더 있습니다.) ② [결혼여부] Are you single yet? (지금도 아직~)

ㅎ

	➡ ⓐ Yes, I am. (예!) ⓑ No, I'm married. (결혼했어요.)

홀

홀아비 신세를 면하게 됐네.	Finally, he's got a lifelong companion. (드디어~)
홀가분합니다.	I feel a load off my mind.

홈

홈페이지 있습니까?	Have you got a webpage? ➡ Sure, we have. (물론이지요, 있습니다.)
홈페이지에 사진을 올려놓았습니다.	I posted the photo on the webpage.

화

화 푸세요.	Don't be upset. = Calm down. = Let off the steam.

화가 났어요.	He's freaking out.
	// He's mad at me. (그가 저한테~)
	// I lost my temper without even realizing it. (저도 모르게~)

화끈하게 놀아봅시다.	Let's paint the town red.
화나게 하지 마세요.	① Do not provoke him. (그 사람~) // Don't rub me the wrong way. = Don't make me angry. (사람~) ② 〈속어〉 Don't piss me off.

ㅎ

화나죽겠어요!	I'm so angry! ➡ Don't be angry. (화내지 마세요.)

화내는 거야?	Are you mad at me?
	// Why are you furious with me? (왜 나에게~)
	➡ Think about what you did to me.
	(네가 나에게 한 일을 생각해봐.)
	// Why are you so mad at him? (어째서 그에게~)
	➡ I'm not mad. (화 안 냈어요.)

화내지 마세요.	Don't be upset. = Don't lose your temper. // Don't be mad at me. = Don't get mad at me. (나한테~)
화낼 줄 모릅니다.	She doesn't easily get mad. (그 여자는~)
화냅니까?	Why are you so mad? = Why are you so pissed off? = Why are you mad at me? = I don't see why you are all hot under the collar? (왜~) ➡ Who is mad? (누가 화냈다고 그래?)
화려한 싱글로 살기로 했어요.	I decided to live cool and single.
화장이 진합니다.	She is wearing heavy make-up. (그녀는~) // She is way too made-up. (그녀는 너무~)
화장 좀 하세요.	Put your make-up on.
화장실 갈 때 마음 다르고 나올 때 마음 다르다.	Danger past, God forgotten. = Once on shore, we pray no more. ☞ 뒷간에 갈 적 마음 다르고 올 적 마음 다르다.
화장실 갔습니다.	① He went to wash his hands. = He went to the washroom. (그는~) ② [집안] He is in the bathroom. ③ [공공장소] He went to the restroom.

ㅎ

화장실 다녀왔습니다.	① [집안] I was in the bathroom. ② [공공장소] I was in the restroom.
화장실 물이 내려가지 않아요.	The toilet doesn't flush.
화장실 좀 다녀오겠습니다.	Let me go to wash my hands. = Excuse me, nature calls.
화장품은 어디서 샀습니까?	Where did you buy the cosmetics? ➡ In Myeong-dong. (명동에서요.)
화장하고 있습니다.	I'm putting on make-up.
화제를 바꿉시다.	Let's change the topic.
화제를 벗어났습니다.	We're off the topic.
화풀이 한 겁니다.	I just took it out on you. (그냥 당신에게~)
화풀이하지 마세요.	Don't take it out on me. = Don't get mad at me without any reason. = Don't get mad at me for no reason. (저한테~)
화풀이 해봤자 소용없어요.	Picking on me won't help.
화해합시다.	Let's make up. = Let's bury the hatchet. (우리~)

확

확률은 반반이야.	The chances are fifty-fifty.
확실한 답을 주세요.	Give me a definite answer.
확실합니까?	[확신] Are you sure? // Can you bet your life on it? (정말~) ➡ ⓐ Yes, I'm sure. = Yes, it's a sure thing. (확실합니다.)

	ⓑ I am one hundred percent sure. (100% 확실합니다.)
확실히 말씀드릴 수 없습니다.	I cannot tell you exactly. // I cannot tell you exactly now. (지금은~)
확실히 해 둡시다.	Let me get this straight. (이건~)
확인해보세요.	Check it, please. = Check it out.
확인해 볼게.	I'll check it. = Let me check it. // Let me double-check. (다시 한 번~)

환

환기 좀 합시다.	Let's open the windows and let some fresh air in. (창문 좀 열고~)
환대해주셔서 감사합니다.	[대접] Thank you for your hospitality.
환불 됩니까?	[반품] Can I get a refund on this? = Can I have my money back on this? ➡ Sure. (그럼요.) ☞ 반품해 주세요.
환송회를 마련했습니다.	[멀리 떠나는 사람을 위해] We prepared a farewell party. // Mr. Na prepared a farewell party for you two. (오늘저녁 나 사장님이 두 분을 위해~)
환영을 받지 못합니다.	I'm not welcome. // You are not welcome in my house. (우리 집에서 당신은~)
환영합니다.	Welcome. = Happy to have you here! // You are welcome anytime. = You are always welcome. = My door is always open to you. (언제든지~)

ㅎ

환율은 얼마입니까?	What is the (exchange) rate of the US dollar? (오늘 달러의 ~) ➡ One thousand and one hundred Korean won for a dollar. (1달러 매입에 한화 1,100원입니다.)
환전합니까?	Where can I exchange money? (어디서~) ➡ At any bank. (아무 은행이나 다 됩니다.)
환전해주세요.	I'd like to exchange money.

홧

홧김에 그랬어.	I did it in a (fit of) rage.

황

황당하네!	① It's embarrassing! ② 〈비속어〉 Shit happens!
황당했어요.	I was embarrassed. = I was stunned. // It made me speechless. (그것 때문에 말문이 막히도록~)
황송합니다.	I'm so grateful.

회

회답을 드리겠습니다.	I will give you an answer tomorrow. (내일~)
회사 그만뒀습니다.	I quit my job. (저는~)
회사 당장 때려치워!	[명령] Quit the job!
회사에 출근합니다.	I go to work.

회사에서 잘린 거야!	You are fired! ➡ Who said that? (누가 그래요?)
회사원입니까?	Do you work at a company? ➡ Yes, I work at a company. (예, 회사원입니다.)
회식이 있습니다.	I have a dinner engagement tonight. (오늘~)
회의 끝냅시다.	Let's call it a day here. (여기서~)
회의중입니다.	① He is in a meeting. (그는 지금~) // The boss is in a meeting now. (사장님은~) ② [표지판] Now in session!

횡

횡단금지	[표지판] No crossing!
횡단보도가 없다.	There's no crosswalk around here. (이 주변에~) ➡ There's one over there. (저쪽에 하나 있네요.)
횡재구나!	What a windfall!

효

효과가 있네!	It really works! (정말~)
효도도 다 때가 있는 법이다.	A son never thinks of his parents until it is too late.

후

후덥지근합니다.	It's hot and humid. // It's very hot and humid today. = It's muggy today. (오늘 매우~)

ㅎ

후반전이 방금 시작됐습니다.	The second half has just started.
후식 드릴까요?	Would you like some dessert? ➡ Sure. (예.)
후회됩니다.	I really regret it. = I'm kicking myself. (정말~) // I regret what I did. = I'm kicking myself for what I did. (제가 저지른 일에 대해~)
후회해도 때는 이미 늦었어요.	It's too late for regrets.
후회해도 소용없습니다.	It's no use regretting. = It's no use crying over spilt milk. ☞ 엎질러진 물이야.

훈

훈계 좀 그만해!	Stop lecturing! (That's enough.)

훌

훌륭한 스승 밑에서 뛰어난 제자가 나온다.	A good teacher makes a good pupil.
훌륭합니다!	☞ 대단하다! // 대단해! ① [칭찬] That's excellent/great! ② [놀라운 행위에 대한 칭찬] That's awesome! ③ [완벽함] You did a perfect job! ④ [최고] You are the best! ⑤ [깊은 인상을 남김] I'm impressed!

ㅎ

훤

훤하다.	I know everything about it. = I am an expert in the field. ☞ 전문이지.

휴

휴가 중입니다.	He is on vacation now. = He is away on leave/vacation. (그는 지금~)
휴대폰을 꺼주세요.	Please turn off your cell phone. // cell phone → cell phones (여러 명에게~)
휴식했습니까?	Did you take some rest? ➡ Yes, I rested for thirty minutes. (30분 쉬었어요.)
휴지 좀 갖다주세요.	① [화장할 때 쓰는 화장지] Please get me some tissue. ② [화장실 휴지] Please get me some toilet paper.
휴지를 함부로 버리지 마세요.	① Don't litter, please. ② [간판] No dumping! = No litter!

흉

흉보지 마세요.	① [글씨체] Please forgive my poor handwriting. ② [선물] Please forgive the humble gift.

흐

흐르는 물은 썩지 않는다.	Running water doesn't decay.
흐린 날입니다.	Today it's cloudy. (오늘은~)

흐립니다.	It's cloudy again. (날이 또~)

흑

흑심이 있습니까?	Do you have a thing for me? (저한테 무슨~) ➡ No, I don't. How dare I? (없습니다. 어떻게 감히!)
흑심 품지 마!	She's off limits! (그녀에게~)
흑자입니다.	We're in the black. = We're turning a profit. = We're making some money.

흔

흔들리지 마세요.	Don't be shaken. = Stick with your resolution. = Do not waffle. (결심~)
흔한 개똥도 약에 쓰려면 없다.	Sometimes it is difficult to get something very common for emergency use. ☞ 개똥도 약에 쓰려면 없다.

흠

흠 없는 사람이 어디 있어?	Nobody is perfect.
흠 잡을 데가 없다.	I can't complain.
흠집이 있습니다.	① [작은 상처] There's a scratch here. (여기~) ② [갈라진 틈] There's a crack here. (여기~) ③ [과일] There's a bruise here. (여기~)

ㅎ

흡

흡연금지!	Smoking-free area! = No smoking area!
흡연석으로 바꿔주세요.	I'd like to move to a smoking seat.

흥

흥!	[혐오 · 질책하는 소리] Pish!
흥미가 없습니다.	I'm not interested in it. (그것에~) // I'm not interested in him. (그에게~)

흥분하지 마세요.	Chill out. = Relax. = Simmer down.
	// Don't be mad.
	= Don't get carried away. (~당신답지 않아요.)
	// Keep your temper. You're not yourself.
	// Relax. Pull yourself together.
	(~차분히 좀 추스리세요.)

흥을 깨서 미안합니다.	I'm sorry for spoiling the sport. = I'm sorry for ruining the mood.
흥정은 붙이고 싸움은 말려라.	You should stop arguing and help bargain.

희

희망사항입니다.	It's just wishful thinking. (그냥~)
희망이 안 보입니다.	I'm hopeless. = There's no hope.
희망이 없습니다.	He is hopeless. (그는~)
희망이 있을 것 같습니까?	Do you think there is hope? ➡ Yes, there is. (희망이 있습니다.)

힌

힌트 좀 주세요.	Give me some clues. = Give me some hints.

힘

힘 빼!	Relax!
힘 좀 내!	[격려] Come on! = Cheer up!
힘 좀 아껴 두세요.	Reserve your energy. = Save your energy.
힘 줘!	Put forth your strength!
힘껏 도와드리겠습니다.	I will help you with all my heart. (저도~)
힘내!	① [응원 · 격려] Cheer up! = Perk up! ② [체력] Keep your steam up! ☞ 기운 내! // 파이팅!
힘냅시다.	Let's pluck up our hearts. (우리 함께~)
힘들어 보입니까?	① [피곤] Do I look tired? ➡ Yes, you do. (힘들어 보입니다.) ② [곤란] Do I look troubled? ➡ No, you don't. (그렇게 안 보여요.)
힘들어 죽겠어요!	[피곤] I'm dead tired! = I'm exhausted! = I'm knocked out!
힘들어서 혼났어요.	It was a really hard day today. (오늘~)
힘들어요!	① [스트레스] I'm stressed out! (정말~) ② [고통] I have a lot of pain! (지금 너무~) ③ [피곤] I'm too tired! (너무~) ④ [어려움] It's so hard! = It's so difficult! ⑤ [고생] I'm suffering hell! (너무~)

ㅎ

힘듭니다.	It's so hard.
	// It is beyond my ability. (제 능력으로는~)
	// This is a bit beyond my ability. (이건 좀~)

힘이 되어 줄게요.	I'll be your strength.
힘이 정말 세구나!	You are so strong!
힘이 하나도 없습니다.	I have no power left in me. = I have no energy.
힘주지 마!	Do not put forth your strength!

색인

MEMO

MEMO

MEMO

MEMO

MEMO

MEMO